Floods of the Tiber in Ancient Rome

Ancient Society and History

Floods of the Tiber

GREGORY S. ALDRETE

in Ancient Rome

The Johns Hopkins University Press
Baltimore

© 2007 The Johns Hopkins University Press
All rights reserved. Published 2007
Printed in the United States of America on acid-free paper
9 8 7 6 5 4 3 2 1

The Johns Hopkins University Press
2715 North Charles Street
Baltimore, Maryland 21218-4363
www.press.jhu.edu

Library of Congress Cataloging-in-Publication Data

Aldrete, Gregory S.
   Floods of the Tiber in ancient Rome / Gregory S. Aldrete.
      p. cm.
   Includes bibliographical references and index.
   ISBN 0-8018-8405-5 (hardcover : alk. paper)
   1. Floods—Italy—Rome—History. 2. Floods—Italy—Tiber River—History.   3. Rome (Italy)—History—To 476.   4. Tiber River (Italy)—History.   I. Title
   DG69.A43 2006
   937'.6—dc22   2006004140

A catalog record for this book is available from the British Library.

To Alicia

Amid all the causes of the destruction of human property, it seems to me that rivers on account of their excessive and violent inundations hold the foremost place. . . . against the irreparable inundation caused by swollen and proud rivers no resource of human foresight can avail; for in a succession of raging and seething waves, gnawing and tearing away the high banks, growing turbid with the earth from the ploughed fields, destroying the houses therein and uprooting the tall trees, it carries these as its prey down to the sea which is its lair, bearing along with it men, trees, animals, houses, and lands, sweeping away every dike and every kind of barrier, bearing with it the light things, and devastating and destroying those of weight, creating big landslips out of small fissures, filling up with its floods the low valleys, and rushing headlong with insistent and inexorable mass of waters.
What a need there is of flight for whoso is near!
O how many cities, how many lands, castles, villas and houses has it consumed!

> Leonardo da Vinci, *The Notebooks of Leonardo da Vinci*,
> ed. and trans. Edward MacCurdy, 652

Contents

List of Figures and Tables   xiii

Acknowledgments   xvii

Introduction: Floods and History   1

One
Floods in Ancient Rome: Sources and Topography   10
    Floods and the Foundation of Rome   10
    Primary Source Descriptions of Floods in Ancient Rome   13
    Geographic Extent of Floods Based on Primary Sources   33
    The Topography of Rome and Floods   39
    Maps of Hypothetical Floods of Different Magnitudes   45

Two
Characteristics of Floods   51
    Flood Types and Basic Hydrology   51
    Hydrology of the Tiber and the Tiber Drainage Basin   54
    Duration of Floods at Rome   61
    Seasonality of Floods at Rome   66
    Frequency of Floods at Rome   71
    Magnitude of Floods at Rome   81
    Conclusion   89

Contents

Three
Immediate Effects of Floods   91
Introduction and Methodology   91
Disruption of the Daily Life of the City   92
Destruction of Property   97
Collapse of Structures   102
Injuries and Drowning   118
Cleaning Up after a Flood: Water, Mud, Debris, Corpses   123

Four
Delayed Effects of Floods   129
Weakened Buildings   129
Food Spoilage and Famine   131
Disease   141
Psychological Trauma   154
Recovery and Reconstruction   160

Five
Methods of Flood Control   166
Drain: The Roman Sewers   167
Fill: Attempts to Raise Ground Level   177
Divert: Canals and Channel Modification Schemes   181
Contain: Roman Embankments   192
Administrative Oversight of the Tiber   198

Six
Roman Attitudes toward Floods   204
Floods and the Urban Fabric of Ancient Rome: Public Buildings   204
Floods and the Urban Fabric of Ancient Rome: Housing   211
Water and the Gods   217
Floods and the Gods: Portents and Divine Anger   219
Flood Reports: Context and Causation   221
Flood Prevention: Costs and Benefits   225

Conclusion: The Romans' Failure to Make Rome Safe from Floods   232

Appendix I: List of Major Floods at Rome, 414 BC–AD 2000   241

Appendix II: The Modern Tiber Embankments   247

Appendix III: A Note on Hydrological Sources   253

Notes   257

Bibliography   303

Index   325

Figures and Tables

Figures

1.1. Representation of Father Tiber   13

1.2. Map of the main geographic features of ancient Rome   34

1.3. The Roman Forum seen through the Arch of Septimius Severus during the flood of 1902   36

1.4. Drawing by J. H. W. Tischbein of the Pantheon during the flood of 1686   37

1.5. Map showing depth of fill and rubble at Rome   42

1.6. Topographic map of Rome at the time of Augustus   44

1.7. Topographic map with 10 masl flood   45

1.8. Topographic map with 15 masl flood   47

1.9. Topographic map with 20 masl flood   48

1.10. Map of Rome with 20 masl flood, flooded sites mentioned in primary sources, and major Augustan structures   49

Figures and Tables

2.1. Typical hydrograph   53

2.2. A section of the Tiber River between Rome and Ostia   55

2.3. A flood marker commemorating the flood of 1530   56

2.4. Map of the Tiber drainage basin   57

2.5. Hydrograph of the flood of December 1870   65

2.6. Frequency of major floods at Rome per century   74

2.7. Estimated population of Rome from 600 BC to the present   78

2.8. The Pons Fabricius during the flood of 1937   87

2.9. The Pons Fabricius at normal Tiber level   88

3.1. Drawing by J. H. W. Tischbein of the interior of the Pantheon during the flood of 1686   94

3.2. The Roman Forum partially flooded during the inundation of 1902   96

3.3. The remaining arch of the Pons Aemilius nearly submerged during an unidentified flood   116

4.1. The commercial Emporium district   134

4.2. The Horrea Galbana   140

4.3. Section of the Aqua Claudia   153

5.1. The outlet of the Cloaca Maxima where it empties into the Tiber   171

5.2. Bust of Marcus Vipsanius Agrippa   172

5.3. Map showing some major Roman drains   174

5.4. Aerial view of the eastern end of the Roman Forum during the flood of December 1900   179

Figures and Tables

5.5. A section of Roman embankment and quay in the Emporium district   195

5.6. The continuous near-vertical walls of the modern Tiber embankments   197

6.1. The Forum Boarium, including round temple, during an inundation   206

6.2. Map of political, commercial, and entertainment centers of Rome plotted against 20 masl flood   207

6.3. Map of major bath complexes plotted against a 20 masl flood   209

6.4. Section of the modern Tiber embankment that protects the city from floods   226

A.1. Section of the Tiber in Rome before construction of the modern embankments   250

A.2. Stretch of the Tiber above the Ponte Garibaldi   251

Tables

1.1. List of known ancient floods   15

2.1. Tiber flood classification scheme   62

2.2. Seasonal distribution of floods at Rome   68

2.3. Frequency estimates of floods at Rome, 414 BC to AD 1870   73

2.4. Major postmedieval floods at Rome with known or estimated peak water levels greater than 15 masl   86

6.1. *Domus* on hills   214

6.2. *Domus* in flood-prone areas   215

A.1. Major floods at Rome, 414 BC to AD 2000   242–246

Acknowledgments

Researching and writing this book were made possible by financial support from several sources. Most prominent among these was the National Endowment for the Humanities, which offered crucial support both at the beginning and end stages of the project. This work had its origins during the summer of 2000 at the NEH Summer Seminar for College Teachers held at the American Academy in Rome, "Representing Geography and Community in the World of Imperial Rome," directed by Richard Talbert and Michael Maas. My preliminary investigations into Tiber floods as a member of that seminar eventually grew into this book. The final phases of writing and revising were also generously supported by the NEH in the form of a full-year NEH Humanities Fellowship, which I was awarded for 2004–5. I would also like to thank the University of Wisconsin–Green Bay for granting me a sabbatical in order to work on the book, and the UWGB Research Council, which contributed funds toward an additional stay in Rome in 2004. I am also grateful to the American Academy in Rome for granting me permission to lodge there as a Visiting Scholar during that trip and to use the wonderful resources of its library and photographic archives.

The personnel of a number of institutions were very helpful and generous with their time in assisting me to gather research for this proj-

Acknowledgments

ect. Among these are the staff of the Interlibrary Loan Office at the University of Wisconsin–Green Bay, especially Mary Naumann; the staff of the Rome office of the Autorità di Bacino del Fiume Tevere; and the staff of the American Academy in Rome, in particular, Alessandra Capodiferro, Lavinia Ciuffa, and Francesca Romoli of the Fototeca Unione.

I am grateful to a number of academic colleagues and friends who, at various stages of the project, have offered advice, insights, or comments on portions of the text, including Joyce Salisbury, Lawrence Morris, Raymond Van Dam, Richard Talbert, Michael Maas, and all of my fellow participants in the 2000 NEH summer seminar. My thanks also to W. T. Courtenay, who met with me and shared his knowledge of the modern Tiber embankment project, and to Albert Ammerman, who answered several of my questions about floods by correspondence. Special recognition is due to David West Reynolds, to whom I am grateful for both his friendship and his advice and insights on matters relating to Roman archaeology.

In the course of writing about some of the technical topics addressed in this book, I have consulted with a number of experts in fields outside the study of the ancient world who have provided invaluable advice. Some of these experts include Professor Kenneth W. Potter, Department of Civil & Environmental Engineering, University of Wisconsin–Madison; Professor Steven Cramer, Department of Civil & Environmental Engineering, University of Wisconsin–Madison; Professor James C. Knox, Department of Geography, University of Wisconsin–Madison; and Dr. Joaquin S. Aldrete, Professor Emeritus, Department of Surgery, University of Alabama at Birmingham. While I have tried to be careful presenting information from fields that are not my own expertise, any errors or misinterpretations that appear in the book are, of course, entirely my own.

Finally, my deepest thanks are to my wife, Alicia. She has acted in the role of research assistant throughout the project, accompanied and aided my investigations during all of the stays in Italy, proofread and edited innumerable drafts of the manuscript, and been a constant source of support and advice. Over the past five years, she has had to live with the topic of Tiber floods fully as much as I have, and it is in grateful recognition of her vital contributions, both material and emotional, to the completion of this project that I dedicate this book to her.

Floods of the Tiber in Ancient Rome

Introduction

Floods and History

Floods and civilization have always been companions.[1] The earliest civilizations, such as those in Mesopotamia, arose along rivers in floodplains. The reasons for settling in such hazardous regions were obvious; rivers offer routes of communication, and the floods themselves can deposit and renew the soil, increasing agricultural yields. The very factors that make these areas attractive for settlement are the same ones that make them vulnerable to devastation caused by floods. The flat floodplains between the Tigris and Euphrates provided fertile ground for the type of intensive agricultural cultivation that would produce the surpluses necessary to support cities and empires, but these lands were also subject to sudden and destructive floods. The most dramatic example of the beneficial effects of floods is, of course, the civilization of ancient Egypt, whose entire economy was based upon the regular annual flooding of the Nile. Throughout history human populations all around the world have tended to cluster most densely along riparian corridors, many of which are prone to violent flooding. Although farmlands situated in such areas may suffer the loss of a crop during a flood yet retain much of the property's intrinsic value once the waters have receded, heavily urbanized areas are a different matter. Not only is population density much higher in urban as opposed to rural settings (with concomitant potential for greater loss of life), but the physical structures of cities themselves represent enormous investments of capital that are vulnerable to a flood's destructive power.

Devastating floods are not just a problem of the ancient world, however. As people continue to settle in floodplains, and as cities grow ever larger and more densely populated, the damage caused by floods continues to rise.[2] In the United States, for example, where there have been decades' worth of massive civil engineering projects aimed at controlling or diverting floods, the annual economic losses from floods are still increasing at a rate of 4% per year in real terms. From 1925 to 1994, the annual damages from floods in the United States, even when converted into 1990 dollars, have steadily increased from an average of around $100 million to more than $3 billion per year.[3] The desire to live in prime real estate and the increasing size and technological complexity of cities have simply provided a richer landscape of expensive targets for natural disasters. In addition, all the technological innovations of the past several centuries and the gigantic and costly efforts at flood control have proved futile against the force of major floods, as evidenced by the catastrophic Mississippi floods of 1993, which inundated 20 million acres in nine states, destroyed 50,000 homes, and flooded 75 towns. The damage from this one meteorological event was approximately $20 billion, resulting from a combination of destruction and harm to property and infrastructure, disruption of transportation, and agricultural losses.[4] In the latter part of the 20th century, more than 80% of the presidentially declared natural disasters in the United States were caused by floods.[5] A study by the U.S. Office of Foreign Disaster Assistance concluded that since 1964, floods outside the United States have killed more than 130,000 people, rendered 70 million homeless, and negatively affected more than 1 billion.[6]

Moving water has huge power. Floodwaters easily have the force to sweep away bridges, topple buildings, and lift boulders weighing several tons. Some idea of the potential power in water can be gauged by the yardstick formula that 1 inch of rainfall dropping from 1,000 feet over 1 square mile has a potential energy equivalent to 60,000 tons of TNT (three times the power of the Hiroshima nuclear bomb).[7] Not least of a flood's harmful effects are the difficulties involved in cleaning up after the waters recede. Added to the physical task of clearing away the debris carried about by the waters are health hazards caused by backed-up sewers spreading dangerous bacteria as well as by the disposal of the corpses of animals and humans killed by the flood. Floods often leave behind vast quantities of silt and mud. The well-known Florence flood of 1966, for example, left the city coated in an estimated 600,000 tons of viscous, stinking mud.[8]

In areas without effective warning systems, the potential for loss of life from floods can be staggering. Perhaps the best illustration of this is found in the records of inundations along the Hwang He (Yellow) River in China. The floods along this river, aptly nicknamed "China's Sorrow," probably have resulted in more deaths than any other. Accounts of hundreds of floods on the Hwang He survive, with the earliest dating back as far as 2297 BC.[9] Some of the greatest losses of life from floods on the Hwang He occurred in relatively recent times and are of truly horrific proportions. The estimated number of combined human deaths from the three Hwang He floods of 1887, 1931, and 1938 is close to 7 million.[10] According to one study of deaths resulting from 16 different categories of worldwide natural disasters between 1947 and 1967, 173,170 people died due to riverine floods as opposed to 216,095 people who died from all other 15 categories of disaster combined, which included hurricanes, tornadoes, volcanoes, blizzards, and earthquakes.[11] In terms of both the economic cost and the human toll, floods probably represent the single most destructive form of natural catastrophe in human history.

Simply put, floods will continue to be a problem as long as people choose to live in areas that are floodplains and, even worse, to build large, expensive cities in such locations. It is within this broader historical context that a study of floods in the largest and most architecturally complex city of classical antiquity is of more than antiquarian interest.

Ancient Rome was an anomaly. By the late Republic, it had reached a population of around 1 million inhabitants and maintained that size for several centuries.[12] This population is absolutely incredible for a preindustrial city—at least twice as large as that of any contemporary urban settlement. Not only was it the largest city up to that point in history but it remained the largest ever to have existed for nearly 2,000 years. The uniqueness of ancient Rome's size is demonstrated by the fact that no other city reached the 1 million mark in population until London hit 1 million inhabitants in the early 19th century.[13]

Rome was notable not merely for the number of people who lived in it but also for the scale, sophistication, and elaborateness of its buildings. Architectural marvels abounded in ancient Rome. As the political capital of an empire, it was the beneficiary of the spoils gained from that empire. The public structures of Rome included vast colonnaded fora and colossal bath complexes. The emperors dwelled in sumptuous palaces covering many acres. The city was adorned with captured artworks and was built out of imported decorative marbles and colored stones from every corner of the Empire. Dozens of temples dotted the urban landscape, the most visible and centrally placed of which boasted a roof covered in gold. Numerous entertainment complexes, such as theaters, amphitheaters, and circuses (all of which were as sophisticated in design as any modern sports arena, and equivalent or greater in size), hosted lavish spectacles. Rome's wealthy lived in beautiful houses whose very floors and walls were coated with fine paintings and intricate mosaics. The poor lived crammed into high-rise tenement apartments, which, while they may have been squalid, overcrowded, and unstable, remain imposing for their sheer scale, many rising more than 100 feet in the air through 10 or 12 stories of close-packed humanity. Even the infrastructure of ancient Rome was impressive, with roads, bridges, aqueducts, and sewers so well made that many are still extant and even continue to be used 2,000 years later.[14]

Rome is famous in the popular imagination as "the city built on seven hills." Of far greater significance, however, is the fact that the small hills of Rome rise out of what was originally low-lying swampy land. The city of ancient Rome was a fabulous artificial landscape erected by human beings, but the Romans chose to build it squarely in an area that nature had designated as floodplain. Throughout the history of the city, therefore, Rome has been subject to frequent and powerful floods.

One anecdote will serve to illustrate Rome's vulnerability. In 13 BC, Lucius Cornelius Balbus dedicated a magnificent new stone theater in the southern section of the Campus Martius. He had earned a triumph for his victory over the Garamantes while serving as proconsul of Africa in 19 BC, and the theater that bore his name was probably constructed using the spoils of this campaign. It was a prime location, with ties both to Rome's glorious past and to its vibrant present. Just across from Balbus's theater stood the venerable temples of the Area Sacra di Largo Argentina, where triumphal processions (including his own) would have begun, while all around the theater, impressive new buildings were being erected by Augustus and his family as part of the emperor's sweeping transformation of the Campus Martius. The grand inauguration of this theater, only the third in the city, would have been an important civic event, and Balbus accompanied the opening of the theater with spectacular public shows lasting several days. Heightening the air of excitement was the fact that, during the course of the inaugural games, news reached the city that Augustus himself was returning to Rome from the provinces, and the senate hurriedly convened in order to bestow various honors upon the returning princeps. Balbus's theater earned him the privilege of casting the first vote in the senate, and Cassius Dio (54.25; Suet. *Aug.* 29) records that this string of highly public successes inflated Balbus's ego.

One note of discord marred Balbus's moment of triumph, however. The Tiber rose from its banks during this time and inundated part of the city. Among the areas flooded was the site of Balbus's theater, and indeed, Dio records that the waters were of such a considerable depth that Balbus was only able to enter his brand-new theater via boat. We can only imagine the inauguration ceremony that was held in the half-submerged theater, presumably with the celebrants clinging to the upper reaches of the *cavea* while the boats that brought them bobbed about in the waters covering the stage. This apparently ignominious aspect of the ceremonies does not appear to have greatly detracted from Balbus's glory, however, and seems to have been accepted by the participants as a matter of course.

This incident illustrates a number of important characteristics of floods in ancient Rome. On the one hand, the Tiber's floods were both frequent and severe, immersing large sections of the city under several meters of water for prolonged periods of time and often causing major buildings to collapse. The areas ravaged by floods were not confined to undesirable or poor sections of the city, but rather extended to many of the most prominent regions, including the Forum itself, so that floods affected Rome's elites as well as the average inhabitants of the city. On the other hand, the attitude of the Romans toward these natural disasters seems to have been surprisingly accepting. The ancient sources mention these floods and their accompanying destruction but do not dwell on them, consistently describing them in a way that suggests they were regarded as a routine aspect of urban life. As in the case of the inauguration of Balbus's theater, life went on despite the flood, with the inhabitants of Rome matter-of-factly making whatever accommodations were necessary to adjust to its presence.

Recently there has been increased interest in evaluating the topography of ancient Rome from a symbolic viewpoint and in Roman concepts of urban space.[15] Humans have always sought to control nature and to impose their will on the landscape through architecture. I would like to reverse this equation and look at some instances when nature violently and dramatically imposed itself on the most densely artificial landscape of the ancient world: the city of Rome.

This book has three main goals. The first is to present what is known and what can be determined about the characteristics of floods in ancient Rome in terms of their geographic extent, duration, seasonality, frequency, and magnitude. Simply collecting this information together in one place should provide a useful reference for those interested in the topic. Particularly for an English-speaking audience, no such reference currently exists. The second goal is to consider what the full range of effects of floods would have been on the inhabitants of the ancient city. Although the extant primary source accounts of ancient floods do not enumerate all the consequences of inundations, these can be reliably reconstructed using comparative and scientific evidence, and this reconstruction must be done in order to properly evaluate the comprehensive effect of floods on the ancient city. The third goal is to examine how the Romans responded to these floods, including their practical attempts to alleviate flooding as well as their attitudes towards floods in terms of causation, responsibility, religion, and preventability. Overall, this book attempts to explore not only the physical consequences produced by these events on the urban landscape, but also how such occurrences were perceived and interpreted by the Romans.

The first two chapters are primarily descriptive and focus on fulfilling the first goal. Chapter 1 centers around an examination of the literary evidence for floods in ancient Rome. It includes a database of 42 primary source descriptions of incidents when portions of the city became inundated with water, ranging in time from 414 BC to AD 398. The information from these written sources is then combined with archaeological and geographical evidence in order to map out a topography of the city that identifies areas prone to flooding. This chapter closes with a consideration of several maps illustrating the extent of flooding of the ancient city that would have resulted from inundations of varying magnitudes. Chapter 2 analyzes the phenomenon of flooding in ancient Rome in terms of a range of significant characteristics of floods. It begins with a survey of the hydrology of the Tiber and the Tiber drainage basin and then proceeds to collect evidence for the duration, seasonality, frequency, and magnitude of floods in ancient Rome. This chapter combines information from ancient sources with principles of hydrology and technical data from the more recent history of the Tiber.

The next set of two chapters addresses the second goal, by offering a description of the full array of effects that floods would have had on the city and making considerable use of modern scientific and comparative historical data to reconstruct the course of an ancient flood and its consequences. Chapter 3 enumerates the immediate physical effects of floods in Rome, including disruption of the daily social, economic, and religious life of the city; the destruction of property; the collapse of structures; and injuries and death caused by floods. It ends with a description of the problems faced by the survivors in cleaning up the water, mud, debris, and corpses left by floods. Chapter 4 investigates the long-term effects of floods, such as weakened buildings, food spoilage, famine, disease, and psychological trauma. It concludes with a brief consideration of the long process of recovery and reconstruction following a destructive flood.

The last two chapters turn toward assessing the Romans' responses to and attitudes toward floods. Chapter 5 examines the various methods by which the ancient Romans reacted to this natural threat, including the construction of drainage systems, spillways, and embankments, as well as attempts to raise the level of certain flood-prone regions and to divert or modify the course of the Tiber itself. In connection with the analysis of different occupation levels, this chapter also considers some aspects of the topography and stratigraphy of the city and surveys the administrative posts that developed over time to supervise and regulate the Tiber and its banks. Chapter 6 turns from these practical aspects of the topic to investigate the Romans' attitudes toward floods. It covers subjects such as the place of water in Roman religion, how floods were sometimes interpreted as portents or divine punishment, and how the threat of flooding affected where the Romans chose to construct various types of structures. It also reconstructs the attitude of the Romans toward these natural disasters through an analysis of how they were reported in the primary sources. One of the mysteries concerning the ancient Romans and floods is that they had the resources and technology to make the city safe from destructive inundations, yet chose not to do so. This chapter suggests some possible reasons for this choice.

The conclusion applies the material presented in this book to evaluate the question of ancient Rome's overall vulnerability to floods. Ultimately this book will argue that while floods were a frequent and destructive force and posed a potentially major threat to the city, ancient Rome possessed a number of unique characteristics that made the city surprisingly resilient in coping with many of the negative effects of flooding. Three brief appendixes serve to connect the history of floods in ancient Rome to the present. Appendix I compiles a list of all the known major floods at Rome, including those of the Roman, medieval, early modern, and modern periods, and illustrates that floods have been a perennial threat throughout the history of the city. Appendix II contains an overview of the Tiber embankment project of the late 19th century, which finally granted the city relative safety from most floods. Appendix III provides a list of hydrological sources for those interested in obtaining more technical information about floods.

One of the earliest construction projects at Rome was the building of the Cloaca Maxima, which served to drain some of the swampy low-lying lands near the Tiber River that were particularly prone to flooding. From the earliest stages of Roman urban history, therefore, efforts to build an artificial environment were constrained by the challenges of dealing with unwanted water. The primary sources attest to the frequency as well as the severity of floods at Rome, describing instances when the streets had to be traversed by boat for days at a time. However, water occupied both a destructive and a benevolent place in the Roman mentality. While floods endangered buildings, supplies, and lives, the Tiber brought necessary food to Rome and the Romans delighted in water, as witnessed by the numerous baths, fountains, basins, and aqueducts of the city, and by the fact that every spring, pool, and river was considered sacred. Ancient Rome depended on water for the functioning of its economy and for its very survival, but at the same time the Tiber could be a violent and unpredictable destructive force. This book investigates the nature of this conflict, and the complex interrelationship between humans and water that was played out amid the urban topography of ancient Rome.

One

Floods in Ancient Rome: Sources and Topography

Floods and the Foundation of Rome

Floods and Rome have been linked since the very beginnings of the city.[1] From Noah's flood to the epic of Gilgamesh, floods have figured prominently in the creation stories of many civilizations and religions, and so too, a flood plays a pivotal role in the foundation narrative of the city of Rome. The famous legend of its foundation focuses on the twins, Romulus and Remus, descended from Aeneas through his son, Iulus. According to the well-known tale, Amulius, one of the descendants of Iulus, became king of Alba Longa by expelling his brother, Numitor, and murdering his brother's sons. His brother's daughter, Rhea Silvia, was forced to become a Vestal Virgin to ensure that she would have no children who might seek revenge against him. Eventually, however, she became pregnant, claiming that she had been raped by the god of war, Mars. She gave birth to twins, Romulus and Remus. The king wanted the twins eliminated but was afraid to kill the possibly divinely engendered babies directly, so he ordered that they be put in a basket and thrown into the Tiber River to drown. The basket washed ashore, however, and the babies were rescued by a wolf, which nursed them and, together with a helpful woodpecker, looked after them (both animals were associated with Mars). Ultimately, the boys were found by a shepherd, Faustulus, who raised them as his own. They grew up into strong young men who performed various noble deeds, such as suppressing bandits, and when Faustulus eventually revealed the secret of their birth, they sought revenge and overthrew the king of Alba Longa.

They then decided to found a new city on the spot where the wolf had discovered them, which became the site of the city of Rome. Almost immediately, however, they fell into an argument over who should be king of the new city, since they were twins and did not know which one was older. In the end, they could not agree, and decided to let the gods choose the king. To do this, each brother went to the top of one of the hills and looked for a sign, Romulus standing on the Palatine Hill and Remus positioning himself on the Aventine. Remus received the first sign when six vultures flew overhead, but shortly afterward twelve vultures flew over Romulus. This left the brothers still arguing, with each claiming the gods had picked him—Remus saying he had received the first omen and Romulus saying he had been granted the better omen. In the end, they could not settle their differences and, growing angry, Romulus solved the problem by murdering his brother. Thus the new city was called Rome after Romulus, and he became its first king.[2]

This much of the story is well-known, and the image of the she-wolf suckling the twins has attained iconic status, but Livy and Plutarch, who provide the fullest versions, stress some additional details which are not as commonly emphasized. The reason that King Amulius's scheme to drown the boys did not succeed was because the Tiber, swollen with winter rains, was in flood at the time, and the man dispatched with the babies was unable to make his way through the standing pools of water to reach the main riverbed (Livy 1.4.4–6; Plut. *Rom.* 3.4). Apparently the maximum height of the flood had passed, although the river was still in flood, and these stagnant pools had been left behind by the peak of the flood. Use of the term "stagnant" suggests that the standing waters were slow to recede due to the geography and hydrology of the area and emphasizes the originally marshy nature of the future site of Rome. Plutarch (*Rom.* 3.4) notes that the man was frightened by the speed and violence of the still-flooding river and so, instead of casting the boys into the torrent, which would have overturned the basket or at least carried them far away downriver and even possibly out to sea, he contented himself with putting the basket down in the calmer water at the edge of the flooded region. The basket floated on the waters and, when the flood receded, was deposited under a fig tree near the Lupercal at the foot of the Cermalus on the slope of the Palatine Hill.[3] These events did not occur randomly, but rather, as Livy (1.4.1) testifies, were directed by divine providence.

In Roman legend, therefore, the love-hate relationship of Rome and the Tiber (fig. 1.1) was present from the very origins of the city. A flood saved the life of Romulus by preventing the king's man from carrying out his task, and the divinely directed floodwaters functioned as the agent by which the actual site of Rome was selected. The importance of the Palatine and Capitoline hills and the region lying between them was already being indicated by the location where the basket was left. The location where Romulus's basket was deposited also draws attention to another less salubrious aspect of the future city's life—that it was to be situated squarely in a floodplain and that some of the most symbolically important regions of the city were doomed to be routinely inundated by water. Ironically, the flood that saved the founder's life also ensured that his city would regularly suffer watery destruction throughout the rest of its history.

The story of Romulus and Remus is, of course, probably more mythological than historical, but at the very least, it is representative of the ideas of the later authors who wrote it down. In this context, it is illuminating to find a flood at the heart of the story, and that the aspects of the account dealing with the flood, from the power and danger of the swollen floodwaters to the geography of the regions that were flooded, are all highly realistic. The authors who described the adventures of Romulus and Remus almost certainly had firsthand experience of the Tiber in flood and must have drawn upon this knowledge in crafting their stories. Living at a time when Rome was a great city, they were likely all too aware that the bucolic fens and marshes that formed the background for this foundation myth would ultimately become the location of a vast, densely artificial urban landscape, but one that would nevertheless periodically return to its original watery state.

what was nearly a torrent, while others, having been soaked in the long-lasting floodwaters, collapsed.

215 BC

Aquae magnae bis eo anno fuerunt Tiberisque agros inundavit cum magna strage tectorum pecorumque et hominum pernicie. (Livy 24.9.6)

In that year there were two great floods, and the Tiber inundated the farms, with great havoc to buildings and destruction of cattle and people.

203 BC

Annus insignis incendio ingenti, quo Clivus Publicius ad solum exustus est, et aquarum magnitudine . . . (Livy 30.26.5)

The year was notable for a great fire in which the Clivus Publicus was burned to the ground, and for floods . . .

202 BC

Inter quae etiam aquarum insolita magnitudo in religionem versa; nam ita abundavit Tiberis ut ludi Apollinares circo inundato extra portam Collinam ad aedem Erycinae Veneris parati sint. Ceterum ludorum ipso die subita serenitate orta pompa duci coepta ad portam Collinam revocata deductaque in circum est cum decessisse inde aquam nuntiatum esset; laetitiamque populo et ludis celebritatem addidit sedes sua sollemni spectaculo reddita. (Livy 30.38.10–12)

Meanwhile, the unusually high water levels were viewed as a portent, for the Tiber so overflowed that the Circus was flooded and preparations for the Games of Apollo were made outside the Colline Gate near the Temple of Venus of Eryx. On the day of the games itself, however, sudden clear weather caused the parade, already having set out for the Colline Gate, to be recalled and dispatched to the Circus when it was announced that the water had receded from it. Restoring the spectacle to its accustomed place enhanced the joy of the people and crowds at the games.

193 BC

Aquae ingentes eo anno fuerunt et Tiberis loca plana urbis inundavit; circa portam Flumentanam etiam collapsa quaedam ruinis sunt. (Livy 35.9.2–3)

In that year, there were great floods, and the Tiber inundated the flat parts of the city. Near the Porta Flumentana, certain buildings even collapsed and were destroyed.

192 BC

Tiberis infestiore quam priore anno impetu illatus urbi duos pontes, aedificia multa, maxime circa Flumentanam portam, evertit. Saxum ingens, sive imbribus seu motu terrae leniore quam ut alioqui sentiretur, labefactatum in vicum Iugarium ex Capitolio procidit et multos oppressit. In agris passim inundatis pecua ablata, villarum strages facta est. (Livy 35.21.5–6)

Attacking the city with greater force than the previous year, the Tiber carried away the two bridges, and many buildings, especially near the Porta Flumentana. Shaken loose, either from the rains or by an earthquake too mild to be otherwise felt, a huge stone fell from the Capitoline Hill into the Vicus Iugarius, and many were killed. All over in the inundated fields, cattle were swept away, and farmhouses were reduced to ruins.

189 BC

Aquae ingentes eo anno fuerunt; Tiberis duodeciens campum Martium planaque urbis inundavit. (Livy 38.28.4)

That year, there were great floods, with the Tiber flooding the Campus Martius and the flat areas of the city twelve times.

181 BC

Τετρακοσίων δέ που διαγενομένων ἐτῶν ὕπατοι μὲν ἦσαν Πόπλιος Κορνήλιος καὶ Μάρκος Βαίβιος ὄμβρων δὲ μεγάλων ἐπιπεσόντων καὶ χώματος περιρραγέντος ἐξέωσε τὰς σοροὺς τὸ ῥεῦμα. (Plut. *Numa* 22.4)

And about four hundred years later, in the consulship of Publius Cornelius and Marcus Baebius, heavy rains fell and the flood tore away the earth mound and dislodged the coffins.

In this passage, Plutarch does not unequivocally say that there was a flood, but only that "heavy rains" caused the coffin containing the body of Numa to become disinterred. Such disinhumations as described here are actually common occurrences during and after floods. In flood-prone areas where the ground water level is close to the surface, such as some parts of China and New Orleans, this is a frequent problem, and corpses and coffins routinely pop up out of the ground after flooding. The disinhumation of corpses and coffins has even been observed in dry climates such as in Los Angeles after flooding or heavy rainfall.[10] Given the mention of severe rainfall and the well-established physical phenomenon of flooding causing disinterment, it seems reasonable to infer that there was probably some degree of substantial flooding on this occasion.

156 BC

> Pontificis maximi tectum cum columnis in Tiberim deiectum. (Iul. Obseq. 16)

> The covering with supports of the great bridge [the Pons Aemilius] was thrown down into the Tiber.

This passage does not explicitly mention a flood, but damage to bridges is most likely to have been caused by high waters. The text surrounding this passage describes a violent storm that struck the city, and it is possible that high winds alone may have been responsible for the damage to the bridge. The issue is clouded by the ambiguity of the term *tectum*. It may refer to some sort of roofing on the bridge, or, perhaps more likely, the earliest version of this bridge had stone piers, while the roadbed and arches were still made of wood.[11] Such a superstructure could easily have been swept away by floodwaters, while the sturdier stone piers survived.

60 BC

> Χειμών τε γὰρ τοιοῦτος ἐξαίφνης τήν τε πόλιν ὅλην καὶ τὴν χώραν ἅπασαν κατέσχεν ὥστε πάμπολλα μὲν δένδρα πρόρριζα ἀνατραπῆναι, πολλὰς δὲ οἰκίας καταρραγῆναι, τά τε πλοῖα τὰ ἐν τῷ Τιβέριδι καὶ πρὸς τὸ ἄστυ καὶ πρὸς τὰς ἐκβολὰς αὐτοῦ ναυλοχοῦντα βαπτισθῆναι, καὶ τὴν γέφυραν τὴν ξυλίνην διαφθαρῆναι, καί τι καὶ θέατρον πρὸς πανήγυρίν τινα ἐκ θυρῶν ᾠκοδομημένον ἀνετράπη, καὶ ἄνθρωποι παρὰ πάντα ταῦτα παμπληθεῖς ἀπώλοντο. (Dio 37.58.2–4)

> For of a sudden, such a storm descended upon the whole city and all the country that quantities of trees were torn up by the roots, many houses were shattered, the boats moored in the Tiber both near the city and at its mouth were sunk, and the wooden bridge [the Pons Sublicius] destroyed, and a theater built of timbers for some festival collapsed and, in the midst of all this, great numbers of human beings perished.

While this passage does not explicitly say that there was a flood, a storm of this intensity would most likely have resulted in some flooding. Furthermore, several of the types of damage described, such as houses destroyed, boats sunk, and the Pons Sublicius (the wooden bridge) demolished, are far more likely to have been caused by rampaging floodwaters than by wind and rain alone. The large loss of life mentioned is also unlikely to have been caused by a storm alone, but is all too probable in the case of an accompanying flood. Therefore, while one cannot say with absolute certainty that this passage provides evidence of a flood in this year, the detailed description of flood-type damages makes it a reasonable assumption. (See the floods of 156 BC and 32 BC for similar situations.)

54 BC

Κἀν τούτῳ ὁ Τίβερις, εἴτ᾽ οὖν ὄμβρων ἄνω που ὑπὲρ τὴν πόλιν ἐξαισίων γενομένων, εἴτε καὶ σφοδροῦ πνεύματος ἐκ τῆς θαλάσσης τὴν ἐκροὴν αὐτοῦ ἀνακόψαντος, εἴτε καὶ μᾶλλον, ὡς ὑπωπτεύετο, ἐκ παρασκευῆς δαιμονίου τινός, τοσοῦτος ἐξαπιναίως ἐρρύη ὥστ᾽ ἐν πᾶσι μὲν τοῖς πεδίοις τοῖς ἐν τῷ ἄστει οὖσι πελαγίσαι, πολλὰ δὲ καὶ τῶν μετεωροτέρων καταλαβεῖν. αἵ τε οὖν οἰκίαι (ἐκ πλίνθων γὰρ συνῳκοδομημέναι ἦσαν) διάβροχοί τε ἐγένοντο καὶ κατερράγησαν, καὶ τὰ ὑποζύγια πάντα ὑποβρύχια ἐφθάρη. τῶν τε ἀνθρώπων ὅσοι μὴ ἔφθησαν πρὸς τὰ πάνυ ὑψηλὰ ἀναφυγόντες, οἱ μὲν ἐν ταῖς τέγαις οἱ δὲ καὶ ἐν ὁδοῖς ἐγκαταληφθέντες ἐξώλοντο. καὶ γὰρ αἱ λοιπαὶ οἰκίαι, ἅτε ἐπὶ πολλὰς ἡμέρας τοῦ δεινοῦ συμβάντος, σαθραί τε ἐγένοντο καὶ πολλοῖς τοῖς μὲν εὐθὺς τοῖς δὲ μετὰ τοῦτ᾽ ἐλυμήναντο. (Dio 39.61.1–2)

Meanwhile, the Tiber, either because excessive rains had occurred somewhere upstream above the city, or because a violent wind from the sea had driven back its outgoing tide, or still more probably, as was surmised, by the act of some divinity, suddenly rose so high as to inundate all the lower levels of the city and to overwhelm even many of the higher portions. The houses, therefore, being constructed of brick, became soaked through and collapsed, while all the animals perished in the flood. And of the people, all who did not take refuge in time on the highest points were caught, either in their dwellings or in the streets, and lost their lives. The remaining houses, too, became weakened since the mischief lasted for many days, and they caused injuries to many, either at the time or later. (Loeb translation)

Romae, et maxime Appia ad Martis, mira proluvies. Crassipedis ambulatio ablata, horti, tabernae plurimae; magna vis aquae usque ad piscinam publicam. Viget illud Homeri: ἤματ' ὀπωρινῷ ὅτε λαβρότατον χέει ὕδωρ Ζεύς, ὅτε δή γ' ἄνδρεσσι κοτεσσάμενος χαλεπαίνῃ, cadit enim in absolutionem Gabini οἳ βίῃ εἰν ἀγορῇ σκολιὰς κρίνωσι θέμιστας, ἐκ δὲ δίκην ἐλάσωσι, θεῶν ὄπιν οὐκ ἀλέγοντες. (Cic. Ad Quint. fr. 3.7.1)

At Rome, and particularly along the Appian Way up to the Temple of Mars, there are amazing floods. The promenade of Crassipes was swept away, and gardens and numerous shops. A huge volume of water reaches up to the public fishpond. That passage by Homer still holds true: "As on a day in late autumn when down in a torrent resistless Zeus pours the rain, in resentment and wrath at the misdeeds of mortals" (for it fits exactly in with the acquittal of Gabinius) "Who in the place of assembly distort without mercy their judgments / Banishing justice from Earth and the voice of the gods never heeding."

44 BC

Iam satis terris nivis atque dirae
grandinis misit Pater et rubente
dextera sacras iaculatus arces
   terruit urbem,
terruit gentes, grave ne rediret
saeculum Pyrrhae nova monstra questae,
omne cum Proteus pecus egit altos
   visere montes,
piscium et summa genus haesit ulmo,
nota quae sedes fuerat columbis,
et superiecto pavidae natarunt
   aequore dammae.
vidimus flavum Tiberim, retortis
litore Etrusco violenter undis,
ire deiectum monumenta regis
   templaque Vestae,
Iliae dum se nimium querenti
iactat ultorem, vagus et sinistra
labitur ripa, Iove non probante,
   uxorius amnis.
(Hor. Carm. 1.2.1–20)

Enough already of dire snow and hail has the Father [Jupiter] sent upon the earth, and smiting with his red right hand the sacred hill-tops, has filled with fear the City and the people, lest there should come again the gruesome age of Pyrrha, who complained of marvels strange, when Proteus drove all his herd to visit the lofty mountains, and the tribe of fishes lodged in elm-tops, that till then had been the wonted haunt of doves, and the terror-stricken does swam in the overwhelming flood.

We saw the yellow Tiber, its waves hurled back in fury from the Tuscan shore, advance to overthrow the King's Memorial [Regia] and Vesta's shrines, showing himself too ardent an avenger of complaining Ilia, and spreading far and wide o'er the left bank without Jove's sanction,—fond river-god. (Loeb translation)

The date of the flood in Horace's poem is not explicitly stated, and in this case is a highly contentious issue. One tradition, following the suggestion of Porphyrius (*Ad Hor. Carm* 1.2), has interpreted the tempests described as being associated with the disasters, supernatural events, and portents that either preceded or followed the death of Julius Caesar in 44 BC. Le Gall places the date of the flood more specifically in late March of 44 BC after the death of Caesar.[12] Most other studies of floods at Rome have accepted the 44 BC date, while often also admitting that it is somewhat uncertain.

The poem itself, however, was composed much later, probably between 29 and 27 BC, and this has caused some to argue for a considerably later date. Gallavotti suggests that Horace's flood should be identified as the one of 27 BC described in Dio 53.20.1. Others, such as Gros, believe that the poem must be describing an otherwise unattested flood that occurred between Actium in 31 BC and the flood of 27 BC, with the spring of 28 or 29 BC being most likely. They base their arguments on the fact that the poem must have been written after Actium, and because a flood is not specifically mentioned in the lists of portents following the death of Caesar given by any other author. Mazzarino has even suggested that Horace's flood should be identified with the flood of 23 BC described by Dio (53.33.5) and that the poem was also composed at this later date.

While the date when the poem was written was probably around 29 or 28 BC, it is not clear why the date of composition and the date of the flood depicted have to be the same. Horace could well be recalling the events of 44 BC. Commager has argued that this is improbable since his contemporaries would be unlikely to remember a specific storm of some fifteen years earlier. He puts forward the possibility that the tempest Horace describes is to be read as a metaphor, rather than as an account of an actual historical flood. Against this interpretation, it could be said that the precise detail of the flood attacking the Regia and shrine of the Vestals suggests a definite flood rather than a metaphorical one. Even here, however, one can offer a counterargument that the mention of these monuments serves an important symbolic role in the poem and thus does not indicate a specific historical flood.[13]

In the end, it is probably not possible to arrive at any definitive answer to the question of the date of the flood in Horace's poem. All of these arguments have some merit, and all are at least possible. If pressed to choose a date for the flood, I would propose the original one of 44 BC as being the most straightforward reading of the poem, and hence perhaps the most probable.

32 BC

καὶ συχνὰ μὲν ὑπὸ χειμῶνος ἐπόνησεν, ὥστε καὶ τρόπαιόν τι ἐν τῷ Ἀουεντίνῳ ἑστὸς καὶ νίκης ἄγαλμα ἀπὸ τῆς τοῦ θεάτρου σκηνῆς πεσεῖν, τήν τε γέφυραν τὴν ξυλίνην πᾶσαν καταρραγῆναι. (Dio 50.8.3)

Much damage was also caused by tempest; thus a trophy that stood upon the Aventine fell, a statue of Victory fell from the back wall of the theater, and the wooden bridge [the Pons Sublicius] was utterly demolished.

Much as in the case of the flood of 60 BC, while this passage does not explicitly state that there was a flood, the damage listed—including the complete destruction of the Pons Sublicius (the wooden bridge)—implies that a flood accompanied the described tempest. The Pons Sublicius is known to have been particularly susceptible to floods and was destroyed by them on at least two (and probably three) other occasions (in 23 BC, Dio 53.33.5; in AD 69, Tac. *Ann.* 1.86; in 60 BC, Dio 37.58.3–4). A storm alone might have destroyed the bridge by a lightning strike that then set it afire, but this was clearly not the case in this instance, since, after he has finished describing the destruction caused by the tempest, Dio separately states that there were also many things destroyed by fires that year. This leaves wind and water as the only possible agents of the bridge's destruction, and of the two, it seems much more likely that the bridge was swept away by floodwaters than that the wind blew it over. It therefore seems a fairly reasonable, although admittedly not absolutely certain, assumption that this passage can be interpreted as providing evidence for a flood, or at least for very high and dangerous waters, in 32 BC. (See also the floods of 156 BC and 60 BC for similar situations.)

27 BC

> ὁ γὰρ Τίβερις πελαγίσας πᾶσαν τὴν ἐν τοῖς πεδίοις Ῥώμην κατέλαβεν ὥστε πλεῖσθαι, καὶ ἀπ᾽ αὐτοῦ οἱ μάντεις ὅτι τε ἐπὶ μέγα αὐξήσοι καὶ ὅτι πᾶσαν τὴν πόλιν ὑποχειρίαν ἕξοι προέγνωσαν. (Dio 53.20.1)

> The Tiber overflowed and covered all of Rome that was on low ground, so that it was navigable by boats. From this sign, the soothsayers prophesied that he [Octavian] would rise to great heights and hold the whole world under his sway. (Loeb translation)

23 BC

> ὅ τε Τίβερις αὐξηθεὶς τήν τε γέφυραν τὴν ξυλίνην κατέσυρε καὶ τὴν πόλιν πλωτὴν ἐπὶ τρεῖς ἡμέρας ἐποίησε. (Dio 53.33.5)

> The Tiber, rising, carried away the wooden bridge [the Pons Sublicius] and made the city navigable by boats for three days. (Loeb translation)

This same flood may also have damaged the Pons Fabricius, which connected Tiber island to the left bank, because an inscription records that a restoration of this bridge was undertaken in 23 BC by the consuls Q. Lepidus and M. Lollius (*CIL* 6.1305 = *ILS* 5892).

22 BC

> Τῷ δ᾽ ἐπιγιγνομένῳ ἔτει, ἐν ᾧ Μᾶρκος τε Μάρκελλος καὶ Λούκιος Ἀρρούντιος ὑπάτευσαν, ἥ τε πόλις πελαγίσαντος αὖθις τοῦ ποταμοῦ ἐπλεύσθη. (Dio 54.1)

> The following year, in which Marcus Marcellus and Lucius Arruntius were consuls, the city was again submerged by the overflowing of the river. (Loeb translation)

13 BC

> καὶ ἔτυχε γὰρ ἡ ἀγγελία τῆς ἀφίξεως αὐτοῦ ἐν ἐκείναις ταῖς ἡμέραις ἐς τὸ ἄστυ ἐλθοῦσα ἐν αἷς Κορνήλιος Βάλβος τὸ θέατρον τὸ καὶ νῦν ἐπ᾽

αὐτοῦ καλούμενον καθιερώσας θέας ἐπετέλει, ἐπί τε τούτῳ ὡς καὶ αὐτὸς τὸν Αὔγουστον ἐπανάξων ἐσεμνύνετο, καίτοι ὑπὸ τοῦ πλήθους τοῦ ὕδατος, ὅπερ ὁ Τίβερις πλεονάσας ἐπεποιήκει, μηδὲ ἐσελθεῖν ἐς τὸ θέατρον εἰ μὴ πλοίῳ δυνηθείς, καὶ ὁ Τιβέριος πρῶτον αὐτὸν ἐπὶ τῇ τοῦ θεάτρου τιμῇ ἐπεψήφισεν. (Dio 54.25.2)

It chanced that the news of his [Augustus's] coming reached the city during those days when Cornelius Balbus was celebrating with spectacles the dedication of the theater which is even today called by his name; and Balbus accordingly began to put on airs, as if it were he himself who was going to bring Augustus back, although he was unable even to enter his theater, except by boat, on account of the flood of water caused by the Tiber, which had overflowed its banks—and Tiberius put the vote to him first in honor of his building the theater. (Loeb translation)

AD 5

... per dies octo Tiberis impetu miseranda clades hominum domorumque fuit. (Cassiod. *Chron.* 604)

For eight miserable days there was destruction of men and homes as the Tiber attacked.

... καὶ ὁ Τίβερις τήν τε γέφυραν κατέσυρε καὶ πλωτὴν τὴν πόλιν ἐπὶ ἑπτὰ ἡμέρας ἐποίησε ... (Dio 55.22.3)

... the Tiber carried away the bridge and made the city navigable for seven days ... (Loeb translation)

AD 12

τά τε Ἄρεια τότε μέν, ἐπειδὴ ὁ Τίβερις τὸν ἱππόδρομον προκατέσχεν, ἐν τῇ τοῦ Αὐγούστου ἀγορᾷ καὶ ἵππων δρόμῳ τρόπον τινὰ καὶ θηρίων σφαγῇ ἐτιμήθη, αὖθις δὲ ὥσπερ εἴθιστο ἐγένετο. (Dio 56.27.4)

The Ludi Martiales, owing to the fact that the Tiber had overflowed the Circus, were held on this occasion in the Forum of Augustus and were celebrated in a fashion by a horse race and the slaying of wild beasts. They were also given a second time, as custom decreed. (Loeb translation)

AD 15

Eodem anno continuis imbribus auctus Tiberis plana urbis stagnaverat; relabentem secuta est aedificiorum et hominum strages. Igitur censuit Asinius Gallus ut libri Sybillini adirentur. Renuit Tiberius, perinde divina humanaque obtegens; sed remedium coercendi fluminis Ateio Capitoni et L. Arruntio mandatum. (Tac. *Ann.* 1.76)

In that year, the Tiber, swollen by constant rains, flowed into the flat areas of the city. Its subsiding was accompanied by the destruction of buildings and loss of life. Therefore, Asinius Gallus proposed that the Sibylline Books be consulted. Tiberius refused, keeping equally secret human and divine affairs. Nevertheless, finding a solution for controlling the river was entrusted to Ateius Capito and Lucius Arruntius.

Τοῦ τε ποταμοῦ τοῦ Τιβέριδος πολλὰ τῆς πόλεως κατασχόντος ὥστε πλευσθῆναι, οἱ μὲν ἄλλοι ἐν τέρατος λόγῳ καὶ τοῦτο, . . . ελάμβανον, ἐκεῖνος δὲ δὴ νομίσας ἐκ πολυπληθίας ναμάτων αὐτὸ γεγονέναι πέντε ἀεὶ βουλευτὰς κληρωτοὺς ἐπιμελεῖσθαι τοῦ ποταμοῦ προσέταξεν, ἵνα μήτε τοῦ χειμῶνος πλεονάζῃ μήτε τοῦ θέρους ἐλλείμῃ, ἀλλ' ἴσος ὅτι μάλιστα ἀεὶ ῥέῃ. (Dio 57.14.7–8)

When now the Tiber overflowed a large part of the city, so that people went about in boats, most people regarded this also as an omen. . . . the emperor, however, thinking that it was due to the great overabundance of running water, appointed five senators chosen by lot, to constitute a permanent board to look after the river, so that it should neither overflow in winter nor fail in summer, but should maintain as even a flow as possible all the time. (Loeb translation)

AD 36

Σέξτου δὲ δὴ Παπινίου μετὰ Κυίντου Πλαυτίου ὑπατεύσαντος ὅ τε Τίβερις πολλὰ τῆς πόλεως ἐπέκλυσεν ὥστε πλευσθῆναι . . . (Dio 58.26.5)

In the consulship of Sextus Papinius and Quintus Plautius, the Tiber inundated a large part of the city so that people went about in boats . . .

Ὁ Τίβερις δὲ τοτε πολλὰ τῆς Ῥώμης ἐπέκλυσεν ὥστε πλευσθῆναι, καὶ πυρὶ μυρία ἐφθάρη. (Zonaras 11.3)

At that time, the Tiber submerged a large part of Rome so that it was navigable by boat . . .

AD 69

καὶ τὸ περὶ τὸν θύμβριν δὲ σύμπτωμα σημεῖον ἐποιοῦντο οἱ μολλοὶ μοχθηρόν. ἦν μὲν γὰρ ὥρα περὶ ἣν μάλιστα οἱ ποταμοὶ πλήθουσιν, ἀλλ' οὔπω τοσοῦτος ἤρθη πρότερον, οὐδὲ ἀπώλεσε τοσαῦτα καὶ διέφθειρεν, ὑπερχυθεὶς καὶ κατακλύσας πολὺ μέρος τῆς πόλεως, πλεῖστον δὲ ἐν ᾧ τὸν ἐπὶ πράσει διαπωλοῦσι σῖτον, ὡς δεινὴν ἀπορίαν ἡμερῶν συχνῶν κατασχεῖν. (Plut. *Otho* 4.5)

The behavior of the Tiber, too, was regarded by most people as a baleful sign. It was a time, to be sure, when rivers are at their fullest, but the Tiber had never before risen so high, nor caused such great ruin and destruction. It overflowed its banks and submerged a great part of the city and especially the grain market, so that dire scarcity of food prevailed for many days together. (Loeb translation)

. . . et primo egressu inundationibus Tiberis retardatus ad vicensimum etiam lapidem ruina aedificiorum praeclusam viam offendit. (Suet. *Otho* 8.3)

. . . and on first leaving the city, he was held back by floods of the Tiber, and at the 20th milestone, he came upon an obstruction of collapsed buildings in the road.

Sed praecipuus et cum praesenti exitio etiam futuri pavor subita inundatione Tiberis, qui immenso auctu proruto ponte sublicio ac strage obstantis molis refusus, non modo iacentia et plana urbis loca, sed secura eius modi casuum implevit: rapti e publico plerique, plures in tabernis et cubilibus intercepti. Fames in vulgus inopia quaestus et penuria alimentorum. Corrupta stagnantibus aquis insularum fundamenta, dein remeante flumine dilapsa. Utque primum vacuus a periculo animus fuit, id ipsum quod parani expeditionem Othoni campus Martius et via Flaminia iter belli esset obstructum, a fortuitis vel naturalibus causis in prodigium et omen imminentium cladium vertebatur. (Tac. *Hist.* 1.86)

But fear, relating both to the current destruction and to future danger, was caused by a sudden flood of the Tiber, which, swollen to an enormous size, pushed over the wooden bridge [the Pons Sublicius] and was turned back by the ruins that blocked the river like a dam. It not only flooded the flat parts of the city, but also parts usually free of such calamities. Many people were carried off in the open; more were trapped in shops and in their beds. The common people starved due to lack of employment and insufficient food supplies. The foundations of apartment buildings were undermined by the stagnant water and then collapsed when the river receded. As soon as people's minds were free from this hazard, the fact itself that while an expedition of war was being prepared by Otho, the Campus Martius and the Via Flaminia which was to be his route were blocked, was interpreted as an omen of imminent catastrophe rather than as due to luck or natural causes.

Floods of the Tiber in Ancient Rome

UNKNOWN DATE DURING THE REIGN OF NERVA

> Eo tempore multo perniciosius quam sub Nerva Tiberis inundavit magna clade aedium proximarum . . . (Sex. Aur. Victor *Epit.* 13)

> At that time, the Tiber flooded much worse than [it had] under Nerva, with great destruction to the nearest shrines . . .

This flood is only indirectly attested by Sextus Aurelius Victor, who in describing the severity of the flood during the reign of Trajan asserts that it was worse than the flood that had struck during the reign of Nerva. Nothing other than this comparative statement is known about this flood, so all that can be said about its date is that it must fall between Nerva's accession in late AD 96 and his death in January of AD 98.

UNKNOWN DATE DURING THE REIGN OF TRAJAN

> Num istic quoque immite et turbidum caelum? Hic adsiduae tempestates et crebra diluvia. Tiberis alveum excessit et demissioribus ripis alte superfunditur. Quamquam fossa, quam providentissimus imperator fecit, exhaustus premit valles, innatat campis, quaque planum solum, pro solo cernitur. Inde, quae solet flumina accipere et permixta devehere, velut obvius sistere cogit atque ita alienis aquis operit agros, quos ipse non tangit. Anio, delicatissimus amnium ideoque adiacentibus villis velut invitatus retentusque, magna ex parte nemora, quibus inumbratur, fregit et rapuit; subruit montes et decidentium mole pluribus locis clausus, dum amissum iter quaerit, impulit tecta ac se super ruinas eiecit atque extulit.
>
> Viderunt, quos excelsioribus terris illa tempestas non deprehendit, alibi divitum apparatus, et gravem supellectilem, alibi instrumenta ruris, ibi boves, aratra, rectores, hic soluta et libera armenta atque inter haec arborum truncos aut villarum trabes atque culmina varie lateque fluitantia. Ac ne illa quidem malo vacaverunt, ad quae non ascendit amnis. Nam pro amne imber adsiduus et deiecti nubibus turbines, proruta opera, quibus pretiosa rura cinguntur, quassata atque etiam decussa monumenta. Multi eius modi casibus debilitati, obruti, obtriti; et aucta luctibus damna. (Pliny *Epist.* 8.17)

> Is the weather as severe and violent around you as with us? Here there are constant storms and repeated floods. The Tiber has risen above its channel and spread out deeply over its low-lying banks. Although drained by a spillway made by the foresight of the emperor, the river covers the val-

leys, swims into the fields, and entirely covers over the flat ground. Then, the streams that it usually receives and, mixing together, bears along with it, it forces to check their course by, as it were, going to meet them. Thus it covers over fields that it is not able to reach by itself with borrowed waters. The Anio, that most delicate of rivers, which seems invited and detained by the villas adjacent to it, has destroyed and carried away the greater part of the groves that shade it. The river has undermined mountains and, blocked by the resulting landslides, destroyed houses and flows over the ruins, attempting to get back to its course.

Those who live in highlands out of the reach of these terrible storms have witnessed, here, the household paraphernalia and weighty furniture of the wealthy, there, the simple tools of the farm, over there oxen, plows, and the plowmen themselves, here herds set free and straying, jumbled among the trunks of trees, or the beams and roofs from villas, and all of it floating about randomly and widely. Nor indeed did these areas, to which the river did not ascend, escape disaster. For constant deluges of rain and whirlwinds thrown down from the clouds have demolished the works that encircle the valuable farms, and have tossed about and even shaken down monuments. Many people have been disabled, buried, and crushed by these disasters, and the property damage has been augmented by mourning for the dead.

As with many of Pliny's letters, the one that describes this flood does not include any information that would enable its date to be fixed. Of those letters containing references that allow dates to be assigned to them, all fall between AD 97 and 108.[14] Furthermore, the books collecting his letters appear to follow a roughly chronological order. Because the letter in question appears in book 8, this chronology suggests a most probable date of AD 107 or 108. Therefore, although it seems fairly likely that this letter describes a flood around AD 108, what can be said with certainty is that the flood occurred sometime between AD 97 and 108 during the reign of Trajan. This flood is also mentioned by Sextus Aurelius Victor, and while his comments might be interpreted as placing it toward the end of Trajan's reign, this is only speculative.

UNKNOWN DATE DURING THE REIGN OF HADRIAN

. . . fuit etiam Tiberis inundatio. (SHA *Had.* 21.6)

There was also a flood of the Tiber.

Any more precise dating for this flood is impossible, since it is mentioned as simply one item in a list summarizing all of the natural disasters and calamities that took place at various points during Hadrian's reign. As such, it could have taken place anytime between AD 117 and 138.

AD 147

   ... fuit et inundatio Tiberis ... (SHA *Ant.* 9.3)

   ... and there was a flood of the Tiber.

   [—] X. K. April. aqua magna fuit. (*Fasti Ost.*)

Ten days before the kalends of April, there was a great flood.

AD 162

   ... sed interpellavit istam felicitatem securitatemque imperatoris prima Tiberis inundatio, quae sub illis gravissima fuit. quae res et multa urbis aedificia vexavit et plurimum animalium interemit et famem gravissimam peperit. (SHA *M. Aur.* 8)

   But interrupting the happiness and rest of the emperor was a flood of the Tiber, which was the most serious of those times. It shook many buildings in the city and drowned many animals and caused a severe famine.

Previous commentators on floods at Rome have all listed this flood merely as having occurred at some indeterminate point during the reign of Marcus Aurelius.[15] It is possible, however, to narrow down the date of this inundation considerably by examining where the account of the flood falls in the sequence of events described around it. The window of time during which the flood could have transpired stretches from the date of the accession of Marcus Aurelius and Verus in March of AD 161 to the departure of Verus from Rome to lead the war against Parthia during the summer of AD 162. Furthermore, it does not seem to have occurred immediately after the accession, since it is said to have taken place after the funeral rites of Antoninus Pius had been completed and after the new emperors had had time to settle comfortably into their jobs. Also, Verus was said to have taken an active personal role in providing relief for the flood victims, so it is unlikely that the flood struck immediately prior to his departure. Therefore, this flood assailed Rome at some point between the fall of AD 161 and the spring of AD 162. If it followed the usual Tiber seasonal pattern, it most likely occurred in late winter or spring, thus making the most probable date early AD 162.

AD 217

καὶ ὅτι ὁ Τίβερις ἐν τῇ αὐτῇ ἐκείνῃ ἡμέρᾳ πληθύσας ἔς τε τὴν ἀγορὰν καὶ ἐς τὰς περὶ αὐτὴν ὁδοὺς τοσαύτῃ ῥύμῃ ἐσέβαλεν ὥστε καὶ ἀνθρώπους παρασυρῆναι. (Dio 79.25.5)

The Tiber rose until it invaded the Forum and the neighboring streets with such violence as to even sweep people away. (Loeb translation)

AD 253

... Tiberis adulta aestate diluvii facie inundavit. (Sex. Aur. Victor *De Caes.* 32)

... at the height of summer, the Tiber overflowed and flooded.

AD 371

Tiberis qui media intersecans moenia, cloacis et fluviis abundantibus multis, Tyrreno mari miscetur, effusione imbrium exuberans nimia, et supra amnis speciem pansus, omnia paene contexit. Et stagnantibus civitatis residuis membris, quae tenduntur in planitiem molliorem, montes soli et quicquid insularum celsius eminebat, a praesenti metu defendebatur: et ne multi inedia contabescerent, undarum magnitudine nusquam progredi permittente, lembis et scaphis copia suggerebatur abunde ciborum. At vero ubi tempestas mollivit, et flumen retinaculis ruptis redit ad solitum cursum, absterso metu nihil postea molestius exspectabatur. (Am. Mar. 29.6.17–18)

The Tiber, which passes through the middle of the city, and flowing together with many sewers and streams mixes into the Tyrrhenian Sea, was swollen by excessive rains. Spreading beyond the appearance of a river, it covered nearly everything. And while all the remaining sections of the city that stretch across the more level plains were submerged, only the hills and certain apartment buildings of outstanding height were protected from the present threat. In order that many people not waste away from starvation, boats and watercraft supplied food in abundance since the depth of the floodwaters did not allow travel by foot. But in fact, when the storms abated, and the river that had broken from its banks returned to its customary channel, fear was banished and no further problems were expected.

AD 398

... aut fluvium per tecta vagum summisque minatum collibus? Ingentes vexi summersa carinas remorumque sonos et Pyrrhae saecula sensi. (Claud. *De Bel. Gild.* 41–43)

Or [why bother describing] the river washing between roofs and threatening the hills? The submerged city knows what it is to experience huge ships, the sounds of oars, and the age of Pyrrha.

THE SUPPOSED FLOOD OF AD 379

One other flood that should perhaps be discussed here is the one that supposedly occurred in AD 379. In all the lists of ancient floods compiled by modern authors, including those of Le Gall, Frosini, Di Martino and Belati, Bencivenga et al., and Bersani and Bencivenga, a flood is ascribed to this year.[16] The citation given for this flood is the *Chronica Maiora* of Bede, which is part of his *De Temporum Ratione*. (Different editions use various numbering systems; the passage in question variously appears as section 589; or lines 2035–40; or section 4671. See also the *Liber Pontificalis* 91.6.) This passage does indeed describe a catastrophic flood of the Tiber that lasted for a week and inundated a broad area.

This flood struck, however, not in AD 379, but rather in AD 716. The account of the flood appears in Bede's chronicle just after an account of Emperor Theodosius III's defeat of Anastasius II at Nicaea, and just prior to the accession of Leo III after Theodosius's brief one-year rule. The flood of AD 716 is particularly well attested, with substantial descriptions appearing in the *History of the Langobards* (6.36) and in the *Liber Pontificalis* (Gregory II, 6). In Bede's chronicle, the described events of AD 715–17 as well as other datable references to people and occurrences exactly match the events in the other primary sources, leaving no doubt that this flood took place in the early eighth century rather than the fourth. The confusion is probably due to a cursory reading of Bede's text, in which the heading of this section, identifying the current ruler, is "Theodosius an. I." According to the conventions of the work, this should be translated as "Theodosius ruled one year," and the subsequent text clearly intends to refer to Theodosius III. Presumably this line was mistranslated as referring to the first year of the reign of Theodosius I, who became emperor in AD 379; thus the flood was ascribed to the earlier date. Even a casual reading of the list of events surrounding this line reveals that the emperor in question is Theodosius III, not Theodosius I, but this seems to be a case of a primary source being read quickly or incompletely, resulting in the flood being attributed to the wrong era. This erroneous date was then repeated in the lists of floods put together by subsequent modern authors so that the mythical flood of AD 379 became enshrined in the literature of ancient Roman floods.

Geographic Extent of Floods Based on Primary Sources

Attempting to create a comprehensive map of ancient flood-prone areas on the basis of the written accounts alone is not easy. The various authors certainly did not write their reports with a journalistic intent to provide a complete and accurate portrait of the event, and many include no geographic information whatsoever. Others who do make reference to the extent of floods are frustratingly vague in their listing of regions inundated, or name monuments whose location is today unknown or contested. Despite these limitations, ancient authors' descriptions of floods do in certain instances plainly identify several regions or sites that seem to have been particularly flood-prone.

The area most commonly identified in the primary sources as being subject to flooding is also the most vague. In nine of the accounts, it is related that a flood inundated the "flat" or "level" (*planus*) region of the city.[17] This phrase is not merely a convention repeated over and over by one author, because the nine accounts that identify the flatlands as flood zones were penned by seven different authors. At first glance, this information does not seem very enlightening, since it simply affirms what common sense would seem to indicate. Is it possible to be more specific about the location of this region? The largest, most extensive flat area near the center of the city is the Campus Martius, the low-lying swampy region enclosed within the bend in the Tiber (see fig. 1.2).[18] Without doubt, the Campus Martius would have been one of the first areas to be covered by rising water, and so perhaps

Floods of the Tiber in Ancient Rome

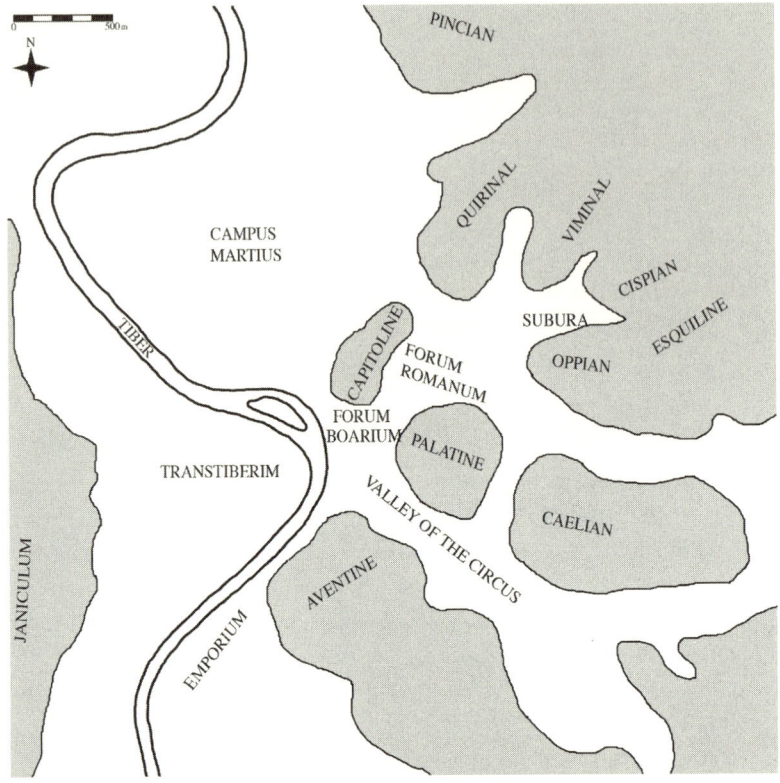

Fig. 1.2. Map of the main geographic features of ancient Rome.

might be the "flatlands" indicated by the sources. Two pieces of evidence argue against such an identification, however. First, the Campus Martius had a well-known name, and there seems to be no reason why the authors would not have employed it in preference to the vaguer designation. Second, in describing one flood, Livy (38.28.4) specifically states that it inundated the "flatlands" as well as the Campus Martius. Also, most of the flood accounts date to periods when, strictly speaking, the Campus Martius lay outside the *pomerium* and thus was not part of the city proper. Thus it seems safest to take the "flatlands" of the sources at face value as generally indicating all the low-lying areas of the city situated between the hills. This zone might be interpreted to include the Campus Martius but should not be identified exclusively with it.

In addition to the general description of "the flatlands," the written sources identify 17 specific sites or monuments that at some point were flooded. Two flood accounts describe buildings being damaged in the region of the Porta Flumentana.[19] This was the gate in the Servian walls opening onto the Tiber from the Forum Boarium, so that these literary sources confirm what seems obvious from geography— that the Forum Boarium, lying so close to the Tiber, was one of the zones most at risk to rising waters. The account of the flood during the reign of Nerva by Sextus Aurelius Victor (*Epit.* 13) may also contain a mention of an inundation of the Forum Boarium area. He says that the flood damaged the "nearest temples." This might well be a reference to the temples in the Forum Boarium because these temples were probably the ones closest to the Tiber, but the allusion is too vague to identify them with certainty.

The written sources also describe floods affecting sites in the valleys extending out of the Forum Boarium to the left and right of the Palatine Hill. Horace (*Carm.* 1.2) paints a vivid picture of the Regia and shrine to Vesta being attacked by floodwaters. These monuments were located near one another at the eastern end of the Roman Forum, squarely in line with the route water would have taken after spilling out of the Forum Boarium and crossing the Velabrum into the region of the Roman Forum. The Forum and nearby streets are also portrayed as being submerged in the flood of AD 217 (Dio 79.25.5) (see fig. 1.3). Three written accounts mention floods inundating the Circus Maximus, which is situated along the valley running to the left of the Palatine from the Forum Boarium.[20] In all three cases, the floods are mentioned because they disrupted games being held in the Circus. Ovid (*Fasti* 2.389–92) specifically describes the legendary flood of Romulus and Remus as covering a section of the city that included the future sites of the Roman Forum, the Forum Boarium, and the valley of the Circus Maximus, and while this cannot be taken as evidence of an eighth-century BC flood of these areas, the list of places inundated would certainly have sounded convincing to Ovid's first-century AD audience.

Fig. 1.3. The Roman Forum seen through the Arch of Septimius Severus during the flood of 1902. (Fototeca Unione, American Academy in Rome, VD 270)

Interestingly, the account of the flood of AD 12 also suggests a limit to the extent of the floodwaters, because the games that were being held in the Circus Maximus were moved to the Forum of Augustus, which apparently was not affected. The valley of the Circus Maximus stretches for quite a distance inland away from the Tiber on a narrow corridor that mirrors the course of the Via Appia. In a letter to Quintus, Cicero describes a flood that extended exactly up this corridor. He

Floods in Ancient Rome

says that it flooded along the Via Appia, with everything up to the *piscina publica* deeply covered, and with floodwaters reaching as far along the Via Appia as the Temple of Mars. The *piscina publica* was located several hundred meters past the southeast end of the Circus Maximus and is almost a kilometer inland from the Tiber. The Temple of Mars actually lay beyond the walls of Rome along the Via Appia more than 2.5 km from the bank of the Tiber. Cicero (*Ad Quint. fr.* 3.7.1) also mentions this flood affecting the promenade of Crassipes, but I have been unable to establish a location for this site. Presumably it was along the Via Appia near the other locations mentioned by Cicero.[21]

The Campus Martius was certainly prone to inundation and a number of sources allude to floods covering the Campus Martius (fig. 1.4). Livy (38.28.4) specifically mentions one flood that swamped the Campus Martius and the flood of 13 BC (Dio 54.25.2) that submerged the Theater of Balbus is also direct evidence for inundation in the Campus Martius because the theater is located in the southeastern corner

Fig. 1.4. Drawing by J. H. W. Tischbein of the Pantheon during the flood of 1686. The Pantheon is located in one of the lowest points of the Campus Martius. (Fototeca Unione, American Academy in Rome, 14130F)

of this region. Ovid (*Fasti* 519–520) recounts that the horse races of the Equirria had to be relocated from the Campus Martius to the Caelian on occasions when the Campus was inundated. The flood of AD 69 was described as blocking the departure of Otho's armies because the Campus Martius and the Via Flaminia were submerged.

As for the other regions of Rome that would seem to have been likely to flood, such as the Transtiberim and the Emporium districts, there are no specific sources that definitely list these areas as having flooded. It is tempting to interpret Plutarch's description (*Otho* 4.5) of the flood of AD 69, which he says flooded the "grain market," as evidence for flooding in the Emporium, which lay along the bank of the Tiber and was the location of most of the major grain warehouses. Tacitus's account (*Hist.* 1.86) of this same flood reinforces this interpretation, because he too notes that as a result of this flood, there was a shortage of food in the city, suggesting that the main food storage sites were involved.

The final set of structures specifically cited in the written sources as being affected by floods are the bridges connecting the left and right banks of the Tiber.[22] Not surprisingly, these seem to have been particularly vulnerable to floods, and no less than seven of the floods are noted as having destroyed or damaged one or more of these bridges. The oldest of the bridges at Rome was the Pons Sublicius, and on five occasions this bridge was swept away by floodwaters.[23] The first stone bridge in Rome, the Pons Aemilius, also seems to have suffered damage from high waters, and on another occasion two unspecified bridges were destroyed. (Iul. Obseq. 16; Livy 35.21.5–6)

The somewhat scattershot evidence for the geographic extent of ancient floods can be augmented by later primary sources. A number of chronicles of medieval floods include fairly extensive descriptions of the areas affected. A particularly elaborate one is the *Liber Pontificalis* account (Benedict III, 23) of the flood of AD 856:

> The river called Tiber left its channel and spread over the plains; it swelled in great spate and entered the city of Rome by the postern gate called St. Agatha's, at the—th hour of the day. Meanwhile in some places it even lapped over and entered the church of St. Silvester, so that of the steps which go up to St. Dionysius' basilica none except the topmost was visible because of the flooding; from there it expanded over the street called Via

Lata and entered God's mother St. Mary's basilica there, and the water swelled so much that this church's doors could not even be seen because of the flooding. Then it went up through the streets and byways as far as the Clivus Argentarius. From there it turned a right angle and entered by the portico in front of St. Mark's church on the 6th day of the same month, the Apparition of our Lord Jesus Christ according to the flesh, i.e. God's Epiphany. Then it made a rush and began to run down into the sewer close to the monastery of St. Silvester and of St. Laurence the martyr's called Pallacinis. From that day and thereafter the water gradually began to diminish and after doing much damage the river returned to its channel. (trans. R. Davis, 1995)

This description depicts the flood flowing into the Campus Martius from the north and submerging it all the way to the foot of the Capitoline, with some waters reaching toward the Roman Forum. Other medieval accounts similarly focus their attention on the flooding of the Campus Martius area and also on flooding along the right bank of the Tiber, which typically reached St. Peter's. (See, for example, *Gest. Lang.* 6.36 and *Lib. Pont.*, Greg. II, 6, on the flood of AD 716; *Lib. Pont.*, Serg. II, 22, on the flood of AD 844; and *Lib. Pont.*, Nic., 15, on the flood of AD 860.) The attention focused on inundations of these regions probably reflects medieval patterns of occupation in the city of Rome.[24] While these medieval accounts can be used to confirm that the Campus Martius would have been one of the first areas to be inundated by rising waters, it must be kept in mind that the ground level at this period was substantially higher than it had been during the Roman era, complicating direct comparisons. This concludes the list of identifiable structures and places mentioned in the written sources as having suffered due to flooding.

The Topography of Rome and Floods

In addition to information derived from primary sources, a second way of determining the extent of ancient floods is to analyze the basic topography of the city. In identifying some of the low-lying, level areas that would have been most flood-prone, two factors to be considered are the elevation of a region, usually expressed as meters above sea level (masl), and how accessible it is to the waters of the Tiber. The second criterion is vital because, no matter how low a district is, if it is completely enclosed by much higher ground, it can remain safe from flooding.

The greatest problem facing a topographic analysis, however, is the fact that the ground levels at Rome vary considerably over time. The unplanned process of rising ground levels occurs through a number of different mechanisms.[25] Among these, disasters of various kinds would have contributed significantly to raising general ground levels. The continual collapse of buildings mentioned by many authors would have produced considerable rubble, and while some was undoubtedly cleared away, at other times, buildings were simply erected upon the ruins of their predecessors. The frequent fires that plagued Rome contributed in an important way to this transformation, because they would have created rubble fields, that—if not cleared away before the next rebuilding—would have served to continually raise the ground level. The most famous fire, that of AD 64, must have generated enormous quantities of debris.[26] The amount of rubble from this conflagration was so great that some of it was loaded aboard empty grain barges going downstream and used to fill in the marshes around Ostia (Tac. *Ann.* 15.443). Floods could have contributed as well, both by depositing layers of sediment and by causing the collapse of buildings. Just the processes of daily life alone, when multiplied by millions of people living on the same spot over a span of many hundreds of years, can create substantial amounts of artificial fill. Centuries of domestic and commercial refuse gradually accumulate, slowly filling in depressions and raising ground levels. Often, a succession of dwellings will be erected on top of one another, frequently employing rubble from a previous phase of construction, but with the inevitable result of a steady rise in occupation level. The most spectacular example of refuse in Rome is, of course, the artificial hill of Monte Testaccio, which is composed entirely of broken amphorae to the height of 35 m.[27] All of these processes taken together have considerable implications for the study of floods at Rome, because areas that once might have been very vulnerable could now be relatively immune from the threat of flooding.

In addition to these unplanned processes, there have also been a number of deliberate efforts to raise ground levels in certain areas and instances, both in antiquity and more modern times, of hills being leveled or partially cut away.[28] The end result is that most of the flat areas of the city and the regions between the valleys are covered with a layer of man-made accretion that is on average between 5 and 10 m thick. In some places, this layer of artificial fill has been found to be as much as 20 m in depth.[29] Many of Rome's most famous archaeological sites, including the Roman Forum and the adjacent imperial Fora, are now located at the bottom of deep pits, far below the current street level. Today, most of the low-lying areas of the city between the hills and in the flood plain of the Campus Martius have an elevation of 18–20 masl. The natural ground levels for these regions were often less than 10 masl, for example, in the Velabrum.[30] Naturally, if the elevation of the Tiber riverbed changed over time as well, then this needs to be considered when assessing the vulnerability of different ground levels. The Tiber is a relatively shallow river, and the level of its bed appears to have remained roughly constant from the Roman period until today, and so is not a substantial factor. It has been suggested that the riverbed may have been 0.5 to 1 m lower in antiquity than today, but even if this is accurate, such a relatively minor difference in height would not make a great deal of difference in flood levels.[31] Figure 1.5 depicts the depth of the layers of fill that exist beneath the modern city.[32]

As figure 1.5 shows, nearly the entire area within the Aurelianic walls is buried beneath a uniform layer of fill that is at least 5 m in depth. The exceptions to this are the tops of the major hills, with the Palatine, Capitoline, and portions of the Esquiline and Quirinal covered to a depth of 2–5 m. The two summits of the Aventine bear the shallowest layer of accretion, with less than 2 m of fill. In a number of areas, the layer is even deeper—lying 10–15 m thick—most notably in a band that runs up the Vallis Murcia, into the nearby valley of the Colosseum, and then extending up roughly along the course of the modern Via Labicana. Spots of the same depth are also encountered in and around the Campus Martius, including just west of Piazza Venezia, around Piazza Pilota, around Piazza di Spagna, along Via Tritone, and along Via Nazionale. Some other places with 10–15 m of fill include a large region around the University district to the west of Termini station, and at the base of the Janiculum Hill in Trastevere. Scattered around the central city are a number of other points with even

Floods of the Tiber in Ancient Rome

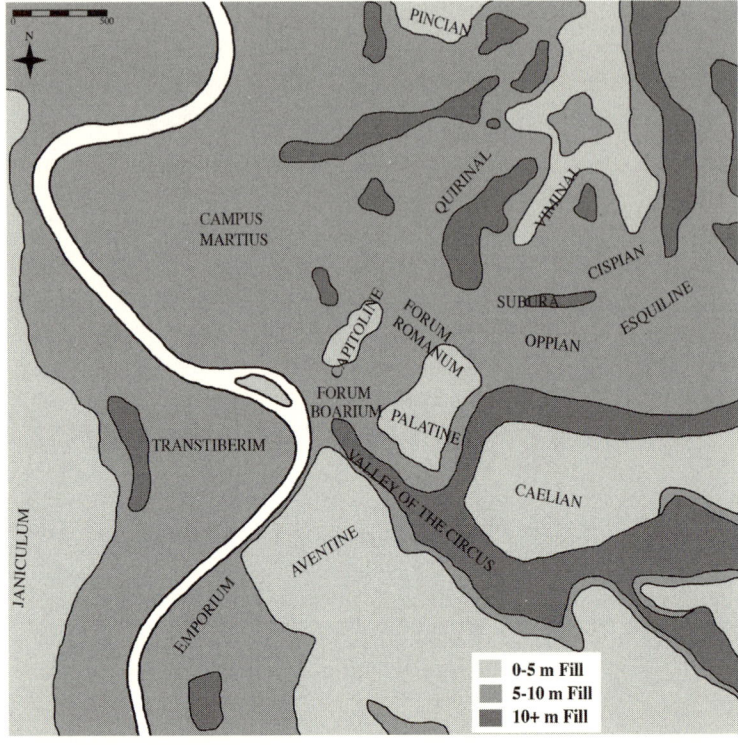

Fig. 1.5. Map showing depth of fill and rubble at Rome.

deeper layers of fill, in excess of 15 m in depth. Outside the Aurelianic walls, the zone of 5–10 m fill extends along both banks of the Tiber as far north as the Ponte Flaminio and south to around San Paolo Fuori le Mura. In general, the area of uniformly deep fill corresponds to the regions urbanized during the Roman era, and the majority of the fill dates to the same period.

Despite all this accumulation, in general the comparative topography of highlands versus lowlands remains roughly similar from antiquity to today, and so a general idea of the areas of the city most likely to flood can be gained by studying a modern map of Rome. For an exact analysis of ancient floods, however, it is necessary to delve into the thorny question of more precisely determining what the ground levels were at specific moments in time. It is not sufficient even to create one map for ancient Rome, because within the Roman period, the ground levels in some regions varied considerably from the time of Romulus to that of Constantine. Ideally, therefore, one would create a whole series of topographic maps showing Rome at various points in the city's development. Unfortunately, while it is possible to more or less reliably recreate the topographic history of certain well-studied areas such as the Roman Forum, or of specific points around the city, the necessary data are lacking to do so for the entire city over a whole range of time periods.

For this book, I have elected to concentrate on creating a map at one important era in time—the reign of the first emperor, Augustus. This moment has been chosen for a number of reasons. The primary consideration is that nearly one-third of all the ancient accounts of floods date to this time period, with a number of others clustering in the neighboring decades; thus creating a topography of the city at this point will facilitate the interpretation of the greatest number of primary source flood accounts. Second, the reign of Augustus is situated midway through the course of Roman history, making a map of the Augustan city a convenient vantage point from which to extrapolate changes in topography both backward and forward in time. Last but not least, this is a period for which there is a comparative wealth of archaeological and topographical data available to draw upon, creating the likelihood that a map for this period will be more accurate than ones for other points in Roman history. The resulting map (fig. 1.6) depicts the topography of Rome recreated roughly at the time of Augustus, with elevations marked in 5 m increments and with the key hills, valleys, and flatlands labeled.[33]

An analysis of figure 1.6 in terms of regions most likely to flood immediately suggests a number of such areas. The Forum Boarium lies next to the Tiber in the region between the Aventine and Capitoline hills. This district would have been extremely prone to flooding. As waters that had flowed into the Forum Boarium proceeded inland away from the river, they would have split left and right around the Palatine Hill. Those waters that spilled around the left flank of the hill would have entered into the Velabrum, the region that lies between the Palatine and Capitoline hills that connects the Forum Boarium

Floods of the Tiber in Ancient Rome

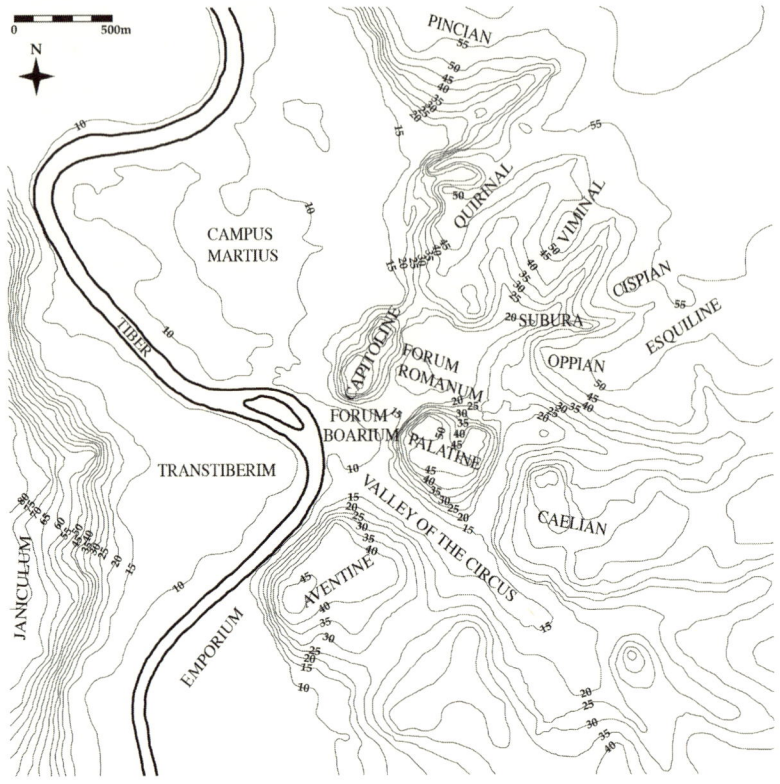

Fig. 1.6. Topographic map of Rome at the time of Augustus.

with the Roman Forum. Water that surmounted the Velabrum would have ended up pooling in the Roman Forum, which is enclosed by a circle of hills. The water that had been diverted to the right of the Palatine would have filled the Vallis Murcia, the long, narrow valley between the Palatine and Aventine hills where the Circus Maximus was constructed.[34] This valley runs fairly straight for a considerable distance, as a narrow channel between higher elevations, and, as noted, the Via Appia was built following its course. A high enough flood might have also caused water in the Circus Maximus area to turn, follow the back slope of the Palatine, and settle in the depression between the Palatine, Caelian, and Oppian hills where the Flavian Amphitheater would eventually be built. To the south of the Aventine, the Em-

Floods in Ancient Rome

porium district along the Tiber bank would also have been susceptible to flooding, as would the peninsula-like region on the opposite side of the river, the Transtiberim, which is bounded to the north, east, and south by the river. Floodwaters could easily have covered this region until they ran up against the high slope of the Janiculum Hill, which forms a north-south wall of high ground. Finally, the entire region of the Campus Martius was, in essence, a floodplain.

Maps of Hypothetical Floods of Different Magnitudes

The following sequence of three maps depicts floods reaching 10, 15, and 20 masl projected onto the topography of Augustan Rome (figs. 1.7–9). Flood magnitude is discussed in greater detail in chapter 2,

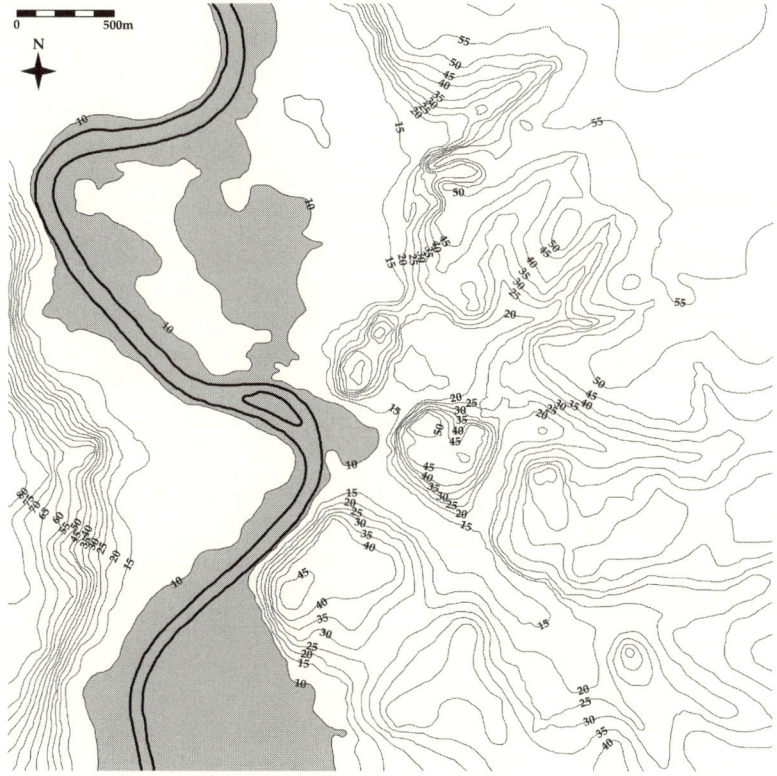

Fig. 1.7. Topographic map with 10 masl flood.

but the normal Tiber level was around 5–7 masl. A flood that reached a maximum depth of 10 masl, therefore, would have been a minor flood, one of 15 masl a major flood, and one of 20 masl an exceptional flood.

The 10 masl flood map (fig. 1.7) highlights the sections of the city most vulnerable to rising waters, although at a level of 10 masl, most of the areas within the *pomerium* would have been safe. The main exception was the Forum Boarium region just below Tiber Island, which would have been inundated for several hundred meters inland from the river. By the time of Augustus, the ground levels in the Velabrum had risen sufficiently so that the floodwaters would have been turned back by its rising ground and would not have poured into the depression beyond where the Forum Romanum lay. Similarly the valley of the Circus Maximus had just barely enough elevation to escape a flood of this modest size. As recent coring work has demonstrated, earlier in Roman history the Velabrum, the Roman Forum, and the valley of the Circus Maximus would all probably have been flooded, as original ground levels in these regions were less than 10 masl.[35] Figure 1.7 also illustrates the vulnerability of the Campus Martius to flooding. Here, although ground levels had also increased by a few meters since earlier times, the Augustan Campus Martius would have suffered extensive inundation for at least 100 m in from the Tiber and also across a broad swath of the central plain. Floodwaters of even 10 masl would have swept onto the Campus Martius at the point where the Tiber begins its curve eastward and then poured south across the entire width of the plain, eventually rejoining the river near Tiber Island. The large flooded basin in the center of the Campus Martius on this map represents the Augustan-era remnant of the earlier Palus Caprae. The slightly higher bank on the east side of the Tiber would have been just enough to provide protection from a flood of this magnitude for most of the Transtiberim region. The final major region of the city that would have suffered complete inundation was the zone south of the Aventine, including the Emporium district that contained many of Rome's docks and warehouses. While causing some disruption, a flood of this magnitude seems not to have affected the dwellings of most of Rome's inhabitants at this point in time, and the life of the city could probably have continued uninterrupted.

Floods in Ancient Rome

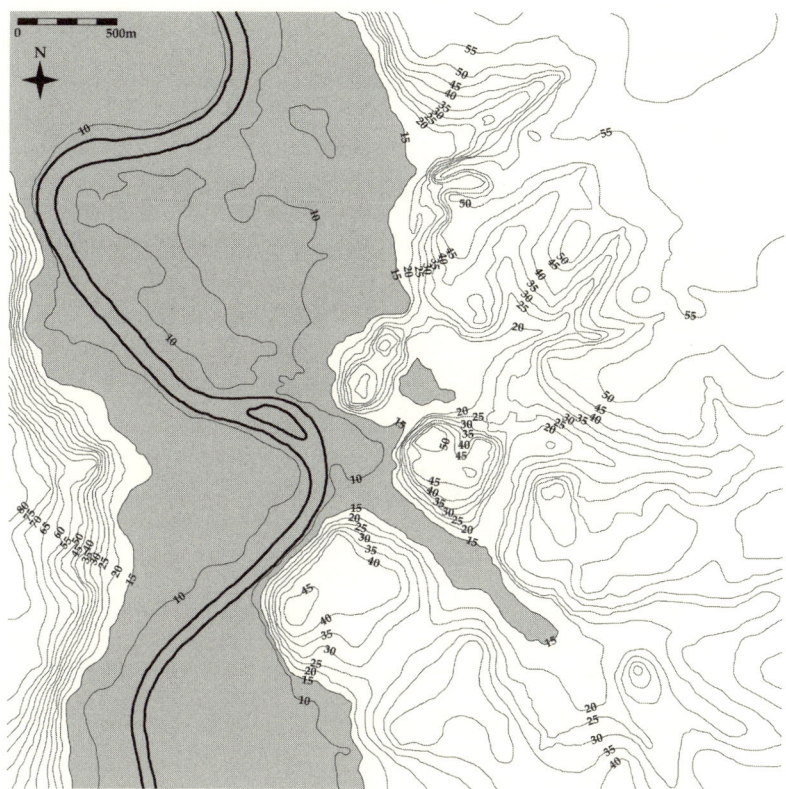

Fig. 1.8. Topographic map with 15 masl flood.

The 15 masl map in figure 1.8 presents a dramatically different picture from the 10 masl projection. This 5 m increase in water depth would have submerged many more regions beneath the floodwaters. The entire Transtiberim up to the foot of the Janiculum as well as all of the Campus Martius up to the Pincian and Quirinal hills would now be affected. Within the city boundaries, floodwaters would also reach right to the base of the Capitoline, Palatine, and Aventine hills and would pour into the low-lying valley of the circus reaching more than a kilometer inland. While the Velabrum might still have been just high enough to deflect floodwaters, the area of the Roman Forum behind it would still have flooded due to river water backing up the Cloaca Maxima. The level of the Augustan-era paving in the Forum varies be-

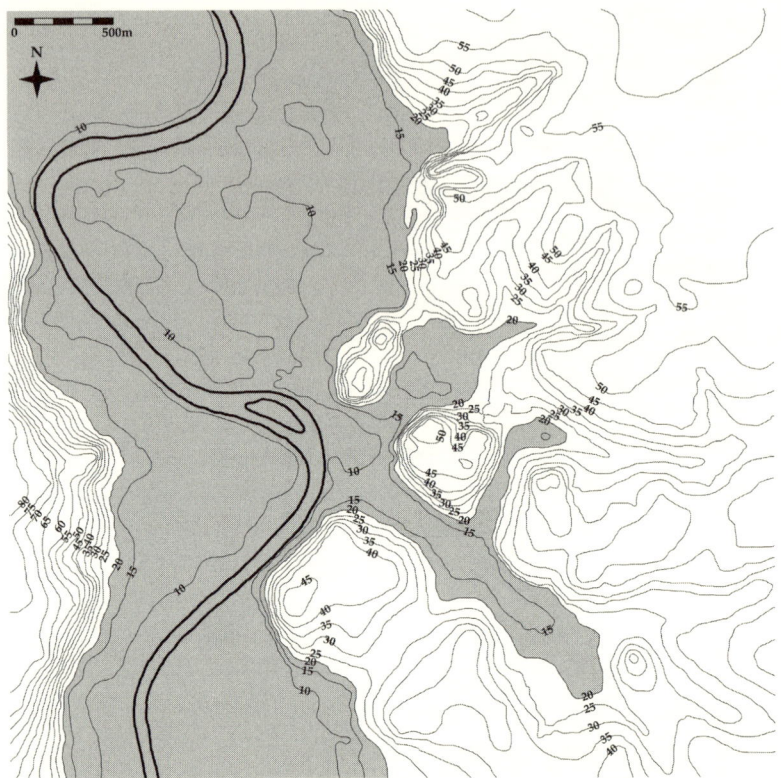

Fig. 1.9. Topographic map with 20 masl flood.

tween around 11–14 masl so that water several meters in depth might accumulate in parts of the Roman Forum. A flood of this magnitude would have been highly disruptive, affecting nearly all the major political, commercial, and entertainment centers of the city.

Although at first glance, the 20 masl flood map in figure 1.9 does not seem to represent as dramatic an increase as the 15 masl flood map did from the 10 masl one, the newly flooded areas include some particularly significant points. The flooded areas on the fringes of the city in the Transtiberim, Campus Martius, and south of the Aventine have not changed much compared with those shown on the 15 masl map because in these places the floodwaters have run up against high hills. Where there are significant differences, however, are in the very heart of the city. At the 20 masl magnitude, the entire region nestled between

Floods in Ancient Rome

the Capitoline, Palatine, Quirinal, and Oppian hills is submerged. This includes the most densely built up regions of the city, among them all of the Velabrum, the entire Roman Forum, the zone of the imperial fora, and a substantial segment of the densely inhabited Subura district. At this level, floodwaters would also have stretched even further up the valley of the circus and would have spilled into the valley between the Palatine and Caelian hills, pooling in the depression below the Oppian where the Flavian Amphitheater would eventually be built. At this level, the Capitoline and Palatine hills are close to becoming islands cut off from the rest of the city. A 20 masl flood would

Fig. 1.10. Map of Rome with 20 masl flood, flooded sites mentioned in primary sources, and major Augustan structures. Key to primary source sites: (1) Campus Martius, (2) Via Flaminia/Campus Martius, (3) Theater of Balbus, (4) Porta Flumentana, (5) Forum Boarium, (6) Roman Forum, (7) Regia and Shrine to Vesta, (8) Circus Maximus, (9) Piscina Publica, (10) Temple of Mars, (11) Emporium district warehouses.

be a catastrophe affecting not just the major public buildings and spaces of the city, but substantial residential districts as well.

A final step is to compare the sites mentioned in primary sources as being flooded with the hypothetical extent of flooding observed by topographical analysis. Such a procedure reveals considerable overlap. Figure 1.10 shows the hypothetical 20 masl flood together with the identifiable points mentioned in primary sources as having been inundated by floods. It also includes some of the major political, entertainment, and commercial structures that had been erected by the end of Augustus's reign. With only the exceptions of the Temple of Jupiter on the Capitoline and Augustus's dwellings on the Palatine, every one of these buildings lay within the flood zone.

This chapter has presented the primary source evidence for floods in ancient Rome and used this information to consider the most basic feature of Roman floods: their geographic extent. The next chapter will build on this foundation by combining ancient and modern data in order to ascertain what can be known about the specific characteristics of these natural disasters.

Two

Characteristics of Floods

Flood Types and Basic Hydrology

Before proceeding to a discussion of the duration, seasonality, frequency, and magnitude of Tiber floods, it will be useful to describe some of the basic hydrological processes of floods in general.[1] A flood can be defined as a high streamflow that exceeds the natural or artificial banks of the stream.[2] Floods are often schematized by their cause. Some of these categories include flash floods, which are the result of sudden, intense rainfall being channeled into a narrow valley; floods created when a dam or reservoir breaks or spills; floods produced by the heavy rains accompanying a hurricane; and floods resulting from tidal waves or tsunamis. A final group of floods consists of those which are caused by heavy rainfall that swells an existing river or stream far beyond its normal levels. The recurrent floods that plagued Rome belonged to this last category.[3]

Such floods are a by-product of the natural hydrologic cycle—a term that refers to the constant global process by which water moves from the oceans through evaporation into the atmosphere, where it condenses into clouds and eventually precipitates back to the Earth's surface as rain.[4] The agent powering the hydrologic cycle is heat from the sun, and the total volume of global water is a constant. At any given moment, the overwhelming majority of the Earth's water is in the oceans, with less than a tenth of 1% in lakes and rivers. Of fresh water, the amount held in the atmosphere and in lakes and rivers is still tiny, but nevertheless the movement of this water creates dramatic effects on the landscape.

When water in the form of rain falls onto land, some evaporates and some is absorbed by the soil. The amount of water that infiltrates the soil is determined by the porosity of the soil, the groundwater level, and the degree of moisture already present in the soil. Soil that already has a high level of moisture, whether due to previous precipitation or other factors, cannot readily absorb new moisture. Once the soil reaches this saturation point, additional rainfall becomes surface runoff. This runoff will follow the contours of the land, finding its way to existing streams and rivers, increasing their flow and, if the water level rises above the banks of the stream, producing a flood. In special circumstances, it is possible to have a flood even when the soil has not reached saturation point. Rainfall may be so intense that it exceeds the absorption rate of the soil, producing surface runoff even before the soil has reached saturation. Soils that have been baked hard by the sun, as is common around the Mediterranean, can also impede the absorption rate, increasing surface runoff. On the other hand, there can sometimes be floods without visible surface runoff in cases where the subsurface flow (or interflow) is substantial, meaning a situation where the water infiltrates the soil and is able to move laterally through it very quickly to the stream channel.[5] Streamflow, known as discharge, is measured in cubic meters per second (m^3/sec) and is the product of the cross-sectional area of the flow multiplied by the velocity. Total streamflow is a combination of surface runoff and interflow. During a typical flood, the discharge of a stream or river fed by surface runoff often increases very rapidly, hits a peak, and then gradually decreases.

A flood can be depicted graphically by a diagram known as a hydrograph, with discharge plotted along one axis and time on the other. Hydrographs are often divided into three periods: the rising limb, when the discharge rate is increasing; the crest, during which it peaks; and the falling limb, during which it decreases back to normal levels.

Characteristics of Floods

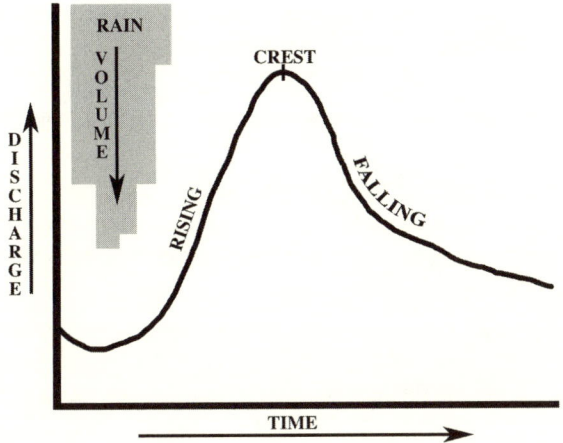

Fig. 2.1. Typical hydrograph.

In the generic example in figure 2.1,[6] the majority of the rainfall occurs prior to much of an increase in the discharge. This effect can be expressed as the lag time, which is the elapsed time between the center of mass of the rainfall and the center of mass of the discharge. The time to peak is the interval from the beginning of the rising limb to the time of peak discharge. The time of concentration is the time it takes for water to travel from the most distant part of the drainage basin to the basin outlet. The drainage basin is the area within which water will concentrate, due to the contours of the topography, into an outlet. A drainage basin can be large or small, but typically includes a river and all the tributaries that flow into it. The shape of the hydrograph is determined by a large number of variables related to the specific characteristics of the drainage basin and the particular rainfall. Every flood will produce a unique hydrograph, and some may have prolonged peaks or even multiple peaks.

Catastrophic floods can be triggered by extreme forms of rainfall, such as the monsoons of southeast Asia, during which there can be sustained, very heavy rains for prolonged periods, or by the briefer but still intense precipitation created by severe weather phenomena such as hurricanes. The extraordinary floods of the Tiber would not have been caused by such single dramatic climatic events but instead by a more subtle combination of factors. In their study of extraordinary Tiber floods of the 20th century, Alessandroni and Remedia have described these floods as resulting from a long preparatory phase typically lasting 90 days during which frequent rains cause the soil to become very waterlogged.[7] This is followed by an antecedent phase of approximately 10 days, during which daily rains further increase the moisture level in the soil, perhaps to saturation point. Finally, there is a short contemporary phase of a few days, during which rains on consecutive days completely saturate the soil and produce high surface runoff, resulting in a flood. Rainfall over a drainage basin can be depicted on a map of the basin by superimposing isohyetal lines over the map. These lines demarcate the different amounts of rainfall that are measured at stations in the basin, and the net effect of such an isohyetal diagram resembles a contour map, with a series of concentric rings showing areas of greater and lesser rainfall.

Hydrology of the Tiber and the Tiber Drainage Basin

The drainage basin of the Tiber has been carefully and extensively mapped by the Italian government. The Tiber River begins at Monte Fumaiolo in the Apennines at a point almost level with, and to the east of, Florence, at an altitude of 1,268 masl. It follows a meandering course bearing generally to the south and eventually empties into the Mediterranean Sea at Ostia (fig. 2.2). The overall length of the river's course is 409 km, although a straight line connecting its source to its mouth would be around 225 km.[8] Several major rivers drain into the Tiber and contribute to the total streamflow of the river. The two most significant of these are the Anio and the Nera, which itself collects the water from a number of subsidiary rivers.

At Rome, the Tiber follows an S-shaped course that encompasses the low-lying area of the Campus Martius on three sides within a broad bend in the river. Tiber Island lies immediately downstream from this bend, and just below the island there is a natural crossing point. Originally there were swamps or even small lakes in the Campus Martius, the Forum Boarium area, the valley of the Circus Maximus, the future site of the Flavian Amphitheater, and the Transtiberim. These watery regions were fed by at least 22 natural springs within the central sec-

Characteristics of Floods

Fig. 2.2. A section of the Tiber River between Rome and Ostia. The riverbank along this stretch is still fairly undeveloped, perhaps presenting much the same appearance as it had during the Roman era. (Photo by author)

tion of Rome, with a number concentrated in the Forum Romanum area. The geology of Rome consists of alluvial deposits from the Tiber of considerable depth, as well as tuffs and pyroclastic formations composing the hills.[9] The location of the city of Rome is an unfortunate one with respect to flooding, because it is situated at one of the most flood-prone sections of the entire course of the river.

Reasonably precise numerical information about the magnitude of floods at Rome is available from the late Middle Ages onward. Hundreds of marble plaques recording high water levels during various floods are scattered throughout the city of Rome (fig. 2.3), with the earliest dating to 1277. In 1704 a marble column at the port of Ripetta was established, noting flood levels. Observations of Tiber levels at Rome began in a systematic way in 1782, when the director of the meteorological observatory of the Collegio Romano started such record

Floods of the Tiber in Ancient Rome

Fig. 2.3. A flood marker located on the facade of the church of Santa Maria Sopra Minerva commemorating the flood of 1530, which was the second highest recorded flood, reaching a height of 18.95 masl at Ripetta. (Photo by author)

keeping, but it really became standardized when the hydrometer of Ripetta was installed in 1821 and daily observations of the level of the Tiber began. The Servizio Idrografico, established in 1917, soon initiated the tradition of collecting hydrographic and meteorological data, and from 1921 onward, detailed hydrological data have been collected from a number of stations within the Tiber basin.[10] These measurements and publications have continued up to the present, and most detailed data sets of Tiber behavior are based on this body of information.

The Tiber drainage basin (fig. 2.4) covers a region approximately 200 km long from north to south and 100 km wide from east to west.[11] The total area of the drainage basin is 17,156 km^2, and it has a median altitude of 524 masl. It is the largest drainage basin in Italy and provides a year-round flow of water in the Tiber. The Tiber drainage basin itself can be divided into four major subdivisions, the drainage basin of the river Paglia and the lower Tiber totaling 5,343 km^2; the drainage basin of the upper Tiber, 6,077 km^2; the region cen-

October	6.40
November	7.01
December	7.17

As might be expected, the average monthly Tiber levels at Rome closely mirror the data for the average monthly discharge, with the peak in late winter–early spring and the low point in late summer. The two charts do not overlap perfectly, because the greatest discharge occurs in February while the highest water level is in March, but they are very close. It must also be kept in mind that the discharge statistics take into account the velocity of the water, which has a great effect on the volume of water. This can be shown by expressing the difference between the highest and lowest water levels and discharge volumes. The difference between the highest average water level in March of 7.24 masl and the lowest in July of 5.77 masl is 1.47 m. This represents a 20% drop in water level. The difference between the highest discharge rate of 356.7 m^3/sec and the lowest of 128 m^3/sec is 228.3 m^3/sec. This is a much more dramatic decline (of 64%) in total volume of water.

The typical level of the Tiber at Rome therefore usually varies on a seasonal basis roughly between 5 and 7 masl. A system of classification for flood levels at Rome proposed by Betocchi has continued to be used (table 2.1).[20] There is some evidence to suggest that the levels of the Tiber may have declined during the 20th century, perhaps due to more water being diverted for irrigation, drinking, and other purposes.[21] While the data presented here about precipitation in the Tiber basin and Tiber volume and level come mostly from the past 200 years and therefore cannot be taken as definitively representing the behavior of the Tiber in ancient times, they at least give a sense of the operation of the hydrology of the Tiber drainage basin and provide benchmarks for comparison.[22]

Duration of Floods at Rome

After having gained a sense of the geographic extent of floods in ancient Rome and the workings of the Tiber basin, the next step is to attempt to estimate the duration of the floods. The duration of a flood

Table 2.1.
Tiber Flood Classification Scheme

Normal	Level of 5 to 7 masl, discharge less than 200 m³/sec
Elevated	Level of 7 to 10 masl, discharge less than 800 m³/sec
Ordinary flood	Level of 10 to 13 masl, discharge less than 1500 m³/sec
Extraordinary flood	Level of 13 to 16 masl, discharge less than 2000 m³/sec
Exceptional flood	Level greater than 16 masl

is a function of multiple variables, including the volume and velocity of water involved, the porosity of the soil, the degree to which the soil is saturated, the duration of rainfall, the extent of rainfall, the area of the watershed, the slope of the ground, and so on. The situation is further complicated in an urban environment such as Rome's where much of the ground is covered by nonporous structures and paving materials and where the capacity of sewage and drainage networks must be taken into account. Also, when floodwaters recede, it is not always a simple matter of the water level dropping and then all the floodwaters draining back into the river. A frequent problem is that high floodwaters can deposit large volumes of water into areas that are cut off by topography from direct drainage back to the river, thus creating sizable standing pools of water that can only dissipate slowly through evaporation or soil absorption.

The duration of a flood is an important factor in assessing the damage it causes, because the length of time that various substances are immersed can dramatically alter the effect that water has upon them. Some foods, for example, might be relatively unscathed after a brief immersion but utterly ruined by prolonged exposure to water. Long-term immersion can also foster the growth of harmful molds and bacteria. Similarly, the materials that buildings are made out of might withstand a few hours' exposure to water without losing structural integrity but, if submerged for prolonged periods of time, could become saturated with water or even dissolve completely, with disastrous consequences. The longer a flood lasts, the greater the resultant interruption of travel and disruption to the economy. Duration of flooding therefore becomes a significant factor in the costs associated with a flood event.

Several of the ancient written sources offer evidence regarding the duration of specific floods. The most dramatic of these was the flood of AD 5, which attacked the city for eight days (Cassiod. *Chron.* 604). Dio (55.22.3) comments about the same flood that it rendered the city navigable by boat for seven days. The necessity of using boats to traverse the flooded streets of the city is a common feature in ancient descriptions of floods at Rome, and Dio (53.33.5) notes that the flood of 23 BC made the city navigable by boat for three days. These are the only ancient accounts that list specific time periods for a flood's duration, but the descriptions of several others imply durations of at least several days. The flood of 202 BC caused the games of Apollo to be moved to a different location, but on the day the games were to be held, a sudden clearing of the weather and recession of the floodwaters enabled them to be held at their original site in the Circus Maximus (Livy 30.38.10–12). This account implies a gap of at least a day or two between the flooding of the Circus and the day of the games. It also suggests that floodwaters could recede with rapidity. The flood of AD 371 was said to have trapped many individuals in their homes and to have threatened them with starvation, so that a system of distributing food to them by boat was instituted (Am. Mar. 29.6.17–18). This again implies a flood persisting for a number of days, because if the flood had lasted only a day or two, starvation would not have been a serious danger. This might have been an unusual incident, however, and not representative of the typical length of floods. The ancient evidence, while admittedly limited, gives the impression that the duration of a typical flood was a few days, with exceptional ones lasting up to a week or more.

The scanty material from ancient authors can be augmented by considering more recent floods in Rome, particularly those from before the construction of the modern Tiber embankments. Indications of duration are noted in the accounts of several medieval floods. The flood of AD 716 was said to have lasted seven days, with the waters described as receding on the eighth (Bede *Chron.* 589; Gest. Lang. 2.6).

The flood of AD 844, by contrast, began inundating the city just after midnight on November 22, covered a substantial section of at least the Campus Martius, and then receded back to the Tiber channel on the following night (*Lib. Pont.*, Serg. II, 22).

From the 13th century onward, numerous stone markers recording floods at Rome have been erected, but these markers are always solely concerned with identifying the highest point that the flood reached. Therefore, while they give a date for the day that the flood peaked and the height the flood attained, they do not mention the duration of the flood. Written accounts of some floods do, however, occasionally note the overall length of a flood in addition to the day it peaked. The flood of 1805 began on the night of January 30 and lasted two full days, although it took a week for the floodwaters to completely leave the city.[23] The Tiber flood that peaked on December 7, 1647, returned to its channel by the 9th.[24] The flood of 1637 began on February 21 and finally receded on the night of the 23rd.[25] The flood of December 24, 1598, maintained high water levels over three days.[26] A contemporary account of the flood of 1310 describes this flood as having lasted an entire week.[27]

The more detailed records of 20th-century floods can also provide comparative information as to how long high water levels persist. In the flood of January 1929, for example, the water level rose above 13 masl on the 2nd, slowly increased to 14 masl over the course of the 3rd, peaked at 14.9 masl late on the 4th, and then rapidly diminished so that by the end of the 5th water levels were back below 13 masl.[28] The hydrograph of the severe and well-documented flood of December 1870 also provides an interesting study (fig. 2.5).[29] After a small peak on the 23rd, the water level returned to a relatively normal level of 8 masl on the 25th. It then began to increase very rapidly, so that by the end of the next day, it had risen to 14 masl. After pausing at this level on the 27th, the water again quickly increased, reaching the peak level of 17.22 masl during the night of the 28th. After sustaining this plateau for a few hours, the water level began to sink even more rapidly than it had risen, falling more than 3 m within a 24 hour period so that by the end of the 30th, the level was back to 14 masl. As it had when increasing, the water level paused around 14 masl, before beginning another swift decline back to 11 masl by the end of January

Characteristics of Floods

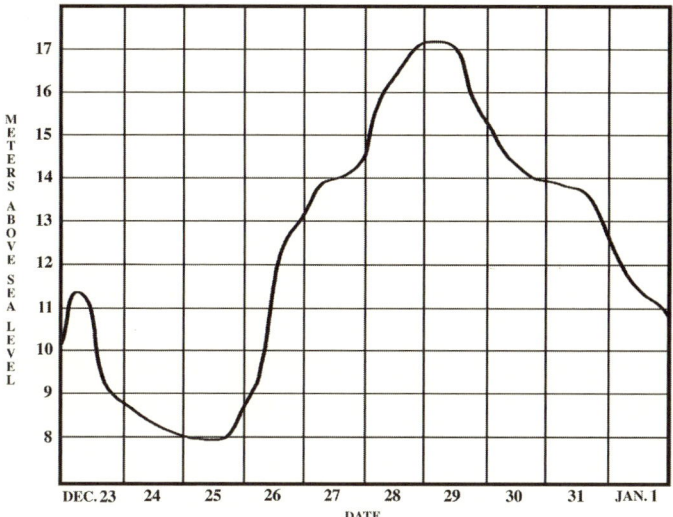

Fig. 2.5. Hydrograph of the flood of December 1870.

1st. The entire cycle of this flood took about a week, and of this time, there was about a 36-hour period when the waters sustained levels greater than 14 masl. This three-day high-water period likely corresponds to the time periods reported for floods in ancient sources, which probably emphasized not the entire duration of the flood event but rather the time period when the waters were truly at high levels.

Other recent floods offer additional data on duration. The flood of 1900 spent 43 hours at a level of 15 masl or greater, the flood of 1915 maintained the same level for a duration of 61 hours, and the great flood of 1937 sustained levels above 15 masl for 70 hours.[30] While all three of these floods sustained high levels longer than the flood of 1870, none of them reached as high a level at its peak. Thus the flood of 1870 is a model of a flood that peaked and declined relatively quickly but that reached very high levels, whereas the floods of 1900, 1915, and 1937 represent floods of longer duration at flood levels but with lower peaks. When one looks at a total time frame of five days for these floods, however, their behavior appears more similar. Within this time span, all four floods rose from and returned to a level of 13 masl. While these floods demonstrate differing patterns in variations

Floods of the Tiber in Ancient Rome

of rates of increase and decrease and in time sustained at certain levels, the overall duration of all four floods was the same—roughly five days.

In general, the postclassical flood accounts reinforce the impression that typical Tiber floods were often relatively quick affairs, with the water rising rapidly over the course of a day or two, the river in full flood for one to three days, and the very high waters then rapidly receding to more normal levels, although elevated water levels and some degree of inundation could persist for some time. The overall duration of serious floods typically seems to be about five days. It is also clear that there may have been occasional floods that followed a different duration pattern, with the city being heavily inundated for an entire week, but no attested flood seems to have lasted much longer than this.

Seasonality of Floods at Rome

The precipitation patterns of the Tiber basin and the measured flow rates and levels suggest that the most likely seasons for floods to take place should be the winter and spring. Conversely the summer, particularly the late summer, would be the least likely time for floods to take place. The historical records of Tiber floods from the Middle Ages to the present appear to confirm these impressions (see table 2.2). Of the 30 known floods between AD 400 and 1699 whose month of occurrence can be identified, 12 were in November, 6 in December, 5 in January, 2 in February, 3 in October, 1 in March, and 1 in September.[31] In the well-documented period from 1700 to the present, of the 76 floods that attained heights of at least 13 masl at Ripetta, 20 were in December, 14 in November, 14 in February, 11 in January, 8 in March, 5 in April, 2 in May, and 2 in October.[32] Two striking patterns are obvious from this data. First, the four consecutive months of November through February account for more than 83% of the historical floods (25 of 30) and more than 77% (59 of 76) of the modern ones. Second, for the past 1,500 years, there seem to have been no major destructive floods between the months of May and September.[33]

When one turns to the seasonal distribution of floods during the Roman period, this neat pattern is challenged. Ancient authors were not very reliable about providing specific dates for the floods they described, and for the majority of ancient floods, it is impossible to determine the season, let alone the month, in which they took place. Of the more than 30 floods between 414 BC and AD 398, less than a quarter can be even tentatively identified by season.

One flood that can be precisely dated was a winter flood. Dio (53.20.1) claims that this flood was interpreted as an omen because it struck on the night of the day after Octavian was granted the title of Augustus, January 16, 27 BC. Similarly, the flood of 13 BC can also be dated by the actions of Augustus because it coincided with his return to the city of Rome, which took place on July 4. The flood of AD 12 was said to have disrupted the Ludi Martiales that were being celebrated in the Circus Maximus, and this information locates the date of the flood as being around May 12 (Dio 56.27). The flood of AD 69 can be placed in mid-March by its coincidence with Otho's preparations for and departure to combat the forces of Vitellius (Plut. *Otho* 4.5; Suet. *Otho* 8.3; Tac. *Hist.* 1.86). The *Fasti* of Ostia give the specific date of March 20 for the flood of AD 147, and the flood of AD 217 was identified as having occurred on the first day of the Vulcanalia, which would place it on August 23 (*Fasti Ostiensis;* Dio 79.25.5). Also worth noting is that although no specific year is identified, the horse races of the Equirria held in mid-March were described as frequently being disrupted by floods (Ovid *Fasti* 519–20). The six specific floods just listed are the only ones that can be precisely dated with certainty, and of them, one was in January, one in May, one in July, one in August, and two in March (see table 2.2).

Several other floods can perhaps be ascribed to various times of the year, although with less certainty than those listed here. If the dating of the flood mentioned by Horace (*Carm.* 1.2) to just after the assassination of Caesar is correct, then this flood would have occurred in the latter half of March 44 BC.[34] The letter of Cicero (*Ad Quint. fr.* 3.7.1) relating the flood of 54 BC was most likely written in very late October or early November of that year.[35] The flood of 202 BC interrupted the Ludi Apollinares, which took place in mid-July (Livy 30.38.10–12). The account of the flood of 192 BC seems to suggest that the inundation happened while the new magistrates were preparing to take office, which would place the flood in March (Livy

Table 2.2.
Seasonal Distribution of Floods at Rome

	AD 1700–2000	AD 400–1699	414 BC–AD 398	
			Floods of Definite Date	Floods of Uncertain Date
January–February	25	7	1	0
March–April	13	1	2	2
May–June	2	0	1	0
July–August	0	0	2	2
September–October	2	4	0	0
November–December	34	18	0	1

35.21.5–6). Finally, the flood of AD 253 may have happened during the summer, but this attribution rests on ambiguities in translation (Sex. Aur. Victor *De Caes.* 32).[36] Further complicating the dating of many of these floods is the problematic nature of the Roman calendar prior to the reforms of Julius Caesar. The irregular use of intercalary months and the difficulties of establishing exact concordance between the 10-month republican calendar and the modern calendar for a given year ensure that any dating of the floods before Caesar will remain open to interpretation and controversy.[37] If, however, these floods of uncertain date were accepted, then there would be an additional two ancient floods in March, two during the summer, and one in the fall. The fourth column of table 2.2 records the ancient floods of uncertain date by season. For the floods from AD 400 to 1699, the table lists all floods whose month of occurrence is known. From roughly 1700 to the present, precisely measured information for the height of floods is generally available, and so for this period the table includes all known instances when water levels of more than 13 masl were recorded at Ripetta. For a complete list of floods in all periods, see Appendix I.

While the records of Tiber floods from the medieval period through the present create an extremely consistent pattern with the overwhelming number of inundations concentrated between November and February, and with none from June through August, the floods from the Roman period offer a very different pattern of seasonal distribution, and one that is at odds with our understanding of the mechanics of the Tiber basin. Not only do Roman floods fail to cluster in the expected winter season, but fully 45% (of an admittedly very small sample) appear to have occurred during the summer. These summer floods are particularly problematic because this is the time of year when the river is usually at its lowest, rainfall is scarcest, and the underground moisture reserves are most depleted. The complete absence of even a single late summer flood from AD 400 to the present makes these Roman summer floods seem even odder.

While looking only at the list of datable ancient floods might suggest that they were most common in the spring and summer, numerous sources describing the flow of the Tiber in general indicate that the primary times of high water were the winter and spring and that the river's level decreased in the summer, a conclusion much more in keeping with the later documentable behavior of the river. Pliny's famous portrait (*Epist.* 5.6.12) of the Tiber states that the flow was greatest in the winter and spring but dried up in the summer.[38] Plutarch (*Otho* 4) noted that winter was the time when rivers were at their fullest, and Horace (*Epod.* 2.25) likewise identified the winter as the rainy season. Even the famous flood involving Romulus and Remus was specifically described as being a winter flood caused by heavy rainfall (Ovid *Fasti* 2.390; Varro 5.54). When Tiberius established a Tiber commission after the flood of AD 15, it was charged with both preventing overflow during the winter and ensuring that the river did not dry up during the summer (Dio 57.14.7–8). Similarly Livy (5.13.1, 2.4.3) notes both an instance when the Tiber was so swollen in the winter that it was rendered too hazardous for travel by boats and an occasion when its flow in summer became greatly diminished, "as is usually the case in midsummer." Thus the impression created by these sources is an image of high water and floods in the winter and spring, and low water levels in the summer.

When attempting to account for the existence of the seemingly anomalous summer floods reported in the primary sources, there are several factors to keep in mind. First, the number of seasonally datable floods is so tiny that it is impossible to draw any mathematically significant conclusions from such a small data set. Also, the very oddity of these floods could well be a contributing reason as to why they were remembered and recorded at all, whereas a much larger number of winter and spring floods could have gone unreported because they were a common, and hence unremarkable, occurrence. There is always the possibility that a couple of freakish intense summer storms did happen, resulting in unseasonable floods. When the Italian soil is extremely dried out, as happens in late summer, it forms a hardened crust that greatly reduces its permeability to water; therefore, in a very sudden and heavy rainstorm, the majority of water would become surface runoff rather than being absorbed, and thus would raise stream levels unusually quickly. Another possible reason for the unseasonable floods at Rome is deforestation of the Tiber basin, a phenomenon that is discussed in more detail in the section on flood frequency.

When taken as a whole, the evidence for floods in ancient Rome suggests a pattern fairly similar to the modern cycle. The ancient Tiber reached high water levels as the result of heavy rains in the winter, the heaviest flooding took place in the late winter and early spring, and then water levels steadily declined, reaching a nadir in late summer. It has been suggested that the frequency of March floods in antiquity as opposed to the more recent pattern of November to February floods was due to heavier and snowier winters that produced great quantities of water from snowmelt in the spring.[39] This seems reasonable but, in the absence of definitive data on ancient snowfall, must remain speculative. The apparent greater deviation in seasonality of ancient floods can be interpreted either as a statistical fluke caused by the very small number of surviving records or as evidence that the behavior of the ancient Tiber was somewhat more unpredictable and variable than it is today. When dealing with such a limited number of ancient data points, with the clear literary descriptions of high water levels in the winter and spring, and given the overwhelming later hydrological information, I am inclined to favor the former explanation.[40]

Frequency of Floods at Rome

The frequency of floods is another essential characteristic to analyze when attempting to assess the impact of these events. If severe floods are extremely rare, they may well not play any role in the consciousness or decision-making process of those who live in a region that floods, for instance, only once every couple hundred years. If, on the other hand, great floods occur relatively often, perhaps several during each person's lifetime, then they will almost certainly affect the way that inhabitants of an area view that region. Frequent floods can have a whole range of effects on a city. They will be more likely to provoke the attention of the government, to be the objects of large-scale projects aimed at reducing their menace, to affect the way that buildings are constructed, to be taken into account when organizing food supply and distribution systems, to influence the way certain districts are viewed, and so on.

Basic flood frequency analysis is often expressed in terms of a flood of such a magnitude that on average it only occurs once over a given time frame. Thus many calculations speak of the 100-year flood. Another way to think about this is that in any given year, there is a 1% chance of experiencing a flood of this size. Such estimates have to be based on reliable measurements of a river over a long span of time; over 1,000 or 2,000 years, the data may even out nicely. As a short-term predictive tool, this analysis is not very useful, because a particular century might experience three or four "100-year floods" while another might have none. As theory, the 100-year flood model seems fine, but in reality, it is problematic over both long and short time scales. As a guide to what might happen in the next year or two, it is obviously uninformative, and current research suggests that over long time periods, severe floods do not spread out evenly either, but instead cluster together, probably as a result of long-term climatic trends.[41]

Rome is one of the few places for which we actually possess reasonable data on flooding recorded over a long time span. Most studies of floods at Rome have done a frequency analysis by simply dividing a given time span by the number of attested floods. For floods from the very late Middle Ages on, some idea of their magnitude can be estimated by the flood markers and hydrometers on buildings that indicate the high water levels reached by each flood, while for the past several centuries, fairly accurate records of flood height and discharge can be consulted. For the Roman and medieval floods, however, their magnitude is hypothetical, and that they were major floods can best be inferred by the fact that they left some memory of their existence at all.

In table 2.3, I have listed the estimates by various authors of the number of major floods at Rome from 414 BC to AD 1870 and then calculated their frequency by dividing this 2,284 year time span by the number of attested floods.[42] The discrepancy in number of floods counted by each author is due to a combination of some using a greater range of sources, and differing opinions over what constitutes a "major" flood. I have followed the convention of several authors when dealing with the floods since 1700 of only counting very large floods that are estimated to have reached heights of at least 15 masl.[43] (See the list of floods in Appendix I.) While my own calculations favor a frequency of one major flood every 28 years, or about four per century, all the estimates fall within the range of one major flood every 20 to 40 years.

Table 2.3.
Frequency Estimates of Floods at Rome, 414 BC to AD 1870

Author	Number of Floods	Flood Frequency 1 per X years
Di Martino and Belati (1980)	58	39
Frosini (1977)	62	37
Alessandroni and Remedia (2002)	65	35
Bencivenga et al. (1995)	66	34
Gregori et al. (1988)	74	31
Aldrete	81	28
Bersani and Bencivenga (2001)	116	20

When flood frequency is mapped out over time, however, a very uneven distribution pattern emerges (see fig. 2.6).[44] While the most common number of floods per century for the 24 centuries being considered is indeed the expected four (occurring six times), the number of floods for particular centuries varies enormously, from a high of eight for the first century BC to several centuries during the Middle Ages with no attested floods at all. Particularly troublesome is a long gap of 320 years between AD 860 and 1180 when there are no recorded floods. Furthermore, the floods seem to cluster curiously, with the floods of the 500-year period coinciding with the height of Roman power (300 BC to AD 200) forming a nice bell curve: 27 floods fall into this period, giving it an overall frequency rate of 1 flood per 19 years. After this, the next 1,100 years from AD 200 to AD 1300 record only 20 floods, for a frequency rate of 1 per 58 years. Finally, the more recent era has witnessed another trend of apparently increasing frequency, with 32 floods occurring between 1300 and 1870 for a rate of 1 per 18 years.

Scholars have advanced various explanations to account for the unevenness of this distribution.[45] One focal point has been speculation regarding different weather patterns over time. Changes in climate, such as shifts to cooler or warmer temperatures, or greater or lesser rainfall, could certainly exert dramatic effects on flood frequency and magnitude. There have been many attempts to detect changes in climate, often with the goal of ascribing the causation of important his-

Floods of the Tiber in Ancient Rome

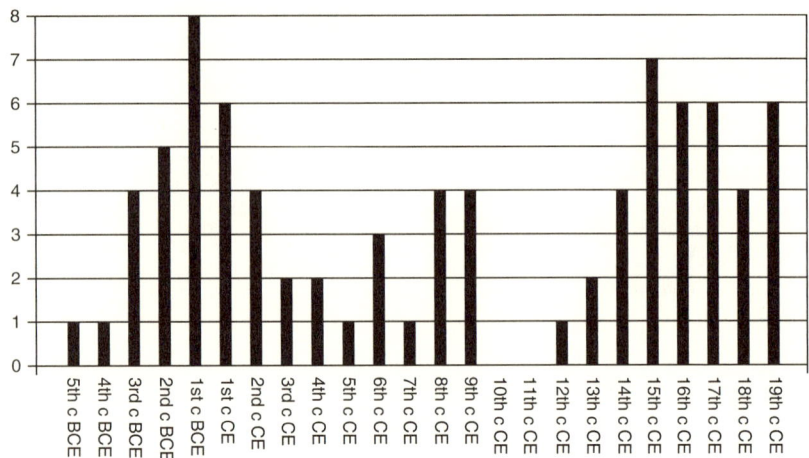

Fig. 2.6. Frequency of major floods at Rome per century.

torical events to climate shifts.[46] The "fall" of Rome itself has frequently been attributed to climatic changes.[47] The evidence cited in such arguments is derived either from references in primary sources to unusually hot, cold, rainy, or dry years, or from interpreting various observable data such as tree rings, sedimentation samples, and pollen residues. In such an attempt, the subjective nature of the primary sources is obviously problematic, but the more scientific investigations hold promise of recreating ancient climate patterns.[48] While certain climate shifts, such as the late medieval Little Ice Age, seem well established, the record of Tiber rainfall for the period in question is more ambiguous, and at least at present, there does not seem to be definitive proof of a pattern of significantly greater rainfall coinciding with the centuries of increased flood frequency in ancient Rome.

Another possible explanation for the apparent peak in the number of floods from circa 200 BC to AD 200 might have to do with anthropogenic changes to the Tiber drainage basin. Some scholars have argued that deforestation of the hills of the Tiber drainage basin from the third century BC onward may be responsible for the increase in the number of floods.[49] Deforestation has often been blamed for an increase in frequency or severity of floods, and while the cause-and-effect relationship between the two has often been oversimplified, removing substantial amounts of trees from a watershed can affect some of the processes that govern flooding.[50] Forests, with their deep and complex root systems, help prevent erosion and severe flooding by holding soil in place. In addition, soils developed beneath forest cover have been shown to have much superior infiltration properties, and the more mature and undisturbed the forest, the greater the infiltration rate of its soil. Particularly on steep slopes, if trees are cut down, the entire layer of topsoil can quickly be washed away. Deep soil acts as a brake on flooding, because more of the moisture from rainfall can be absorbed by the soil, where it slowly makes its way to the drainage stream through infiltration. On the other hand, bare, rocky ground lacking soil does not absorb much moisture, and nearly all rainfall becomes surface runoff that quickly makes its way to the stream, increasing its discharge and, hence, the volume of a flood. The dense vegetation composed of the trees and other plants in the forest also increases evapotranspiration, and itself can hold moisture or slow down the process of infiltration in the soil. One study suggests that when a dense forest is clear-cut, the volume of moderate floods can be increased by as much as 30% as a result.[51] In mountainous areas with substantial snowfall, forests can also play a role in reducing flooding caused by rapid snowmelt when temperatures suddenly increase. The forest cover causes the snow to melt more gradually and over a longer time period, thus reducing sudden peaks in stream discharge. One study in Colorado suggests that removing the forest cover caused an increase of 50% in the peak stream discharge as a result of more rapid melting.[52]

Originally, the Tiber basin, like much of Europe, was densely covered by forests.[53] The city of Rome required vast amounts of forest products, especially for construction, to fashion objects, and for fuel.[54] Early in Roman history, lumber was the main component in construction, and even when many buildings were being built out of concrete and brick, wood was still employed for doors, lintels, roof beams, and scaffolding. Wood was used for all manner of tools, utensils, containers, and furnishings. In the absence of other readily available sources of fuel, wood was burned in fires used to bake bricks and make mortar. Individuals burned wood as fuel in fires used for heating and cooking, and much wood was also transformed into charcoal that ultimately served the same purposes. Charcoal was an essential item and probably accounted for the great majority of wood consumed. In underdeveloped countries today, close to 90% of wood consumed is used to produce charcoal.[55] Rome's public baths alone would have used huge amounts of charcoal or wood to heat their waters. Forests were also the source of numerous other important products and materials, such as cork, pitch, tar, oils, resins, medicines, nuts, and spices.

The thick woods of Etruria, Latium, and Umbria seem to have been heavily exploited by the Romans to provide wood for the city of Rome. The easiest way by far to transport felled trees is by water, and the forests along the banks of the Tiber and its tributaries would have been the first places where Roman loggers concentrated their efforts. After the trees were cut down, they were stripped of branches and rolled down to the nearest stream, where the logs were fastened together to form timber rafts. These timber rafts were then floated down the Tiber by the current until they reached Rome, where they could be further processed. Strabo (5.3.7) stresses the essential transport role that the Tiber and its tributaries played in providing timber to Rome, and Pliny (*HN* 16.202) records that in his time the standard price for such a raft of timber was 40,000 sesterces. The Romans do not seem to have been too concerned about the ecological cost of clear-cutting the Italian forests and in fact, up until the second century BC, offered incentives to anyone who would clear woodlands and transform them into farmland.[56]

Rome's insatiable demand for timber appears to have required that supplies be brought considerable distances, suggesting that local resources had been exhausted. Strabo (5.2.5) records that the forests around Pisa had been destroyed in order to feed the demands of the construction industry at Rome. By the third century AD, there are signs that the closest and most accessible supplies of timber may have been depleted. Alexander Severus concerned himself with ensuring an adequate supply of wood for Rome's baths, and by the middle of the fourth century AD, African shippers who brought timber to Rome were being granted imperial privileges (SHA *Alex. Sev.* 24.5; *Cod. Theod.* 13.5.10). In this time period, deforestation of the areas around Rome and a subsequent increase in erosion are also indicated by stratigraphic pollen analysis of cores taken from lakes Nemi and Albano.[57]

Because it was precisely the forests of the Tiber drainage basin that were probably being most heavily logged, it appears highly suggestive that the period when this logging was at its peak, from 200 BC to AD 200, was also the same time when the frequency of floods apparently increased and peaked. The erosion of the soil in the Tiber basin that would have followed the clear-cutting of the forests would have left bare hillsides, which could have increased the frequency and magnitude of floods. The Romans do not seem to have been completely unaware of the link between deforestation and flooding. Pliny (*HN* 31.30) observes that "often devastating torrents unite when from hills has been cut away the wood that used to hold the rains and absorb them."[58] Deforestation might also have potentially been the cause of the anomalous summertime floods, which seem so aberrant in light of the Tiber's normal strongly seasonal pattern of winter and spring flooding. All four floods that can be securely identified as having occurred in the summer—those of 202 BC, 13 BC, AD 12, and AD 217—fall into the period when the logging of the Tiber basin was probably most intense. The disruption caused to the normal hydrological operation of the Tiber drainage basin by deforestation during this period could have been a strong contributing factor to these atypical floods. By the early Middle Ages, the Italian forests apparently had begun to recover or at least had stabilized, and by the Renaissance, they were again providing large trees for Roman construction projects.[59]

The evidence for deforestation as the cause of the apparent increase in flood frequency is suggestive but by no means definitive. While deforestation of the Tiber basin probably exercised at least some intensifying effect on the magnitude, and perhaps the frequency, of Tiber flooding, it is much more difficult to quantify that effect, or to identify this as the sole cause of a dramatic change in flood behavior. Could deforestation alone have been responsible for an apparent eightfold increase in the frequency of floods from the fourth to the first century BC? In the end, while deforestation does perhaps seem a potentially good explanation for the anomalous summer floods, it was at most probably only one of a multiplicity of factors contributing to the numerous floods from 200 BC to AD 200.

While the reasons listed may help to account for some perturbations of the flood frequency pattern, I would argue that the main ex-

Floods of the Tiber in Ancient Rome

planation for the unevenness of the flood frequency pattern is also perhaps the simplest—the spottiness of the surviving sources. It is probably no coincidence that the highest number of attested floods comes from the first century BC, which is one of the most well-documented eras in terms of the amount of surviving primary sources; conversely, the medieval lacuna falls during the "darkest" of the "dark ages" for Rome, when the population of the city plummeted, and our sources are fewer. Despite the plethora of climate-focused explanations that have been put forward to explain this pattern, I believe no factor is as important as the sporadic nature of the surviving sources. In assessing flood frequency, I think one must take into account the number and completeness of the available primary sources.

This interpretation gains credence from a direct comparison between flood frequency and the rise and fall of Rome's population. Figure 2.7 shows rough approximations of the city's population over the past 2,600 years.[60] The points of greatest- and least-attested flood frequency correlate very well with the increases and declines in the population of Rome. Both graphs show the same bell curve positioned around the height of Roman power and the same increase in the modern period. Thus, the apparently increased tempo of flooding during the high point of ancient Rome may actually be a reflection of the fact that at that time there were more people living in the city and therefore more potential for damage and loss of property and life. Around AD 1000, the population of Rome is estimated to have dwindled to

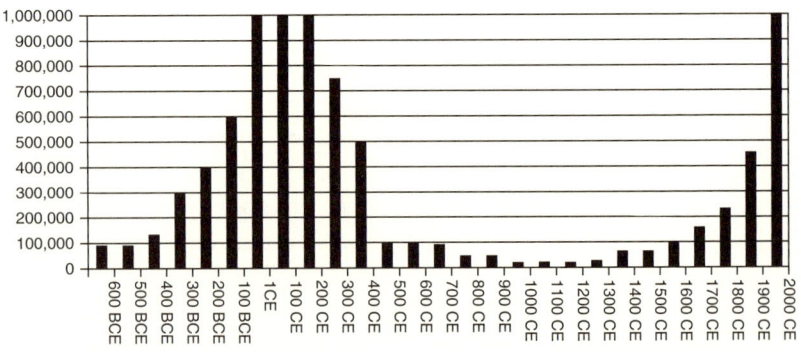

Fig. 2.7. Estimated population of Rome from 600 BC to the present.

less than 20,000 inhabitants, and this low point in population precisely coincides with the time of no reported floods. At such a time, even if floods did strike the city, there were simply not many people who would have been affected. In eras of low population, more of the inhabitants could also have been living atop the hills, thus rendering the city itself less vulnerable overall to the destructive effects of flooding. Viewed in this light, the variation in flood frequency may well be due less to an actual change in the number of times the river rose than to differences in the number of structures present to be affected by, and people to record, such events.

An assessment of the ancient sources reveals that they often only bother to report a flood if it coincides with some important event of which it is interpreted as a portent. Thus many floods that did not happen to occur near the death or accession of an emperor or some other notable event may have gone unrecorded. Furthermore, there are several instances of multiple floods being reported in the same year, but these are never taken into account individually when ancient flood frequency is calculated. Livy (24.9.6, 38.28.4) noted that in 215 BC there were two floods that struck the city and also recounted that in 189 BC the Tiber flooded the city an astonishing twelve times. If just these two cases of multiple floods per year were factored in, the frequency rate would be dramatically increased. The assumption that floods were more common than is attested in the surviving sources can also be inferred from a passage in Ovid's *Fasti* (519–520) where he states that, when the horse races of the Equirria were disrupted by flooding, it was customary to move them from the Campus Martius to the Caelian. No actual account of a flood that disrupted the Equirria is extant, but the fact that Ovid bothers to mention that there was a standard alternative site suggests that there were multiple such instances that have left no trace in the sources.

When looking at the modern data, there is no question about floods going unreported due to incomplete or lost documentation. There are other problems, however. One complicating factor is the effect that occurs when the ground level has been raised in many areas of the city, without as great a corresponding rise in the streambed level of the Tiber. The ground level in much of modern Rome is easily 5 m higher than it was in republican Rome. This steady increase also means that more recent floods have had to rise to higher levels than ancient ones in order to inundate the ground to the same depth. For the past several hundred years, we possess accurate measurements. Therefore, an inundation that would have caused widespread flooding in ancient Rome would today leave the city relatively unscathed. The best modern data come from the past hundred years, after the Tiber embankments were constructed, when only a truly extraordinary flood would be able to surmount them. Between 1870 and 2000, there were 57 instances when the Tiber levels rose to at least 13 masl. (See the list of floods in Appendix I.) Due to the embankments, only a few of these resulted in serious flooding, but in ancient Rome a water level of 13 masl would have constituted a substantial flood. The presence of the embankments themselves no doubt contributed to the height of these measurements, but these statistics nevertheless suggest that the Tiber may have risen to dangerous levels in the past more frequently than is usually asserted.

All of this information indicates that rather than the commonly cited rate of two to three floods per century, the actual frequency of floods in ancient Rome was much higher. What, then, was the typical frequency of floods at Rome? I am inclined to accept a flood frequency rate for ancient Rome that is much higher than those usually quoted by other modern scholars. For the period when there seems to have been a fairly reliable continuous record of major inundations (1300 to the present), there has been an average frequency of one major flood every 19 years.[61] During the best documented ancient Roman period of 250 BC to AD 250, a nearly identical rate of one flood every 18 years is observed.[62] Even more striking is if one looks at the period since 1700 when there have been very accurate measurements of Tiber levels. If one includes for this period not only the exceptional floods of more than 15 masl, but also all times when the Tiber reached a significant flood level of 13 masl, one finds no fewer than 77 such incidents, or about one every four years.[63] The best documented ancient and modern periods therefore both suggest an average periodicity of one exceptional flood every 19 years, or about 5 per century. Recent Tiber data further suggest that minor floods occurred even more frequently, on the order of every 5 years, or 20 per century.[64] I believe that the much lower flood frequencies recorded for other time spans are the direct result of the paucity of sources for these periods rather than being indicative of drastic differences in the frequency of flooding.

A realistic estimate for Tiber flood periodicity, therefore, is one exceptional flood every 20 years, and for every exceptional inundation there were likely 4–5 lesser but still significant floods. Such a rate would have made floods a serious hazard, and one that would on average have given inhabitants of the city quite frequent direct experience with moderate flooding and have made them witnesses to exceptional inundations two or three times during their lives.

Magnitude of Floods at Rome

For all the other characteristics of floods discussed in this chapter—extent, duration, frequency, and seasonality—it has been possible to draw upon at least some precise evidence from ancient sources in order to evaluate them. The information from these sources has often been supplemented with later data in order to develop a more fully rounded or complete understanding. About the final characteristic, magnitude of floods, however, the ancient data are much less specific. While numerical information on the height that floodwaters reached is available from the late Middle Ages onward, prior to this time no such records survive. The magnitude of modern floods is expressed in terms of the height of the water and the volume of discharge of the stream. There are subjective descriptions from ancient authors stressing the violence or scale of certain floods, but it is nearly impossible to translate these impressions into concrete terms.

While no ancient source gives numerical quantification of Tiber levels, the Romans surely did make such measurements. Frontinus's detailed analysis of aqueducts demonstrates that some Romans had both the inclination and means to amass extensive data related to the hydraulic affairs of the city. Hydrometers to measure river levels were certainly well known in the ancient world, as the famous nilometers of Egypt attest. The simplest form such a device would have taken at Rome would have been a numerical scale inscribed along the vertical face of a wall that abutted the Tiber. The various embankments within the city or perhaps a pier of one of the bridges would have been natural locations. Although no such device survives in its entirety, a block of marble recovered from beneath the modern Ponte Sisto strongly suggests that the Romans did have such hydrometers.[65] It is a trapezoidal block of fine travertine measuring 2.4 by 1.12 by 7.82 m that has been interpreted as originally forming part of the pilaster of a bridge pier. Inscribed along one face is what seems to be a vertical scale marked in Roman feet. The surviving portion includes the number VI enclosed between two horizontal lines, and at a distance of one Roman foot from this number is inscribed the numeral VII similarly framed. While not enough remains to reconstruct a complete picture of the positioning and functioning of this device, it at least illustrates that the Romans did make rudimentary measurements of the Tiber's level.

Returning to what can be gleaned from the primary sources, it is possible to make some general observations about the depth of water implied by these accounts. One indication of depth can be inferred from the numerous times the sources stress that one had to travel through the streets by boat. This certainly suggests that the water on these occasions was of a depth of at least half a meter or so. The streets of the city were said to have been navigable by boat on no less than eight occasions. These were the floods of 27 BC, 23 BC, 13 BC, AD 5, AD 15, AD 36, AD 371, and AD 398 (Dio 53.20.1, 53.33.5, 54.25.2, 55.22.3, 57.14.7–8; Dio 58.26.5 and Zonaras 11.3; Am. Mar. 29.6.17–18; Claud. *De Bel. Gild.* 41–43). The water level of the flood of AD 69 is also described as having risen so quickly that people were trapped in their dwellings by the high water, a situation that recurred in AD 371, when it necessitated that food be brought to the stranded people by boat (Tac. *Hist.* 1.86; Am. Mar. 29.6.17–18).

The waters of the floods of 54 BC and AD 69 were said to have attained sufficient force and depth to sweep people off their feet and drown them in the streets (Dio 39.61.1–2, 79.25.5). Again, this suggests a probable depth of at least half a meter.[66] During several floods, the water was plainly deep enough to cause the widespread death by drowning of cattle in the fields. Livy (24.9.6, 35.21.5–6) states that the floods of 215 and 192 BC were so deep and violent that cattle were swept away, and the flood of AD 162 is likewise described as having caused many animals to drown (SHA *M. Aur.* 8). In all of these cases, the details mentioned by the authors illustrate that over wide areas the floodwaters achieved and maintained depths of at least half a meter and almost certainly considerably more.

In accounts of medieval floods, there are several instances where the authors attempt to give an indication of water depth. The flood of AD 716 is described by two different authors as having reached a depth of one and a half times a man's height along the Via Lata (*Gest. Lang.* 6.36; *Lib. Pont.*, Greg. II, 6). The Via Lata runs through the Campus Martius toward the Roman Forum area, and while it would certainly be one of the more flood-prone regions of Rome, this description suggests a considerable floodwater depth of around 2.5 m in this area. The flood of AD 856 was said to have completely covered the doors of a church located along the Via Lata, which seems to imply a depth similar to that of the AD 716 flood (*Lib. Pont.*, Ben. III, 23). The account of the flood of October of AD 860 repeats the phraseology used to describe the AD 856 flood almost exactly, including the indication of depth as measured by covering this church's doors, suggesting that these accounts may be more formulaic or derived from a single original than they are accurate descriptions of specific, separate floods (*Lib. Pont.*, Nic., 15).

Although no ancient author expressed information about the magnitude of a flood in concrete numerical terms, combining the literary descriptions with what can be reconstructed of ancient topography allows for some tentative estimates to be made. For example, the floods during or near the time of Augustus that inundated the Roman Forum, such as that of 44 BC, would have had to reach a height of at least 14 or 15 masl (Hor. *Carm.* 1.2.13–20). The flood of 13 BC that interrupted the inauguration of the Theater of Balbus could have been of a lesser magnitude because the theater is situated in the central depressed area of the Campus Martius (Dio 54.25.2). A flood of only 8–9 masl would have been sufficient to cover this area with water, although the need to travel to the flooded theater in boats indicates that the water was probably deeper than this.

The flood of AD 12 is described as having inundated the Circus Maximus, resulting in the Ludi Martiales being moved from the Circus to the Forum of Augustus (Dio 56.27.4). This is particularly useful information because it suggests both a minimum and a maximum for this flood. At this date, the floodwaters would have had to reach a height of at least 13 and probably more like 15 masl to fully inundate the Circus. The Forum of Augustus, which remained dry enough for horse races to be held in it, is situated at an elevation of around 17 masl. Thus we can estimate that the flood of AD 12 was in the range of 15 to 17 masl. For spectators to be able to reach the Forum of Augustus, presumably the lower-lying approaches to it had to be relatively dry as well, suggesting that the flood was actually toward the lower end of this range, perhaps around 15 to16 masl.

One of the most interesting flood accounts to subject to this sort of analysis is the flood of 54 BC described by both Cicero (*Ad Quint. fr.* 3.7.1) and Dio (39.61.1–2). This seems to have been an especially large flood. Dio notes that it flooded not only the "lower levels" of the city but that it also reached many of the higher portions as well. Cicero offers the information that an "amazing flood" had struck Rome and that it inundated the valley of the Circus Maximus "on the Via Appia to the Temple of Mars." He also states that "a huge volume of water reaches the public fishpond." The *piscina publica* lies several hundred meters past the Circus Maximus at an elevation of around 15 masl. Cicero's description of a "huge volume" of water reaching this far suggests that the flood was of a greater magnitude than 15 masl because it did not merely reach this point but deposited a substantial amount of water there. Some idea of this flood's ultimate extent is given by his statement that the water proceeded along the Appian Way up to the Temple of Mars. This temple has traditionally been identified with a location just outside the Porta Appia of the later Aurelian Wall. If such an identification is correct, this would place the temple at an elevation of more than 30 masl, and a flood that even approached this site would be by far the greatest ever recorded at Rome. A flood of this magnitude seems so much greater than other known inundations, however, that it is scarcely believable. This suggests that the flood was of lesser magnitude and either that Cicero merely meant that the flood extended along the Appian Way toward the site of the temple, or that the temple itself was located closer to Rome on a lower elevation. The site of the temple is in fact a matter of dispute among scholars, and the ancient sources themselves offer contradictory information about its location.[67] On the other hand, the Latin is sufficiently vague that Cicero may have just been indicating that the waters were extending toward the temple without actually reaching it. In either case, to be at all reconcilable with topography, the flood would have had to reach a height of 20 masl or even slightly more, and thereby is the greatest attested flood at Rome in the ancient period whose magnitude can be estimated.

If we turn to more modern floods in order to get a sense of Tiber flooding, the flood markers and hydrometers attached to some buildings make it possible to quantify the exact depth of many of the postmedieval floods at Rome. The 38 floods that attained known or estimated levels of 15 masl or greater at Ripetta are recorded in table 2.4. The two columns on the left list the floods in chronological order from the earliest at the top of the table to the most recent at the bottom, while the two columns on the right list the same floods but with the flood attaining the highest peak water level at the top of the table down to that with the lowest at the bottom. The highest ever measured level for a flood at Rome was 19.56 masl, which is almost three times the historical average level of 6.7 masl (see figs. 2.8, 2.9). Interestingly, the five top recorded levels all occurred in the 16th or 17th centuries.

The other measure of flood magnitude is the discharge, or volume of water, expressed in flow rates of cubic meters per second. Data for this statistic are even more limited and restricted to relatively modern times than those for water height. The first such reading dates from June 1821, when the Tiber was recorded as having a discharge of 244 m^3/s. The historical average from this time to the present, as noted previously, is 232.49 m^3/s. The highest measured discharge rates in the 20th century were 2,730 m^3/s during the flood of 1937, 3,100 m^3/s during the flood of 1915, and 3,300 m^3/s during the flood of 1900.[68] While we cannot know what levels or discharge rates were reached by ancient Roman floods, the modern statistics do provide an indication of actual water levels achieved by the Tiber, and certainly any of the flood levels listed in table 2.4 would have produced disastrous consequences in ancient Rome.

As if constructing much of the city in a floodplain were not problematic enough, the very presence of the city itself exercised an intensifying effect on the severity of the floods. There were several different factors that contributed to this effect, and which hold true for any city built in a floodplain, not just ancient Rome. First, covering the ground

Table 2.4.
Major Postmedieval Floods at Rome with Known or Estimated Peak Water Levels of Greater Than 15 masl

Listed by Year		Listed by Height	
Year	Height (masl)	Year	Height (masl)
1180	>16	1598	19.56
1230	>16	1530	18.95
1277	>16	1557	18.90
1310	>15	1606	18.27
1345	>15	1637	17.55
1376	17.00	1476	17.41
1379	17.00	1422	17.32
1415	>15	1438	17.22
1422	17.32	1870	17.22
1438	17.22	1660	17.11
1476	17.41	1379	17.00
1485	>15	1376	17.00
1488	>15	1495	16.88
1495	16.88	1937	16.84
1514	>16	1805	16.42
1530	18.95	1647	16.41
1557	18.90	1846	16.25
1589	>16	1900	16.17
1598	19.56	1915	16.08
1606	18.27	1686	16.00
1637	17.55	1180	>16
1647	16.41	1230	>16
1660	17.11	1277	>16
1686	16.00	1514	>16
1688	>15	1589	>16
1700	>15	1750	15.58
1702	15.41	1809	15.47
1742	15.02	1702	15.41
1750	15.58	1878	15.35
1805	16.42	1843	15.34
1809	15.47	1742	15.02
1843	15.34	1310	>15
1846	16.25	1345	>15
1870	17.22	1415	>15
1878	15.35	1485	>15
1900	16.17	1488	>15
1915	16.08	1688	>15
1937	16.84	1700	>15

with buildings, streets, and paving creates a large impermeable surface where there used to be permeable soil.[69] Thus all rain that falls within this area becomes runoff and adds to any floodwaters rather than being partially absorbed by the soil. In modern cities, which coat huge expanses with an impermeable layer of asphalt, concrete, and buildings, this can become a major problem if generous drainage systems are not incorporated into the city's design.

Second, the actual buildings of the city can occupy a substantial amount of the area of the floodplain, forcing floodwaters into a smaller space and thus increasing their depth. For example, suppose there were a floodplain that was regularly inundated by floods to a depth of 5 m. A city was then constructed in this floodplain whose buildings covered 35% of the ground. If a flood of the usual magnitude subsequently struck, the presence of the buildings would have the effect of forcing the same volume of water into a smaller space, with the result that the depth of the inundation would be increased from the usual 5 m deep to 7.7 m deep.

Fig. 2.8. The Pons Fabricius during the flood of 1937, which reached a recorded height of 16.37 masl. This is the best preserved Roman bridge, and part of the original inscription is visible on the arch. (Fototeca Unione, American Academy in Rome, 574)

Floods of the Tiber in Ancient Rome

Fig. 2.9. The Pons Fabricius today, with a normal water level of around 5 masl. A good sense of how high the Tiber can rise can be gained by comparing this photograph with figure 2.8. (Photo by author)

Heavily built-up urban environments can intensify floods in yet another way as well. When confronted with the restrictions of an urban landscape instead of an open floodplain, rather than reacting by increasing in depth, floodwaters can sometimes respond by increasing the velocity of the water flow. This most often happens when waters are channeled through streets of decreasing width. In some respects this can be even more destructive than an increase in depth because the force exerted by water increases by the square of the velocity. In other words, water flowing at a velocity of 6 meters per second has four times the force of water flowing at 3 m/sec, and water flowing at a velocity of 9 m/sec has nine times the force of water flowing at 3 m/sec. Due to these effects, the larger and more built up a city becomes, the greater and more powerful are the floods that it suffers.

By the end of the second century AD when much of the Campus Martius had been covered by monumental buildings, ancient Rome was an intensely built-up urban environment. Although some regions were given over to gardens, by this point in time these were located more toward the outskirts of the city, and the areas lying in the floodplain were mostly covered with architecture. The narrowness of many of ancient Rome's streets would also have exacerbated the urban intensification effect on floods. Wide, straight streets might have served as conduits to channel floodwaters safely through a city, but the narrow, often twisted streets of ancient Rome would have been transformed into turbulent and dangerous torrents in which the depth of the waters was increased by the city's architecture. Given all these factors, we should expect to see increases in flood frequency, magnitude, and damages as the city itself grew and became more densely built up. Such a pattern may be detectable in the increase in numbers of floods reported during the first centuries BC and AD.

Conclusion

The vivid descriptions of ancient flooding found in the primary sources testify to the scale of ancient floods. Floods of sufficient magnitude to submerge the city's streets for multiple days, destroy buildings, and sweep away and drown large numbers of humans and animals were clearly major floods that were at least comparable with, and perhaps even greater than, the better-documented floods of the modern era.

While much remains unknown about floods in ancient Rome, by combining the hints offered by the primary sources with comparative historical data on flooding at Rome, and viewing this information through the perspective of modern knowledge of hydrology and the current behavior of the Tiber basin, it has been possible to gain a reasonable understanding of the major characteristics of ancient floods. These floods affected large portions of the city of Rome and nearly all the most intensively built-up regions. They occurred with sufficient frequency to be a part of the urban experience of most of the inhabitants of the city and to necessitate consideration in urban planning. There were definite patterns to their seasonality and duration, and, perhaps most significant, floods were of a scale to result in widespread disruption and destruction. The damage caused by these inundations encompassed a wide range of effects, both during the event itself and for a long period of time subsequently, and these effects form the subject of the next two chapters.

Three

Immediate Effects of Floods

Introduction and Methodology

The goal of this chapter and the next is to examine both the immediate and the delayed physical effects of floods on the ancient city of Rome and its inhabitants. This task poses a considerable challenge because there is very little in the primary sources about these consequences beyond a few nonspecific allusions to buildings destroyed and lives lost. These chapters will, nevertheless, present a step-by-step reconstruction of the effects of a "typical" flood in ancient Rome and the problems and challenges that such an event would have created. These include not only the immediate effects of the floodwaters themselves but also the long process of cleaning up after the disaster and dealing with its aftereffects. No comprehensive account of a single ancient flood survives in the primary sources, but by combining the existing descriptions with scientific and comparative data, it is possible to assemble a reconstruction of the range of effects that ancient floods must have caused.

In recreating such a "virtual flood," these chapters will of necessity frequently describe phenomena and actions in hypothetical terms using a great many "must have been" or "would have been" grammatical constructions. It should be emphasized at the outset, however, that such statements are not simply an exercise in imagination, but rather are based on concrete scientific data. When dealing with a physical phenomenon like floods, just because something is not explicitly mentioned by an ancient author does not mean that one is left uncertain whether it occurred. One of the advantages of writing the history of a physical phenomenon such as floods is that it is possible to make many definite statements about the behavior and effects of these inundations despite the scarcity of information derived from primary sources. The physical laws of nature, such as the behavior of water under the influence of gravity, can be precisely described through mathematical equations, and the resulting description of the movement of floodwater is as valid for ancient Rome as it is today. To my mind, it would be irresponsible to pretend to offer a meaningful analysis of the topic of floods that failed to address important effects of flooding just because someone like Cicero did not happen to mention them. Naturally, we always wish that ancient sources would be more informative about the subjects that interest us, but their silence about a topic is not sufficient excuse to simply ignore it, if we hope to gain a more meaningful understanding of the ancient world. In this case, it is possible to make definitive statements about the effects of floods in ancient Rome based on comparative and scientific evidence. The reconstructive approach employed in these chapters is necessary in order to provide a framework within which to examine the various stages of problems that a major flood would have caused and how these might have been dealt with. While often expressed in terms of a hypothetical "typical" ancient flood, all of the effects, problems, and incidents described would have occurred every time that a major flood struck the city.

Disruption of the Daily Life of the City

The most basic effect of a flood on ancient Rome would have been the disruption of the daily life of the city. During the period of high water and the recovery and reconstruction phase following the flood itself, normative activities would have been suspended, ordinary routines altered, and many of the usual proceedings of the city canceled or delayed. Much of the economic functioning of the city would have ground to a halt as businesses closed and workers failed to show up at their jobs. Instead of attending to their usual occupations, people would have wholly devoted their energy to such tasks as finding shelter, rescuing possessions, and locating family and friends. These types of disruptions affecting the inhabitants of the city are not specifically recorded in ancient sources, but they would nevertheless have constituted a major hardship and might have had a significant impact on the economy of the city. When they do mention the interference of floods with the urban life of Rome, the primary sources tend to focus on two specific areas: disruption of movement through the city, and interruption of major public rituals.

One of the main ways in which floods would have created problems is by disrupting normal routes of movement through the city. Regions that were submerged beneath deep or swiftly flowing water would have been impossible to traverse by foot. The streets would have been transformed into impassable raging torrents of water, isolating survivors on hilltops or in tall buildings, and different areas of the city would have been cut off from one another.

In such conditions, the only feasible means of transportation is by boat, and the Romans seem to have readily resorted to using watercraft to move about the submerged city (fig. 3.1). Indeed, mention of traveling about the inundated city by means of boats is one of the most common features of ancient flood accounts, appearing in more than one-quarter of them (9 out of 33). These were the floods of 27 BC, 23 BC, 13 BC, AD 5, AD 15, AD 36, AD 371, and AD 398 (Dio 53.20.1, 53.33.5, 54.25.2, 55.22.3, 57.14.7–8; Dio 58.26.5 and Zonaras 11.3; Am. Mar. 29.6.17–18; Claud. *De Bel. Gild.* 41–43). Six of these accounts clearly state that boats were used to move about the submerged city or that the city was "navigable" by boats (Dio 53.20.1, 53.33.5, 55.22.3, 57.14.7–8, 58.26.5; Zonaras 11.3). Dio's chronicle (54.25.2) of the flood of 13 BC includes the detail that Balbus could only visit his newly constructed theater by boat, which seems to imply that boats would also have been necessary for others. The flood narrative of AD 371 describes a famine relief scheme that involved bringing food by boat to people trapped in buildings by the water (Am. Mar. 29.6.17–18). The report of the flood of AD 398 relates that the underwater city knows what it is like to experience ships and "the sounds of oars"

Floods of the Tiber in Ancient Rome

Fig. 3.1. Drawing by J. H. W. Tischbein of the interior of the Pantheon being visited by men in boats during the flood of 1686. Travel through the streets of Rome by boat is frequently attested during floods. (Fototeca Unione, American Academy in Rome, 14133F)

(Claud. *De Bel. Gild.* 41–43). Information is twice given about the length of time that the city was navigable by boats: for three days during the flood of 23 BC, and for seven days during the flood of AD 5 (Dio 53.33.5, 55.22.3). As a riverine city with port facilities, Rome would have had a fair number of small watercraft that could have been pressed into service during such emergencies. Many of the "boats" that flood survivors would have employed on these occasions, however, were probably impromptu craft cobbled together from whatever materials were at hand and probably resembled rafts more than true boats.

Ancient Rome was a city with a rich ritual life, and this too was disrupted by flooding. From complex religious observances to spectacular public entertainments to small family ceremonies, various forms of ritual structured and gave meaning to daily life. Parades, sacrifices, speeches, funerals, athletic contests, gladiatorial combats, purification ceremonies, augury taking, theatrical presentations, chariot races, benefactions, beast hunts, and legal proceedings were all staged in the spaces of the city and served to regulate its operation. The great public religious and political rituals could be massive affairs lasting for days, accompanied by spectacular shows, and observed by tens of thousands of spectators. By the second century AD, the annual calendar was dotted with an array of holidays and festivals, most of which demanded substantial public and/or private rituals. Given the number of these events, it seems likely that the occurrence of floods would have overlapped with some of these, and, indeed, specific descriptions of flooding interfering with public rituals provide a recurrent theme in flood accounts (fig. 3.2).[1]

One of the earliest records of a flood, that of 363 BC, already includes such an instance: a flood inundating the Circus Maximus, halting some unspecified games being held there (Livy 7.3.2). The flood-prone nature of the Circus made games that were traditionally held there particularly susceptible to disruption, and such was the case in 202 BC, when the planned staging of the Ludi Apollinares was jeopardized by a flood that submerged the Circus. In response, preparations were made to hold the games outside the Colline Gate near the Temple of Venus of Eryx instead, and on the day of the games, the parade set out for this alternate location. A sudden clearing in the weather, however, resulted in a withdrawal of water from the Circus Maximus, and the parade was redirected to the original site. Livy (30.38.10–12) records that the joy of the celebrants was increased on this occasion by the unexpected return of the games to their customary setting. In 13 BC the planned inauguration of the newly constructed Theater of Balbus was disrupted by a flood that submerged

Fig. 3.2. The Roman Forum partially flooded during the inundation of 1902. This flood reached a recorded height of 14.39 masl and demonstrates that even after the Romans had raised the paving level numerous times, the Forum, the site of many of the most important urban rituals of the city, remained vulnerable to flooding. (Fototeca Unione, American Academy in Rome, VD 267)

the theater itself (Dio 54.25.2). Flooding in the Circus was again the cause of the relocation of games in AD 12 when the celebrations of the Ludi Martiales had to be transferred to the Forum of Augustus. Because of the halting of the ceremony, custom prescribed that the games had to be held again, and a second celebration featuring the slaughter of 200 lions was held in the Circus once the floodwaters had dissipated (Dio 56.27.4). These are the specific instances when a flood is known to have interfered with a public ritual, but it is likely that many similar interruptions took place but went unrecorded. Evidence of this is suggested by an offhand remark of Ovid (*Fasti* 3.517–22) that the horse race of the Equirria held in the Campus Martius was often interrupted by flooding, but that when this happened, it was customary to move the races to the Caelian Hill.

In general, the Romans displayed considerable flexibility in dealing with the interruptions to the ritual life of the city that were caused by flooding. The floods appear to have been accepted as a natural part of the urban landscape, and ceremonies either proceeded as best as possible or else were relocated to drier ground. Only in the earliest incident does the flood seem to have been interpreted as evidence of divine displeasure related to the festival itself. (This is also the only recorded case when the festival may not have been relocated or otherwise continued to its conclusion.) While the celebrants of the Ludi Apollinares of 202 BC were pleased when the games were able to be held in their usual site, they do not seem to have been concerned that the inundation of this location was somehow an indictment of the planned ceremony. Floods were a part of life in ancient Rome, and even when they intruded into significant public spectacles, the Romans simply adapted to the situation and proceeded with their intended rituals.

Destruction of Property

Following a flood, the destruction of personal property would have been an additional hardship endured by Rome's inhabitants. The majority of people probably only had rather meager possessions to begin with, and these would no doubt have been essentials for daily living. Restoring or replacing these could have been a serious problem for many flood victims. It is difficult to say what a "typical" Roman's personal belongings consisted of, but even relatively poor households most likely had a couple items of clothing, bedding, footwear, a lamp or two, assorted cookware and implements, and some rudimentary furniture. Juvenal's inventory (3.203–8) of the belongings lost in a fire by one poor inhabitant of an *insula* must certainly be viewed with caution, but is probably indicative of the sorts of things that people owned. The sum of this man's worldly goods is described as consisting of a too-short bed, a cupboard, an old storage chest, six cups, a flagon, and a statue. Wealthier Romans owned a much wider range of possessions, and, as evidenced by finds from elite homes at Pompeii and Herculaneum, had a full range of often decorative tables, pots, pans, chairs, beds, cabinets, chests, lamps, and so on.[2]

Floodwaters typically cause loss of property in three main ways: items are directly broken or smashed by the water; they are ruined or spoiled by contact with or immersion in the water; or they are swept away by the floodwaters and lost to their owners. Small household objects made out of bronze or other metals would have been fairly resistant both to being broken and to water damage. The wide assortment of ceramic items that might be found in a Roman household, such as cups, plates, flasks, lamps, and urns, would have been unaffected by immersion in water, but would have been highly susceptible to breakage. Additionally, objects used in the storage, preparation, and eating of food or liquids, even if they survived being shattered by the floodwaters, would have been contaminated with the many disease-causing organisms that typically permeate floodwaters and would have required thorough cleaning before they could be safely used again.[3] Sturdy objects made from wood, such as furniture or chests, would have been somewhat more immune from breakage unless the waters were flowing swiftly (which is not unlikely in a flood) and they were thrown against walls or other debris. Textiles such as clothing and blankets that became soaked by floods could be dried out, but even more so than ceramic or wooden items, these would have been very difficult to cleanse of the dangerous bacteria that would likely have been present in the waters. Foodstuffs that were in waterproof containers might survive a flood, but anything that came into direct contact with the water would be ruined or rendered unfit for consumption.

Simply sifting through the chaos within one's dwelling created by a flood would have been a challenge. All of one's possessions would have been tossed about by the water and jumbled together with one another and with the other debris present in the water. Adding to the problem would have been the mud and sediment typically carried in floodwater and deposited thickly wherever the waters reached. Simply extracting property from this muck and cleaning it off can be a formidable task. Floods do not have to be of great depth to cause havoc in a household. Modern flood damage assessment studies suggest that the majority of household items will be affected by any flood that inundates a dwelling to a depth of only 0.8 m, or roughly the height of a table.[4] Finally, there would have been damage to the dwelling itself.

Wall coverings made of porous materials, including mud, plaster, unfired clay, and wood, could either disintegrate outright or else suffer long-term rot. These materials would also have been prone to the same kinds of contamination with disease-causing organisms as textiles. More substantial types of structural damage are addressed in the next section.

If property was neither destroyed nor ruined on site by a flood, but rather was picked up and carried away from one's dwelling by the waters, finding and recovering it would have presented an even greater challenge. Rapidly flowing currents can easily scour a room of its contents and carry off everything within. Floodwaters possess surprising force, enough to bear away very heavy and even seemingly immovable objects. Even the largest items of household furniture can be shifted or transported by relatively shallow floods. Today automobiles are washed away by floods of only half a meter in depth if the water is flowing with some velocity.[5] Floodwaters powerful enough to carry away cars would certainly have been sufficient to sweep away most items of personal property or furniture likely to be found in the homes of the inhabitants of ancient Rome. These possessions would have become separated from one another and mingled together with other people's goods, as well as with the general detritus being borne by the flood. If the local eddies and currents of the flood brought an item into one of the main streams, it could have been carried along for kilometers and, conceivably, even swept out to sea.

If one were so fortunate as to have one's possessions transported only a short distance, the odds of stumbling across them were slim, and even if one miraculously recognized an item, there was then the issue of establishing legal possession. In most cases, being able to prove definitively that a particular amphora, lamp, bed, or table plucked out of the mud in a street really was one's former property would have been all but impossible. The issue became even more complicated if the object had not been deposited in a public space, but instead had lodged within a building or on a piece of property belonging to another. Roman legal texts actually address such a situation and offer fascinating insight into what must have been a common occurrence after a flood as people went searching for their belongings that had been carried away by floodwaters: "When the Tiber flooded and carried a great deal of property belonging to many people into other people's dwellings, an interdict was granted by the praetor to prevent force being used against the owners to stop them taking away their possessions, provided they gave security for possible damage" (*Dig.* 39.2.9.1, Ulpian 53 *ad ed.*).[6] Similarly, Roman legal commentators also considered a situation in which the river carries off a boat belonging to one person and deposits it on land belonging to another (*Dig.* 39.2.9.3, Ulpian 53 *ad ed.*).

Most accounts of ancient floods do not directly address the destruction of personal property but instead focus on the collapse of buildings and loss of life. However, Pliny's narrative of a flood that struck during the reign of Trajan contains a remarkably evocative description of the terrible jumble of possessions and debris that was created by a raging flood:

> Those who live in highlands out of the reach of these terrible storms have witnessed, here, the household paraphernalia and weighty furniture of the wealthy, there, the simple tools of the farm, over there, oxen, plows, and the plowmen themselves, here, herds set free and straying, jumbled among the trunks of trees, or the beams and roofs from villas, and all of it floating about randomly and widely. (*Epist.* 8.17)

This is an excellent and timeless description of the chaos left behind by a flood and the task that faced survivors attempting to rebuild their lives and possessions. For the average ancient Roman, the financial loss represented by the damage and destruction of personal property would have been a serious problem, and finding the funds to replace even essential clothing and household items may have proved impossible.[7]

Another category of specialized flood damage also appears in the sources. Due to their proximity to the river, the port areas of the city would naturally have been particularly hard hit by flooding, and the docks and quays themselves were likely to suffer damage. Harbors and ports such as those found along the Tiber in Rome and at the river mouth at Ostia require large numbers of minor watercraft for their day-to-day operation. Rome's port would have had its share of ships, barges, lighters, ferryboats, rowboats, rafts, and bumboats. This assortment of watercraft would have been vulnerable to a rapidly rising river that could carry away or sink them. Exactly this seems to have happened during the flood of 60 BC, when, Dio (37.58.3–4) records, "the boats moored in the Tiber both near the city and at its mouth were sunk." While this is the only explicit mention of damage to the city's boats, every flood would have taken its toll on Rome's watercraft.[8]

Finally, although they were not located in the city of Rome per se, the farms that lay in the alluvial plain along the length of the Tiber were often damaged by floods, and this fact is stressed in a number of accounts of ancient floods. These farms suffered destruction to buildings, infrastructure, crops, and livestock. Six flood reports relate some sort of damage to farms: the floods of 414 BC, 215 BC, 192 BC, 54 BC, AD 162, and the flood during the reign of Trajan (Livy 4.49.2–3, 24.9.6, 35.215–16; Dio 39.61.1–2; SHA M. Aur. 8; Pliny Epist. 8.17). Only the earliest of these specifically notes damage to crops in the field, although, depending on the season, agricultural losses must have been a significant negative consequence of many floods. Most crops, and especially grains, are quickly ruined by immersion in water. Citations of the demolition of farm structures also cluster among the early floods, with farmhouses or buildings being listed as lost in the floods of 414 BC, 215 BC, and 192 BC. The flood during the reign of Trajan was said to have devastated the structures that encircled the farms, presumably walls or fences.

The most common type of farm resource cited as having been destroyed by floods was not crops or buildings, however, but livestock, particularly cattle. No less than five flood narratives by four different authors mention the loss of farm animals as one of the most important effects of these floods. Cattle were certainly valuable animals that represented a considerable investment of resources. Even if a crop were ruined by a flood, the field could be replanted the next year so that the loss to the farmer would represent only one year's worth of labor and investment. If a herd of cattle were drowned, however, this loss would constitute multiple years' worth of investment and husbandry. Cattle were specifically identified as being victims of the floods of 215 and 192 BC (Livy 24.9.6, 35.21.5–6). As described in these accounts, the cattle perished by being swept away and drowned in the floodwaters, so that their owners likely could not even have recovered the carcasses to salvage whatever meat might be cut off before they spoiled. Farm animals such as cattle seem to be particularly susceptible to drowning, even in floods where the majority of humans are able to escape. While this might be expected in countries with large commercial cattle operations where hundreds of cattle can be trapped inside buildings, it is also commonly observed in less-developed countries where the cattle are not as constrained and each farmer has only a handful of cows to look after. For example, in India during flooding in 1978, 2,000 people died but more than 40,000 cattle were lost, and in a 1988 flood in Bangladesh, 2,379 people drowned but more than 172,000 cattle perished.[9]

Other important animals raised by Roman farmers as food, to give milk, or for their products, such as eggs and wool, included goats, sheep, swine, and poultry.[10] In a major inundation of a farm, all of these animals would have drowned. It was said that in the flood of 54 BC "all animals perished," and similarly the flood of AD 162 "drowned many animals" (Dio 39.61.1–2; SHA *M. Aur.* 8). Perhaps the most devastating animal loss of all was the death of oxen used to plow fields, since such a loss might affect an entire farming community whose ability to plant the next season's crops would have been severely impaired. Oxen for plowing were quite expensive and required lengthy training. The loss of the village oxen to a flood might well have spelled disaster and starvation for the entire community. Pliny's description (*Epist.* 8.17) of the detritus floating in the aftermath of a flood includes farm tools, plows, oxen, and the plowmen themselves. For the subsistence farmers of antiquity, whose margins of survival were narrow even in a good year, the destruction of crops or animals by a flood would have been catastrophic. The only consolation they might have found in such natural disasters was that, if they were able to survive the immediate crisis, the sediments deposited by the floodwaters would have enriched future crop yields.

Collapse of Structures

Perhaps the most dramatic immediate effect of a flood is the collapse of large buildings. Fully 61% of the accounts of floods in ancient Rome (20 out of 33) include some reference to structures damaged or destroyed by the floodwaters.[11] A range of specific types of structures are named in these sources. Damage to farms or farm buildings is mentioned a number of times, including the floods of 414 BC, 215 BC, 192 BC, and the flood during the reign of Trajan (Livy 4.49.2–3, 24.9.6, 35.21.5–6; Pliny *Epist.* 8.17). Destruction of private homes (called either *domus* or *oikos*) is singled out as having happened during the floods of 60 BC, 54 BC, and AD 5 (Dio 37.58.3–4, 39.61.1–2; Cassiod. *Chron.* 604). Shops (*tabernae*) were said to have been swept away by the flood of 54 BC, and apartment buildings (*insulae*) were named as having been undermined and having fallen as a result of the flood of AD 69 (Cic. *Ad Quint. fr.* 3.7.1; Tac. *Hist.* 1.86). Various monuments were damaged by the floods of 54 BC, 44 BC, 32 BC, and the flood during the reign of Trajan (Cic. *Ad Quint. fr.* 3.7.1; Hor. *Carm.* 1.2.13–20; Dio 50.8.3; Sex. Aur. Victor *Epit.* 13). The bridges over the Tiber were frequently victims of floods, including those of 192 BC, 156 BC, 60 BC, 32 BC, 23 BC, AD 5, and AD 69 (Livy 35.21.5–6; Iul. Obseq. 16; Dio 37.58.3–4, 50.8.3, 53.33.5, 55.22.3; Tac. *Hist.* 1.86). Perhaps the most unusual edifice identified as having been demolished by a flood was a temporary wooden theater erected for a festival in 60 BC (Dio 37.58.3–4). Most commonly, however, the accounts do not specify a particular type of structure, but simply state that numerous unidentified buildings were either swept away or collapsed. In fact, harm to physical structures is the most frequently cited effect of flooding in ancient sources, appearing even more often than citations of human fatalities. Some of the standard Roman construction techniques may have considerably heightened the vulnerability to water damage of structures built using these methods.

There are definite patterns to the types of structures that seem to have been susceptible to flood damage. When floods swept through the streets of the city, plainly some buildings collapsed while others remained standing. The accounts normally do not describe flood damage in terms of all of the structures in a flooded area being obliterated, but rather they state that some were. The most impressive buildings of the city were the famous monumental public ones, which, on the whole, do not seem to have been much affected by floods. Both ancient and modern authors who describe the architecture of ancient Rome tend to focus almost exclusively on such awe-inspiring edifices as temples, porticoes, theaters, circuses, baths, amphitheaters, aqueducts, arches, warehouses, fortifications, and palaces. Part of the reason that these sorts of buildings loom so large in our image of ancient Rome is that they were indeed impressive, and ancient writers emphasized them, but we also know a lot about them simply because they were built so soundly that examples of them have survived up until the present.

This same solidity of construction that ensured their fame through longevity also rendered these types of buildings relatively impervious to serious damage or ruin from floodwaters. Indeed, not a single such monumental structure is ever attested as having been destroyed by a flood (aside from the special case of bridges), despite the fact that these types of buildings clustered thickly in the floodplain. The Circus Maximus, for example, was flooded on multiple occasions, but in none of the accounts is there any mention of the building itself being demolished or even damaged. Similarly, while the flood of 13 BC disrupted the inauguration ceremonies for the brand-new Theater of Balbus, there is no hint that the building incurred any serious harm from its immersion (Dio 54.25.2). Massive monumental public buildings such as these were simply too well built to be at risk from floods. Particularly from the first century BC onward, such buildings routinely had cement walls many meters thick resting upon enormous concrete foundations reaching deep into the soil. Certainly plasterwork or wall paintings may have been spoiled, but the basic structure was relatively invulnerable.

Roman sources consistently display pride in the architectural marvels of the city, and judging from the detailed accounts given by ancient authors, whenever a major public building was damaged or destroyed (as, for example, by fire), it seems to have been regarded as an event worthy of being recorded. If important public buildings were routinely being seriously harmed or demolished by floods, it seems almost certain that the sources would have made note of this; thus in this case, the silence of the sources can reasonably be inferred to indicate that such buildings were not being affected by floods. Of what type, then, were the unidentified buildings named in the sources as having been destroyed by floods? The narratives of the floods of 241 BC, 193 BC, 192 BC, 54 BC, AD 5, AD 15, AD 69, the flood during the reign of Trajan, and the flood of AD 162 all include mention of the destruction of unidentified buildings. The word most commonly used to refer to these structures is the generic term *aedificia*.[12] Logically, the buildings that would have been affected by floods first were those constructed out of the flimsiest materials, made with poor workmanship, or possessing intrinsic flaws in engineering. These characteristics exclude most of the best-known buildings of ancient Rome.

The city was not made up of just impressive monumental structures, however, but also the shops and dwellings of the ordinary inhabitants. It is these buildings that probably fell victim to the force of the floodwaters. The characteristic urban dwelling of the average person of ancient Rome was the *insula*, a building sometimes occupying an entire city block—hence the name, literally meaning "island."[13] *Insulae* both great and small often combined commercial and residential functions, with the ground floor containing shops or taverns and the upper floors housing renters in apartments. These residents could span a wide range of differing socioeconomic classes. The lower-floor apartments would have been rented out to the wealthiest tenants, who did not want to have to trudge up many flights of stairs to reach their dwellings.[14] As one climbed up the levels of the *insula*, the wealth of the tenants declined and the number of people per room increased. The cheapest rooms were located under the eaves of the roof, sometimes up many flights of stairs.

Such *insulae* are the prime candidates for the type of building that was destroyed by floods, and their vulnerability is due to a number of interconnected factors. As they were owned by landlords who themselves usually did not live on the premises and whose goal was to maximize their profit, *insulae* were notorious for being constructed quickly and out of inferior materials. Juvenal famously portrayed the lamentable condition of such buildings perpetually on the verge of collapse, with gaping cracks that the manager tried to cover over and with the whole edifice only narrowly prevented from falling down by struts placed against the walls (3.193–96); such crumbling buildings are a recurrent motif (3.7–8). This does not seem to have been merely rhetorical exaggeration, as Seneca (*De Ben.* 6.15.7) described the existence of a group of professional "underpinners" who apparently specialized in propping up collapsing structures for relatively cheap fixed prices. He also vividly portrays the crumbling, cracked, and out-of-line walls typical of poor people's dwellings in a passage where he contrasts this type of architecture with the well-made homes of the rich (*De Ira* 3.35.5; see similarly *De Ben.* 4.6.2). Cicero (*Ad Att.* 14.9, 14.11), who was a highly successful slumlord, is utterly unfazed by the collapse of one of his properties and sees it merely as an opportunity to rebuild and obtain higher rents.

Cicero is an interesting case study, as he was the owner of multiple *insulae* from which he obtained substantial rents (100,000 HS from one property alone).[15] His callousness and lack of concern for the safety of his tenants were probably typical of the attitudes of Roman upper-class landlords and go a long way toward explaining the shoddy construction of many of these buildings. The *insulae* put up by owners such as Cicero were all too likely to use inferior materials and to be structurally unsound. Because most of the owners did not live on the premises but instead employed middlemen to manage them, they had little or no contact with the tenants and no personal incentive to ensure the safety of the structure.[16] The spontaneous collapse of poorly constructed buildings such as these was a constant event in ancient Rome, as attested by Strabo (5.3.7), who stresses the need for a continual flow of supplies of timber and stone to the city in order to replace the incessantly collapsing dwellings.

Another factor contributing to the instability of *insulae* was the heights that they could sometimes attain. Martial (1.117) relates that he lives in an *insula* up three flights of stairs, and his poems (1.108, 3.30, 8.14) repeatedly make references to himself and other poverty-stricken individuals living in attic rooms atop such structures, where cold winds blow through holes in the walls. The most dramatic of these instances is Martial's mention (7.20) of an acquaintance who has to trudge up 200 stairs to reach his garret apartment, which would seem to imply an edifice with more than 10 stories.[17] Before dismissing such heights as simply the exaggerations of a satirical poet, it is worth noting the efforts by emperors to pass legislation limiting the height of structures. Augustus set a maximum of 70 Roman feet on buildings, which implies that this height was being exceeded often enough to require regulation (Strabo 5.3.7). As part of his attempt to make the city safer and more resistant to fire, Nero similarly ordained a height restriction after the great fire of AD 64, and a few decades later

Trajan lowered the maximum height to 60 Roman feet (Tac. *Ann.* 15.43; Sext. Aur. Vict. *Epit.* 13.13). The repeated passage of such laws indicates that the height restrictions were routinely being disobeyed by builders who were continually pushing the limits set by the emperors. A residential building of 70 Roman feet would probably have been at least seven stories high, and such towering *insulae* seem to have been common. Today, only a handful of *insulae* from ancient Rome survive in even partial form, but among these, there are three that had at least four stories and one with five.[18] Such heights were necessary because the populace of Rome was crammed into a relatively small area. Vitruvius traces the trend toward taller buildings:

> But with the present importance of the city and the unlimited numbers of its population, it is necessary to increase the number of dwelling places indefinitely. Consequently, as the ground floors could not admit of so great a number of people in the city, it has been necessary to find relief by increasing the height of the buildings. In these tall towers built up with piers of stone, walls of fired brick, and partitions of rubble, and with floor piled upon floor, the upper stories can be usefully partitioned off into separate rooms. Therefore walls are erected to great height exceeding numerous stories and the Roman people have excellent places to live. (2.8.17)

Vitruvius's optimistic opinion about the high quality of these structures may represent more of an ideal than the reality, but his account of the need for more lodging and its consequent effects on architecture clearly presents the interrelationship between these developments.[19]

Enormous multilevel *insulae* such as these would have housed many hundreds of tenants.[20] The high rents that could be obtained from them would have made it tempting for a landlord to add a story or two onto the top of an existing *insula* in order to increase the number of apartments and collect even more rent.[21] Such additions, however, might then exceed the load-bearing capacity of the lower walls, resulting in stress fractures and, ultimately, even in the collapse of the whole edifice. This tendency to add onto perhaps already precarious structures is another factor that probably made *insulae* prone to collapse. Burdening a building with balconies, overhangs, new internal partitions, and entire additional levels could substantially add to the load being borne by walls that might not be able to meet the task. Adding to the problem was legislation that supposedly restricted the walls abutting public property to no more than one and a half Roman feet in width in order to save space in the crowded city (Vitruvius 2.8.17). Vitruvius notes that this law placed limitations on the types of materials that can safely be used in multistory constructions.

At this point it is worth considering some of the common Roman construction techniques and materials that were likely employed in erecting these structures and that might have increased their vulnerability to flood damage. The sturdiest buildings would have had a concrete core faced with brick. If the bricks had been properly fired, and the elements in the mortar had been properly proportioned and mixed, these buildings would have been quite solid and resistant to damage from flooding. There are many steps involved in the making of the sundry components that go into such a structure, however, and consequently also numerous opportunities for errors that undercut the strength of the end product. Fired bricks are made by mixing clay, sand, and water; forming this material into bricks in a mold; and then firing the bricks in a kiln.[22] When this is done properly, the resultant brick will be extremely durable and resistant to water. If, however, the bricks do not reach the necessary temperature in the kiln, they will remain soluble in water or be prone to crumbling. For this reason, the upper layers of bricks in the kiln, which often are not heated to as high a temperature as the others, are frequently discarded. If such flawed bricks were used in a building, either through negligence or deceit, they would render the structure vulnerable to moisture and subsequent collapse. Roman mortar was formed by mixing lime with aggregates and water.[23] Again, all the steps must be done correctly for the end product to possess the desired strength and permanence. If the lime is incompletely burned or mixed in the wrong proportions, the result can be disastrous. The role of properly mixed aggregates is particularly important because without these, the lime, which naturally shrinks during drying, will crack, and the necessary adhesive bond will not form. In truly bad mixes, the core will not even set but instead remain amorphous, causing severe settling and slipping that will destabilize the whole structure.

By default, the examples of Roman architecture that have survived until the present are those in which the workmanship is excellent and the materials first-class. A sense of less ideal Roman construction can be obtained, however, by examining many of the buildings of Pompeii that were preserved by the volcanic eruption. These structures reveal a much less perfectionistic reality in which incompetent workmanship was often concealed behind a superficial facade of high-quality but structurally irrelevant plasterwork. The Romans had a consistent propensity for concealing lesser-grade materials beneath veneers suggesting finer ones—for example, the many panels of "decorative marbles" in Roman private homes that are in reality wall paintings. In a sense, even the standard use of thin marble facings attached to brick and concrete core buildings could be considered a form of this practice. The widespread employment of plaster and paint to finish walls invites such deception, because they can be applied over solid stone or brick inner cores as readily as they can be over far flimsier wattle-and-daub or timber-framed construction.[24] In many of Pompeii's walls, the interior core, which should be a solid and impermeable mass of mortar and aggregate, is instead merely a crude mixture of rubble and clay that, when exposed to water, crumbles away and turns into sludge.[25] Vitruvius (2.8) refers to such poorly made walls and notes that at Rome a number of buildings are collapsing due to the mortar having lost its strength, which causes cracks, with the result that the joints split. If Rome's buildings were constructed with similarly lax quality control, then an imposing *insula* would be hiding a fatal flaw at its core; as soon as moisture seeped into the center of the walls, they would lose their structural integrity and come crashing down.

The specific details mentioned by ancient authors are indeed suggestive of these various structural flaws. In his account of those whose profession it is to prop up buildings, Seneca (*De Ben.* 6.15.7) depicts structures that are unstable because they are showing cracks near the foundation. This could describe the situation where too much weight was put on a building, perhaps by the addition of further stories, so that the walls were then inadequate to support the load. In such a case, stress fractures such as those described by Seneca would develop at the bottom, where the loads were greatest. In another passage (*De Ira* 3.35.5), he characterizes walls of some *insulae* as crumbling, cracked, and out of alignment (*exesos, rimosos, inaequales*). Whereas the previous example of foundational cracks could refer to a sound building that was overloaded, this one is suggestive of some of the poor workmanship flaws described above. In particular, the crumbling would be symptomatic of a poor mortar mixture, and the misaligned walls indicative of excessive settling, which again would be typical of poorly set mortar.

Thus far, the type of construction considered has been high quality and the focus has been upon flaws in design or execution, but much of Rome's populace probably lived in structures made of much simpler materials. One time-honored and widespread mode of construction around the Mediterranean was the employment of the most humble material, clay.[26] One way in which clay was used was to combine it with water and a tempering agent, such as grass, straw, or chaff, and then form it into bricks. After an extended period of drying, these bricks could be piled up to form walls. Vitruvius (2.3–4) begins his discussion of construction materials with a detailed description of proper mixtures to use when fashioning sun-dried clay bricks, standard brick dimensions, and warnings that they must be thoroughly dried before use in order to prevent cracking and settling. He recommends a drying period of at least two years, a stretch of time that, in the bustling construction atmosphere of Rome, it must have been tempting to abbreviate. Alternatively the clay could be used for wattle-and-daub construction, in which the mixture is tamped down around or within a wicker or wooden framework. A somewhat more substantial variant on this is timber-frame construction, in which the spaces between solid timber members are filled in with clay.[27]

All these methods are relatively cheap and fast and require only minimally skilled workers, which makes them very useful in quickly constructing dwellings. Walls made using any of these methods can easily be plastered and painted over so that from the outside, they give the appearance of being solid and of high-quality workmanship. Finally, the resultant walls are comparatively light and therefore are suitable for use in constructing upper stories of buildings where weight is a concern. The upper floors of *insulae* were undoubtedly built in just such a way, and unscrupulous landlords might well have been tempted to have as much of the structure as possible built out of such cheap yet fragile materials in order to save money.

The great drawback to all of these methods, however, has to do with the basic nature of unfired clay, which is that it will readily crumble and dissolve back into mud if exposed to water. Dried clay is extremely porous and will soak up moisture, causing it first to swell substantially and eventually to simply melt away. Because of this, anything made of unfired clay must be carefully protected from getting wet. Moisture normally comes from three sources: rising damp from the ground, rain from above, and direct absorption from humid air. The clay can be insulated from the ground by the use of a damp-proof course of masonry as a foundation, topped by a wooden sill. To protect them from rain, the walls should be capped by an upper sill and then waterproof tiles of fired clay that overhang the tops of the walls as much as possible. Direct absorption from the air can be reduced by covering the walls with plaster and paint. This sort of structure requires fairly frequent repair and maintenance for it to retain structural integrity. If any of these protections fails, then fatal moisture can enter the wall and reduce it to a formless heap of muck.

While we know from sources such as Vitruvius that buildings made using these techniques were common in ancient Rome, all examples have long since utterly vanished due to the highly perishable nature of the components themselves. Once again, however, the entombing effects of the volcanic burial of Pompeii and Herculaneum have preserved a few examples. Timber framing was extensively used in these cities for the upper levels of buildings and for internal partitions within them.[28] It does not seem to have been employed at these sites for ground-level exterior walls, probably both because it would not have formed as solid a foundation to support upper levels and because thieves could have simply gouged through the walls to gain entry to a dwelling. Pompeii and Herculaneum were also relatively elite towns with disproportionate populations of wealthy inhabitants, and presumably at Rome these construction techniques would have been more widely employed by poorer inhabitants who could not afford more expensive options. These types of buildings would have been terribly vulnerable to flooding. When such structures were immersed in floodwater, the moisture would quickly find its way past the external plastering (if present) to the core of the walls and cause them to dissolve.

It is perhaps significant that the only time when a flood is described as having leveled all the buildings in an area rather than just some is in the account of the relatively early flood of 241 BC (Orosius 4.11.6; Aug. *De Civ. Dei* 3.18). At this date, the buildings of the city would have been constructed primarily using the less-water-resistant building methods, and thus would have been more susceptible to wholesale devastation. The date at which fired bricks and more durable forms of concrete came into widespread use is a matter of considerable debate; while individual examples can be attested by the last several centuries of the Republic, these forms of construction seem not to have truly become standard until the late Republic and early Empire.[29] In this context, Augustus's famous boast that he found Rome built of brick and left it made of marble may be even more dramatic if "brick" is here interpreted to mean "sun-dried brick" (Suet. *Aug.* 28.3). Sometimes it is suggested that after Nero's rebuilding of the city following the Great Fire of AD 64, the quality of the construction was much higher, and while this is certainly true for some structures, there was still plainly a great deal of shoddy building that led to collapses.[30] In one dramatic example from the fourth century AD, an *insula* of what must have been a very considerable height spontaneously toppled over, with the ruins actually falling into the Forum of Trajan (Sym. *Epist.* 6.37). The vivid portraits of rickety, tottering high-rise *insulae* by authors such as Martial and Juvenal date to after the Great Fire, indicating that this sort of poor construction was a perennial problem not just restricted to the period when most construction was sun-dried brick.

Finally, the truly impoverished and the homeless of Rome would have cobbled together whatever shelter they could out of basic materials such as sticks, mud, timber, and rubble. Human ingenuity can fashion huts, lean-tos, and other basic shelters out of the most unpromising materials, as is amply demonstrated by modern examples, such as the bustling improvised shantytowns erected on the fringes of Mexico City atop the city's garbage dumps. This type of settlement has become a standard feature of large cities in Third World countries today, where they have developed into a significant form of urban housing.[31] Whether labeled shantytowns, squatter settlements, or, as the United Nations categorizes them, "improvised habitation," they are an important part of the landscape of large cities. While almost comically prim, the UN definition of these structures is, nevertheless, quite descriptive: "an independent makeshift shelter or structure built of waste materials and without a predetermined plan, for the purpose of habitation. . . . This type of housing unit is usually found in urban and suburban areas, particularly at the peripheries of the principal cities."[32] A further characteristic of these settlements is that they are often found on the lowest-lying and least desirable land in the city, which is most prone to flooding. The famous Ciudad Nezahualcoyotl settlement in Mexico City, for example, occupied a low point of the topography and, during heavy rainfalls, turned into a toxic lake contaminated with raw sewage and pollution.[33] In places such as Manila, Calcutta, Kuala Lumpur, Bangladesh, and Delhi, squatters are being forced to settle in marginal lands that are the most vulnerable to flooding, such as along riverbanks and on floodplains.[34]

In Rome itself, during the Middles Ages and later, the most flood-prone regions adjacent to the Tiber became stigmatized as the dwelling places of Jews and other marginalized groups. In recent decades, the strips along the Tiber at the base of the embankment walls have become a location where homeless persons have erected lean-tos and shanties.[35] While admittedly only speculative, it is easy to envision such improvised dwellings dotting the banks of the ancient Tiber, cropping up in the shelter of structures such as aqueducts and bridges, and clustering in marginalized areas such as the Transtiberim or the Campus Martius prior to its formal development. Naturally no trace of these dwellings survives, but given the Roman elites' preference for hilltop housing, the less fortunate would have been driven into the low-lying areas where their insubstantial shelters would have been demolished by even mild flooding.

There are several main ways in which floods destroy or damage structures. The most straightforward is that the horizontal stresses applied by the direct force of the floodwaters can simply push down a wall or walls and collapse a building. Floodwater can actually either partially or entirely float a structure off its foundation, causing it then to collapse or sometimes carrying away the whole building. These are immediate effects caused by the water itself, and many structures in ancient Rome would have succumbed to the force exerted by even modest floods. In general, walls are very good at bearing vertical loads such as those resulting from the weight of the building itself, but they are extremely vulnerable to horizontal loads such as those produced by wind or floodwaters. The accounts of the flood of 241 BC include the evocative detail that where the floodwaters rushed in a swift-moving "torrent," buildings were "pushed over and collapsed" (Orosius 4.11.6; Aug. *De Civ. Dei* 3.18). In 60 BC a temporary wooden theater built for a festival was washed away and destroyed by the force of a flood (Dio 37.58.3–4).

Water exerts two main types of horizontal forces on structures that it encounters. In a pool of still water, the weight of the water itself will create hydrostatic pressure pushing against a wall; if the water is in motion, there will be additional pressure as a result of the velocity effect. In a standing pool of water, the horizontal force due to hydrostatic pressure increases with the square of the depth. In other words, the pressure being applied to the walls of a building that is immersed in still water that is 2 m deep will be four times greater than the pressure that would be applied if the water were only 1 m deep. If the water were 3 m deep, the pressure would then be nine times greater than if it were 1 m deep. Because of this exponential effect, the height of a flood is a crucial factor in determining the damage that the floodwaters will cause to structures. Of course, if the interior of the building flooded, the hydrostatic pressures inside and outside would cancel each other out.

If the water is moving, then there is an additional velocity effect. The pressure exerted by moving water on a wall is greatly affected by the angle at which the water strikes it. If the water is moving parallel to the wall, there will be almost no velocity effect, but if the flow is perpendicular to the wall, then the force is proportional to the velocity squared. Thus water moving at 2 m/sec will exert four times the horizontal force as water flowing at a velocity of 1 m/sec, and so on. Due to various factors, the velocity of naturally flowing water usually does not exceed a rate of about 9 m/sec. At even a fraction of this extreme velocity, however, flowing water can exert enormous forces on objects that it encounters, and if directly in the path of such a current, many structures would, as the Roman sources relate, simply be "pushed over."

One type of structure at Rome that had to bear the full brunt of direct horizontal force from floodwaters was the bridges spanning the Tiber. Floodwaters would have attacked these bridges in four main ways. First, the direct horizontal force of the swiftly moving current pushing against the piers of the bridge could be enough to push them over and bring down the whole edifice. Second, the same strong current could scour away at the foundations of the piers underwater, causing them to become destabilized, again resulting in collapse. Third, if the waters rose high enough, they might reach the superstructure of the bridge, including the actual spans and the roadway, which would have been even more susceptible to horizontal stresses than the piers and would have easily been toppled. Fourth, and perhaps most dangerous, was the detritus being swept along in the floodwaters. Large trees or pieces of structures potentially weighing many tons and being carried in the water could crash into a bridge, either smashing it outright or at least severely weakening it. Huge balks of timber striking the bridge end-on would act like battering rams, except that they would be propelled by the rushing current with greater than human force. The force exerted at the point of impact by such waterborne missiles could be enough to pulverize the piers; bridges today are often equipped with protective fenders to deflect just such dangerous projectiles.

Not surprisingly, Rome's bridges are recorded as having suffered damage or destruction on numerous occasions as a result of floods. The oldest of the bridges at Rome was the Pons Sublicius, usually identified in the primary sources as "the wooden bridge," which was located just below Tiber Island, probably at the point of the Porta Flumentana entrance to the Forum Boarium.[36] It was first built by Ancus Marcius, supposedly without any metal components, and, apparently out of religious considerations, the Romans seem to have rebuilt it several times to the original specifications. This insistence on fashioning the bridge out of wood rather than stone may have contributed to its vulnerability, as it was the bridge most frequently destroyed by floods. At least four times—in 60 BC, 32 BC, 23 BC, and AD 69, and probably again in AD 5—this bridge was swept away by floodwaters.[37] The first stone bridge in Rome, the Pons Aemilius, constructed in 179 BC, also suffered damage from high waters. In 156 BC its "*tectum*" was torn

Floods of the Tiber in Ancient Rome

Fig. 3.3. The lone remaining arch of the Pons Aemilius (today called the Ponte Rotto) nearly submerged during an unidentified flood, with Tiber Island in the background. Roman bridges were destroyed by floods on a number of occasions. (Fototeca Unione, American Academy in Rome, 586)

away and thrown down into the Tiber (Iul. Obseq. 16). This term may refer to some sort of superstructure, or more likely, the earliest version of this bridge had stone piers, while the roadbed and arches were still made of wood.[38] This may be a case where very high waters reached the less resistant wooden superstructure of the bridge and swept it away, but the stronger underlying stone piers endured the force of the water and remained intact (fig. 3.3). One additional account states that two bridges were destroyed in the flood of 192 BC (Livy 35.21.5–6), but which bridges this refers to is impossible to tell. At such an early date, the only major bridge definitely known to have existed was the Pons Sublicius, but there were almost certainly other temporary or pontoon bridges at various points, connecting, for instance, Tiber Island to the right and left banks of the river.

Somewhat surprisingly, the most frequent method by which floods destroyed buildings according to the ancient sources was not actually by direct action of the water pushing over the structure. Instead, the most commonly cited reason for collapse was a more gradual process beginning when buildings were immersed in slow-moving or stagnant pools of water. The structures are described as absorbing the water, which subsequently causes them to crumble and collapse. So, for example, it was said of the flood of 241 BC, "in those places where the floodwaters were slow-moving, the buildings became soaked and crumbled" (Orosius 4.11.6). Of the same flood, Augustine (*De Civ. Dei* 3.18) says in nearly identical terms, "other buildings, having been soaked in the long-lasting floodwaters, collapsed." In the flood of AD 15, the destruction of buildings was said to have happened not at the height of the flood but rather when the waters subsided. A few decades later, in AD 69, Tacitus (*Hist.* 1.86; also *Ann.* 1.76) further relates, "The foundations of apartment buildings were undermined by the stagnant water and then collapsed when the river receded." Finally, Dio (39.61.1–2) adds an important detail about this process in his narrative of the flood of 54 BC where he explicitly identifies bricks (presumably sun-dried) as being vulnerable to floods: "The houses, therefore, being constructed of brick, became soaked through and collapsed."

All these accounts are clearly describing the results of the construction techniques possessing great vulnerability to water previously outlined in this chapter. Unfired bricks when immersed in water would dissolve in just the manner depicted by Dio, with the disastrous consequences that he relates. Water seeping into walls made with poorly mixed or set mortar, or with clay infill, would cause these materials to revert back to a semiliquid form, resulting in the crumbling and eventual collapse noted by these authors. Both our understanding of Roman construction techniques and the descriptions in the ancient sources paint a consistent picture of floods wreaking havoc upon buildings via a two-pronged attack. The flimsiest structures, including improvised dwellings, would have immediately succumbed to the direct force of the currents and been knocked down or washed away, while others, including those made of dried-brick or with improperly mixed or set mortars, would have absorbed water, causing the walls to dissolve gradually and to crumble. The time frame for this second mechanism varied, but it often seems to have taken place while the floodwaters either were still standing or else while they were in the process of receding. This slight delay could have posed yet an additional hazard to people returning to their homes or attempting to salvage their possessions from the flooded buildings, because they might be injured or killed by the suddenly falling structure.

Injuries and Drowning

In addition to the damage and destruction to property that floods can produce, they frequently have a human cost through injury and death. Modern analyses of morbidity and mortality as a result of floods tend to focus on postflood illnesses caused by communicable diseases, contamination of water and food supply, and environmental issues. Certainly these problems result in the greatest number of flood-related deaths, from causes such as gastrointestinal diseases and malaria, and these long-term effects will be considered in the next chapter. In the short term, however, floods exact a human price through two main mechanisms: trauma injuries and death by drowning.

Most flood deaths stem from events such as flash floods or floods caused by a dam breaking. In these incidents, a swift-moving wall of water strikes a populated zone with little or no warning, resulting in high mortality rates among those directly in its path. This type of flood was not the sort encountered in ancient Rome. Tiber floods were a comparatively slow-rising phenomenon, and while the waters could eventually achieve considerable depth and velocity, there was not a sudden wave of water sweeping across previously dry ground. In this sort of flood, some people might drown from being trapped within confined spaces that filled with water, but the main cause of death resulted from those who were caught in floodwaters deep and strong enough to render them unable to maintain their footing, with the outcome that they fell into the water and either drowned or suffered death from traumatic injuries.

Floodwaters of much less than a meter in depth are more than sufficient to cause the death by drowning of those caught in them. This depth may not sound like much, but water, particularly if flowing with some degree of speed, can exert considerable force on people attempting to wade through it. Water levels do not have to be higher than one's head to result in drowning, because the real danger is that the force of the water or unstable footing will cause a person to fall over and be unable to regain his or her footing. In such a situation, it is altogether possible to drown in relatively shallow water. The force of the water is determined by a combination of depth and velocity.

Studies of human instability in flood flows show that it does not take much of either variable for floodwater to cause people to lose their balance. In elaborate tests on a range of adult male and female human subjects, the greatest velocity of water in which a person was able to remain standing was 3.05 m/sec, but this was at a depth of only .43 m.[39] The greatest depth at which a subject was able to retain his footing was 1.2 m, but in this particular situation the water had a velocity of only 1.21 m/sec. The researchers used a formula combining depth and velocity to assess how successful the test subjects were at maintaining their balance. The most impressive achievement was by a 30-year-old male, 1.8 m tall and weighing 91 kg, who was able to remain upright until the water reached a combination of 2.91 m/sec velocity and .73 m in depth. Height and weight were clearly important variables in assessing an individual's ability to remain standing.[40] This study suggests that any flood with waters more than 0.5 m in depth or velocities greater than 1 m/sec creates a situation where those caught in the water are in serious danger of losing their footing and drowning.

The success in maintaining footing achieved by these test subjects, however, was almost certainly far superior to what actual flood victims would be able to hope for. The test subjects were all adults between 19 and 54 years of age who were in good health and "considered to be well-coordinated."[41] The experiments took place in a laboratory with bright lighting, the underwater surface was smooth and free of obstacles, the water was clear and warm, there was no debris present in the water, the subjects were dressed in unrestrictive clothing, and they were not burdened by carrying anything. Finally, they were attached to a safety harness that caught them when they fell, the presence of which enabled them to better maintain their footing by allowing them to "take risks in maneuvering that might not normally be taken without safety equipment."[42] In real life, flood victims might be infirm or injured, would likely be carrying children or valuables, would constantly experience being struck by floating debris, would be struggling over uneven ground, and all of this often in the dark and in frigid water. This has led other flood researchers to conclude that in any flood with a velocity exceeding 0.5 m/sec it must be considered probable that many people would be swept away.[43]

Floodwaters pose far greater hazards than such idealized laboratory conditions or even than normal streams due to the presence of debris and high levels of sediment in the water. Sediment makes the water opaque so that it is difficult to see submerged obstacles or to detect uneven footing or even sudden drop-offs. Interviews with the urban poor of metro Manila who routinely experience flooding readily yield stories of such hidden dangers: for instance, one man almost died when he dropped into an open manhole concealed beneath the muddy waters.[44] Debris in the floodwaters, such as trees, lumber, pieces of houses, and rocks, becomes dangerous waterborne missiles that can strike people, knock them down, and injure them. Because floods can occur at any time of day or night, attempting to negotiate such an environment in dim lighting, at night, or during a storm greatly increases the difficulty and danger. Other nonenvironmental factors may also play a significant role in intensifying a person's susceptibility to drowning. For example, in 5 out of 16 drownings that took place as a result of flooding in Maryland in 1972, the consumption of alcohol by the victims was apparently a factor.[45]

Finally, exposure to cold water can quickly sap the endurance of flood victims, decrease their ability to press through the waters, or even cause death. Because most Tiber floods take place in the period from late fall through early spring, the temperatures of the air and water can become major factors in determining survival. Water removes heat from the body 25–30 times faster than air, and flood victims who find themselves immersed in water can have their core body temperatures rapidly reduced, leading to hypothermia and death.[46] In water below 5°C, death can result in minutes, and from 5–10°C, survival is estimated to be no more than 3 hours. Also, this assumes that the victim remains motionless in order to conserve heat, but if he or she is forced to move or swim, time of survival is drastically reduced. Even in relatively warm water there is a risk of hypothermia, and it is estimated that half of the drowning deaths in the United States actually result from fatal effects due to water temperature rather than from water entering the lungs. For victims of a winter flood in Rome having to struggle energetically through cold water to save themselves and their families, death from exposure would have been a very real threat. Even after a flood victim managed to climb out of the water, the effects of water contributing to hypothermia would have continued, because wet and sodden clothing increases heat loss to the air by a fivefold factor over dry clothing.

No ancient author's description of a flood lists actual numbers of people who drowned in the disaster. Nevertheless, general allusions to human fatalities are one of the most common features of these accounts, appearing in 27% of them (9 out of 33). Most of these are very terse and contain little detail about how the deaths occurred, but some do offer insights. The earliest reference to flood fatalities appears for the inundation of 215 BC, where Livy (24.9.6) simply notes that people were killed; Livy (35.21.5–6) also records that many people perished in a series of natural disasters that struck Rome in 192 BC. Dio (37.58.3–4) provides a bit more information for the flood of 60 BC, stating that "great numbers" of humans died in the calamity. His narrative (39.61.1–2) of the flood of 54 BC cites a significant death toll, but this time he adds that those who died were those who were overtaken by the waters in their houses or in the streets. From this point on, there are a number of examples of people explicitly being swept off their feet by floodwaters and drowned. Cassiodorus (*Chron.* 604) says that the Tiber carried people away in the flood of AD 5, and Tacitus (*Hist.* 1.86) similarly relates that those caught in the open were borne away by the floodwaters during the inundation of AD 69. Most specific is Dio's description (79.25.5) of the flood of AD 217, in which he says that the floodwater rushed through the Roman Forum and the surrounding streets with such force that those caught in its path were swept away. A different mechanism of death is named for the flood of AD 15 when Tacitus (*Ann.* 1.76) states that great loss of life resulted from buildings collapsing as the waters receded. Finally, when discussing a flood during the reign of Trajan, Pliny (*Epist.* 8.17) grimly describes what must have been a common sight in the aftermath: the bodies of the drowned bobbing in the waters, ignominiously mingled together with animal carcasses and sundry other flotsam.

Some idea of the order of magnitude of mortality that might have been experienced in ancient Rome as a result of a flood can be inferred from later accounts. The great flood of 1530, for example, was said to have caused the deaths by drowning of 3,000 people.[47] This flood occurred at a time when the population of the city was probably one-tenth of what it had been at its height during the Roman era. The population density in ancient Rome would also have been greater. Thus it can be shown that floods at Rome had the potential to result in the deaths of thousands, but any more precise estimation would be speculative.

One fact to note about Rome, however, is that the particular topography of the city may actually have helped to reduce somewhat the death toll from drowning. Rome's many hills ensure that most places in the city are less than a few hundred meters from high ground where people could have taken refuge from rising waters. From the standpoint of their city providing safe zones from floods, the inhabitants of Rome were fortunate; the city's topography was such that hills were scattered throughout the city rather than being confined to one area, and the hills themselves, while often fairly small, were of sufficient height to provide safety from floodwaters. Even in a situation of rapidly rising water, the vast majority of Rome's inhabitants could have run to high ground in a few minutes. The account of the flood of 54 BC mentions that those who drowned were those "who did not take refuge in time on the high points," implying that others did seek and find safety on the hills (Dio 39.61.1–2). The area most lacking high ground was the Campus Martius, and even there, the furthest one could be from a hillside was only approximately a kilometer. The situation in Rome can be contrasted with that of the deadly Hwang He (Yellow) River in China, where a key reason why so many people have been killed by floods is because the flat floodplain extends for hundreds of kilometers and there is literally nowhere to run for safety when floods strike.

While data on fatalities from ancient Roman floods are sketchy, information on injuries suffered by flood victims is nonexistent. Even today, less evidence is available on the types of nonfatal injuries sustained by those caught in floods than on those who were drowned. Nevertheless, it is possible to make some reasonable assumptions about what kinds of trauma would have been inflicted. The majority of these injuries would have resulted from people being tossed around in the water, scraped along the ground, flung up against walls, or struck by flood-borne debris. These impacts would have caused a range of trauma injuries, such as broken bones and lacerations. One study on flood injuries conducted by the Center for Disease Control and the Missouri Department of Health on injuries sustained by victims of the 1993 Missouri floods revealed a pattern of just such types of traumatic injury as would be expected. Of approximately 250 flood-related injuries, the top categories were sprains or strains (35%), lacerations (24%), abrasions or contusions (11%), puncture wounds (9%), and animal or snake bites (2.4%).[48] While no statistics about injuries sustained by ancient Roman flood victims survive, the physics involved in a human being tumbling about in swift-moving water through an urban setting are no different today than they were 2,000 years ago, and ancient Romans no doubt suffered a similar set of injuries. With modern medical care, the ratio of deaths to injuries resulting from a flood is estimated at approximately 1:6.[49] In ancient Rome, with less efficient public warning systems and inferior medical care, the death ratio would presumably have been somewhat higher.

Cleaning Up after a Flood: Water, Mud, Debris, Corpses

Once the floodwaters had receded and the Tiber had returned to its normal channel, the survivors would have faced the daunting task of cleaning up after the flood. While it might seem that a flood would wash out and cleanse the city, the opposite is actually the case, because floods tend to deposit thousands of tons of mud, silt, and debris in their wake. Even before any reconstruction can take place, the immediate process of cleaning up after a flood has several phases. Among the most important tasks that the survivors must tackle are eliminating the remaining pools of water, drying out buildings and property, removing mud and debris, salvaging possessions, and disposing of corpses. In modern cities, a high priority is usually placed upon the restoration of public services such as electricity, gas, and telephones, but in ancient Rome, simply cleaning up the liquids and solids left behind by the flood would have been the primary concern.

The vast majority of the water that submerged the city during a flood would have simply drained back to the Tiber. Nevertheless, substantial pools would have remained, for example, in low-lying areas that were surrounded by slightly higher ground. Deep floodwaters would have easily flowed into and inundated such spots, and the local topography would then have trapped some of this water and prevented its return to the Tiber. If there were no drains connecting these areas to the Roman sewers, these pools could have remained for days or weeks and would have posed considerable problems for the inhabitants attempting to return their city to normalcy. Standing water will eventually disappear through natural processes, chiefly evaporation of moisture into the air and infiltration of water into the ground. Direct exposure to strong sunlight will speed up evaporation while high humidity levels can prolong the process. Infiltration into the ground is a particular problem in an urban environment. If the pool of water is located in a place where the ground is mostly covered with impermeable stone or cement rather than exposed soil, as is often the case in the midst of a city, then infiltration is prevented and the rate of disappearance of the pool of water is enormously prolonged. If pools of water are so large that it is impracticable to wait for natural processes to remove them, then people can attempt to drain or pump away the water. While the Romans possessed sufficient hydrological technology to construct pumps, there is no definite evidence that they were applied to this specific situation. However, it does seem that there were workers who specialized in somehow draining or drying up floodwaters. In a list of unscrupulous contractors, ranging from temple builders to slave auctioneers, Juvenal (3.32) includes "those who dry up floods."[50] How such groups operated and what methods they employed must remain speculative, but the fact that they existed at all is suggestive of the scale of Rome's hydraulics.

The very building design patterns favored by the Romans also would have exacerbated the challenge of removing water from the city. In Roman residential architecture, both individual houses and apartment buildings tended to be built as a hollow square around a central open courtyard. The standard Roman house pattern featured a high exterior wall with few openings for windows or doors and lined on the inside by rooms. In the center was one or more courtyards open to the sky that served to provide light to the residence. Many high-rise *insulae,* or apartment buildings, had a similar design, with rows of cubicle-like rooms forming a square around a central open courtyard, which again was the principal source of air and light for the building's inhabitants. Such an *insula* could be huge, covering an entire city block. Even when these buildings did not occupy the entire block, a group of apartment buildings might collectively form a ring around a communal open space in the middle of a city block, as is still common in Rome today. In all these cases, there is usually little or no direct access connecting the central courtyard to the street. While this design pattern of city blocks as hollow squares offers certain benefits, the Romans could not have settled on a worse design in terms of flood proofing the city. During a flood, the central courtyard will fill up with a pool of water that, lacking a ready outlet, can remain trapped long after the main floodwaters recede. A study of how best to design a flood-resistant city notes that "for intensive high rise buildings open isolated premises are better than closed blocks built around interior courtyards. This latter type should be banned from flood-prone areas because center blocks remain useless for flood conveyance. Water remains inside these blocks for weeks before drying out."[51] The closed block design favored by the Romans would not only have inhibited the flow of water through the city, thus slowing down the recession of the floodwaters, but would also have greatly prolonged the amount of time it took for these buildings to dry out. As will be seen in the section on disease, speed of drying out after floods is a crucial factor in preventing potentially fatal diseases.

Once the water from a flood had been drained, dried, or otherwise removed, the next cleaning challenge would have been to dispose of mud and sediment deposited everywhere the waters had reached. The Tiber was plainly a river bearing considerable sediment loads, as evidenced by recurrent problems with the harbors of Ostia and Portus silting up. Strabo (5.3.5) refers to this as a severe problem, while Augustus (Suet. *Aug.* 30) and Aurelian (SHA *Aur.* 47.2–3) undertook efforts to dredge the river in order to maintain its navigability, which may also have been one of the duties of the *curatores* in charge of the

Tiber and its banks. The current coastline at the delta of the Tiber is nearly 5 km from where it was in Roman times, and in recent times the river has continued to bear huge loads of silt—for example, an estimated 10.6 million metric tons per year from 1873 to 1878.[52] Floodwater tends to carry a higher level of sediment than ordinary streamflow. The flood wave erodes, transports, and deposits large quantities of sediment, often to such an extent that the actual morphology of the river and floodplain is changed. The quantity of sediment that can be carried by a river is partially dependent on the velocity of the water. During a flood, as the water flows out of the swift-moving channel onto neighboring land, the water velocity tends to slow down, and the particles of dirt and sand fall out and are left behind on the land. This is why when floods recede, they often leave behind such large deposits of mud. The famous Arno River flood of 1966 left the city of Florence coated in more than 600,000 tons of mud, which the river deposited in the streets and buildings of the city.[53] In places, the layer of mud reached a depth of a meter. The Florentines were able to employ bulldozers and heavy mechanized equipment to remove the mud left by this flood, but the inhabitants of ancient Rome would have had to dig out their city by hand.

Survivors attempting to clean up after a flood also would have had to contend with various types of debris left behind when the waters departed, mixed together with the mud and sediment deposited by floods. Floodwater has an astonishing power to carry and deposit huge objects, including trees, bushes, debris from buildings destroyed by the flood, rocks, and even boulders. Although it is probably an extreme case, the 1952 flood that sliced through the English town of Lynmouth left behind some 200,000 metric tons' worth of boulders within the city that the waters had carried down from a nearby hillside. Some of these boulders weighed as much as 15 metric tons.[54] While a typical flood might not drop multi-ton boulders that would have to be removed, the rubble from collapsed buildings would still have to be cleared. All floods would probably have carried heavy debris made up of material with buoyant properties, such as logs, detritus from wooden buildings, and even entire trees, which would have had to be chopped up or hauled away.

One of the greatest threats to the survivors laboring to clear their streets and dwellings of the mud and debris from a flood would not have come from direct injury as a result of manhandling these materials, but rather from the invisible threat posed by bacteria, viruses, and parasites carried and spread by the floodwaters, a topic that is treated in detail in the next chapter, which considers the long-term effects of floods. Another hazard confronted when cleaning up the debris after a flood is the possibility of encountering potentially dangerous animals displaced by the floodwaters. One type of creature that frequently causes trouble for workers in the aftermath of a flood is rodents, especially rats.[55] They are driven into buildings by the rising waters and additionally are often made more aggressive by the unfamiliar situation and surroundings. When people reenter flooded buildings and begin to pick through the piles of debris, there is considerable danger of their being bitten by disturbed rodents.[56] Because rats carry many diseases and parasites that can infect humans, these bites, or even just physical contact with the animals, can result in disease. So pronounced is the postflood rat problem that the standard U.S. government-issued guidelines for flood cleanup crews begin by urging workers to enter a flooded structure only if equipped with a "solid rat club." Even if the rats are not encountered directly, their presence can pose serious health risks for people cleaning up after a flood. It is common for there to be outbreaks of leptospirosis following a flood, because the disease can be transmitted to humans wading through floodwater when their skin comes into contact with water that has been contaminated with rat urine.[57]

Another animal often found in unusual locations after a flood is snakes. In areas where there are poisonous snakes, this can be a considerable hazard. There are accounts from India of people fleeing floodwaters by climbing trees, only to be bitten by poisonous snakes, such as cobras, which have also sought refuge there. While such poisonous snakes may not have posed as great a risk to the inhabitants of ancient Rome, the buildings of the city must have supported a healthy rodent population.[58] Rodents would have thrived in *insulae,* where the dense crowding, unsanitary conditions, and poor construction would have offered shelter, food, and easy access. Juvenal (3.207) exploits the ubiquity of rodents in *insulae* for satiric purposes by describing mice chewing on the meager possessions of a tenant, and to emphasize the decrepitude of one of the slums that he owns, Cicero (*Ad Att.* 14.9) remarks that even the rats have fled his crumbling structure.

The final aspect of the cleanup process following a flood would have been disposal of the corpses of humans and animals drowned in the floodwaters.[59] If these bodies were not quickly removed, they would have posed a further health hazard as they began to decompose. Some corpses would have been deposited wherever the floodwater reached and then have been left behind when the water receded. Others would have sunk to the bottom of pools of water, or have been trapped within buildings or caught in underwater debris. Depending on various factors, chiefly temperature, drowned corpses typically become buoyant within a week after death and float to the surface due to the gases produced in the gastrointestinal tract during the process of putrefaction.[60] In Europe, a body will typically surface after two or three days during the summertime, and after three to five days in the spring and fall, whereas in winter the process can be delayed up to six weeks.[61] Thus new corpses would likely be appearing for a few days to several weeks after the end of a flood. Presumably those bodies which were identified and recovered by family members or friends would have received some form of burial. The ignominious fate of many anonymous corpses was probably to be thrown back into the Tiber.[62] How Rome's inhabitants disposed of the carcasses of animals both large and small that had been drowned in a flood is uncertain. Several accounts relate that many cattle were killed by floods, and if one of these carcasses washed up in a neighborhood and was still relatively fresh, it may simply have been butchered and eaten on the spot. More decomposed animal remains might have been dragged to the nearest sewer opening or cast into the Tiber.

Even after the flood had subsided and the water and debris had been cleared, the inhabitants of the city were not safe because the harmful effects of floods continued long after the Tiber had returned to normal. While the majority of the physical destruction may have occurred during and immediately after an inundation, the toll in human life had just begun. In the aftermath of a flood, survivors would often have had to face famine and disease, which posed even greater risks to their health than the floodwaters themselves. These dangerous long-term effects of flooding are the subject of the next chapter.

Four

Delayed Effects of Floods

Weakened Buildings

Long after the immediate crisis of a flood had passed, the waters had largely receded, and the cleanup process had begun, floods would have continued to have serious consequences for the inhabitants of the city. These delayed effects of a flood could in many cases prove more severe and could result in more deaths than the actual disaster itself. Even if a building that was flooded did not collapse immediately or show obvious signs of damage, its structural integrity could have been weakened or fatally compromised. While the dramatic destruction of buildings during a flood would have been catastrophic enough for Rome's inhabitants, these delayed effects meant that floods had consequences that extended far beyond the actual period of high water.

In cases where the constituent materials of a building did not dissolve outright, their immersion in water for periods of several hours to several days could ultimately have brought down even fairly well-made structures.[1] During such prolonged periods of immersion, water would have had ample opportunity to seep into cracks in the facings of walls, thus reaching the potentially more vulnerable cores or simply being absorbed directly through the surfaces in contact with the water. Many building components will eventually soak up some water, which can have a range of destructive effects. A number of the most commonly used building materials such as timber and concrete are porous, which causes them to swell when they absorb water. The high-quality Roman hydraulic cement made with pozzolana is extremely water-resistant, but most concretes will soak up varying degrees of water depending on their particular mix of mortar and aggregate and the various materials used for these. When immersed, wood will similarly absorb water, causing a certain amount of swelling. While these materials may not necessarily lose their structural integrity if waterlogged, the swelling does tend to lead to the formation of cracks as substances of different porosity expand at different rates. Cracks and gaps will open up between building components of differing materials and within sections made up of compounds of various substances. These cracks can become focal points for erosion, cause the bonds between structural components to be broken, and produce slipping and settling, possibly resulting in the building becoming destabilized. Another problem with external cracks is that, unless they are filled, they offer routes of ingress for future moisture that can exacerbate all the previously mentioned threats. Even if cracks or gaps do not produce immediate problems, they can serve as the source of later destruction in cold weather when moisture that has worked its way into the structure freezes and expands. This will either widen the existing cracks or result in a whole network of new ones, further weakening the building and creating yet more vulnerable areas. Further compounding the problem, when different parts or components of the structure dry out at different rates, this creates more opportunities for cracks to develop as various parts expand and shrink.

A danger particular to wood that has been immersed in floodwater is the threat posed by decay or rot. This results from various types of fungi that feed on the wood and cause it to become soft and spongy. In advanced states of rot, the wood no longer has any structural integrity whatsoever but simply crumbles away. The fungi causing wood rot require a certain level of moisture to be active (if the moisture level is less than 20%, the fungi will usually stay dormant). Wood rot can be an insidious problem because the affected members are often buried deep within the structure where they are least exposed to sunlight and air that could dry them out, and are also hidden from view so that they cannot be inspected directly in order to detect the rot. Thus an apparently solid building with no damage or weakness visible from the exterior can be concealing a rotten and unstable core. In the hot and dry Mediterranean summer, moisture-laden timbers would probably dry out rapidly enough so that rot would not be a serious threat, but in the rainy fall and winter seasons, once saturated, timber might retain high levels of moisture, encouraging the fungi.[2]

A final long-term effect of flooding on buildings is the possibility of the foundations being undermined by the scouring action of the water. Floods often cause severe erosion along riverbanks and in floodplains, and any large structures located near these areas can find themselves resting on destabilized soil. The famous Florence flood of 1966, for example, carried away long stretches of the Arno embankment. In these conditions, nearby structures settle, which can create cracks, misaligned walls, or in extreme cases, collapse.

While we can say with near certainty, on the basis of our knowledge of the behavior of materials, that these sorts of long-term flood damages occurred, once again this is confirmed in the primary sources. In assessing the flood of 54 BC, Dio (39.61.1–2) adds the detail that the buildings that were not immediately destroyed became weakened and that this resulted in many people being injured at a later time. Some of the sudden and apparently spontaneous collapses of buildings that were so characteristic of ancient Rome may well have been the delayed result of flood damages. In this way, the inhabitants of Rome continued to be the victims of floods even long after the last pool of floodwater had dried up.

Food Spoilage and Famine

A significant aftereffect of flooding was a shortage in food resulting from the disruption of transportation and the spoilage of stored food supplies. In instances when large quantities of stored food were destroyed, or new supplies were not readily available, these shortages could even lead to widespread famine and starvation. Even with modern transportation methods, food shortages that are caused by flooding can be deadly. In Africa in 1974, for example, a food shortage produced by widespread flooding resulted in more than 30,000 deaths.[3] In ancient Rome, there are seven times in the primary sources when a Tiber flood is explicitly linked to food shortages: 54 BC, 23 BC, 22 BC, AD 5, AD 69, AD 162, and AD 371.[4]

Most of these instances fall nearly within a century of one another. In 54 BC a sudden flood caused extensive destruction, including spoiling much of the stored grain. The ensuing shortage was so severe that Pompey left the city in order to personally supervise the efforts to bring supplies of food to Rome to alleviate the situation (Dio 39.63.3, 39.61.3). The years 23 and 22 BC seem to have been marked by a nearly continuous string of disasters, including floods, fires, and an epidemic, during the collective course of which large numbers of people were said to have perished (Dio 53.33.4–5, 54.1.1–3). The grain shortage following the flood of 22 BC prompted rioting in the streets. A mob besieged the senate in the senate house, threatening to burn it down, and then beseeched Augustus to become dictator and take charge of the grain supply (Dio 54.1.2–4). He turned down the dictatorship but did take measures to provide adequate food to relieve the shortage, such as distributing supplies at his own expense, so that he could state "within a few days I delivered the whole city from fear" (*Res Gestae* 5). Augustus was again forced to contend with a famine as a result of the flood of AD 5 (Dio 55.22.3; Cassiod. *Chron.* 604). The following year, when the city still may have been suffering due to the ruination of stored food by the flood, saw one of Rome's most severe food crises. Augustus even went so far as to attempt to reduce the population by banishing various groups from the city, and he also made multiple distributions of grain at his own expense (Dio 55.26.1–3). In AD 69, a flood submerged much of Rome, including an area identified by Plutarch (*Otho* 4.50) as the place where grain was sold; the result was a severe shortage of food for many days. Tacitus (*Hist.* 1.86) also describes this flood and the subsequent famine, adding that a lack of employment opportunities further contributed to the widespread starvation.

After this concentration of famine-causing floods, there are only two attested later instances. The flood that took place in AD 162, which was said to be the most destructive of the era, produced a severe food shortage (SHA *M. Aur.* 8). Again there is evidence of direct imperial action to relieve the crisis, as Marcus Aurelius and Verus were said to have personally alleviated the situation. Finally, the response to the flood of AD 371 contains an interesting variant on the food shortage-caused-by-flood theme. The long-persisting deep waters of this flood trapped many people in their dwellings, and there were fears that they would starve before the waters receded. The author of this account notes that all of the city was submerged except for the hills and the upper stories of high dwellings (presumably *insulae*). To meet the anticipated food shortage, boats and watercraft were organized to bring supplies to the stranded people. Ultimately, however, the Tiber returned to its channel, and the feared famine did not materialize (Am. Marc. 29.6.17–18).

Of these seven instances when a flood definitely caused a shortage of food, none occurred earlier than 54 BC, and five of them fall within a narrow span from the middle of the first century BC to the middle of the first century AD. This raises the same problems of interpretation as the record of flood frequency discussed in chapter 1, because the number of floods seems to have peaked in this same period. As previously discussed, there is debate whether this apparent peak was due to better and more complete documentation for this period, a shift in climate, or an actual increase in the number of floods and famines. In addition, except perhaps for the incident of AD 371 (which was not really a food shortage anyway), all the other incidents correspond with the period when Rome's population was at its maximum and therefore most vulnerable to disruptions in the food supply. With the city's population at its peak and the food supply system strained to maximum capacity, there would have been less margin of error for losses caused by floods to be made up, and so shortages would have been more common. The increased incidence of food shortages may be due as much to the size of the population as to any other factor for this period.

The size of Rome far outstripped local resources and its enormous populace could be fed only through the importation of food on an enormous scale.[5] The main staple food was wheat, and by the time of the Empire a substantial monthly ration of wheat was being distributed free of charge to the citizens of the city. Of the various wheat species, the most widely grown in the ancient Mediterranean of the Roman period were probably several naked varieties: *triticum durum* and *triticum turgidum* of the emmer group, and a species of spelt, *triticum vulgare.*[6] The amount of these grains plus other foodstuffs being shipped to Rome at its height must have been well in excess of 400,000 metric tons annually.[7] This food did not arrive in the city spaced out evenly over the year, however, because the prime sailing season in the Mediterranean is a relatively short 100-day period falling mostly during the summer; most ships avoided sailing at all during the dangerously stormy winter.[8]

The half million tons or so of food that arrived during the summer had to be stored somewhere and then distributed to the populace of Rome over the course of the rest of the year. To hold the vast quantities of grain and other goods that poured into Rome during the sailing season, colossal warehouses were constructed both at Ostia and at Rome itself, particularly along the left bank of the Tiber downstream from the Aventine. This area, known as the Emporium district (fig. 4.1), eventually became a dense warren of gigantic warehouses abut-

Fig. 4.1. The commercial Emporium district as recreated in the Gismondi model at the Museo della Civiltà Romana. The Aventine Hill is in the upper left, and just below it is the long roof of the Porticus Aemilia. In the center is the Horrea Galbana, with Monte Testaccio visible on the far right. (Photo by author)

ting the Tiber embankment, which was equipped with quays for the ships and lighters to tie up at and unload their cargoes.[9] It is impossible to tell exactly how much of the food was immediately sent upriver to Rome and how much remained at Ostia (and later Portus) for more gradual transport upriver. The considerable storage capacity of even the relatively small number of known warehouses is a clear indication that these buildings were holding more than just a short-term supply of food.

Most Roman warehouses, or *horrea,* followed a standard plan in which a series of small inward-facing storage cubicles were arranged around a central open courtyard.[10] The design of many of these *horrea* suggests that they were specially built for the storage of grain. Grain must be kept cool, dry, and free of excessive moisture, which can cause it quickly to go bad. Some granaries were built with raised floors and large openings between adjoining rooms to provide free circulation of air, which helps to keep down the moisture levels. The walls were very thick, often a meter wide, which would have been necessary in order for them to resist horizontal pressures if the grain were stored loose. There was also great concern with keeping the grain safe from thieves, and *horrea* were built with only a bare minimum of external openings. Windows to the outside for ventilation were small and situated high up on the walls, and there were typically only a couple of relatively narrow doors connecting the complex to the outside. Elaborate systems of locks and bolts secured these doors. *Horrea* could have multiple stories, and some of them were truly gigantic; for example, the Horrea Galbana at Rome, whose ground floor was 167 by 146 m and possessed no fewer than three internal courtyards lined with more than 140 separate storage rooms, covered a total area of more than 20,000 m^2. The Regionary Catalog lists more than 300 *horrea* scattered around Rome, and some were found in all of the 14 districts of the city.[11] These warehouses constituted the food larder of the city, and the survival of the populace literally depended on safeguarding the year's supply of grain stashed within them.[12]

Although *horrea* are attested all over the city, evidence such as the fragments of the Severan Marble Plan suggests that the largest warehouses were located close to the Tiber, particularly in the Emporium region on the left bank and the corresponding section of the Transtiberim on the right. These locations are perfectly logical, because proximity to the river would have facilitated the rapid unloading of the watercraft that had brought the grain upriver from Ostia and Portus. However, the desire to locate the main warehouses near the Tiber also meant that these buildings were located squarely in the floodplain, where their precious contents were at greatest risk from flooding. It seems reasonable to assume that nearly all of the major floods at Rome would have inundated the main storage areas for Rome's food supplies.

Stored grain is very vulnerable to wetness because once the moisture content exceeds a certain level, mold will begin to grow in the grain. It is usually recommended that if grain is to be stored for periods longer than a month, as was the case in ancient Rome, the moisture content should be less than 13% in order to prevent the growth of mold.[13] The grain would probably be safe up to about 15% moisture content, but above this, there would ultimately be some mold growth. Another important factor is the temperature, because molds will not propagate at cold temperatures. The temperature of the grain is not always determined solely by the outside conditions, because the growth of mold itself can create heat; thus it is possible for mold cultures to thrive inside a pile of grain, even when the outside temperature would appear to be too cold. The ideal conditions for mold propagation occur when moisture levels are above 18.5% and temperatures are 20–30°C; at these levels, mold can multiply very rapidly, spoiling the grain in a matter of days. Mold can begin to grow, however, at temperatures as low as 5°C as long as the moisture content is greater than 14%. Some molds, including the most dangerous varieties, can thrive in cool temperatures, but no mold can grow in grain without at least 13% moisture content.[14] Thus, moisture is the key factor that must be considered in preventing stored grain from becoming moldy.

The spores from which molds grow are almost always present on wheat, but they lie dormant until moisture levels and temperature are sufficient to promote reproduction. Molds can produce mycotoxins which, if consumed by people or animals, can cause a range of health problems, sometimes even resulting in death.[15] The best-known historical mycotoxin was a parasitic fungus produced by *claviceps purpurea,* which caused ergot.[16] Although largely eradicated in humans today, this disease, known as St. Anthony's Fire during the Middle

Ages, killed thousands. Sufferers of the gangrenous form of ergotism could have their limbs literally fall off, and another strain often produced nervous seizures and psychosis. The mortality rate of those who contract ergotism is very high. In the epidemics that struck Russia during the 19th century, more than 40% of those infected died of the disease.[17] Ergot most commonly affects rye, which was not widely cultivated in the Roman world, but it can strike any grain crop. Today the most common mycotoxins of grains include the aflatoxins and the orchratoxins, both of which can cause problems including vomiting, gastric irritation, and hemorrhaging, and which possibly play a role in promoting cancers. Another significant category of mycotoxins found in cereals are the trichothecenes that are produced by Fusarium molds and cause alimentary toxic aleikiia, a disease of humans that can be fatal, particularly among those whose diet consists primarily of grains.

The Romans were plainly aware of the danger posed by moisture to stored grain, as evidenced by the distinctive design of *horrea* and attested in the treatises of agricultural writers. Various authors give detailed instructions about how grain should be stored and stress the need to separate the grain from possible sources of moisture. Columella (*De Ag.* 2.11, 1.9.10) warns that grain "deteriorates more rapidly in damp places" and recommends that grain be stored suspended in lofts so as to protect it from the damp rising from the ground. Pliny the Elder (*HN* 18.301) suggests a variety of strategies to safeguard grain from spoiling, ranging from burying the grain in specially insulated pits to hanging a toad by one of its hind legs before storing the grain. The Romans also seem to have understood the link between consuming moldy grain and disease. Often it is difficult to identify diseases with certainty based on the symptoms given by ancient medical writers, so that the evidence from these texts alone is open to interpretation. Other evidence is more clear-cut, however, such as Julius Caesar's account of the siege of Massilia during the Civil Wars. He recounts that toward the end of the siege, the Massiliotes were suffering severe food shortages and were driven by desperation to eat old stocks of grain that had become moldy. Caesar (*BC* 2.22.1) specifically states that as a result of consuming this bad grain, a pestilence broke out that further weakened the populace, leading to the capitulation of the city.

The Romans were well aware of the dangers of eating grain that had spoiled and was no longer fit for consumption by humans or animals. In AD 62, for example, Nero ordered that the entire stored grain reserves of the city be dumped into the Tiber because they had gone bad (Tac. *Ann.* 15.18).[18]

In ancient Rome, if a granary flooded and temperatures were moderate or warm, the grain reached by the waters would have been ruined quickly by the propagation of molds. Grain that has been immersed in water for a period of several days will have a moisture content of 30–50%. In warm temperatures, grain with such high degrees of moisture will become moldy in only a few days. This does not even take into account the factor that the floodwater itself would probably have been loaded with organic pollutants. The many disease-causing organisms in the dirty floodwaters would on their own have thoroughly contaminated any grain that was immersed, rendering it completely unfit for consumption.[19]

One potentially positive aspect of flooded granaries is that it might have been possible to salvage any grain that was above the high water level. If, for example, a bin in which loose grain was piled 2 m high flooded only to a depth of 1 m, the dry grain on top might be saved. Water does not readily "wick" through grain, so only the grain immediately above the water level will be affected by direct seepage. While the dry grain will probably remain usable for several weeks, it should be separated from the wet grain as soon as possible because the mold that will quickly grow in the moistened portion can eventually spread upward and the proximity to damp areas can also increase the moisture level in the dry grain. In a study of a wheat bin that had been flooded to a depth of only one foot, measurements taken a month later showed the affected wheat was solid with mold, and moisture and mold were detected spreading to the unflooded sections.[20] After 30 days, the rest of the wheat was still usable but plainly deteriorating. Insects can exacerbate the problem, because grain that has been partially chewed is more susceptible to mold growth.[21] Additionally, the very presence of insects can increase moisture levels, perhaps pushing them into the critical range. Insects and mold can form a self-encouraging cycle, because both thrive in moister and hotter environments;

the greater the insect population, the higher the moisture, and thus the greater the mold, which in turn raises the temperature, encouraging more active insects, and so on.

Another problem in the warehouses that could have resulted from flooding has to do with the absorptive quality of grain. Grain that has soaked up water will swell considerably in volume, and the swollen grain can exert powerful horizontal pressure on the walls of a granary. Due to this effect, modern grain silos often experience torn and stretched sides and bent and broken doors after a flood.[22]

In addition to keeping grain safe from theft, the design of Roman warehouses may have had a further benefit. Although many of the most important *horrea* were located in a highly flood-prone area, the design of these buildings could have offered considerable resistance to floodwater and even may have been able to keep their contents dry and safe from all but the most severe floods. The rectangular, fortress-like construction of many of the *horrea* presented solid walls on all four sides with no windows or openings except high up (fig. 4.2). Sometimes the only external ground-level opening was a single doorway, which was itself of massive construction. In a flood, buildings such as these could literally become islands, completely surrounded by water perhaps several meters deep but remaining dry on the inside. Nearly all the stereotypical elements of *horrea* construction would have contributed to making these buildings highly flood-resistant. The thick walls would have been well suited to withstanding the horizontal pressure of floodwaters, and the pressure exerted by loose grain on the interior would have helped to counterbalance the external pressure of the water. The lack of low-level windows and openings would have minimized points of ingress for water. The few doorways could have been barricaded with sandbags (or perhaps handy sacks of grain) to make them relatively waterproof. In *horrea* equipped with raised floors in the storage cubicles, the grain would have been kept safe from modest amounts of water that did manage to penetrate the complex. (The dwarf walls that supported the raised floors were usually about 40 cm in height, so that in such buildings, a substantial amount of water could seep in before the water level reached the lowest grain.)[23] With such construction, a *horrea* might have formed a dry pocket even when

Floods of the Tiber in Ancient Rome

Fig. 4.2. The Horrea Galbana from the Gismondi model. The fortress-like construction of many *horrea*, with minimal entrances and small, high windows, is evident. (Photo by author)

surrounded by deep floodwaters and may well have been able to hold out against the water's siege for many days until the flood finally receded.

These aspects of *horrea* design may explain why food shortages after floods were not more common. With so much moisture-sensitive wheat being stored so near the Tiber, one would expect that every flood would destroy some, if not all, of the stored grain. This does not appear to have been the case, and one possible explanation is that the large imperial *horrea* were able to resist the floodwaters and preserve their contents. It is probable that some food was indeed ruined in every flood since by no means all *horrea* were as water-resistant as described, but as long as sizable grain reserves remained untouched, there were time and opportunity to avert a potential famine. It seems likely that Ostia was also prone to Tiber flooding and that a flood of great enough magnitude to ruin food at Rome would also have affected the supplies stored in Ostian warehouses. Thus it might not have been possible to avert a postflood famine at Rome by simply bringing up more food from Ostia. It is tempting to try to assess the relative scales of ancient floods by assuming that those which resulted in food shortages due to the spoilage of stored grain must have been of greater magnitude than others. This may be the case, but there are so many unknown variables, such as the time of year, the amount of stored food, and whether the previous or current harvest had been good or bad, that this factor alone cannot be used to make comparisons among floods.

Although wheat was probably the main staple of the ancient Roman diet, accounting for the greatest percentage of daily caloric intake, other foods were significant as well. Among these were olive oil and wine, both of which seem to have been consumed in nutritionally significant quantities even by ordinary Romans.[24] Due to olive oil's many nonconsumptive uses in cooking, lighting, bathing, and a myriad of other activities, the volume of olive oil imports to Rome was impressive.[25] These liquid commodities were typically transported and stored in large ceramic amphorae which might have been piled up in *horrea*.[26] If warehouses containing amphorae or *dolia* were flooded, the contents of the jars should nonetheless have remained safe from contamination, provided that the waterproof seals closing the mouths of the jars had been properly applied. There would have been a danger that the mouths of jars that had been submerged in water containing disease-causing organisms might retain some of these contaminants. As long as these areas were cleaned off before the jar was opened, this danger would have been averted. The *dolia* should have remained relatively impervious to floods, but there is a chance that loose amphorae might have been picked up by the floodwaters, and possibly smashed if the current were strong enough. In general, however, the food products stored in these jars should have survived inundations with minimal ill-effects.

Disease

One of the most potentially destructive aftereffects of a flood is disease. The health hazard posed by floods was greatly intensified by Roman burial and sanitation practices—or, perhaps more accurately, the frequent lack thereof. As a result, the streets of Rome were breeding grounds for numerous disease-causing organisms due to the widespread presence of human and animal cadavers in various states of decomposition as well as the copious quantities of raw sewage deposited in the streets.

The normal course of events resulted in enormous numbers of dead bodies, many of which were not properly disposed of.[27] The truly impoverished who could not afford to join a burial club or who lacked nearby family members to dispose of their bodies, along with Rome's large population of homeless and beggars, simply lay where they dropped, or else were thrown into the Tiber or into open pits just outside the city. It has been estimated that the city of Rome produced perhaps 1,500 such unclaimed bodies per year.[28] Various literary anecdotes vividly illustrate the presence of both bodies and scavenging animals in the streets of the city. The poet Martial (*Epigrams* 10.5) describes the gruesome death of a beggar whose last moments are spent trying to fend off the dogs and vultures that have gathered to feed on him. Suetonius (*Vesp.* 5.4) mentions an incident when a stray dog ran into the room where the emperor Vespasian was dining and deposited a human hand beneath the table, and a partially eaten corpse was hauled through the Forum itself by a pack of scavenging canines (Oros. *Adv. Pagan.* 7.41–42).

Although Rome possessed some sewers, their purpose was more to provide drainage than to actually carry away waste.[29] While latrines were sometimes present in buildings, *domus,* and *insulae* at Rome, most often they were not, suggesting that people relieved themselves in the streets or in chamber pots. Unfortunately most city inhabitants appear to have emptied their chamber pots by simply dumping them out the windows of their dwellings. Much of Rome's garbage and sewage seems to have ended up in the streets. This was no small problem, because at its height, Rome's human inhabitants were producing on the order of 50,000 kg of excrement per day.[30] Roman law offers an insight into sanitation and living conditions through laws that attempted to regulate what was obviously a common practice: pouring feces and garbage from one's window into the streets (*Digest* 9.3.1, 43.10.1). Rome's animals certainly also contributed to the general level of filth, and the streets of the city probably more closely resembled open sewers than our modern notion of roadways.

The garbage and excrement that were thrown or deposited onto the roadways would have been trampled together with mud and refuse to form a layer of sludge coating the street surface. The continual flow of water from streetside fountains and basins may have served to wash this waste into the sewers to some extent, but it would also have covered the surface of the streets with a perpetually moist and unpleasant muck. In connection with this, it is perhaps worth noting Martial's description (5.22) of the steps leading up from the Subura as being always wet and filthy, and Juvenal's account (3.247) of a trip through the streets during which his legs (not merely his feet) became entirely splattered with mud. This foul accretion would have been scoured off by floodwaters and would have mingled with, and been dissolved into, the waters. The result was that floodwaters were transformed into a highly infectious soup filled with disease-causing organisms. Because the Roman drainage networks and sewers did not possess valves to prevent backflow, the contents of these sewers would also have been washed up into the city by the floodwaters and carried everywhere that the waters reached. Added to this deadly liquid mixture were the bodies of dead humans and animals already present in the streets; these cadavers, in varying degrees of decomposition, would have been, in essence, biological bombs loaded with pathogens, which would have contributed their share of disease-carrying organisms to the floodwaters as well. Finally, in the days following the flood, the corpses of humans and animals drowned in the disaster itself would have begun to putrefy, serving as fresh vectors of disease and contamination via the standing water.

Everything touched by the befouled waters would have been contaminated by this mixture. Excrement can harbor a large number of different organisms that cause disease in those who come into contact with it. People infected by these diseases then spread the bacteria, parasites, and viruses in their feces and urine. If water comes into contact with this infected excrement, the pathogens are easily spread to other people, usually by oral transmission. These dangerous organisms, which fall into four groups, result in various diseases whose effects range from mild gastrointestinal distress to death.[31]

One group of organisms in excrement consists of enteric viruses such as rotaviruses, parvoviruses, and at least 67 different varieties of enteroviruses. The most common health hazard posed by these viruses is gastroenteritis. Testimony to the ease with which it is spread is that even today, viral gastroenteritis, which typically results in severe diarrhea, fever, and nausea, is the second most common disease in the United States. Victims of gastroenteritis usually recover, but it can be fatal to infants, elderly people, and those whose health has been weakened by other factors. Flood survivors, who might not have access to food, clean water, or shelter, would be particularly susceptible. Some of the enteroviruses also cause meningitis, which can result in blindness, brain damage, and, frequently, death. Also in this category is the virus causing hepatitis A, a highly infectious form of the disease that causes episodes of fever, lassitude, vomiting, and jaundice that can persist for weeks.

The next group of disease-causing organisms abundantly present in feces is bacteria. These include the common *Escherichia coli* bacterium, which causes the familiar "traveler's diarrhea" form of gastroenteritis. Another common bacterium found in feces is salmonella, producing salmonellosis, which results in the usual array of gastrointestinal ailments, but can sometimes invade the respiratory, cardiovascular, and nervous systems as well. Even today, the mortality rate from salmonellosis is around 4%. Yet more serious is typhoid fever, which is caused by a bacillus of the Salmonella family, and which would have proved particularly dangerous to flood survivors due to the other stressors that these people were suffering from. Victims of typhoid are struck with fever, chills, malaise, and diarrhea, and the disease can rupture the intestines. About 5% of those affected continue to shed typhoid bacilli in their urine or feces for up to a year, and some will continue to do so for the rest of their lives, as was probably the case with the famous "Typhoid Mary."

The third category of organisms is certain parasitic protozoans that, when transmitted to the gastrointestinal tract, cause diarrhea and infection. These include *Giardia lambli* (which causes giardiasis), *Entamoeba histolytica* (causing amebiasis), and *Balantidium coli* (which causes balantidiasis).

The final group is parasitic worms. The most common of these are nematodes, such as hookworms, threadworms, roundworms, pinworms, and whipworms, and cestodes, which are various species of tapeworm. Although most of these parasitic worms are usually not fatal to their hosts, their presence can cause a variety of health problems and substantially weaken infected individuals. On occasion death might even result, as when roundworms sometimes agglutinate in sufficient quantity to block the bile duct, resulting in jaundice, or even to produce a fatal obstruction in the small intestines.

All four categories of infectious organisms would have been common in the sewage-contaminated waters of ancient Rome. Even in modern Western cities, flooding or heavy rainfall often overwhelms local sewer systems, causing outbreaks of waterborne diseases. During the great midwestern floods of 1993 in the United States, the sewage system of Milwaukee, Wisconsin, was compromised by floodwater with the result that 403,000 cases of waterborne intestinal illnesses and 54 fatalities were recorded.[32] A comprehensive study of the 548 serious outbreaks of waterborne disease in the United States from 1948 to 1994 found an extremely high statistical correlation between these outbreaks and unusually heavy rainfall or flooding.[33]

One of the most dangerous waterborne diseases, cholera, does not seem to be definitively attested in ancient Rome, although it plainly existed in ancient India. If it was present in the ancient Mediterranean, it seems to have vanished by the Renaissance before reappearing in Europe in the great cholera epidemics of the 19th century. The vagueness of ancient descriptions of disease makes it difficult to identify diseases for certain, but if cholera was present in ancient Rome, the mortality rates would have been quite high.[34] The entire range of digestive tract diseases grouped under the general term "dysentery" that all result in inflammation of the intestines and cause severe diarrhea would have been prevalent in the postflood landscape of ancient Rome. Whether resulting from a bacterium, a protozoan, or a parasitic worm, disease due to fecal contamination of the water would have brought considerable suffering to the survivors. Of these diseases, bacillic dysentery tends to be the most severe form, causing bloody diarrhea, but is shorter in duration than amoebic dysentery, which lasts longer but with less severe symptoms.

As the waters containing all of these various organisms washed through the dwellings, monuments, and structures of the city, they would have tainted everything that they reached. Stockpiles of food would have been particularly vulnerable to contamination and, unless sealed within watertight containers, would have been rendered unfit for consumption. Even after the flood receded, the invisible contamination carried by the waters would have remained behind. Any porous substance—including clothing, textiles, and wooden furniture and furnishings—would have harbored these potentially deadly organisms, and typically all it would take to infect a person would be for him or her to touch the lips or mouth after handling any of these items.

In modern floods, even when the water causes sewage backflow into buildings, the level of fecal contamination in the water is much less than it would have been in ancient Rome, where the unsanitary contents of the streets themselves would have contributed to very high levels of contamination in the water. Even in modern floods, the health hazard presented by contaminated water is so severe that the standard guidelines for dealing with a postflood environment where there might be contamination from sewage dictate that the affected buildings and property must undergo extensive decontamination procedures in order to render them habitable and usable. The level of risk is suggested by the fact that these guidelines stipulate that workers undertaking the decontamination have to be equipped with rubber boots, gloves, and splash goggles and should wear respirators with high-efficiency particulate air cartridges.[35] Nonporous surfaces have to be wiped down with strong disinfectant chemicals such as bleaches, ammonium compounds, phenol, or hydrogen peroxide. Items made of semiporous materials such as wood, ceramic, and plaster require similar treatment. Ideally, porous items, including carpet, clothing, and bedding, should be thrown away, as it is very difficult to remove biological contaminants.[36] In ancient Rome, where such extensive decontamination could not have been undertaken, many people must have become infected during the cleanup process, and many more from subsequent contact with contaminated clothing and other items.

Even when the majority of the floodwaters had drained away, the continuing dampness of the moisture-saturated soil and the buildings and objects that had been immersed in the water would have served to prolong the life-span of the disease-causing organisms. For example, in normal situations, the organisms causing typhoid and dysentery will survive in feces for one to two weeks. If deposited in very dry soil, they will die off quickly, but in moist conditions, they have been found to survive in an infectious state for periods of up to several months.[37] This is why it is essential for areas and items affected by flooding to be dried out as rapidly and as completely as possible.

The high levels of moisture and humidity commonly encountered in parts of buildings that have been flooded and that do not have ready access to sunlight or strong ventilation not only serve to prolong the life-span of disease-causing organisms but can also promote the creation of additional ones. Such damp environments encourage the growth of a variety of molds and fungi, many of which can cause further diseases or pose health hazards. Such molds and fungi frequently produce or intensify allergies and respiratory ailments, and the very young and old are especially vulnerable. Recently, for example, the Center for Disease Control determined that the *Stachybotrys atra* mold has caused dozens of cases of pulmonary hemorrhage, some of which were fatal, in infants in the United States following floods.[38]

The construction of Roman residential dwellings—in particular, *insulae*—would have exacerbated the problems posed by high levels of moisture. These buildings were often densely inhabited warrens of tiny rooms lacking direct access to sunlight and ventilation. In such an environment, drying out the mud brick, plaster, and wood used to build the structure would have been an extremely difficult and prolonged process. In the aftermath of a flood, mold, mildew, and fungi must have been rampant within the humid, airless cubicles at the core of such buildings.

Another delayed health hazard from flooding would have been a potential increase in the population of mosquitoes.[39] The numerous small pools of standing water left behind by a flood would constitute ideal breeding grounds for the incubation of mosquito eggs. The life cycle of the mosquito from egg to adult takes between 7 and 12 days depending on the species, so that a week or two after a flood, the survivors would have been plagued by swarms of mosquitoes. In addition to the annoyance factor caused by these insects, they would of course have posed the risk of transmitting additional diseases to humans, including malaria and encephalitis.

Malaria is caused by sporozoan parasites of the plasmodium group, which in turn are carried by the *Anopheles* mosquitoes. When an infected mosquito bites a human, the parasites are transmitted to the bloodstream and establish themselves in the liver, where they multiply and further infect the bloodstream. Although malaria is usually not a fatal disease, bouts are often lengthy and debilitating, and those stricken suffer recurrent episodes of enervating fever and malaise. Of the 12 mosquito species found in Italy today, just 3 in the maculiponnis group of anopheline mosquitoes pose a significant threat of transmitting malaria to humans. Of these, 2 prefer to breed in the type of stagnant pools of water that might be left behind by a flood.

There is some question concerning when malaria reached Europe, but it seems reliably attested in the eastern Mediterranean, probably by the fifth century and certainly by the third century BC.[40] Malaria is a disease characteristic of the stagnant water found in swampy regions, and the inhabitants of the ancient world had formed strong associations between marshes and diseases, although usually ascribing this connection to "bad air" rather than to insects.[41] Columella (1.5), for example, warned that dwellings should not be placed near marshes, "from which are often contracted mysterious diseases whose causes are beyond the understanding of physicians." Malaria has sometimes been identified as the principal agent in the decline of various ancient civilizations, and while this view is probably too extreme, it was plainly a serious problem whose victims may have included such notable individuals as Julius Caesar and Augustus.[42] Juvenal (*Sat.* 4.56–57) testifies to its presence in ancient Rome, and the disease seems to have been a major health threat that killed large numbers of the city's inhabitants outright and weakened many more, leaving them susceptible to other diseases. Studies of the seasonality of deaths in the city of ancient Rome reveal a strong peak in mortality during August to October, which probably correlates to the malaria season.[43]

Horace (*Epist.* 1.7.8–9) specifically identifies the low-lying Roman Forum as being one place where there was a high risk of contracting malaria. In the early modern period, a number of observers have left detailed accounts of areas of Rome that were unhealthy due to malaria and those that were relatively salubrious. Not surprisingly, the low-lying regions, especially those near the Tiber, were repeatedly identified as being the disease-ridden ones, with the hills being the safe zones.[44] These commentators also attribute malaria outbreaks to Tiber floods that left large standing pools of water, a perfect breeding ground for mosquitoes.

There is also comparative evidence to support an increase in mosquito-borne diseases such as malaria in the aftermath of floods. One 1983 study of malaria in Peru, for example, showed a dramatic 7-fold increase in the number of cases following floods, which was attributed to the increase in mosquito breeding sites caused by postflood pools of water and the greater exposure of people housed in temporary lodgings.[45] During 1963 in Haiti, a 13-fold increase in cases of malaria was attributed to flooding.[46] In Bolivia as well, receding floodwaters have been identified as a significant source of mosquito breeding grounds.[47] Such outbreaks in ancient Rome would probably have been confined to times of moderate or warm weather, and so would not have been a factor in winter floods, but could well have been a significant threat following floods that occurred during times of warm weather.

Another small winged insect, the fly, can also pose particular problems after a flood.[48] Flies feed upon and lay their eggs in animal or human feces so that small fragments of excreta containing disease-causing organisms often become caught in the stiff hairs of a fly's legs and body. When the fly then lands on food, these fragments can fall off, infecting the food. While flies would have been a constant and familiar presence in Rome's filthy streets, when floodwaters carried excrement to areas where it was not usually found, flies would have followed, breeding and fossicking in places where they normally would not have been as prevalent. Among the most common diseases transmitted by flies are typhoid and shigellosis.

Leptospirosis is another fever-causing disease that is frequently encountered in the aftermath of floods. It is carried by a variety of animals, but the strain that most often infects humans is borne by rats and is spread through ingestion of food or drink that has been contaminated by rat urine. It can also be contracted merely through exposure to or immersion in water infected by rat urine, entering the body through, for example, cuts or scrapes in the skin or the conjunctiva. As far back as the 19th century, it was recognized as being prevalent among those who work in sewers or in swampy environments, leading to its common names of "swamp fever," "mud fever," and "rat fever." Epidemic outbreaks of leptospirosis are standard following floods because the rat-contaminated water found in sewers mingles with the floodwaters and is then spread throughout the urban environment. Those caught in the floodwaters, as well as rescue workers, cleanup crews, and people returning to the postflood but still muddy environment, are at risk. Brazil, for example, routinely records its highest annual incidence of leptospirosis following floods in urban areas. In 2000, after a series of floods struck northern Thailand, there was an outbreak of leptospirosis and the Thailand Ministry of Public Health identified 1,639 cases of the disease. In the aftermath of similar flooding the previous year, there was a comparable epidemic that eventually resulted in 130 fatalities. Increasingly, leptospirosis is being recognized as a significant threat following floods, and as a disease responsible for many of the illnesses that arise in a flood's wake. In August 2002 the Department of Health of the Philippines issued proclamations intended to educate the public about the need to wash with soap after being exposed to floodwaters. They also announced that several hundred cases of leptospirosis had been identified that summer associated with exposure to waters infected by rat urine and that these had resulted in a number of deaths.[49]

The hygienic conditions present in ancient Rome are probably most similar to those experienced by many of the poor inhabitants of lesser-developed modern regions. One such possible comparanda is Bangladesh, which is highly flood prone, and a study of the morbidity and mortality that followed the severe floods of 1988 might offer insight into the distribution of illnesses resulting from flooding in such an urban environment. Of some 46,740 patients who were seen by doctors after the floods of 1988, 34.7% were suffering from diarrhea, 17.4% from infections of the respiratory tract, 10.1% from intestinal worms, 6.5% from fever, 5.8% from skin infections, 5.1% from injuries that had become infected, and the remaining 20.45% from a variety of other diseases.[50] These results are very much in keeping with an environment where contamination of the water by various disease-bearing organisms poses a serious threat.

The same study also examined the causes of death among the 154 reported fatalities from the 1988 floods. In Bangladesh, which lies

Delayed Effects of Floods

mainly in the delta of the Ganges, Jamuna, and Meghna rivers, the river floods typically rise slowly over several days so that there is time to flee to high ground. This produces a comparatively low rate of death by drowning from these floods, and indeed, only 5.8% of the fatalities in the flood of 1988 resulted from drowning. The chief causes of death were diarrhea (27.3%), respiratory tract infections (13%), "old age" (11%), and accidents, including drowning (9.7%).[51] While drowning overall only accounted for 5.8% of deaths, it was the cause of 16% of the reported deaths among children.[52] Survivors of floods are highly susceptible to illness simply because of factors such as lack of shelter or food. After flooding in Pakistan in 1980, a study found that fully 60–75% of the survivors fell sick with a wide variety of illnesses.[53] In addition, nearly every family had at least one member who became so ill that they were bed-ridden for months.[54] The pattern of disease seen in densely populated Third World regions such as Bangladesh, with high levels of death and disease caused by waterborne infections, may be the closest modern equivalent to the situation in ancient Rome.

The final health hazard posed by floods, and perhaps one of the most serious, is contamination of the water supply. A shortage of potable water is one of the greatest problems facing modern cities inundated by flooding.[55] In less-developed nations with open sewer systems (not unlike ancient Rome's), increases of 150% in gastrointestinal illnesses and up to 100% in total mortality have been documented following floods.[56] The Romans did not fully understand the link between providing a clean water supply and preventing disease; indeed, public and government concern over hygiene and water did not become intense until the 19th century.[57]

In ancient Rome, all the fountains, cisterns, pipes, baths, basins, and reservoirs reached by floodwaters would obviously have been contaminated by the virulent stew of disease-bearing organisms present in these waters. Under the fully developed system, Rome's freshwater supply came from a network of 11 major aqueducts supplying around 1 million m^3 of water per day to the city.[58] This water was deposited by the aqueducts into settling tanks called *castella*, which were distributed throughout the city, and from there the water flowed on to secondary *castella* and to fountains or open basins where the city inhabitants could fill their jars. By the end of the first century AD, there were 247 *castella* and 591 basins scattered throughout the city. Most ordinary people would have gotten their water for drinking and cleaning from these distribution points. A major consumer of the water coming to the city was the dozen or so huge public baths and several hundred private ones. The majority of the Roman water network was a continuous flow system in which water flowed constantly through many of the pipes, fountains, and basins—even at night, when use of water would presumably have been much lower. This seems wasteful from a modern perspective, but this overflow may have served a useful health purpose by continually washing out drains and gutters. Rome also possessed a number of freshwater springs and wells that could have served as potential sources of water.

At first glance, this system appears fairly vulnerable to contamination by floodwaters. The many open channels, basins, fountains, and pools of water would easily have been contaminated by floodwater bearing fecal matter and disease-causing organisms. Not only would the water currently in these reservoirs have been contaminated, but the containers themselves could have retained harmful organisms unless thoroughly purged.

Although ancient Rome was inferior to modern standards in many aspects of public health and engineering, in terms of the vulnerability of the water supply to contamination and the speed with which it could recover from contamination, the peculiar nature of Rome's water supply system may actually have made the ancient city unusually resistant and quick to recover. First of all, the continual-flow nature of Rome's water supply system would have ensured that contaminants did not linger in the pipes and basins, but were instead flushed out fairly rapidly and prevented from settling in standing pools of water within the system. The volume of water passing through Rome's water supply system was enormous, exceeding the per capita water consumption rates of most modern cities. Once floodwaters receded below the level of any given fountain or basin, the constantly flowing water supply would have washed out the basin and, while perhaps not rendering it completely free of contamination, would at least have greatly reduced the concentration of dangerous organisms quite rapidly.

Another quirk of Rome's water supply is that the majority of water

Delayed Effects of Floods

Fig. 4.3. Section of the Aqua Claudia. Rome's water supply system brought a constant supply of fresh water to the city. (Photo by author)

did not originate locally but was transported a considerable distance to the city by aqueducts (fig. 4.3). Most of these aqueducts brought water directly from springs located on high ground up in the foothills of the Apennines. These water sources would have been completely unaffected by local disasters such as floods, so that their water would have remained pure and uncontaminated. Thus, no matter how severe a flood occurred at Rome, its inhabitants would have been assured that a constantly flowing supply of millions of liters of good, drinkable water was on its way to Rome.

In contrast, modern cities often get their water from local sources; water from an adjacent lake, stream, or river goes through filtration plants, which have huge, open reservoirs of water that are extremely vulnerable to contamination that is not readily removed. Similarly, local wells that have been contaminated by floodwaters can take a long time to become pure again because the contaminated water is constantly seeping downward and refouling the well water. Also, modern water systems that rely on pumping to distribute water are often knocked out of commission due to failure of the city power grid. With a loss of power and of pumps, water in a modern system can sometimes flow in the wrong direction, bringing contamination to other parts of the system and spreading these contaminants. Rome's water distribution system, on the other hand, operated by gravity, and so again was relatively immune to these problems. Parts of the system in low-lying areas might have been affected by floodwaters, but water would have always been flowing down into these areas and thus limiting the spread of the contamination. Due to the reliance on distant water sources, the continual-flow nature of the system, and the gravity-powered distribution of water, ancient Rome's water supply would have been fairly resistant to contamination by flooding, relatively quick to flush out contaminants and restore the flow of safe water, and generally more resilient when faced with the hazards posed by flooding than almost any other large city in any era.

Psychological Trauma

All the effects of floods described in this chapter thus far have been based on the constant laws and principles of physics, hydrology, biology, and engineering. Therefore it has been possible to make comments about what would have happened in ancient Rome with some degree of assurance, even when direct written or archaeological evidence for such effects has been lacking. The final category to be considered, however, deals with neither physical effects that can be scientifically described nor experimental data that can be reliably reproduced, but rather involves the transitory mental states of human beings. Making statements about the emotional responses of people from another culture who lived in the distant past based on the reactions of human beings from a 20th-century industrial society is obviously a procedure fraught with possibilities for error. Even among modern psychologists and sociologists, there is considerable disagreement about the intensity and duration of the psychological trauma suffered by victims of natural disasters. While attempting to guess at the Romans' emotional and psychological responses to floods is a highly speculative enterprise, simply to ignore this important aspect of floods would be even more unsatisfactory.[59] Therefore, in the interest of thoroughness, the final section of this chapter presents modern findings on the psychological effects of flooding on survivors while fully acknowledging that such data may not be comparable to the experiences and mentalities of the ancient Romans. Instead, this information should be taken as suggestive of the range of possible responses that disasters provoke among those who have had the misfortune to experience them.[60]

One of the common stereotypes about behavior during disasters is that many people become "unhinged" or hysterical and that there is widespread panic. Various studies have consistently found this not to be the case.[61] While people experience high levels of fear and stress, they usually continue to act in a rational manner and to take reasonable steps to preserve their own lives and the lives of others. Interviews with disaster victims and the accounts of rescue workers reveal that of those people caught in a disaster, far more display considerable initiative and ingenuity in dealing with the event than succumb to panic. One of the few situations that does seem to cause people to lose their composure is the specific circumstance when large numbers are somehow trapped in a space with limited egress and severe injury or death is imminent, as in a fire in a theater or on a rapidly sinking ship.[62] Floods normally do not produce such conditions, so it should not be assumed that there would have been widespread panic in ancient Rome when flooding struck the city.

Perhaps the most disturbing reaction to a disaster is exhibited by those who attempt to exploit it for their own gain. One of the most frequent forms this profiteering takes during the aftermath of a disaster is when unscrupulous entrepreneurs sell vital supplies such as food, water, or clothing to survivors at grossly inflated prices. This sort of opportunism certainly took place in ancient Rome with regard to foodstuffs, especially grain. There are numerous instances of legislation and price controls enacted in order to prevent rampant inflation of grain prices during food shortages.[63] During a food crisis in AD 19, for example, Tiberius set limits on grain prices, and after the Great Fire of AD 64, Nero imposed a maximum price of three sesterces per modius of grain (Tac. *Ann.* 2.87.1, 15.39.3). There was a long tradition at Rome of speculation and price manipulation of vital food supplies, and at least some merchants would certainly have taken advantage of food shortages caused by flooding to increase their profits.

Even during a disaster itself, it is not unknown for people to seek ways to exploit the calamity. During a flood in Australia in 1918, boat owners approached flood victims stranded in trees or on rooftops and offered to rescue them, but only in exchange for a considerable sum of money. If the unfortunate victims declined this offer, they were left to the mercy of the flood.[64] Extreme behaviors such as this do not appear to be very common, but they typically receive much media attention, causing them to be overemphasized in accounts of disasters. Similarly, the modern media accounts of disasters often include sensationalized descriptions of rampant looting. While there are well-attested examples of such behavior, sociological studies of this subject again suggest that its frequency and severity are often exaggerated.[65]

The experience of living through a natural disaster such as a flood can be extremely traumatic. While most people display considerable resilience during the disaster itself and in its aftermath, it is not unusual for feelings of numbness or shock to develop once the immediate crisis is past.[66] It is notoriously difficult to quantify amorphous conditions such as stress. One indication can be gained by comparing the stress experienced during one event with that caused by another. When a group of people who had lived through a flood of the Mississippi were asked to compare the level of stress from this event with that experienced from other traumatic life occurrences, they rated the flood as even more stressful than such events as giving birth, imprisonment, losing a job, or getting divorced.[67] In fact, the only events that they collectively cited as being more stressful than the flood were prolonged serious illness, a serious accident, or the death of a loved one. Many of those interviewed stated that the flood was the "worst" or "most horrible" experience that they personally had ever had. The anxiety and stress manifested themselves in a very wide range of symptoms, including physical ones such as headaches, dizziness, body pains, and nausea, as well as others such as difficulty sleeping, nightmares, and problems interacting socially with people.[68]

Certain specific circumstances seem to greatly intensify the levels of stress experienced by flood victims. One of the most significant of these factors is if the flood takes place at night.[69] The additional confusion and fear resulting from being woken up or having to flee in the dark appear to make the overall experience considerably more stressful. Other stress-enhancing factors include a lack of warning, suddenly rising waters, and coldness of the water.[70] Conversely, prior experience of a natural disaster seems to reduce significantly the amount of stress that is felt.[71] Thus, in flood-prone areas where it is likely that the inhabitants will live through several episodes of flooding during their lifetimes, there may be a cumulative stress-reducing effect. Familiarity with the effects of flooding and the knowledge that one has already survived a similar calamity seem to provide people with a certain degree of confidence when facing a current disaster. In ancient Rome, where it is not unlikely that one might have experienced multiple Tiber floods, this effect may have helped mitigate the psychological trauma inflicted on the populace by floods.

How prolonged or pervasive the aftereffects of a flood are remains a matter of controversy. One comprehensive analysis that reviewed 15 other studies concerning the link between disasters and health found a strong correlation between increased levels of stress and poorer health among those who had experienced a disaster.[72] The main debate over this issue does not center around whether there is some link between stress and poor health in disaster victims, but on the degree of severity and the length of post-traumatic effects.[73] At one end of the spectrum, some studies have found that as many as 71% of flood victims still reveal symptoms of post-traumatic stress three months after the flood, while others estimate that a much lower figure of 15–20% of the victims of a natural disaster suffer from symptoms of post-traumatic stress disorder.[74] Even if the actual figure lies toward the lower end of these estimates, this would still indicate that post-traumatic stress disorder is a major problem for a substantial number of people in the aftermath of a flood. Furthermore, it seems that the negative psychological effects that result from experiencing a flood do not dissipate quickly. Even after more than a year, the levels of stress among victims remained significantly elevated from their preflood levels.[75] The levels of stress in flood victims were comparable with those measured in people who had experienced other natural disasters, such as tornadoes and earthquakes, and did not seem to be related to demographic factors such as income, gender, and age.[76] There were some variables that did seem to predispose certain people to be more susceptible to higher stress. These included preexisting elevated levels of anxiety and poor health. Those who had physical or mental conditions before the flood often had these exacerbated by the event.[77]

One particularly acute type of trauma associated with floods is that stemming from loss of personal possessions and damage to people's homes. The destruction of objects imbued with deep personal significance can be devastating. Possessions and memorabilia serve many important purposes, such as linking people to their own histories, functioning as treasured reminders of events and people with happy or meaningful associations, and giving people a sense of connection to their ancestors. Commonly the loss of personal possessions is singled out by victims as the single worst long-term effect of a flood, and they continue to actively mourn for these irretrievable items long after the other traumas linked to the flood have lessened.[78] Some disaster victims have even stated that the loss of such objects was more grievous than the death of family members.[79]

Among victims of modern disasters in industrialized nations, often the specific objects whose loss is felt most acutely are photographs, especially those of family members who are already deceased.[80] The fervor of the emotions attached to these items is frequently very intense. The photographs have plainly become powerful symbols for the missing person, which, by preserving his or her image, helps to keep alive his or her memory. It would be interesting to determine whether, in societies lacking photographic technology, other objects are imbued with similarly powerful meanings and emotions, or if the intensity of feeling attached to photographs stems from their unique ability to record the exact image of a person. Perhaps one type of object of analogous importance in Roman society might have been the wax death masks, *imagines,* which preserved the visages of a family's ancestors. These masks were displayed together in the home and were at the center of many important familial rituals. The extreme Roman reverence for one's ancestors was manifested in the significance ascribed to these images and the vital role they played in ceremonies such as funerals.[81] The *lares* and *penates,* small figurines representing the gods of the family and household, could also have been items with enormous symbolic and emotional significance for Romans. The damage or destruction of any of these objects in a flood could well have been a traumatic event.

Most of the readily available studies of flood victims focus on floods in Western industrialized nations, but investigations of the reactions of poor people in less-developed nations might provide a better comparison with ancient Rome. The intensity of the feelings of loss that flood victims describe in regards to their possessions may partially reflect the fact that inhabitants of more-developed countries simply tend to own more stuff than poor people in less-developed countries. According to studies of flood experiences in developing countries, there does not seem to be as much focus on the emotional trauma resulting from the loss of possessions. The narratives of flood victims, such as those of inhabitants of shantytowns in Manila, address at length the severe economic hardships caused by losing their possessions and having to try to fix or replace them, but do not specify whether additional emotional trauma resulted from the loss of treasured items.[82]

An individual's sense of self-identity and place-identity is also often severely compromised by the destruction of his or her home. People typically invest their homes with powerful emotional associations. The home functions as a locus of nurturing and security, a setting for positive memories of family and friends, and serves as an emotional refuge from the outside world.[83] When this sanctuary is invaded and destroyed by a disaster such as a flood, it can undermine an individual's sense of self and leave him or her with a heightened feeling of insecurity and rootlessness. Even after their homes have been rebuilt—often to exactly the same specifications—many flood victims no longer feel the same sense of security or attachment that they previously enjoyed.

Finally, there can be a ripple effect of psychological disturbances among those who did not actually experience the disaster itself, but had to deal with its consequences. The most obvious way that this can happen is when a person is killed in the event, and his or her family members and close friends have to contend with the standard range of emotions associated with such a loss, including grief, denial, anger, and shock. Particularly if they themselves had been absent and did not experience the disaster, their grief might be compounded by feelings of guilt stemming from a belief that perhaps they might have been able to save the loved one if they had been present. Another factor that can add to survivors' emotional distress, and which is especially common in a disaster such as a flood, is that the bodies of the dead often are not recovered.[84] Victims of drowning in Rome might well have been swept off by the floodwaters and carried a considerable distance away. In such cases, friends and family would have had to endure a long period of uncertainty as to the fate of their loved ones.

Eventually they would have had to assume that the missing person was in fact dead, but without the finality of a body, they might have had difficulty accepting this. In these circumstances, flood victims can find themselves in a kind of suspended animation, unable to move on with their lives or commit to new activities and relationships. Another group of people highly prone to post-traumatic stress syndrome, while not actually being direct victims of a disaster, comprises those involved in the rescue and cleanup operations following the event. Witnessing the aftermath of a disaster, and especially dealing with injuries and corpses that are often severely mutilated, has been documented as frequently producing serious emotional distress and dysfunction among relief workers.[85]

Recovery and Reconstruction

Modern disaster researchers tend to organize their analyses of these events by dividing them into a number of distinct phases that extend both before and for some time subsequent to the actual calamity. This compartmentalization facilitates examining disasters as a process and makes possible comparisons of data from different disasters. While different researchers favor schemes with varying numbers of phases and labels, they usually employ a number of categories corresponding to the predisaster period during which warnings are issued and precautions taken, the time period of the disaster itself, the immediate aftermath, and the long-term efforts at recovery. The labels applied to these phases vary depending on whether the focal point of their interest is the actions taken during disasters or the emotional reactions of people caught up in them. Thus one typical scheme might have categories such as "Warning, Threat, Impact, Inventory, Rescue, Remedy, and Recovery" while another will emphasize stages such as "Fear, Heroism, Euphoria, Altruism, Honeymoon, and Disillusionment."[86]

The actions taken and responses felt during these phases can be summarized fairly quickly.[87] Many disasters occur without any advance warning, but in those that are preceded by an alert or warning signs, there is often a formal or informal Threat or Warning phase during which people are aware that dangerous conditions are present or that a disaster is imminent. The emotional response in this phase is usually apprehension, and there may be attempts to safeguard possessions or to escape to a safer zone. The Impact period spans the actual disaster, and it is within this period that death, injury, and destruction occur. Responses to this phase typically include fear and shock. The Rescue period is when the survivors' attention turns to ensuring their own safety and that of their loved ones as well as rescuing other victims and helping the injured. People frequently exhibit heroic behavior during these efforts, and immediately after the disaster, many experience feelings of euphoria stemming from the fact that they escaped injury or death. In the Remedy and Inventory period, the survivors energetically take stock of their losses, organize temporary shelter, and receive assistance and aid from external government or private sources. In this "honeymoon" period, there is often strong community bonding and altruistic behavior as people help one another and receive attention and aid from outside sources. The Recovery or Reconstruction period is usually the longest in duration and covers the slow process of rebuilding damaged structures, replacing lost possessions, and attempting to return to a normal existence. As the scope of the losses becomes apparent, the novelty of the situation wears off, and external attention and assistance taper away, people often experience feelings of disillusionment and depression during this phase.

Another more basic system of periodization has just four phases: the Emergency period, which encompasses the disaster itself and the time during which normal activities are suspended; the Restoration period, during which basic services are restored and normal activities resume; the Replacement and Reconstruction period, during which population, structures, and infrastructure are returned to their pre-disaster state or levels; and the Commemorative, Betterment, and Developmental Reconstruction, in which major projects improve the community or city, often including elements commemorating the previous disaster and steps to alleviate or prevent future ones.[88] The amounts of time required for each of these phases often exist in a kind of logarithmic relationship to one another. The Emergency period is usually over in a matter of hours or days, the Restoration period typically is measured in days or weeks, the Replacement and Reconstruction period lasts months or at most a year or two, and the final phase frequently spans multiple years.[89]

The response of the ancient Romans to Tiber floods follows roughly these four phases. The actions known to have been taken during the Emergency and Restoration periods that encompass the flood and its immediate aftermath have mostly been described earlier in this chapter. In these phases, the Romans were concerned with reaching safety, salvaging whatever they could of their possessions, and, once the waters began to subside, beginning the cleanup process. There is not much direct evidence for state intervention or assistance during these phases. Today, providing early warning of disasters is viewed as one of the main obligations of the government, but it is unlikely that any sort of early warning system existed in ancient Rome. Awareness of flood conditions was probably transmitted through direct observation or word of mouth.

The principal immediate requirements of disaster victims are usually food, water, shelter, and medical care. In regard to flooding, the evidence in ancient sources about state efforts to provide these necessities after an inundation is scanty. There was a well-established precedent at Rome of the government directly concerning itself with ensuring adequate food supplies for the city's inhabitants, and, as we have seen, magistrates and emperors actively took steps to provide food in the aftermath of flooding. The clearest examples of this were Pompey's efforts after the flood of 54 BC (Dio 39.63.3, 39.61.3), Augustus's relief measures following the flood of 22 BC (Dio 54.1.2–4), and the actions of Marcus Aurelius and Verus after the flood of AD 162 (SHA *M. Aur.* 8). It seems that the plan to distribute food by boat to prevent the starvation of those trapped by the flood of AD 371 must have been organized by government officials, but explicit evidence to support this conclusion is not given in Ammianus's account (29.6.17–18). The restoration of a clean water supply, which is typically one of the most vital duties of modern governments, would not have required much effort from Roman officials because the natural operation of the continual-flow system would have served to wash out the contaminants in the system. If aqueducts or pipelines were broken by the flood, then repairs would have been necessary. Imperial Rome possessed a well-developed bureaucracy to oversee the water system, and such repairs would have fallen within the normal duties of the *curatores aquarum* and their staff.

Various government agencies and officials probably would have been involved in postdisaster rescue, cleanup, and aid operations simply as an extension of their normal duties.[90] By the early Empire, the professional, full-time officials, slaves, and employees whose duties were related to maintaining the water supply numbered at least 700. Added to these were the several thousand members of the *vigiles,* the state-organized night watch and fire-fighting brigade. While their primary responsibility was combating conflagrations, they would have constituted a natural source of skilled manpower to assist in emergency activities during a disaster. Various other city officials, such as the *prefectus annonae* (prefect of the grain supply), the *curatores operum publicorum* (supervisors of public works), the *curatores riparum et alvei Tiberis* (supervisors of the Tiber and its banks), and, especially, the urban aedile would all have been directly concerned with dealing with and alleviating the effects of a flood. Each of these officials had his own staff and gangs of slaves and underlings who had professional expertise that would have been valuable in the aftermath of a flood and who could have been dispatched to assist survivors and restore services. The Praetorian Guard posted on the outskirts of Rome from the time of Tiberius onward could also have been summoned in an emergency, at least in the capacity of maintaining order in the disaster zone. Finally, the considerable personal resources of the emperor could have been brought to bear on a disaster. Calamities such as floods and fires represented not just problems for a ruler but also opportunities for him to display his munificence and enhance his reputation through ostentatious shows of benefaction. It seems probable that the state could have mustered considerable resources to combat the effects of a disaster such as a flood. In and around the city of Rome, more than 10,000 trained government employees (at a minimum) were present who could have been mobilized in the immediate aftermath of a disaster. It must be admitted that explicit descriptions of these workers being deployed on disaster relief missions after floods are not extant, but such actions seem to fall well within the established duties of all of these groups.

Although detailed information about state responses to floods is limited, more comprehensive accounts can be found in respect to another category of natural disaster often encountered in ancient Rome: fires.[91] During the Empire, Rome's rulers seem to have routinely taken a very active role in providing aid to victims of fires. The original formation of the *vigiles* by Augustus in AD 6 suggests that they may have been organized to provide general aid to the public during disasters. Dio (55.26.4–5) states that Augustus "organized a company of freedmen in seven divisions to render assistance on such occasions and appointed an *equites* in command over them, expecting to disband them in a short time. He did not do so, however, for he found by experience that the aid they gave was most valuable and necessary." The sorts of aid that were supplied following disaster may be suggested by the actions taken after the horrific collapse in AD 27 of a temporary amphitheater a few kilometers from Rome that resulted in thousands of deaths and injuries. Within a day of this accident, houses of the wealthy were opened to the victims, doctors made available to the wounded, and in general there was supposedly an outpouring of assistance to the victims (Tac. *Ann.* 4.63).

The most ostentatious way in which emperors aided disaster victims was through direct distributions of money to the victims. For example, after a fire devastated the entire Caelian Hill, the often stingy Tiberius received public acclamation for giving money to the victims in order to compensate them for their losses (Tac. *Ann.* 4.64). Toward the end of his reign, in AD 36, when a fire ravaged the area of the Circus and the Aventine, Tiberius again provided financial aid by giving full replacement costs to the owners of all the private homes and *insulae* lost to the fire. He supposedly expended 100 million sesterces on this munificence and, as Tacitus (*Ann.* 6.45) notes, by doing so he "converted the disaster into his own glory." Future emperors followed this model, as when Caligula distributed money after a fire in AD 38 (Dio 59.9.5). The emperor's largess was not confined to survivors of disaster in Rome but sometimes also extended to other cities, as when the colony of Bononia received 10 million sesterces after a fire in AD 53 (Tac. *Ann.* 12.58).

The greatest disaster in the city of Rome's history and the one that receives the most detailed coverage in the sources is the Great Fire of AD 64, which blazed for a week and consumed most of the city (Tac. *Ann.* 15.38–46). The official actions taken in response to this catastrophe addressed the vital requirements of the survivors. Because so many buildings had been burned down, shelter was an urgent need, so Nero opened the Campus Martius, the public works of Agrippa, and his own gardens to the populace in order to provide temporary lodging. With normal city life disrupted, food was also a concern, so supplies were brought upriver from the warehouses of Ostia, and the price of grain was fixed at three sesterces per modius. The steps taken by the administration during the Emergency and Restoration periods of these disasters were quite similar to those typically initiated in disasters today, in which the most urgent concerns are food, shelter, and medical assistance. The account of the Great Fire also continues with details of the actions taken during the subsequent Replacement and Restoration phases. Nero famously took advantage of the space cleared by the fire to construct his Golden House, but in rebuilding the rest of the city, he had the streets broadened and straightened and enacted a number of measures in order to make the new buildings more resistant to fire (Tac. *Ann.* 15.43).

These steps aimed at preventing or minimizing future disasters carry the story of the Great Fire into the final phase of actions following a disaster, the Commemorative, Betterment, and Developmental Reconstruction period. This phase is characterized by efforts to improve the city and to make it less susceptible to recurrences of the disaster. In regard to floods, the Romans did attempt a number of different strategies to protect the city from inundations of the Tiber. These efforts, which were pursued with varying degrees of determination and success, are the subject of the next chapter.

Five

Methods of Flood Control

Floods can be prevented or mitigated by a wide variety of methods. Historically, the emphasis has been on structural flood control involving works of engineering such as levees and dams, but more recently it has been realized that modifications in land use and vegetation cover can have equally significant effects on controlling flood hazards.[1] The four main categories of structural flood control are levees, floodways, channel improvement and stabilization, and reservoirs.[2]

Levees include a range of embankments, walls, and mounds, whose purpose is to provide a physical barrier to high water levels and to channel floodwaters between the levees. Earthen levees or concrete flood walls are perhaps the most common antiflood structures and are effective in protecting specific areas, such as a city, so long as the bank is not overtopped by the flood. Their disadvantages are that they restrict access to the stream, they trap water if the wall is overtopped, they are unsightly, and they do not address any of the underlying causes of flooding. Floodways or spillways are special channels employed during times of high channel discharge to divert some of the volume of flow and thus decrease the water level in the main channel. Channel improvement and stabilization covers various modifications to the main streambed, such as dredging, removal of debris and obstacles, alterations in channel shape and path, and improvements to the banks. Clearing out debris and obstacles allows the water to flow more smoothly and increases the stream capacity. Stabilizing the channel through the construction of works such as revetments prevents erosion, protects against bank slippage at times of high discharge, and guards against severe scouring or undercutting of the bank during floods. Alterations to the actual course of the channel are usually undertaken in order to create a more direct path for the water. When there is a bend in a river, a cutoff may be formed across the base of the bend, which usually has the effect of increasing the velocity of the flow, enabling a greater volume of water to be discharged while maintaining the same water depth. Increasing the depth and width of a channel also allows greater volumes of water to be carried without flooding the surrounding areas. Reservoirs are most commonly created by dams, serve to store high discharge levels during flood stage, and then gradually release this water at safe discharge levels over a longer period of time. Reservoirs can also reduce sediment in the main channel. The ancient Romans employed a number of these strategies with varying degrees of success and, at different points in time, entertained plans to enact yet others.

Drain: The Roman Sewers

Before the Romans could even begin to consider methods for dealing with occasional high Tiber levels, they had to confront the hydrological problems posed by the site of Rome itself. In early Rome, while hills such as the Capitoline and Palatine provided useful sanctuaries and dwelling sites, the intervening valleys were very low-lying and swampy. A combination of factors would have contributed to the watery nature of these depressions. Rainfall would have run off the steep surrounding hills and pooled in the valleys between them, numerous springs lay within these areas, the water table was not far below the surface, and Tiber inundations would have reached these sites easily and might have been slow to drain. Just how wet these regions were during Rome's early history, however, is difficult to determine. It seems certain that several streams ran through these valleys toward the Tiber, such as along the Vallis Murcia where the Circus Maximus would eventually stand, and that there were probably some areas that were originally lakes or fens, such as the Palus Caprae in the center of the Campus Martius.

Roman literature gives the impression that much of these low-lying regions was perpetually covered with swamps or open water. Varro (*Ling.* 5.43–44) describes the areas around the Aventine Hill as being nearly entirely submerged beneath swampy pools and streams, necessitating that these regions be traversed by boats, and he claims that there was an established ferry that plied between the Aventine and the Roman Forum and Palatine, crossing through the Velabrum. The Velabrum, the valley lying between the Capitoline and Palatine and running from the Roman Forum to the Tiber, is consistently portrayed in literature as being fenlike. Propertius (4.9.5) refers to it as being the site of a stagnant body of water through which boats traveled. In Ovid's *Fasti* (6.395–417), a character delivers a lengthy monologue on the original swampy nature of the center of Rome, in which it is stated that the Velabrum was overgrown with willows and reeds, the fora were covered in swamps, the Lacus Curtius was an actual lake, and the whole region was so marshy as to be impassable by foot. Plutarch (*Rom.* 5.5), too, mentions the ferry running through the Velabrum and emphasizes the swampy nature of this region.

All of these references create a somewhat extreme image of the original site of Rome as an uninviting and, indeed, nearly uninhabitable morass. If the site was so waterlogged, it is difficult to imagine how significant numbers of people lived and built structures in such an environment. While the consistency of the portraits of Rome's swampiness offered by ancient authors suggests that these must have possessed at least a fair measure of accuracy, it should be noted that all of the authors were writing at least several hundred years after the period being described. In addition, a way to reconcile the image of Rome as a swamp and the fact that it was becoming an urban center is to factor in the very pronounced seasonal regime of Rome's rainfall and of the inundations of the Tiber.[3] What the sources are describing is probably not the year-round condition of these sites, but rather their nature during the rainy winter season or in the aftermath of a flood. Plutarch (*Rom.* 5.5) specifically states that the ferry service was put into action "when the river overflowed." Such inundations would proba-

Methods of Flood Control

bly have been quite common during the rainy season, and, coupled with the usual winter rains, might well have ensured that the low-lying areas of the city did indeed remain damp or even submerged for prolonged periods during the several months of the rainy season. These same areas, however, would also probably have dried out by the late spring and certainly during the hot, dry summer months. Recent investigations of the Velabrum, which involved taking cores that bored from the modern street level of around 20 masl down to the original pre-Roman level of around 5–7 masl, support just such a seasonal alternation between wet and dry conditions.[4] These cores also show evidence of sediment deposits from frequent Tiber flooding up to a level of 10 masl, but they do not yield the sorts of soil and residues that would be found in a true year-round, permanent swamp.[5] Thus the ferry described by Varro and others would have operated during the damp season, but for long stretches of the year, these parts of the city would have been reasonably dry land and available for use.

Despite the seasonal nature of the wetlands in the valleys between Rome's hills, there would have been an understandable reluctance to build structures on land that was so liable to becoming sodden. Areas such as the Velabrum, Forum Boarium, and Roman Forum were natural sites for commerce and trade because of their location at important intersections but, at this point in history, were so low-lying that they would have suffered multiple floods on an annual basis. Buildings constructed out of the types of materials used during this period, such as timber, mud brick, and wattle and daub, would have been particularly susceptible to damage or destruction by water. Thus the entire future development of the city of Rome hinged on rendering these key areas at least somewhat drier on a year-round basis. This requirement led to the first great public works project in Roman history, the construction of the first version of what, even in the city's most developed form, would continue to be viewed as one of its greatest marvels—the Roman sewers.

Strictly speaking, the Roman sewers were not sewers at all, since they were not intended to carry away waste, but were instead drains whose function was to draw off accumulated water and to channel excess water from springs and rainfall into the Tiber. Over time, these conduits would take on a dual purpose as both channels for carrying off water and as receptacles for sewage, but drainage always remained their primary role. Modern cities tend to split sewage systems and drainage networks, but for much of history these functions have been combined, and even today, many cities retain dual-purpose sewers.

The earliest drain, which would evolve into the Cloaca Maxima, seems to have followed the natural meandering course of the stream that ran through the Roman Forum, between the Palatine and Capitoline, and then emptied into the Tiber.[6] Originally, this work probably took the form of an open canal with subsidiary channels bringing water to the main one. Pliny (*HN* 36.105) records that the Cloaca Maxima collected together the water from seven tributaries. Although later authors conflated the stages of its construction and ascribed a fully covered underground drain to its first incarnation, the fact that as late as the third century BC there are still allusions to open portions of the drain in the Forum area (Plaut. *Curc.* 476) demonstrates a more realistic and gradual development in which the open culverts were slowly covered over as the area became more urbanized. The intent of this first drainage project is clearly stated by Livy (1.38.6): "to drain the lowest parts of the city about the Forum, and the other valleys between the hills which were too flat to carry off the floodwaters easily." It is interesting that the problem identified by Livy in this passage is not that the area was inherently too swampy for use, but rather that it was too slow to drain after flooding.

The construction of the Cloaca Maxima, attributed to Tarquinius Priscus by Pliny (*HN* 104–108) and to Tarquinius Superbus by Livy (1.38.6, 1.56.2), was a difficult and lengthy task utilizing the labor of the urban plebs. It may be that the project was an ongoing one, with additional culverts being added and connected to existing ones, so that substantial works were completed during both king's reigns. According to legend, the excavation was so arduous that some of the conscripted workers committed suicide rather than continue the labor, prompting cruel compulsory tactics by the king. The extant system reflects later rebuildings, most notably that of Agrippa's aedileship in 33 BC, when he renovated the entire drainage system, even traveling through the sewers by boat for a personal inspection (Dio 49.43.10; Pliny *HN* 36.104). In its final form, the Cloaca Maxima runs for 1,600 m and drains the entire region lying between the Quirinal and Es-

Methods of Flood Control

Fig. 5.1. The outlet of the Cloaca Maxima where it empties into the Tiber. (Photo by author)

quiline hills. The irregularity of its course, with many jogs, turns, and circumventing of various structures, is indicated by the fact that a straight line drawn from its beginning to where it joins the Tiber covers only 900 m. The size of the conduits varies in different sections, but all are impressive in scale, some in excess of 4 m in height and 3 m in width. Pliny's assertion (*HN* 36.108) that it was possible to drive a fully loaded wagon through the sewers may be an exaggeration, but not much of one. The standard of workmanship of these drains is high, with the extant version having Gabine stone walls and a brick and concrete vault. The Cloaca Maxima ultimately empties into the Tiber through an orifice measuring 4.5 m wide and 3.3 m high still visible today in the Tiber embankment, situated at an altitude of 4.7 masl (figs. 5.1, 5.2).

The Cloaca Maxima and its tributaries were ultimately supplemented by additional sewers. One of the most important of these ran along the floor of the valley of the Circus Maximus.[7] Originally there seems to have been a natural stream flowing through this valley that drained the surrounding hills. This drain emptied into the Tiber a

Floods of the Tiber in Ancient Rome

Fig. 5.2. Bust of Marcus Vipsanius Agrippa. He played a key role in the development of Rome's water system, including renovating and constructing sewers, fountains, and aqueducts. (Photo by author)

short distance downstream from the outlet of the Cloaca Maxima. Remains of this sewer have been identified near its outlet, but although it is routinely depicted running beneath the Circus Maximus, firm archaeological evidence for its exact course has yet to be found. Some have reconstructed its course extending inland along the route of the Via Appia and even branching into the depression between the Palatine and Aventine, and it seems reasonable that the Romans would have extended their drainage network to service these areas as the city expanded.[8]

Another significant drainage conduit that began as a natural stream and was eventually monumentalized in stone and covered over served to drain the central and southern Campus Martius. This stream, known as the Petronia Amnis, constituted a ritual boundary and seems to have originated with one or more springs on the slopes of the Quirinal.[9] Its course meandered through some of the low-lying areas of the Campus Martius and it emptied into the Tiber just north of the Pons Fabricius across from Tiber Island. The construction of more modern drains and sewers from the Renaissance onward has obscured much of the earlier Roman network, but the existence of a number of other Roman drains has been inferred from the courses of the later drains coupled with occasional archaeological traces. These may have included a drain below the Aventine in the Emporium district, others in the northern and southern Campus Martius, and eventually perhaps even several on the right bank of the Tiber serving the modern regions of Trastevere and the Vatican (fig. 5.3).[10]

A number of ancient writers recorded their admiration for this system. Pliny (*HN* 36.104–8) identifies the sewers as the most noteworthy aspect of the city and marvels at both their extensiveness, because they constitute a subterranean world beneath the city, and the sturdiness of their construction, which is able to resist earthquakes, building collapses, the pounding of heavy traffic overhead, and the violent force of the waters themselves. Dionysius of Halicarnassus (*Rom. Ant.* 3.67.5) similarly ranks the sewers alongside the roads and aqueducts as the greatest wonders of Rome. Even in the sixth century AD, the sewers continued to be cited as one of Rome's greatest accomplishments by Cassiodorus (*Var.* 3.30.1–2), who described them as mighty enclosed rivers and posed the challenge, "What other city can compare with Rome in her heights, when her depths are so incomparable?"

Despite all the praise lavished on the Roman sewers, note should be made of their limitations as well. First of all, they combined the functions of drains and sewers so that excrement and waste were mingled with excess water. Because of the need for frequent openings in the streets in order to provide drainage, this dual purpose design meant that Rome's inhabitants were exposed to the fumes emanating

Floods of the Tiber in Ancient Rome

Fig. 5.3. Map showing some major Roman drains.

from the sewers. The mixture was then emptied directly into the Tiber, fouling the river's waters within the city. These features have often been criticized,[11] but this system was much preferable to the alternative, which would have been the absence of any real provision for removing waste and excrement.

The Roman sewers would have contained a constant flow of water from the springs and natural rivulets that they originally encased, but eventually a potentially more significant flow would have resulted from carrying away the enormous amounts of water that were brought to the city by the aqueduct system. Although the flow would have varied seasonally and there are a number of difficulties in calculating estimates of volume, Rome's aqueducts had the potential to supply around 1million m^3 of water per day to the city. In addition to water that was directly routed into the sewers from, for example, the baths, the constant overflow from the hundreds of fountains and basins dotted throughout the city, which received water from the aqueduct system, might have poured onto the streets, and from there found its way into the sewers. This mechanism would have served to provide at least some degree of cleansing of the accumulated debris and excrement dropped or poured onto Rome's roadways. The continual-flow nature of Rome's water system was an important factor in cleaning the city because it would have helped to prevent the buildup of waste in the drains.[12]

A more significant drawback of the system than the mingling of waste and water was the lack of any means to prevent water from backing up through the system when the Tiber flooded. The Roman drains were not equipped with valves or other mechanisms to thwart such an occurrence, and it is clear that when the Tiber rose, flow in the system reversed direction and the drains became a path through which water flooded the city.[13] With the mouth of the Cloaca Maxima situated at a relatively low height of 4.7 masl, even modest rises in the river level would have caused water to begin creeping up the system, and in a full-fledged flood with water levels at 10 or 12 masl, the sewers would have been transformed into conduits carrying the floodwaters up into the heart of the city. Pliny (*HN* 36.105) referred to such events in the course of his description of the sewers and described the underground struggle between the rising floodwater forcing its way up the system colliding against the normal drainage flow toward the Tiber. This was a battle that the floodwaters would have won, and it must have been a disconcerting experience for the Romans to find water bursting up out of the sewers and inundating the city. Not least among the negative effects of this backflow is that along with the water, all the waste, excrement, and vermin that had been down in the sewers would have been regurgitated up into the streets and dwellings of the city, posing serious health hazards.

Discussions of the Roman sewers tend to fixate on their function in carrying away waste, but they did play a vital role in regards to flooding. While the drains would have done nothing to prevent flooding and in fact might have exacerbated the problem by allowing floodwaters to travel backward up the system, they would have been essential in helping the city recover from inundation quickly. An underappreciated purpose of the drains was to remove floodwater from the city and direct it through established channels back into the Tiber once the river's level had fallen back to normal. The sewers would have been especially important to this drying-out process in regions of the city where large standing pools of water would otherwise have been trapped by the topography and prevented from flowing directly back to the river. The topography of Rome, with its many hills, creates a number of bowl-like depressions where low ground is surrounded by slightly higher regions. While a large flood would have covered wide areas, when the water receded, lakes could have been trapped in such depressions with no natural outlet. Parts of the central Campus Martius, the depression where the Flavian Amphitheater would be constructed, points along the Vallis Murcia, and, perhaps most important of all, the Roman Forum itself might have been left under sizable pools of water, if no means were available to give the water an outlet. The drainage system, however, provided just such outlets for water in exactly these areas. Thus, vital portions of the city that might otherwise have remained submerged for days or even weeks would have been drained of their floodwater in a matter of hours or, at most, a day or two. The large cross sections of many of the conduits forming the sewer system were far greater than necessary to carry away any amount of waste, or even the normal flow of water, from the aqueducts, but in the aftermath of a flood, this large potential carrying capacity would have greatly aided in rapidly draining away the unwanted waters.

The Roman sewers were a noteworthy achievement of engineering whose primary purposes were closely linked to the Tiber and the hydrology of the site of Rome. By providing drainage for the natural watercourses of the area, they made possible the year-round habitation of the vital low-lying regions that developed into many of the commercial and political centers of the city. They also played at least some role in improving the hygiene of the city and removing waste matter. Finally, although many have commented negatively on the manner in which the sewers offered access to floodwater, it should not be overlooked that floodwaters would have flowed in both directions through these pipes, and that in the aftermath of a flood, they would

Methods of Flood Control

have played an essential part in removing water and quickly restoring the city to a more normal, less aquatic state.

Fill: Attempts to Raise Ground Level

Another way to render an area less prone to flooding is to raise the actual ground level so as to make a region immune to (at least minor) floods. As described in chapter 1, such an increase in ground levels often happens naturally over long stretches of time in regions that are densely populated, as debris piles up and layers of settlement are superimposed on top of previous ones. This effect is dramatically illustrated at Rome, where nearly all the flat areas of the central city are coated by an artificial layer more than 5 m in depth consisting of accumulated fill and rubble. In addition to this unplanned process of steady accretion, a second way that the ground levels in parts of Rome were elevated was through deliberate efforts to fill in low-lying areas so as to make them drier and less flood-prone. If carried out over a large expanse, this strategy requires enormous quantities of fill, but it is clear that on a number of occasions, the Romans adopted precisely such a policy.

Perhaps the earliest deliberate attempt to elevate the ground level of a region as a flood control measure took place in the Roman Forum itself. The natural land surface elevation in the center of the Forum basin was around 6–7 masl. This level was quite low, roughly the same as that found in the Vallis Murcia on the other side of the Palatine Hill, and both areas were highly flood-prone. In the Forum, the ground level seems to have risen rapidly to around 9 masl, and immediately following this, the first gravel paving of the Forum was laid down. Ammerman has proposed that this rapid rise was due to a deliberate effort to raise the level of the Forum basin that took place at the end of the seventh century BC or perhaps at the beginning of the sixth century BC.[14] Such a project would have entailed the movement of a huge quantity of fill, with minimum estimates on the order of 10,000 m^3 of material. Ammerman's argument—that this fill was undertaken in conjunction with the construction of the Cloaca Maxima drainage system, and that together these works were necessary in order to render the central Forum area more habitable and safe from regular annual inundation—seems compelling. These efforts would not have protected this area from major floods that might have occurred every few years, but they might well have put an end to the annual transformation of the area into a marshy region every rainy season.

Not only are there considerable differences between the ground levels in antiquity compared with those of the present; even within the Roman period, there were significant changes. The history of the Forum offers a good example of the process of gradual buildup, with as many as eight successive layers of Roman era paving being laid down on top of one another.[15] After the gravel paving at around 9 masl, the first areas of stone paving are found at 10.6 to 10.9 masl. A subsequent comprehensive repaving thought to date to 179 BC raised the Forum floor to 11.8 to 11.9 masl. Later Sullan and Augustan repavings further elevated the level of the central Forum surface to 12.6 and 12.6–14 masl respectively (fig. 5.4).

How rapidly levels could increase is illustrated by the successive versions of the Pantheon in the Campus Martius. The remains of Agrippa's structure have been detected about 2.5 m beneath the Hadrianic version built only about a century later. Visitors to the Pantheon today who walk around to the rear of the building can readily see how Hadrian's building lies considerably below the modern street level.[16] Similarly, the superimposition of temples in the Largo Argentina and the successive layers of paving around them testify to steadily rising ground levels from the Republic to the Empire. Today, the remains of these temples also lie at the bottom of a pit more than 4 m below the busy surrounding streets, which are now at an elevation of around 18 masl.

A series of major fill projects, some of which seem to have been undertaken expressly for the purpose of raising ground levels as a protection against flooding, took place in the northern Campus Martius. This area just south of the Mausoleum of Augustus would have been particularly flood-prone, not only because of its low elevation, but also because this is where the Tiber takes a sharp turn to the right, forming the beginning of the bend that encloses the Campus Martius. In times of raging floods, when the Tiber level had risen above its banks, the water would naturally have had a tendency to proceed straight at this point, pouring into the Campus Martius from the north. Augus-

Fig. 5.4. Aerial view of the eastern end of the Roman Forum with the remains of the Temple of the Deified Julius Caesar and the Regia during the flood of December 1900. This flood reached a height of over 16 masl, which, as can be seen in this photo, was sufficient to cover all the paved areas in the center of the Forum. (Fototeca Unione, American Academy in Rome, 3219F)

tus dramatically transformed this region with the construction of his mausoleum, the Horologium, the Ara Pacis, and associated structures. Over the next century, the ground levels in this region were raised substantially by a succession of projects that seem to have occurred in three stages.

Central to interpreting the history of this area are two superimposed *pomerium cippi* of Vespasianic and Hadrianic date respectively. The Hadrianic one was found 4.15 m below current ground level and the Vespasianic one 2.95 m deeper than this.[17] At the nearby Ara Pacis, there is also evidence of a 2.35 m difference between the Hadrianic and Vespasianic levels. This very dramatic increase in ground level over a relatively short period is most likely evidence for a Hadrianic project to raise the ground level in this region. He seems to have constructed a long dike cutting east-west across the northern Campus Martius, substantially raising the ground levels with fill. Vespasian's earlier reworking of the *pomerium* may have elevated certain areas above the Augustan levels, and Domitian certainly rebuilt at least parts of the Augustan Horologium and raised levels in some areas by 1.6 m. The Hadrianic fill superseded these projects and uniformly raised the levels all across the northern Campus Martius. These works would have had the effect of erecting a greater barrier to floodwaters pouring into the Campus Martius at the bend of the Tiber and, given the increasing urbanization of this region, seem a logical expedient to render the area safer from inundation.

An alternate flood-proofing strategy to the labor-intensive approach of raising the ground levels over an entire area was to place important buildings atop raised podia. One of the typical differences between Roman and Greek temple architecture is the Roman predilection for positioning their temples atop high podia, which is thought to derive from Etruscan precedents. While there may be traditional or aesthetic reasons for such a design, it is nevertheless notable that a large number of the early temples that were constructed at Rome near the Tiber or in highly flood-prone areas were equipped with particularly high podia that elevated the temples above the level of all but the most severe floods. For example, the republican temples of Portunus, Vesta, and the three that are now incorporated into St. Nicola in Carcere (the temples of Janus, Spes, and Juno) were all situated near the Tiber on sites that would have been very vulnerable to floods. All five of these temples, however, were perched atop very high podia that raised the level of the temples themselves to a fairly secure elevation of around 15 masl.[18]

Whether or not the platforms of these temples were intentionally constructed this high primarily to protect them from floods is impossible to prove conclusively. The high podia would certainly have given them an impressive appearance, and while this may have been the main inspiration for their design, it seems hard to believe that the builders would have been completely unaware of the beneficial side effect that such podia would have had in helping to protect these sacred buildings from destruction and damage due to flooding. This is particularly the case due to their locations so near the bank of the Tiber.[19]

Divert: Canals and Channel Modification Schemes

Another category of flood control involves changing the volume or path of water through a river system. Through engineering works, people can attempt to decrease the amount of water flowing through a channel, alter the course of the channel, or otherwise modify the flow of water. Common ways of accomplishing these goals include constructing artificial canals to completely deflect the course of a river away from valuable or vulnerable areas, diverting a part of the flow so as to make flooding less likely, or making physical alterations in the path, dimensions, or characteristics of the main channel. There is evidence, often sketchy in nature, that the Romans contemplated a number of these strategies at various points, although only a few of these schemes were ever carried out.

In the brief span of years between his victory in the civil wars and his assassination, Julius Caesar instituted a number of dramatic reforms and building projects and had plans for many more. Both Suetonius (*Caes.* 44) and Plutarch (*Caes.* 58) record a long list of ambitious endeavors that Caesar was said to have been contemplating. A number of these were bold hydrological schemes, including draining the Pomptine marshes, draining the Fucine Lake, cutting a canal across the Corinthian isthmus, and constructing safe harbor facilities at Ostia. In addition, two other hydrological proposals were mentioned, both of which involved diverting the course of the Tiber through artificially dug channels.

One of these was a fantastic scheme to divert the Tiber just below the city and excavate a canal running parallel to the coast, which would have emptied into the sea just past the Circeian promontory near Tarracina. The reason given for this plan was to provide a safe passage for merchant ships bringing supplies to the city (Plut. *Caes.* 58). At this time, the harbor at Ostia was not a safe anchorage for ships, and many were unloaded in the superior port facilities of Puteoli. Also, the river between Ostia and Rome was only navigable by smaller ships, necessitating the transferal of cargo from large merchantmen into river barges. Thus there was a need for a more secure and navigable waterway to Rome. This pathway would have run through the Pomptine marshes and so presumably might have been able to save on labor by incorporating or deepening existing waterways. It could also have served the subsidiary purpose of providing drainage to these areas and reclaiming some of the land for agriculture. Despite these potential benefits, this grandiose scheme seems more fanciful than realistic; it would have involved carving out a waterway more than 60 km in length through very difficult terrain, and it is therefore hard to believe that this plan ever amounted to more than idle speculation.

The diversion of the Tiber to Tarracina would have done little to alleviate flooding at Rome, but Caesar's second Tiber proposal was directly aimed at securing the city from inundation. This plan is known primarily through a description given by Cicero in a letter to Atticus dated to July of 45 BC (*Att.* 13.33.4).[20] In this proposed scheme, the Tiber would have been diverted just north of Rome near the Mulvian Bridge and redirected through an artificial channel around the high ground of the Vatican hills, presumably rejoining the original riverbed south of the city.[21] According to Cicero, the Campus Martius would then be incorporated as a built-up part of the city, and the Vatican Plain would have become the new "Campus Martius," taking over the functions traditionally held in its open expanses. This proposal would have had a number of benefits. First, it would (in theory) have made the city completely safe from flooding by the radical solution of completely removing the source of flooding. With this plan, Caesar also seems to have acknowledged the need for expansion room for the growing city and to have realized that it was inevitable that the open expanse of the Campus Martius would be a logical site for urbanization. The greatest drawback of this space, however, was its highly flood-prone nature, and so this plan would have simultaneously gained room for expansion and rendered the area safe from inundation.

The sketchy description of this plan makes it hard to evaluate, and there are a number of significant uncertainties. Because there would still have been a need for urban drainage to carry away rainwater, spring water, and water from the aqueduct system, presumably these waters would have continued to empty into the old channel of the Tiber, which would then have rejoined the main course of the river downstream, but this is not specified. Also, some water would probably have been allowed to continue flowing from the north through the old channel of the Tiber in order to provide sufficient water to carry away the city's waste. Most problematic is the actual course of the proposed canal. It seems that the most likely path would have been if it ran in front of the Vatican hills following a fairly straight north-south course and cutting off the left-hand meander of the river below the Mulvian Bridge as well as the two sharper bends enclosing the Campus Martius and the Transtiberim. If a more radical deviation that went around the back of the Vatican hills was envisioned, it seems difficult to reconcile this topographically with the high range of hills that would have had to be traversed, particularly if the canal were to begin near the Mulvian Bridge, as Cicero reports.

A canal across the front (east side) of the Vatican hills would have given the water a straighter path than the original channel, and because the water would have been falling the same altitude but over a shorter distance, the slope of the riverbed would have been slightly increased. This would in turn have had the effect of causing the water to flow faster, enabling a somewhat greater volume of water to pass at an equivalent water level (if we assume that the new canal was the same as the old Tiber in terms of area of cross section). Even if it were possible to construct this canal, its utility as a flood preventative in times of high water is at least somewhat questionable. It seems dangerously likely that water would have overtopped the new canal and still spread out toward the city over the old flood plain. Much would have depended on the capacity of the canal and the height of its embankments.[22]

Some later canals were constructed whose purpose was ostensibly to alleviate flooding.[23] An Ostian inscription of AD 46 records that, as part of his work creating a new harbor for Rome, Claudius had constructed a canal that supposedly had the additional effect of making the city of Rome safe from inundation (*CIL* 14.85).[24] It is thought that this inscription refers to the canal or canals that were dug to connect Claudius's new harbor with the Tiber.[25] How such a canal situated near the mouth of the river was supposed to protect Rome—which was located considerably upstream—is not clear, but plainly Claudius believed this would be the case. Le Gall has proposed an explanation for this curious Roman belief that constructing canals at the Tiber's outlet would alleviate upstream flooding.[26] He suggests that the Romans thought that the tidal water coming in from the sea could force back the river's water, resulting in the system "backing up" and causing upstream flooding. They also seem to have imagined that the wind might similarly play a significant role in pushing water against the current of the river, causing it to pile up further upstream. While today we understand that this would not have been hydrologically possible, perhaps the Roman belief is understandable given their experience with the sewers of Rome, where the normal direction of flow did indeed on occasion get reversed and move in the opposite direction, with flooding as the result.

The idea that providing canals near the river mouth would alleviate flooding upstream seems to have inspired a later emperor to undertake a similar project. While describing a flood during the reign of Trajan, Pliny (*Epist.* 8.17.2) notes that this inundation had occurred despite the efforts of the emperor, who had built a canal in order to drain the river and prevent such events. This canal of Trajan is also the subject of an inscription that, like Claudius's, claimed that it would protect the city from the threat of Tiber floods (*CIL* 14.88).[27] Trajan built a new harbor for Rome, in the course of which some of his projects were superimposed over parts of the earlier Claudian ones. There is debate concerning whether the Trajanic canal referred to in this inscription mentioned by Pliny constituted a refurbishing of Claudius's canal or was an entirely different one associated with the construction of his new harbor. From the perspective of flood prevention, the solution to this debate is not relevant. Whether it was a reworking of Claudius's canal or, like his, was a new canal also dug near the mouth of the Tiber, it would either way have had no effect in preventing or mitigating flooding at Rome. If, on the other hand, Trajan's canal was dug upstream from Rome, then it might have had some effect on flooding, but no discernible traces of such a canal have been identified. Additionally, because the inscription commemorating Trajan's canal was found in proximity to other Ostian inscriptions, it seems much more likely that this canal was either a restoration of Claudius's or a new one in the same vicinity. In either case, what these accounts make clear is that floods continued to pose a serious threat, provoking concern and direct intervention from the emperor. Unfortunately, the location chosen for these works rendered these responses ineffectual.

Another category of proposal involving the diversion of water in order to alleviate flooding at Rome centered around reducing the discharge of the Tiber by lessening the amount of water that the Tiber's tributaries poured into it. Diverting water from tributaries or alternatively damming some of these streams would have been ways to achieve better control over the discharge of the Tiber at Rome. The flood of AD 15 seems to have spurred the Romans to take action in order to reduce flooding. According to Dio (57.14.7–8), after this flood, Tiberius set up a commission of five senators who were charged with ensuring the even flow of the Tiber and preventing both flooding and drought. Tacitus (*Ann.* 1.76) does not mention the five-man commission, instead saying that Tiberius gave the task of regulating the river to Ateius Capito and Lucius Arruntius. Ateius and Arruntius seem to have taken their charge seriously and soon brought before the senate an ambitious plan. They hoped to lessen the chance of flooding at Rome through a series of engineering projects along the Tiber's tributaries intended collectively to reduce the amount of water being discharged through the river (Tac. *Ann.* 1.79). It is not known how many projects were proposed by Ateius and Arruntius, but three can be reconstructed from Tacitus's comments. They proposed that the flow of the Clanis (Chiani) River should be diverted from the Tiber and redirected into the Arnus (Arno), that the Nar (Nera) River should somehow be split and its waters dispersed, and that the outflow from the

Veline lakes, which had been emptied into the Nar through an artificial spillway, should be dammed up and prevented from doing so.

The redirection of water from the valley of Lake Trasumennus (Trasimeno) toward the Arnus rather than the Tiber might have been feasible, because both river systems have tributaries originating in this valley. Whether such a diversion would have resulted in an appreciable reduction in the Tiber's volume is another question, and one that cannot be definitively answered without much more detailed knowledge of the hydrology of these rivers and the region in which they originated during the period in question. As best as can be estimated, however, it does not seem too likely that the effect of such a diversion on the discharge of the Tiber at Rome would have been very dramatic.[28]

The next proposals involved preventing the Nar from adding its waters to the Tiber through a twofold strategy of dispersing the waters of the Nar in the plain of Terni and reducing the water it received from other rivers. How the Nar's water was to be dissipated is unclear, but perhaps the commissioners envisioned a network of canals. Such a plan seems dubious and might well have only resulted in creating a large swamp.[29] The second stage of the Nar plan involved keeping the outflow from the Veline lakes from reaching the Nar. The background to this proposal concerns a long-standing dispute over how to deal with these waters. The Lacus Velini was fed by the waters of the Avens (Velino), Himella (Salto), and Tolenus (Turano) rivers, and there was not a natural outlet for the accumulated water, which resulted in local flooding problems. As a solution, this water was directed through artificial channels over the cliff at the northern end of the Peidiluco valley (probably by the end of the second century BC), thereby creating the Marmore Falls, which plunge 165 m into the Nar River below.[30] The inhabitants along the Nar below the falls were not pleased at this, claiming that, as a result, their lands suffered flooding due to the increased flow of water.

The conflicts between those living above and below the falls seem to have been the source of recurrent disputes. In 54 BC there was a consular senatorial commission that investigated the situation and mediated in a dispute between Reate (Rieti), located upstream from the Lacus Velini, and Interamnate (Terni), situated downstream from the falls on the Nar, concerning the discharge of water over the Marmore falls. Cicero was enlisted by the people of Reate to plead their case, leading him to visit the area personally in order to assess the situation (*Pro Scauro* 27; *Att.* 4.15). As part of the plan of AD 15, Arruntius and Ateius proposed that the outflow from the lake should be dammed and prevented from reaching the Nar. Such a procedure, while probably possible from an engineering standpoint, would certainly have created serious flooding problems for the people around Reate as the excess water accumulated. In addition, calculations suggest that the diminishment of the Nar's flow into the Tiber might not have made a substantial difference to flooding at Rome.[31]

Whether these plans were practicable or would have achieved their purpose is moot, since the proposal was met with heavy opposition from those cities which would have been affected. The Florentines protested that the diversion of the Clanis to the Arnus would bring catastrophic flooding to their city; the Interamnates lamented that their fertile fields would be inundated by the dispersion of the Nar; and the Reatines similarly pleaded that damming the falls would bring disaster to their region (Tac. *Ann.* 1.79). Several other interesting arguments were voiced in opposition to this plan. The claim was made that Nature had provided the optimum arrangement of streams and rivers and that therefore humans should not interfere with their proper courses. There were religious objections to meddling with hallowed streams and their accompanying sacred sites, which had witnessed rituals performed by the ancestors. Finally, it was asserted that to reduce the flow of the Tiber was to lessen the majesty of Father Tiber. The net result of these objections was that Piso made the motion that "nothing be changed." This motion was approved (Tac. *Ann.* 1.79).

The history of this proposal reveals a number of points about the difficulty of dealing with the problem of flooding. First of all, it amply illustrates the truism that a river and its tributaries form a complicated and interconnected system. It is not always easy to estimate how alterations to one part will affect other sections, and furthermore, changes that benefit one region can often result in deleterious consequences for another. The Tiber commission based at Rome produced a plan that in theory would have helped the capital city, yet the fears of the colonies that this plan would bring disaster upon their lands were probably well founded. In one sense, the commission's approach was laudable because they were seeking solutions that addressed the root of the flooding problem at its sources and they were considering the entire Tiber drainage system rather than just focusing in a reactive way upon the city and its attendant stretch of the Tiber. In their efforts to craft a solution to flooding at Rome, however, the Romans were handicapped by their incomplete understanding of riverine hydrology as well as by their inability to mathematically model both the current behavior of the Tiber and the proposed modifications. Without this ability to calculate the effects of changes, the Romans simply were not able to properly assess the pros and cons, let alone the feasibility, of their ideas. Finally, this episode illustrates that seeking solutions to flooding was not merely a practical problem involving engineering, but was also greatly complicated by other issues, chiefly religious concerns. Given the sacred identity ascribed by the Romans to nearly all rivers, streams, springs, lakes, ponds, and other bodies of water, any modifications to the natural flow of these entities constituted not just an experiment in engineering, but also a meddling in divine affairs.[32] In planning a project, Roman hydraulic engineers faced considerable challenges, since they had to be concerned with the risk of incurring the disfavor of the relevant divinities as well as with the practical aspects of their craft.

The debate over blocking the water from the Veline lakes raises the issue of another method of flood control, which it is appropriate to discuss here—the construction of dams and reservoirs. This has been (and continues to be) one of the most widely employed means by which the flow of water in a river is regulated. The reservoirs created by dams serve to absorb the high volume of water that would cause a flood, and then the excess water is gradually released by the dam so that water levels remain safe. The technology of dam construction was certainly available to the Romans, and they constructed many dams with various designs and materials all around the Mediterranean.[33] They did not, however, seem to have built many dams in Italy itself, and in fact only one set of three closely spaced dams is known from all of Italy.

These dams were located on an important tributary of the Tiber, the Anio (Aniene), but appear not to have been constructed for purposes of flood control. Nero had a villa situated on the banks of the Anio just upstream from Sublaqueum (Subiaco). He apparently had three concrete dams placed on the Anio near his villa in order to enhance the visual beauty of the site with artificial lakes (Pliny *HN* 3.12).[34] The middle dam, which remained standing until 1305, may have been the tallest known Roman dam, with an estimated height of more than 40 m.[35] Although the motivation behind the construction of these dams seems to have been aesthetic rather than practical, they did end up serving an important function for the city of Rome. The Anio Novus aqueduct completed by Claudius in AD 50 had not been a success because its water, taken directly from the river, was muddy. Under Trajan, the source of the aqueduct's supply was shifted to the reservoir created by the largest of Nero's dams. The reservoir acted as a settling tank and, from this point on, the waters of the Anio Novus ran clear (Frontinus, 2.93). The dams at Subiaco (as well as others around the Mediterranean) illustrate that the Romans possessed the engineering skill to erect sound dams and create reservoirs but that, at least in Italy, they elected not to pursue this method of flood control.

A final form of channel modification involves neither changing the path nor altering the volume of a river, but rather simply increasing the carrying capacity of the channel itself or improving the flow of water in it. These goals are usually accomplished by dredging the channel to clear or deepen it or by cutting away the embankment to widen the stream. Roman efforts of this type are demonstrated by the actions of Augustus, another emperor who concerned himself with Tiber flooding. His solution was to dredge the channel of the river, to clear out the debris that was clogging it, and to remove structures that were constricting its flow (Suet. *Aug.* 30).[36] Suetonius states that the express purpose of these measures was to prevent flooding, and such endeavors could indeed have actually been quite helpful in improving the flow of the river and in lessening the likelihood of at least minor floods overflowing into the city. If the river's channel were substantially deepened or widened by the dredging, then this would allow a greater volume of water to pass through without flooding; removing accumulated debris could also help.[37]

The Romans routinely used the Tiber as a convenient way to dispose of the city's rubbish, including corpses.[38] In this capacity, the river served as a practical way to get rid of the large numbers of animal carcasses produced on a day-to-day basis by butchers and sacrifices. Even if all the usable meat was removed for consumption, there would still have been a considerable volume of bones and viscera that would have needed to be thrown out. The great spectacles and animal hunts resulted in thousands of carcasses that seem to have ended up in the Tiber. The river also had a traditional role as the repository for the corpses of humans who had been executed as criminals. Political victims were often cast into the Tiber, and these could be very numerous, as in 121 BC when Gaius Gracchus and some 3,000 of his followers were slaughtered and flung into the Tiber (Plut. *G. Gracch.* 17.5; Vel. Pat. 2.6). In addition to being a convenient repository for such disposals, the Tiber seems to have played a purifying role in these instances.

As alarming as the prospect of several thousand human corpses being simultaneously dumped into the Tiber is, and as insalubrious as this would have been from the standpoint of hygiene, such events would not have significantly clogged the river physically in a meaningful long-term way. Attested instances of large-scale dumping of other types of material are rare but not unknown. For example, in AD 62, Nero had the stored grain supplies of the city poured into the Tiber because they had gone bad (Tac. *Ann.* 15.18). Most troublesome, however, would have been the collective actions of a million inhabitants routinely dumping their rubbish into the river. Over time this habit would have contributed to a buildup that would have affected the flow of water. If the river were used as the dumping ground for heavy types of debris such as rubble from collapsed or demolished buildings, such deposits would certainly build up and would have eventually seriously constricted the flow of water as well as posing navigation hazards. It was probably rubbish of this type that was the focus of Augustus's efforts to dredge out the river and clear its channel.

The tradition of dumping refuse into the Tiber was so well established that it even made its way into Roman legend in connection with the creation of Tiber Island. As related by Livy, the island was formed when, during the reign of Tarquin, a crop of grain grown on the Campus Martius could not be used as food due to religious reasons and so the harvested grain was thrown into the river, where it combined with other debris to form the foundations of Tiber Island (Livy 2.5.3–4; see also Dion. Hal. 5.13.3–4 and Plut. *Publicola* 8.1–3). Interestingly,

Livy's account stresses that the reason the grain was not simply swept downstream as it was thrown in was because the river was very shallow during the heat of midsummer, so the grain stuck in the mud. This realistic detail raises an important point when evaluating the buildup of debris in the Tiber—that the seasonal variation of the water level would have had a great deal of influence on how problematic Tiber dumping would have been for navigation, flood control, and health. During the spring and winter when there were typically a greater depth of water and a stronger current, even large objects could have been tossed into the river with the assurance that they would be swept downstream. During the drier seasons, especially late summer, the river's flow would have decreased. At such a time, bodies that were cast into the Tiber might have stuck in the shallows, creating a visual and olfactory nuisance and a serious health hazard, while larger objects would similarly have lodged in the mud or combined with other debris to block navigation channels. Because the season of reduced streamflow overlapped with the prime sailing season and the time of the year when much of Rome's supplies were being delivered via Tiber boats and barges, river dredging and the removal of obstacles would have been an especially vital task during these months.

Suetonius's account of Augustus's actions also refers to the removal of structures that impeded the flow of the river. Over time, private buildings, mills, and landings could certainly encroach into the river and alter its navigability. Roman law is quite explicit in forbidding such actions: "You are not to do anything in a public river or on its bank, nor put anything into a public river or onto its bank which make the landing or passage of a boat worse" (*Digest* 43.12.1). The subsequent sections of the *Digest* lay out the rules concerning construction in or on the banks of rivers, and the concern is clearly to maintain navigability and smoothly flowing waters (*Digest* 43.12.1.12–15; see also 39.1.1.17). Augustus seems to have tackled the issue of ensuring the Tiber's flow on all fronts, dredging the channel, removing debris and obstacles from the river, and clearing its banks of obstructions.

There is only one other literary account of a specific instance of dredging and clearing out of the riverbed. This occurred in the late third century AD and was one of the actions of the emperor Aurelian. In a list of activities through which he boasts that he has increased the grain supply for the city, he includes building up the riverbanks and digging out the shallow spots in the riverbed (SHA *Aur.* 47.2–3).[39] He somewhat optimistically prefaces this comment with the statement that these measures will provide a permanent benefit to Rome, but the incessant silting up of the river and continued dumping would have required constant dredging in order to maintain a clear channel.

Although these are the only specific mentions of the dredging of the Tiber channel at Rome, it is certain that periodic channel clearing must have occurred on other occasions as well, and was likely a perennial task. Supervising such works would have naturally fallen under the duties of the curators of the Tiber, and it would not have been improbable if they kept a gang of workers fairly constantly employed on dredging projects.

Contain: Roman Embankments

Perhaps the oldest method of protection from floods is the construction of walls along part of the course of a river in order to guard a specific region from high waters.[40] Whether such structures are termed floodwalls, embankments, or levees, this strategy is comparatively cheap and effective in achieving its immediate goals. Earthen levees are typically fashioned out of the materials at hand (often alluvial deposits) and have gradually sloping sides in order to maintain the stability of the loose materials from which they are composed. The wet slope typically needs a ratio of 1:3 to 1:5 height to width, and the reverse dry slope requires even greater ratios of 1:4 to 1:7 in order to counteract the hydrostatic pressure that might be exerted during times of flooding. Such earthen levees are often better suited to protect farmland rather than urban areas, because within cities space is usually at a premium, and it is not practical to lose the use of the large basal footprint necessary for a stable earth levee. Due to space constraints, embankments in cities are frequently built out of reinforced concrete and thus more closely resemble walls rather than the low-mound appearance of earthen levees.

Despite the advantages of floodwalls in terms of ease of construction and low cost, there are also significant drawbacks to this form of flood protection. If properly built, they can provide total safety for an area, but only for floods that do not exceed the height of the wall. If overtopping occurs, the floodwall is rendered useless and, even worse, serves to trap water within the very areas it was intended to safeguard. Such walls can give residents of an area a false sense of security, so that when a major flood that overtops the walls strikes, the inhabitants are caught unprepared. Another problem is that while floodwalls may protect one specific area, by constricting the flow of a river, they can create higher flood stages in other parts of the river and increase the velocity of the water as well. Finally, the walls themselves cut off access to the river, occupy valuable space, and are often unsightly.

Within the city of ancient Rome, substantial sections of the banks of the Tiber were lined with concrete embankments by the second century AD. The motivation behind these works, however, seems to have been dictated more by the requirements for providing port facilities rather than from concern about flooding. The ancient Tiber embankments appear to have been constructed in a sporadic fashion in response to the need for quays and sites for unloading the hundreds of riverine craft bringing supplies to Rome. There does not ever seem to have been a systematic plan to erect a continuous line of embankments along the river. The embankments that were built would, in some cases, have served a secondary function in providing a degree of protection from floods to certain regions, but they must be viewed primarily as port facilities rather than floodwalls. The history of Rome's ancient river embankments is further complicated by the sketchy nature of the archaeological evidence. Most of the ancient embankments have been either obliterated or buried by the construction of the modern Tiber floodwalls in the late 19th century. In addition, the traces of Roman embankments that were uncovered at that time were often incompletely preserved or recorded, and even later excavations were sometimes published in only a partial manner.[41]

When the city of Rome began to grow rapidly during the middle and late Republic and its population soared, it became necessary to transport gigantic quantities of foodstuffs to Rome in order to keep its inhabitants fed. One side effect of the creation of this transportation system was the development of port facilities in and around the city.[42] While some form of embankment or quays existed during the early phases of the Republic, the beginning of the second century BC witnessed a number of major projects aimed at providing better port facilities. In 193 BC, the curule aediles, M. Aemilius Lepidus and L. Aemilius Paullus, constructed a portico along the Tiber together with an adjoining quay, in addition to a number of other works (Livy 35.10.12). The censors of 179 BC, M. Aemilius Lepidus and M. Fulvius Nobilior, seem to have undertaken a general refurbishing and standardization of the riverside quays (Livy 40.51). Similarly, the censors of 174 BC, Q. Fulvius Flaccus and A. Postumius Albinus, undertook repairs of the warehouses near the Tiber and added to the quays (Livy 41.27).

The net result was that during the Republic, a number of stone embankments were constructed in key areas, such as near the Forum Boarium, at the base of the Aventine below the Pons Sublicius, and downstream from the Aventine in the Emporium district. Traces of these structures show that in their simplest form, they consisted of a low, vertical embankment topped with a walkway, with paired flights of stairs leading down from the walkway to the water. All of this was solidly constructed out of tufa and travertine. Ships were secured to the bank by means of large, circular stone mooring rings, and the ships would have had to lie broadside to the bank to unload. These facilities were plainly erected in order to facilitate the transfer of cargoes from riverboat to shore, and their low height would have provided little protective capacity in the event of a flood, although these structures would have helped prevent scouring and erosion along the bank.

Subsequent rebuildings maintained the same basic design, albeit with a steadily increasing complexity of facilities. Some of the quays being built by the end of the first century BC have been reconstructed featuring elaborate lifting devices and adjacent storage rooms. A second major phase of building, which seems to have been Trajanic in date, resulted in larger and more sophisticated dock facilities. The portion excavated along the Lungotevere Testaccio reveals a solidly built concrete core structure with a 5 m high sloping embankment wall leading up to a paved travertine quay surface that, in turn, is backed by several levels of barrel-vaulted storage spaces. Huge travertine mooring rings stud the face of the embankment and are often flanked by pairs of steps or ramps connecting the top of the quay with the surface of the water (fig. 5.5).

Methods of Flood Control

Fig. 5.5. A section of Roman embankment and quay in the Emporium district. The stairs, ramps, and mooring rings that were used in unloading watercraft are visible. (Fototeca Unione, American Academy in Rome, 3208F)

Ultimately, embankments lined much of the riverbank within the ancient city walls and for some distance downstream. Remains of wharves have been discovered along the banks of the Tiber all the way from the Forum Boarium area down along the slope of the Aventine through the Emporium district and stretching for almost another 2 km downstream. The region immediately south of Rome seems to have possessed considerable port and warehouse facilities, such as in the area of Pietra Papa. Traces of other port facilities have been identified in the Transtiberim and the Campus Martius. Several fragments of the Severan Marble Plan include what appear to be depictions of quays, such as Fragment 25, which shows a quay with two flights of steps leading down to the river backed up against the Horrea Lolliana, and Fragment 27, which represents a dockside in the Transtiberim with a very elaborate system of stairs (or perhaps ramps).[43]

Although Rome clearly had well-made and extensive port facilities, it is questionable what role these quays and embankments may have had in safeguarding the city from inundation. One major difficulty is that, while the remains uncovered to date give the impression of an unbroken line of embankments extending over large portions of the riverbank, it is by no means certain that these works were indeed continuous. Because any sort of wall system relies on presenting an unbroken front to floodwaters, any gap in the line of embankments would have nullified their efficacy as flood protection. While certain flood-prone areas (such as the valleys to the north and south of the Aventine) seem to have been equipped with a solid line of embankments, other high-risk zones (such as the northern Campus Martius) do not appear to have been similarly protected. The sporadic nature of these works testifies to the fact that their main purpose as envisioned by the Romans was clearly to serve as an aid to commerce; any flood protection they may have offered was purely incidental.

Given these rather severe limitations in construction and intent, did the embankments provide any measure of security from flooding? In those areas where the embankments were not continuous, the answer can only be no. Along the stretches of the riverbank where the line of quays was unbroken for a considerable distance, the relevant factor becomes the height of the works. In their most developed form, dating to the second century AD, the most substantial of the quays featured a sloping wall consisting of a concrete core faced with *opus reticulatum* and with a vertical height of approximately 5 m. Together with other elements of the dock, the entire quay structure would have presented a barrier of perhaps 5–6 m above the usual level of the Tiber. Such an embankment would have offered protection from elevated water levels and even minor floods that attained peaks of less than 10 or 11 masl. Even at its most formidable, the barrier offered by the ancient Roman quay system seems to have been at least a full 5–6 m lower than the modern Tiber embankments (which in most parts of Rome have a height of at least 18 masl; see fig. 5.6). Thus, while the ancient Roman embankments may in certain areas have provided a measure of relief from ordinary high water levels and even from minor flooding, they would have been severely overmatched and essentially useless when confronted with major floods. Nevertheless, the

Fig. 5.6. The continuous near-vertical walls of the modern Tiber embankments, which reach a height of approximately 18 masl in the central section of Rome and protect the city from inundations. (Photo by author)

construction of the ancient Roman dock facilities demonstrates that the Romans did indeed possess the engineering skills necessary to have constructed embankments of sufficient size to prevent flooding, if they had chosen to do so. Therefore, the inability to protect the city from inundations of the embankments they did erect is not the result of a failure of engineering but must instead be viewed as a conscious choice.

Administrative Oversight of the Tiber

While major construction initiatives like those previously described seem to have usually originated with emperors or powerful politicians such as Caesar, there was also a need for day-to-day administrative oversight of the Tiber and its banks. Over time, a network of somewhat overlapping bureaucratic offices developed to fulfill this administrative function. These agencies and their magistrates are known largely through epigraphic evidence commemorating specific works or erected as honorific monuments. The organization and evolution of the offices charged with oversight of the Tiber—and of related areas including the sewers, the aqueducts, and the food supply—have already been treated with considerable thoroughness by other scholars, so it should suffice for the purposes of this book to present a general outline of the development and duties of these offices.[44]

During the Republic, there was presumably some attention given to the maintenance of the navigability of the Tiber and the provision of suitable quays and facilities for riverine traffic, but little is known about who was in charge of such areas and how they operated. The aediles, who oversaw urban maintenance in general, may well have played some role. It is evident that the censors, whose duties included the construction of public works, were clearly involved with labor along the Tiber. Nineteen surviving *cippi* erected along the banks of the Tiber by the censors of 55 BC, P. Servilius Vatia Isauricus and M. Valerius Messalla Niger, refer to them as *curatores riparum* (*CIL* 6.31540 = *ILS* 5922). Terminal *cippi* such as these, which were used to demarcate boundaries between public and private zones along the riverbank, provide valuable evidence concerning those who took a role in regulating the Tiber.[45] In 8 BC the activities of the consuls C. Asinius Gallus and C. Marcius Censorinus were recorded by additional riverine *cippi*, of which 20 are extant (*CIL* 6.31541 = *ILS* 5923). Twenty-two additional *cippi* dating to the subsequent year were erected by the emperor Augustus (*CIL* 6.31542 = *ILS* 5924).

Augustus may have been instrumental in establishing (as he was in so many other areas) a permanent administrative department charged with the oversight of the Tiber. Suetonius (*Aug.* 37) relates that, along with the *curatores* of the public works, the grain supply, the water supply, and the roads, Augustus appointed a man to be in charge of the channel of the Tiber (*curator alvei Tiberis*). This account is contradicted by Cassius Dio (57.14.7–8) and Tacitus (*Ann.* 1.76), who ascribe the creation of this office to Tiberius, in reaction to the destructive flood of AD 15. It may be that the Augustan office was incorporated into the Tiberian one or perhaps superseded by it. In any event, in AD 15 a permanent board composed of five senators was definitely established and charged with regulating the Tiber so that it neither flooded during the winter nor dried up during the summer (Dio 57.14.7–8). This was also the year of the special commission of Ateius Capito and Lucius Arruntius, whose plan to reduce the Tiber's flow was rejected by the senate (Tac. *Ann.* 1.76, 1.79).

The Tiber board in its five-man incarnation lasted until the reign of Vespasian, when a single man of consular status was appointed as the curator of the Tiber. This administrative position continued well into the fourth century. The actual title of the men serving in this post appears to have varied over time, and while some of the changes seem purely bureaucratic, others may suggest extensions or restrictions of the position's responsibilities. The five-man board members were identified as the *curatores riparum et alvei Tiberis* (curators of the banks and channel of the Tiber), and the one-man version retained the same title in the singular. Under Trajan, the responsibilities of the office were extended to the oversight of the sewers of the city and, accordingly, from AD 100 on the title was amended to *curator alvei et riparum Tiberis et cloacarum urbis* (curator of the channel and banks of the Tiber and the sewers of the city).

How far upstream and downstream from Rome the jurisdiction of the curators reached is uncertain.[46] The portion of the Tiber that undoubtedly received the most attention from the curators was that near the city itself and down to Ostia, and their jurisdiction plainly covered this stretch of the river. In order to carry out the charge assigned to the original board of preventing winter floods and ensuring adequate summer water flow, the curators would most likely have had at least some responsibility for and power over the entire Tiber drainage basin.

Due to the many surviving *cippi*, the best known of their duties was to mark boundaries concerning the riverbanks.[47] In addition to demarcating between public and private land, they seem to have had some degree of jurisdiction over private lands that adjoined the Tiber when this was necessary in order to safeguard river traffic. The curators played a role in settling disputes concerning riverine boundaries, as indicated by an inscription on one *cippus* (*CIL* 14.4704c). These tasks were complicated by the behavior of the river itself, which could—and apparently did—often shift its course. Within Rome, the section of bank that seems to have been particularly unstable and prone to such shifts was the stretch of the river adjoining the northern Campus Martius. Some of the back-and-forth shifts of the Tiber can perhaps be recreated by tracing the lines of boundary *cippi* at various points in time.[48] The curators could grant the right for individuals or groups to occupy or use land along the river that was in the public domain. A *curator alvei et riparum Tiberis* is thanked on an honorific inscription erected by a guild of Tiber boatmen, the *lenuncularii traiectus Luculli* (*CIL* 14.254, 5320). This was a guild of ferrymen who, as recorded in this inscription, were apparently constructing some sort of building near the Tiber and therefore had to seek the permission of the curator. A second inscription commemorates a similar event involving the same guild and Ti. Julius Ferox, who was the *curator alvei Tiberis et riparum* from AD 101 to 103 (*CIL* 14.5320). Both these instances involved the construction by guilds of buildings along the banks of the river, and so, rather than interpreting these inscriptions as evidence for a general supervisory role of the curator over the guilds or corporations of workers associated with the Tiber and the supply system, it seems more likely that he was simply exercising his control over the riverbanks.[49]

Not surprisingly, the curators also seem to have played a part in the building and maintenance of the quays and embankments where cargo ships docked and unloaded at Rome. This duty of the curators is recorded in two inscriptions commemorating the restoration of quays that had fallen into disrepair, one from the first century AD (*CIL* 6.31543) and the other dating to around AD 300 (*CIL* 6.1242).[50] The first of these records the names of the initial five-man Tiber board and that the work was undertaken by order of the senate, whereas in the second there was only a single curator operating under the direction of the emperor. These two inscriptions simultaneously illustrate the transformation of the organization of the office over time, as well as continuities in its duties.[51] Finally, the curator had to maintain the navigability of the Tiber. The two main components of this responsibility were removing obstacles both man-made and natural, such as shipwrecks or trees, and ensuring that the channel was of sufficient depth, which could have been accomplished by dredging.[52]

The curator was based at Rome but, because the most important function of the Tiber for the city was in the transportation of foodstuffs, it is not surprising that he had an office at Ostia as well (*CIL* 14.5384, 6.1224).[53] It appears that the Ostian office was eventually headed by an assistant to the curator. In the second century AD, a deputy of equestrian rank, styled the *adiutor curatoris alvei Tiberis et cloacarum* (assistant to the curator of the channel of the Tiber and of the sewers), is attested as being based at the Ostian office (*CIL* 14.172, 5345).[54] This departmental organization mirrors that of the food supply system, in which there was a *praefectus annonae* in overall command who was aided by an assistant labeled an *adiutor*. Of the staff that served under the curator of the Tiber, less is known, but presumably he would have been attended by the usual assortment of scribes, accountants, messengers, and functionaries. A funerary inscription of such a man survives: a freedman who is identified as having served as a secretary or accountant (*commentariensis alvei Tiberis*) in the office of the curator of the Tiber and its banks (*CIL* 2.6085). The maintenance of the embankments and sewers in proper working order would have necessitated at least a modest gang of workers and perhaps an engineer, and any major initiatives, such as new construction, substantial refurbishing, or dredging of the river, would of course have required a much larger work force. Other groups that the curator would have needed in his employ, or who might have been hired occasionally, include boatmen and divers. The curator of the Tiber and the sewers would have had to work closely with other officials, such as those involved in the supply system and especially the *curator aquarum,* the official in charge of the aqueducts, because the aqueducts provided much of the water that ended up in the sewers and was necessary for flushing away the waste deposited in them.

Many methods can be used to lessen or prevent harmful inundations, and throughout the long course of their history, the Romans experimented with nearly all of the major categories of structural flood control, including altering or diverting streamflow, improving drainage, erecting embankments, and raising ground levels. The Romans, therefore, had practical empirical experience with a range of possible strategies that could have been employed to render their capital city safe from the threat of inundation. The main problem with the Romans' flood control efforts, however, was that, in all periods, these works remained sporadic, uncoordinated, and incomplete. They consisted of an irregular sequence of individual projects and initiatives aimed at specific problems or vulnerabilities, but there was never a single, overarching, coordinated effort aimed at preventing or lessening flooding in general. An emperor or administrator might occasionally raise ground levels in one place, build small embankments in another, or undertake some dredging of the Tiber's channel, but these endeavors were always limited in extent and narrow in focus.

The Romans' responses to issues involving the river in their midst were generally passive in nature. When a problem arose, such as blockages obstructing the channel, they would remove these obstacles; when there was a need for quays along a stretch of bank, they would construct a concrete embankment for that section. Even on the rare occasions when the Romans directly considered the problem of flooding in broader terms, this was usually a reaction to a specific event, such as a recent, particularly destructive flood. The Roman response to the Tiber's ravages was fundamentally piecemeal in nature; what was missing was the big project—the single, large effort that would solve the problem once and for all.

Given the amount of practical experience accumulated by the Romans through their minor flood relief projects, the impediment to a major flood control plan was neither expertise nor technology. The Romans had the engineering ability to safeguard their city, but chose not to do so. In order to understand how they came to this surprising de-

Methods of Flood Control

cision, it is therefore necessary to look, not to the Romans' technological knowledge, but rather to their attitudes toward the Tiber and its floods. The answer to why the Romans did not do more to prevent flooding must be based on how they viewed the river in both practical and symbolic terms, and on the perceived costs, risks, and benefits of meddling with it. Before we can return to the basic question of why the Romans did not do more to prevent inundations, these attitudes toward floods and the river itself must be explored—an investigation that is the subject of the next chapter.

Six

Roman Attitudes toward Floods

Floods and the Urban Fabric of Ancient Rome: Public Buildings

In evaluating the Romans' attitudes toward floods, one of the most basic questions is how the flood-prone nature of the city's location affected the way that the physical city developed. Was flooding a significant factor in determining where the Romans chose to build various types of structures? Can we detect patterns in the man-made topography of the city that represent a response to the threat of inundation? The somewhat extreme nature of the topography of Rome, with its many steep hills, deep valleys, and swampy depressions—all of which were situated within a relatively small square area—creates an urban landscape of great variety. Locations that would have been subject to frequent flooding lie within a few meters of others that would have been completely safe. Therefore, the Romans had available to them a great diversity of building sites. There are usually many factors that combine to determine where structures are erected, and it is certainly worth considering how significant the threat of flooding was in this decision-making process. Some of the basic categories of building in ancient Rome were political centers, commercial structures, religious monuments, entertainment complexes, and residential buildings. It may be possible to perceive trends in the urban fabric of Rome in regard to what kinds of buildings were erected where. This chapter begins its examination of the Romans' attitudes toward flooding by plotting these categories of structures against the map of flood-prone areas in order to identify possible patterns concerning where the Romans chose to place these different types of structures.

The most important political center of the city was, from early on, the Roman Forum. It included such important civic structures as the *curia,* the usual meeting place of the senate, the *comitium,* the space where many assemblies and elections were held, and the various speakers' platforms from which significant orations were delivered to the public. The Forum originally was a swampy zone crisscrossed by streams, and even when drained by sewers such as the Cloaca Maxima and with its level raised by fill, the area remained flood-prone. The later imperial fora extend in a line stretching away northwest from the Roman Forum and were situated on slightly higher ground, but were still not safe from major floods.

The commercial centers of the city, where goods were stored, bought, and sold, shifted over time. Despite its name, the Forum Boarium was probably not the main center of cattle trade, but it did lie along the main salt trade route and certainly was the site of early commercial activity at Rome (fig. 6.1). Early on, the Roman Forum likely also served as a marketplace, and during the Republic the Campus Martius would have made a better area for the cattle trade. The main food market of republican Rome, the *macellum,* was situated near the Forum on the site of what would be the future Forum of Augustus. During the Empire, there was probably a shift to local markets rather than one centralized one, but the vast quantities of foodstuffs that had to be imported by sea to supply the city fostered the development of the Emporium district, which became the center of commercial activity and came to include elaborate quays and gigantic warehouses. Warehouses seem to have clustered across the river from the Emporium district as well. What all of these sites of commercial activity had in common was that they were in low-lying areas vulnerable to floods. Naturally the location of commercial zones was often dictated by the necessity of having ready access to the Tiber, which was the most efficient way to move large quantities of goods, but unfortunately this

Floods of the Tiber in Ancient Rome

Fig. 6.1. The Forum Boarium, including round temple, during an inundation. This low-lying region near the Tiber would have been one of the most flood-prone parts of the city. (Fototeca Unione, American Academy in Rome, 2817HF)

requirement ensured that high-value perishable goods were concentrated in flood plains.

The entertainment centers of the city likewise tended to be situated in low-lying areas. The sites of the two largest entertainment structures, the Circus Maximus and the Flavian Amphitheater, were at one time either streambeds or swamps, and the Circus remained one of the most frequently flooded parts of the city. Rome's theaters were in the Campus Martius, where they, too, were subject to recurrent flooding. During the early Empire, this entire region eventually became filled with magnificent public structures. Again, there are sound practical reasons for the decision to construct these buildings on the sites where they were located. Huge edifices such as the Circus demand a large, flat surface to build upon. Greek theaters were often constructed on hillsides, taking advantage of the slope's natural shape to form the seating areas for the audience, but at Rome, all the theaters were built up from flat surfaces. The distribution of Rome's religious structures is more complicated. The many temples and shrines were more evenly distributed, with some—most notably the Temple to Jupiter Optimus Maximus—located atop hills, but with many others situated in flat or low-lying areas.

Rome's major political, commercial, and entertainment centers, then, were almost exclusively concentrated in those areas of the city that were most prone to flooding (fig. 6.2). When these spaces and structures are plotted onto a map of flood-prone areas, there is a striking correlation, with nearly all of them lying squarely within the reach of major floods.[1] This geographic distribution either suggests an amazing indifference to the threat of natural disasters or else reveals the in-

Fig. 6.2. Map of political, commercial, and entertainment centers of Rome plotted against 20 masl flood.

fluence of other positive characteristics of these locations that must have outweighed the threat of occasional flooding. Another factor that probably helps to explain the positioning of these buildings in flood zones is that the original site of Rome was along the banks of the Tiber, and even when it expanded considerably inland, through a combination of tradition, central location, and ease of transport, the city center remained near the river; therefore most major public buildings were constructed in proximity to the river as well. Religious structures such as temples and shrines also seem to have been built without regard to floods. When temples are located on hills or high ground, it is usually for obvious reasons related to the specific cult or divinity. When there was not a compelling religious motivation for placing a temple on a hill, the Romans seemed just as happy to situate them in valleys.

While the Romans do not appear to have been concerned about any of these building types being placed in flood zones, there is one type of monumental public structure that reveals a very different pattern. Figure 6.3 shows the major public baths plotted against a 20 masl flood. The two earliest of these baths, those of Agrippa and Nero, were in the central Campus Martius, which was certainly a flood-prone region. All of the subsequent baths, however, were erected on sites whose elevations would have kept them safe from flooding. Whereas all other types of public buildings cluster in the flood plain regardless of their date of construction, from the 2nd century AD onward, no major bath complex was placed where floodwaters could reach it. It is unlikely that such a pronounced pattern as this is accidental. Rather it suggests that large bath complexes were somehow more vulnerable to flood damage than other categories of public buildings. Grand imperial *thermae* such as the baths of Diocletian and Caracalla harbored thousands of meters of intricate plumbing within their walls, consisting of a maze of pipes, conduits, and drains delivering to and carrying away from assorted pools and basins water of various temperatures. Such a complicated internal network would have been more vulnerable to becoming clogged with silt or debris from floodwater than other types of urban water systems such as aqueducts or sewers. Because many of a bath complex's pipes were inaccessibly located

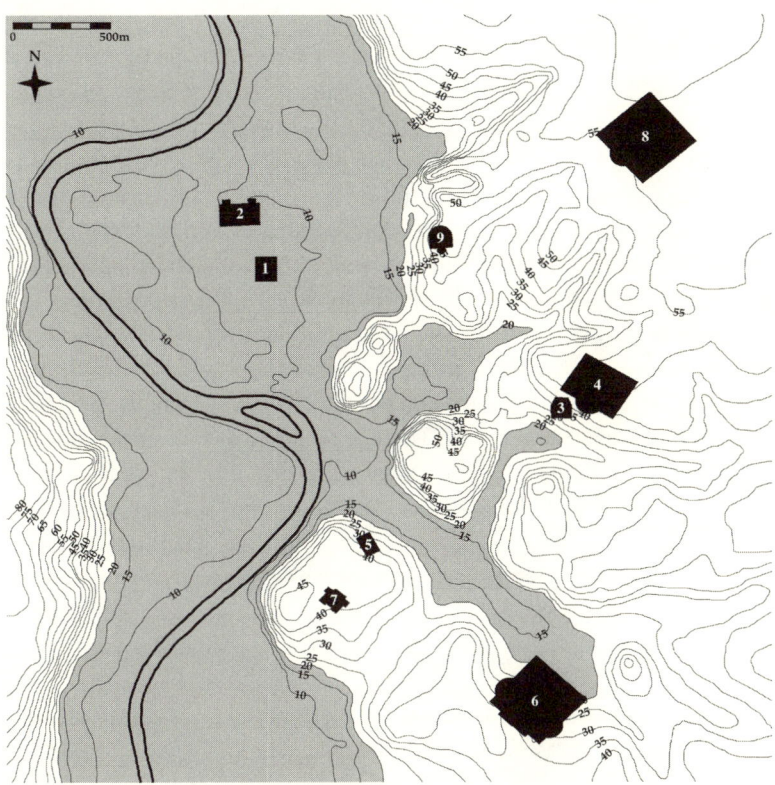

Fig. 6.3. Map of major bath complexes plotted against a 20 masl flood. Baths numbered in order of date of construction: (1) Baths of Agrippa, (2) Baths of Nero, (3) Baths of Titus, (4) Baths of Trajan, (5) Baths of Sura, (6) Baths of Caracalla, (7) Baths of Decius, (8) Baths of Diocletian, (9) Baths of Constantine.

within the walls of the structure, they would also have been extremely difficult and expensive to unclog and clean out.

The chronological pattern of bath development suggests that the earliest grand public baths were built, as were all other structures, without regard to flooding. Negative experiences with these baths during floods must then have dictated that future bath complexes be placed out of reach of floodwaters. A number of objections might be raised against this interpretation, including the fact that Rome had hundreds of smaller public and private baths, a few of which are known to have been located in the flood zone. On the other hand, while there is ample evidence for there having been a large number of baths in the city of Rome, there is relatively little evidence for where these were situated, and if we could somehow learn the location of all of these baths, it is possible that there would be a preference for higher ground. Also, the internal plumbing in a small neighborhood or private bath would have been far less complicated and correspondingly easier to flush out and clean in the aftermath of a flood, making the location of such small baths less of an issue. Another possible objection is that by the time the later baths were constructed, all of the available sites near the flood-prone center of the city had already been taken, necessitating that they be built further away from the river simply due to space limitations. There is probably some truth to this, but emperors certainly had an established record of finding ways to construct large new buildings in already built-up areas if they desired.

In addition, most of the later bath complexes seem to cling to the very edges of the flood zones, as if their builders were trying to locate them as close as possible to the center of the city while still keeping them on safe ground. The baths of Caracalla, Titus, Trajan, Decius, Sura, and Constantine all perch on hillsides, less than 100 m from flood zones. It would have been easier to build a number of these baths, such as those of Titus or Caracalla, a little further inland where there was flatter ground, but instead they were erected on awkward slopes. What such locations did accomplish was to bring them as near as could be to the densely inhabited central region of the city while still skirting the dangerous 20 masl flood zone. Only the Baths of Diocletian are situated well away from the flood zone, but this complex was clearly constructed in order to provide a nearby public bath for those living in this region as the city grew and expanded to the northwest.

It could be argued that the location of the later bath complexes can be explained entirely by the basic requirement to serve the outlying regions of the city that did not already possess adequate public baths. Therefore, as the city population grew and expanded onto the eastern ring of hills, there was a pressing need to provide baths in these newer (and higher) areas of the city. An analogy to the shift in location of large bath complexes to regions farther from the city center can be found in the development of the aqueduct system. The earliest aqueducts served areas close to the Tiber, but as the city spread, they brought water to zones successively farther to the east and on higher ground. In this interpretation, the placement of both aqueducts and baths can be explained by simply following the shifts in population over time. I agree that providing bath facilities to newly developed regions of the city was a major—perhaps the dominant—factor in determining the general location of bath complexes. What I am focusing on, however, is the specific places chosen, which often seem to hover just above the flood danger zone. In a number of cases, shifting these sites just 100 m would have brought them within reach of floodwaters. Thus, while the general placement of later bath complexes was dictated by need and population, the specific spots on which they were erected may have been influenced by concerns about floods. One final benefit that would have been reaped by positioning large bath complexes just outside the flood zone is that these structures would have been logical choices to serve as refugee centers for Rome's inhabitants after an inundation. Their basic design features made them admirably suited to provide clean water, food, and shelter for displaced Romans who needed emergency lodging for a few days while waiting for floodwaters to recede.[2]

It could additionally be argued that the layout of the aqueduct system itself, whose pipes and conduits (like those of baths) would be damaged or contaminated by floods, reflects a concern for flooding. Many aqueducts (especially later ones) end above the flood zone, and all of them tend to cling to the ridges of high ground for as long as possible before descending into flood-prone areas. Naturally, this also has very practical hydraulic advantages for distributing water in an open flow system, but this could be another case in which one decision reaped benefits in two unrelated areas.

Floods and the Urban Fabric of Ancient Rome: Housing

The distribution pattern of another type of urban structure—the actual dwellings of the city's inhabitants—might indicate if residences in Rome were built with regard to flood-prone areas. Modern urban planners divide (and often formally zone) cities into distinct districts based upon the type of activities that occur within them. Thus we can speak of the industrial, commercial, residential, and entertainment sections of a city. These areas are often separated so that there is minimal overlap among them. Many cities, for example, have a downtown commercial zone that is heavily populated with workers during the day but becomes an empty wasteland at night when nearly all the employees disperse to their homes in the primarily residential suburbs. Another typical distinction characterizing modern cities is residential areas that are sharply defined according to income levels. Rich people tend to live near other wealthy people, and the poor are often compelled to live in neighborhoods consisting of other poverty-stricken individuals. Rarely are sumptuous luxury homes found intermingled with run-down, low-income tenements.

By contrast, one of the standard truisms about ancient Rome is that the city did not have such extremely pronounced divisions between residential and nonresidential areas, with residential zones clearly demarcated from commercial and industrial zones. Nor was there the sharp divide between rich and poor neighborhoods that typifies and defines many modern cities. In ancient Rome, homes and apartment buildings were jumbled together with public structures, and a decrepit tenement might be found immediately next door to the lavish *domus* of a consul, or a glittering temple. The Subura district probably came the closest to possessing the distinct character of a densely crowded, "inner city," poor residential area, but even this region abutted immediately upon the magnificent structures of the imperial fora, and several famous upper-class Romans are known to have lived in houses in the Subura. While there was not strong regional differentiation between rich and poor, Roman cities were characterized by vertical stratification, whereby the wealthier inhabitants might occupy the lower levels of a structure, while progressively higher floors were inhabited by increasingly poor dwellers who had to trudge up multiple flights of stairs.[3]

The two main types of housing in Rome were private homes (*domus*) and apartment buildings (*insulae*). The fourth-century AD Regionary Catalogs provide the much-quoted statistic that, at that time, there were some 1,790 *domus* and 46,602 *insulae*.[4] The discrepancy between numbers of private homes and communal dwellings may seem extreme, but probably accurately reflects wealth distribution in Roman society, where a tiny minority of extraordinarily affluent individuals and an enormous mass of very poor people coexisted, with not much in between. The number of *insulae* has been the subject of considerable controversy, as many scholars have expressed doubts concerning the reliability of this figure, suspecting that it is too high to be believable.[5]

A hint as to where Romans lived and whether their dwellings were in flood zones can be obtained by dividing the number of *domus* and *insulae* per region by the square area of that neighborhood in order to determine the density of residential dwellings. Such density plots of the 14 traditional Augustan regions of the city have been done based on data from the Regionary Catalogs, and these reveal that there were not marked differences between the distribution of these two types of residential buildings among the various regions.[6] Both are found in high densities near the city center, and both taper off in density in outlying areas. The three regions with the highest concentrations of *domus* (Regio VIII: Forum Romanum, Regio X: Palatium, and Regio XI: Circus Maximus) are the same three regions with the highest density of *insulae*. These districts also contain some of the greatest numbers of monumental political, commercial, religious, and entertainment structures, which supports the view that rich and poor were intermingled with one another among the monuments and public buildings of the city. These areas are all near or adjacent to the Tiber, and although containing several hills, they also encompass many of the main flood zones, suggesting that Rome's prime residential neighborhoods may also have lain in frequently flooded locations.

A further question is whether there is actually any pattern to the locations where rich and poor Romans lived. Anecdotal literary evidence gives the impression that *insulae* tend to have been built mostly in flat areas while many aristocratic homes were on hills, but there are also notable examples of rich men living in low-lying districts. The Regionary Catalogs offer no help in answering this more detailed question because their data only extend to distinguishing dwellings according to which of the 14 Augustan regions they were situated in, most of which contain areas of both high and low ground. One can, however, compile a list of all the *domus* at Rome whose location can be identified either through mention in literary sources or by archaeological evidence, and then divide these up according to whether they were located on a hill or high ground, or in a low-lying and flood-prone location. While the resultant survey is obviously subject to the idiosyncrasies of the sources and to flukes of survival, if the numbers are large enough or the trends pronounced enough, such an enterprise may offer a crudely accurate portrait of where the wealthiest Romans lived.

The outcome of such an analysis, depicted in tables 6.1 and 6.2, reveals a striking pattern. Of the 228 *domus* whose locations can be reasonably guessed at, fully 194 (85%) were situated on hills or high ground, and only 34 (15%) were in flood-prone areas.[7] The hill with the most known *domus* was the Palatine, with 45 (20%), and the one with the second most was the Quirinal, with 39 (17%). Just the five hills or regions of high ground with the most private dwellings—the Palatine, Quirinal, Esquiline, Aventine, and Caelian—together account for 156 (68%) of the total. Of the areas that are known to have been subject to flooding, the most common site of *domus* was the general area of the Roman Forum, with 10 (4%), followed by the Campus Martius, with 9 (4%).

In reality, houses may well have been distributed more evenly around the city than these data suggest, but what these statistics prob-

Table 6.1.
Domus on Hills

Location	Number	Percent of Total *Domus*
Palatine	45	20
Quirinal	39	17
Esquiline	26	11
Aventine	23	10
Caelian	23	10
Carinae/Oppian	14	6
Viminal	11	5
Pincian	6	3
Capitoline	5	2
Cispian	2	1
Total of Domus on Hills	194	85

Table 6.2.
Domus in Flood-Prone Areas

Location	Number	Percent of Total *Domus*
Forum Romanum Area	10	4
Campus Martius	9	4
Transtiberim	7	3
Subura	3	1
Valley of Flavian Amphitheater	2	1
Near Circus Maximus	1	<1
Near Porta Metrovia	1	<1
Near Thermae Antonianae	1	<1
Total of *Domus* in Flood Prone Areas	34	15

ably do accurately reflect is where the houses of the very richest and most powerful Romans were located. In fact, members of this elite group are probably overrepresented in these data because, due to their very fame or influence, they were the most likely to be mentioned in the primary sources. As the people with the most resources, they could also be most selective about where they chose to live; thus their extraordinarily strong preference for dwelling on hilltops offers a clear indication of what neighborhoods of Rome were viewed as most desirable to live in.

There were several compelling reasons for such a preference. Originally, the attraction of hilltop sites was the very practical one that they are more easily defensible. It was probably for this reason that the early settlements of Rome clustered on the Palatine. By the time Rome had become a major city (from which the overwhelming majority of the data on residences dates), defensive considerations were no longer relevant. A dwelling on a hill, however, would have had better access to light and fresh air—no small considerations in a densely packed city like Rome. There would also have been the possibility of a view, although given the inward focus and relatively small windows of Roman domestic architecture, this may well have been less of a concern than it is today. In addition to these aesthetic factors, hills would, of course, have offered refuge from floods. While it cannot be said with certainty that the threat of flooding was the primary reason for Roman elites' inclination for living on hills, it must have been a significant factor at the very least. One notable disadvantage of living atop a hill was having to climb up and down an incline to reach one's own house or those of hill-dwelling friends. Martial (5.22) vividly describes his exhaustion from having to trudge uphill from the Subura to visit a friend who lived on the Esquiline (as well as his annoyance at the wasted effort when the friend proved not to be at home).

The most coveted residential location of all was the Palatine. It may have possessed some residual attraction as a desirable address on the basis of traditions established during Rome's very early history, when it was the site of some of the first settlements, but it was also simply the most convenient place from which to gain access to the central areas of Rome. In view of all of these factors, it is not surprising that the Palatine eventually became the site of the emperor's palace which, over time, expanded enormously until it engulfed nearly the entire upper surface of the hill.

If the distribution pattern of *domus* can be taken as an indication of where Rome's elite dwelt, the distribution of *insulae* might suggest where the poorer inhabitants of Rome lived. Unfortunately, a reasonable analysis of *insulae* distribution does not seem as practicable because the number of *insulae* whose locations are definite is smaller. On the other hand, the total number of *insulae* was much larger than that of *domus*, and they seem to have been built more or less anywhere that there was room. Various fragments of the Severan Marble Plan show *insulae* crammed together and often immediately abutting monumental public buildings; for example, Fragment 29 depicts *insulae* with rows of *tabernae* pressed up against the Forum of Trajan.[8] While it can be argued that *domus* locations reflect the decisions made by people who had the ability to make choices about the placement of their dwellings, *insulae* were, by contrast, inhabited largely by those whose options were far more restricted.

This comparison of the sites of the main political, commercial, religious, entertainment, and residential centers of Rome with the zones of the city that were vulnerable to flooding yields some interesting patterns. The regions of Rome that lay within zones prone to frequent flooding included most of the important political, religious, commercial, and symbolic monuments and spaces of the city. Common sense might seem to suggest that valuable political, commercial, religious, and entertainment structures would not be constructed in zones prone to natural disasters, but this was not the case in ancient Rome. As discussed previously, these monuments were so massively built that they were largely immune to many of the harmful effects of flooding. Therefore, while public structures (with the exception of baths) do not seem to have been situated with regard to floods, private domestic buildings offer a very different pattern. The very topmost strata of Roman society evinced a strong preference for locating their private residences on high ground, and the emperors, surely the elite of the elite, followed this model. By modern standards, the urban texture of ancient Rome was unusually integrated, with public and private structures jumbled together, with the modest and the spectacular side by side, and with rich and poor to a large extent intermingled; yet within this urban mélange, there were still distinctions, and one of the most pronounced seems to have been the elites' preference for high, dry ground.

Water and the Gods

Given their reverence for water and rivers generally, and in light of the important role the Tiber played in Rome's economy, it is necessary to consider the Tiber in terms of its religious associations. The personification of the river as Father Tiber was regarded as both an important and a potent deity by the inhabitants of the city. The connections between the Tiber and religion and the nature of the cults associated with the river are topics that have drawn the most extensive attention from scholars interested in Rome's river. Particularly noteworthy are the classic studies of Le Gall and Holland, which investigate in detail the role of Father Tiber in Roman religion as well as other cults associated with the river. While these works have thoroughly explored these general topics, I consider here a more narrow question concerning religion and the Tiber: how were floods of the Tiber interpreted by the ancient Romans in terms of their religion?

The general association between water and the sacred is a strong one, not just in Roman religion, but across most ancient cultures.[9] This link is more powerful yet when the water concerned is actively flowing rather than still, and perennial rather than seasonal. For the Romans, nearly every body of water was sacred to some degree, and every river, spring, and rivulet might be the preserve of a numinous spirit. This attitude is neatly encapsulated by Servius's simple statement (*Ad. Aen.* 7.84) that "there is no spring that is not sacred." Such aquatic entities could take offense if proper respect was not shown to them or if their waters were misused. Rivers commonly demarcated boundaries both political and religious, and the crossing of these barriers had to be accompanied by suitable prayer and propitiations. In cosmology, rivers were inevitably envisioned as forming the boundaries between the lands of the living and those of the dead; crossing these rivers was never taken lightly and could only be accomplished with appropriate ritual. Those souls who were not interred with a coin to pay the ferryman, Charon, were condemned to a miserable existence forlornly wandering the banks of the Styx. Water played a key role in the use of magic as well. In folklore, streams or rivers often formed a protective barrier that evil spirits could not cross. Curse tablets were commonly deposited in wells or springs, and the deity inhabiting the water was often among the entities invoked to inflict punishment on the object of the curse.[10] Even when Christianity replaced paganism, water retained its mysterious potency in rites of baptism and the powers ascribed to Holy Water.

In view of these attitudes, bridging a river was a momentous act. The construction of a pathway over a previously unbridged river was a notable feat, and one that was perceived as a way for great rulers to assert their supremacy. The actions of Darius in bridging the Bosphorus, Xerxes the Hellespont, Caesar the Rhine, Caligula the Bay of Naples, and Trajan the Danube were clearly intended as more than merely practical engineering projects, but also as symbolic and literal expressions of these rulers' power. These works have been construed as representing a triumph over nature, an interpretation that is reinforced by the Roman propensity for erecting victory monuments on bridges.[11] By spanning a body of water, one was, in a sense, conquering it, and care again had to be taken in order not to offend the spirit of the waters.

If bridging a river could anger its deity, then affecting its flow by altering its course could also incur divine wrath. The Romans' reverence for allowing water to choose its own path is vividly illustrated by the convoluted course of the Cloaca Maxima, which follows the meandering path of the original rivulet that flowed from the Forum to the Tiber. A purely practical engineer would surely have straightened out some of its twists and turns, but even when the original stream was utterly transformed by being wholly enclosed within stonework and buried underground, the Romans were reluctant to alter its course. Similarly, changing the nature of a river by such actions as reducing its flow or diverting its tributaries could be taken as an offense by the affiliated deity. As noted in the previous chapter, fear of "reducing the majesty of Father Tiber" was one of the reasons successfully put forward in defeating proposals to divert some of the Tiber's tributaries (Tac. *Ann.* 1.79).

Floods and the Gods: Portents and Divine Anger

For the Romans, therefore, the Tiber was not simply a body of flowing water, but also a potentially dangerous divinity who demanded respect. When such an entity erupted from its normal confines, bringing wide-scale destruction, it would have been tempting to see such an event not as a random occurrence but instead as a deliberate statement from the gods. How, then, did the Romans view Tiber floods in terms of religion? Pliny the Elder (*HN* 3.5.55) offers his unequivocal opinion on this question in his famous description of the Tiber; he states that the river "is looked upon as a prophet of warning, its rise being always construed as a call to religion rather than as a threat of disaster." This clear linkage between Tiber flooding and the gods is reinforced by the ancient accounts of floods in which inundations are frequently associated with or ascribed to the actions of the gods.

There are two main ways in which this association is usually presented. The first and most common of these is that a flood is described as constituting a portent that foretells some momentous event, such as the death of an emperor. An example is the flood of AD 36, which was seen as prophesying the death of Tiberius (Dio 63.27.1). Roman authors were certainly fond of reporting long lists of bizarre, unusual, or destructive events and interpreting these occurrences as omens. In the course of his history, Livy (43.13) offers a justification of such interpretations: "I am aware that men nowadays, through lack of religious feeling, do not believe that the gods foreshadow events through portents and, for this reason, unusual and miraculous occurrences are no longer publicly announced or recorded in histories. However, in writing of events long ago I somehow get into an old-fashioned frame of mind and am gripped by a certain religious scrupulousness, so that I consider worthy of inclusion in my history what those wise men of old thought should be matters of public concern."

In more than half of the flood accounts (23 of 42), a flood is portrayed in this manner as being a portent.[12] Sometimes this is stated by the author directly, as in Livy's comment on the flood of 202 BC that "the unusual height of rivers was interpreted as a portent" (30.38.10–12), Plutarch's report that "the behavior of the Tiber [the flood of AD 69] was regarded by most people as a baleful sign" (*Otho* 4.5), and Dio's stating (of the flood of 32 BC) that "many clear portents were shown by the gods" (50.8.1). In describing the corruption of certain politicians during the late Republic, Dio (37.58.3–4) offers an even lengthier comment by prefacing his description of the destruction caused by the flood of 60 BC with the observation, "Heaven was not ignorant of their doings, but then and there revealed very plainly to those who could understand any such signs all that was to result later because of them. . . . These signs were revealed in advance as an image of what should befall the people both on land and on water." As befits their destructive nature, floods are usually interpreted by ancient authors as foretelling negative events.[13] There is at least one instance, however, in which a flood is portrayed as anticipating a positive (or at least somewhat ambiguous) one. When relating the rise of Augustus, Dio (53.20.1) notes about the flood of 27 BC that "from this sign the soothsayers prophesied that he would rise to great heights and hold the whole world under his sway."

The second way that floods were interpreted in regards to religion was as constituting a form of divine punishment for some transgression. Of the 42 accounts, 9 contain an explicit statement of this type, indicating that the flood is an expression of the anger of the gods.[14] When a flood interrupted games in the Circus Maximus in 363 BC, Livy relates that "the people were filled with fear" because it seemed that "the gods had turned away, rejecting the proffered appeasement of their anger." Interestingly, the deeds that were seen as provoking divine wrath often were not religious offenses against the gods directly but rather political actions of which the gods disapproved. For example, Dio states that the flood of 54 BC was interpreted as indicating the gods' anger over Gabinius's unauthorized restoration of Ptolemy to the throne of Egypt (Dio 39.61.1–2). In his account of the same flood, Cicero (*Ad Quint. fr.* 3.7.1) first quotes a tag from Homer—"Zeus pours the rain in resentment and wrath at the misdeeds of mortals / Who in the place of assembly distort without mercy their judgments / Banishing justice from earth and the voice of the gods never heeding"—and then despairingly comments that this seems to perfectly describe the recent acquittal of Gabinius at his trial over the Egyptian settlement.

Not surprisingly, a number of flood narratives also include mention of actions intended to appease or placate the gods. Such attempts at propitiation occur in 8 out of the 42 flood accounts.[15] The flood of 193 BC, together with other portents, prompted a frantic round of appeasements, among them a consultation of the Sibylline Books, a nine-day sacrifice, a supplication, and a purification of the entire city (Livy 35.9.2–6). The Sibylline Books were also consulted after the flood of 54 BC, and either purifications or supplications were held after the floods of 192 BC and AD 69 (Dio 39.61.1–2; Livy 35.21.5–6; Tac. *Hist.* 1.86).

Flood Reports: Context and Causation

It is important to our understanding of how the Romans viewed floods to note the particular contexts in which floods were reported by ancient authors. Floods are rarely described on their own as significant events, but instead are usually linked to other related occurrences. In 12 of the 42 accounts, the flood in question is recounted merely as one item in a longer list of supernatural portents.[16] These omens span the usual range of natural and unnatural events, including buildings and monuments being struck by lightning, monstrous births, talking animals, statues rotating of their own accord, eclipses, and such oddities as snakes eating themselves. A brief but typical example of this type of context for flood reporting is how Dio (53.33.5) mentions the inundation of 22 BC: "And just as it usually happens that some sign occurs before such events, so on this occasion a wolf was caught in the city, fire and storm damaged many buildings, and the Tiber rose . . ." Usually, as just noted, these omens are identified as prophesying some specific event, but occasionally floods are mentioned more generally as part of a list of all misfortunes or prodigies that occurred during a given span of time, typically an emperor's life.[17]

Another frequent context for flood accounts is as one item in a list of disasters that struck in a given year. In annalistic authors such as Livy or Dio, this is the most common way that floods are reported. Out of the 42 flood accounts, 18 associate a description of a flood with other natural disasters that transpired that year, most typically fires, earthquakes, and diseases.[18] In these contexts, floods and other catastrophes are sometimes interpreted as having supernatural significance or being caused by the gods, but in other instances they are related as natural events. At times, a flood is simply reported among an inventory of notable happenings, positive or negative, that took place during a given year. The floods of 189 BC, for instance, are placed among a motley list of the year's events, which includes the results of a census, details of contracts being let for public works, and the results of a Campanian delegation to the senate (Livy 38.28.1–4).

The frequent association in primary sources between floods and the gods leads to the important question of whether floods were viewed by the Romans as divine acts that could not (or perhaps even should not) be prevented, or as natural disasters that might be remedied by engineering. This has direct relevance to any assessment of the Romans' efforts at flood control, because if floods were viewed primarily as portents and as a way that the gods sent messages, then it might be sacrilegious to interfere with this mechanism through man-made works intended to alleviate flooding. If, on the other hand, floods were seen as primarily random natural disasters, then it would be less problematic in terms of religion to attempt flood control measures.

Whether a flood is identified as having divine causation is not simply a function of which author happens to be reporting it. Both Livy and Cassius Dio, who together account for almost half of the extant flood narratives (20 of 42), at times report floods as being instigated by the gods in retribution or as warnings, while in other instances they record them as simply having occurred, or include them in lists of natural disasters or notable events. Livy 5 times specifically associates inundations with the gods, but 3 other times he does not, while Dio ascribes 10 floods to divine causation while mentioning 2 others without making such a link.[19] The remaining 22 flood narratives, which are from 16 different authors, are similarly mixed, with 8 associating a flood with the gods while 14 do not.

At times it seems surprising that an author does not interpret a flood as reflecting or foretelling contemporary events. One such notable omission concerns the two floods that struck in 215 BC. These inundations are recounted by Livy (24.9.6), who elsewhere demonstrates no reluctance to portray floods as supernatural omens. On this occasion, despite the fact that these inundations occur during the Hannibalic invasion of Italy, and, in fact, took place only a year after the catastrophe of Cannae, Livy does not interpret the floods as having any supernatural meaning. Instead, at the end of his narrative of events for the year, he simply states without further comment that there were two floods that year that destroyed many buildings and killed many people. Overall, while just over half (23 of 42) of the flood accounts do link an inundation in some way to the supernatural or to the gods, that leaves nearly another half in which no such connection is made.

The primary source accounts, therefore, seem to present an ambiguous message in regard to the question of the gods as the cause of floods, which leads to further questions about whether the Romans truly believed that the gods routinely sent messages through portents, and even how deeply they believed in the gods at all. This is not the place to delve into the thorny (and perhaps overly simplistic) issue of whether the Romans literally believed in their gods. The reality of ancient Roman religious belief was certainly a complex and at times contradictory one that incorporated a wide spectrum of degrees of belief and adherence to ritual. The ambivalence of the flood narratives themselves—in which there is not a consistent attitude expressed toward the causation of floods, and inundations are sometimes seen as divinely directed and at other times not, even by the same author—probably accurately mirrors the multifaceted nature of Roman religious belief itself.

The range of possible ancient opinions toward floods is even explicitly addressed in the two accounts of the flood of AD 15. Concerning this flood, Dio (57.14.7–8) reports that "most people regarded it as an omen." He then adds that "the emperor, however, thinking that it was due to the great overabundance of surface water appointed five senators . . . to look after the river so that it should neither overflow in winter nor fail in summer." Here we have one source presenting two conflicting interpretations for the causation of this flood—a popularly held one that ascribes it to divine action, and Tiberius's explanation, which is an attempt at a rational, scientific one. Which explanation was accepted as the primary cause of the flood is of great significance because the rival interpretations would have demanded radically different reactions on the part of the Romans. If the inundation was divine in nature, then some form of prayer or sacrifice was called for, whereas if Tiberius was correct, then an appropriate response required engineers and analysis rather than priests and rituals. Tacitus's account (*Ann.* 1. 76) of this same flood also records this split in opinion over what caused the disaster and how to respond to it. He emphasizes the severity of the flood and then records that "Accordingly, Asinius Gallus moved that the Sibylline Books be consulted. Tiberius objected, preferring secrecy on earth as in heaven, yet the job of regulating the river was entrusted to Ateius Capito and Lucius Arruntius."[20] Seeking guidance from the Sibylline Books would have been a standard way to respond to a major flood, but Tiberius instead prescribed a practical response rather than a spiritual one.

The tension reflected in these accounts, between a desire to make the city safer from destructive flooding through practical actions and a fear of meddling with possible divinely inspired occurrences, probably accurately represents the complex nature of Roman attitudes toward the gods. The Romans seem to have been content to have "hedged their bets" by following both courses. In all periods, they remained open to the possibility of interpreting floods as supernatural messages or as being divinely caused, and at times responded to floods with religious rituals of purification or appeasement; however, at the same time, they investigated and experimented with a range of practical measures aimed at reducing the extent and damage of floods. Such an apparently contradictory attitude was, in fact, just the opposite—it was a way of maximizing the chances for the best possible outcome by covering all the possibilities.[21] The evidence also suggests that the Romans made distinctions as to how offensive various actions were in religious terms based on how much they affected the fundamental nature of the stream. While Romans, therefore, do seem to have harbored some religious scruples about possible flood control methods that would have changed the course or altered the volume or flow of the Tiber, they do not seem to have felt such concerns about more passive methods, such as building up the riverbanks.

Flood Prevention: Costs and Benefits

This once again brings us back to the central issue of the Romans' failure to enact effective flood control measures. Although the Romans' understanding of hydrology appears to have been incomplete, it was nonetheless sufficient for them to have been able to identify some measures that would have been likely to affect flooding in a beneficial manner. Many of the schemes that the Romans did undertake, such as raising ground levels, were effective and could have been even more so had they been carried out on a larger scale. The solution ultimately selected to prevent flooding at Rome—the embankments built at the close of the 19th century (fig. 6.4)—were well within the ancient Romans' technological ability and could just as well have been constructed in the second century AD. The Romans were demonstrably capable of crafting high-quality stone or concrete embankments, as can be seen by the remains of such structures in the Emporium district. Additionally, as a passive response to flooding that did not alter the fundamental nature of the river, embankments should have been immune from potential objections or criticisms based on religious scruples. If only the Romans had erected a continuous line of such embankments at the proper height over the entire course of the Tiber within Rome, the city would have achieved security from most floods 2,000 years earlier than it did.

One obvious possible reason why the Romans may have elected not to build such embankments is the cost in money, manpower, and materials required for such a major construction project. Lining the Tiber with sufficiently high embankments would have demanded an enormous amount of work. Thousands of laborers would have had to be employed digging, hauling dirt and stone, and erecting the embankments. Their wages and the necessary raw materials would have

Floods of the Tiber in Ancient Rome

Fig. 6.4. Section of the modern Tiber embankment which protects the city from floods. The Romans could have constructed similar walls. (Photo by author)

placed a heavy burden on the state treasury, and the undertaking itself would likely have required years to complete. It is worth considering, therefore, if this could be the reason why (or even a major factor in explaining why) the Romans did not build such embankments.

The investment in resources, though certainly large, would still have been well within the demonstrated capabilities of the Romans. The Romans even seem to have had a propensity for undertaking mammoth public works. Neither high cost, nor prolonged construction time, nor great manpower demands were deterrents, if the Romans were resolved to build something. Particularly in the last century of the Republic and the first two centuries of the Empire (a period during which there were at least 18 major floods), the Romans embarked upon numerous massive public works projects. During these centuries, the city of Rome was completely transformed and rebuilt several times, acquiring many of its most famous and substantial monuments, but little was done to prevent floods.

One factor that might help to explain why the Romans were unwilling to devote substantial resources to a project such as embankments could be that a major motivation for the elites who financed such structures was to gain prestige from them. However, a practical undertaking such as embankments might yield less fame than, for instance, a highly decorative temple or theater. Against this hypothesis can be placed many examples of practical infrastructure that were constructed, such as roads and aqueducts. The eponymous Via Appia and Aqua Claudia certainly brought considerable renown to their builders. The resources that the Romans were willing to expend on such structures are staggering. The Aqua Marcia was reported to have cost 180 million sesterces, and the Anio Novus / Aqua Claudia project 350 million sesterces (Front. *De Aq.* 1.7; Pliny *HN* 36.122).[22] The immense expense of public works becomes evident when these figures are compared with other well-known costs, such as a legionary's annual pay of 900 HS under Augustus, or the minimum senatorial qualification of 1 million HS. Nor did the time required to complete such works daunt the Romans. The Claudian aqueducts, for example, took almost 14 years to complete.

Another major project that took place during the reign of Claudius, the draining of the Fucine Lake, makes for an especially interesting comparison with a hypothetical Tiber embankment project. Both were large-scale undertakings involving the channeling of unwanted water. Given the Romans' uncertainty concerning the cause of Tiber flooding, the outcome of both projects would have been at least somewhat in question at the time they were begun. The intended goal of draining the Fucine Lake was to expose valuable farmland, which was to be accomplished by boring a tunnel 6 km in length through the rock of a mountain. Ultimately, digging this tunnel required the constant labor of 30,000 workers for 11 years (Suet. *Claud.* 20.2–3).

The draining of the Fucine Lake once again illustrates the scale of public works that the Romans accomplished during this period, the patience that they had in undertaking projects that would require many years to complete, and the resources they were willing to expend in order to accomplish them. While it is not recorded how much this endeavor cost, merely paying for 30,000 laborers over that time span would have represented a substantial commitment.[23] If Claudius was willing to spend so much to obtain some additional farmland, from a modern perspective it seems that he should have been willing to commit an equal (or lesser) amount to rendering his capital city safe from destructive inundations. While the farmland exposed by the draining of the Fucine Lake was no doubt welcome, the benefits obtained from making Rome free from flooding would have been no less tangible.

Nor was it only in or around the city of Rome that the Romans were willing to undertake such massive projects. The provinces were full of impressive and expensive feats of Roman engineering. An example of such an imperial project requiring substantial investment in manpower and resources that was located on the very edge of the Empire is Hadrian's Wall in Britain. A potential Tiber embankment project should have been a relatively attractive one when compared with many other large-scale public works that the Romans actually built. Given the importance of the city of Rome as the focus of power in the Empire and the residence of the emperor, anything that enhanced the city brought additional status and glory to both the Empire and to its leader. If the Romans were willing to pour out resources for huge construction schemes on the remote fringes of the Empire, they certainly would not have hesitated to expend comparable or lesser sums on beneficial projects within the capital itself. Therefore, while the resources in terms of time, money, and manpower necessary for a Tiber embankment project would have been substantial, it is hard to imagine that they would have been any greater than those expended on such public works as a major aqueduct, Claudius's or Trajan's harbors, the draining of the Fucine Lake, or even on more focused undertakings such as Trajan's Forum, Nero's Golden House, or the Flavian Amphitheater.

Just because the Romans were financially and logistically capable of undertaking a major flood prevention project is not reason enough for them to have done it. They also had to have sufficient motivation to commit themselves to undertaking it. Today such a project would be subject to a cost-benefit study, and while it is unlikely that the Romans would have subjected possible flood prevention schemes to such a formal analysis, they certainly would have had a general sense of some of the potential benefits. Evaluating how the Romans would have perceived these benefits, however, is especially difficult from a modern perspective, both because the Romans did not have the economic tools available to them to model and evaluate such projects as we would and, more importantly, because of significant cultural differences. For example, the Romans would likely have anticipated that a flood prevention project would eliminate financial losses resulting from the destruction of stored goods such as grain, but would they have considered the economic losses arising from lost workdays or disruption of travel? Even more problematic is attempting to assess the actions taken by a modern versus an ancient state to prevent natural disasters in regard to more abstract considerations and attempting to guess the motivations and assumptions behind those actions.

An area where such factors are particularly acute is evaluating how strong the protection of the inhabitants of the city was as a motivating factor for the Romans. Today, the preservation of human life is the paramount concern for those who plan for natural disasters. This motivation is so powerful that it frequently overrides other factors, such as economic ones. The desire to minimize casualties and to swiftly bring aid to victims dominates to a marked degree modern thinking about what actions are appropriate (or necessary) to take in order to prevent natural disasters. It is worth remembering, however, that this priority may not have been fully shared by ancient administrators. It does seem that there was at least somewhat of a lesser degree of concern for the loss of human life as a result of natural disasters on the part of the state and those in charge than would be tolerable today. I am not suggesting that individual Romans did not feel emotions of loss or grief as keenly as people today, but it does seem safe to say that the state placed less value on individual lives. This was especially the case for the poor or lower-class citizens, foreigners, and slaves who would certainly have made up the vast majority of casualties in a flood.

This difference can plainly be seen in how floods are reported in ancient sources versus modern news accounts. Today the most emphasized and lengthiest sections of flood narratives in the media concern deaths, injuries, and stories about those who were rescued. Overwhelmingly, the modern focus when reporting natural disasters is the toll in human life. Ancient sources, on the other hand, concentrate most heavily on the event as a religious portent and on damage to buildings. While deaths and injuries are occasionally mentioned by ancient authors, these are plainly not the primary focus of their accounts.[24] Not a single ancient flood account contains the type of narrative of an individual's death or rescue that is the staple of modern disaster reporting.

The issue of who were the principal victims of Roman floods is, therefore, a significant one in assessing the Roman state's interest in preventing floods. There is evidence to suggest that those living closest to the Tiber, and consequently at greatest risk when it flooded, tended to include a large proportion of marginalized groups. The low-lying section of the southern Transtiberim, for example, has a long history of being associated with foreigners and marginalized groups. It seems to have housed a substantial portion of Rome's early Jewish community (at least four synagogues were built in the Transtiberim) as well as being the region where a large number of foreign cult centers were located.[25] Certain businesses whose operation created unpleasant smells or by-products, such as tanneries, were also concentrated here—perhaps by official decree, as is suggested by several literary references (Martial 6.93; Juv. 14.203). Another marginalized business that seemingly thrived across the Tiber was prostitution, and this region is known to have harbored a number of brothels and seedy taverns (Tac. *Ann.* 14.15). On the left bank of the Tiber where the main city lay, some areas adjacent to the river may also have been similarly marginal in character, such as the commercial Emporium district below the Aventine. In later times, a number of strips alongside the riverbanks became clearly delineated ethnic ghettos, such as the famous Jewish Quarter, and although the existence of such districts cannot be extrapolated with certainty back to the Roman era, it is certainly a common urban trend across cultures and time periods for poor or marginalized groups to be relegated to the areas closest to rivers.[26] Many of Rome's poor were also crammed into the lower regions of the city in the valleys between the hills, such as the Velabrum and the Subura district. Those who ran Rome's government would have worried much less with these groups constituting the main victims of flooding than if they themselves had been the ones principally affected.[27]

From the perspective of some of Rome's elites, the destruction caused by floods in these neighborhoods could perhaps even have been perceived as a beneficial phenomenon. By literally washing away undesirable people and establishments, floods might have been viewed as constituting a crude but effective form of urban renewal. Open space was at a premium in the heart of the city, and if a flood caused a few rickety *insulae* to collapse or unsavory taverns to be demolished, the resultant cleared zone might become the site of a more luxurious apartment building from which greater rents could be extracted, or even of a new monument or public work that would immortalize and bring fame to its donor. Roman legal codes contained provisions that could make it difficult to demolish existing buildings, so if a flood helpfully performed this service, it would have presented a welcome opportunity for those eager to erect new structures in already heavily developed areas of the city.[28]

Such attitudes alone, however, are a completely inadequate explanation of the Romans' surprising failure to do more to prevent flooding in the city. While the Romans did take some actions to lessen the effects of floods, they did not take the steps necessary to prevent them. The inescapable conclusion remains that while the Romans had both the technology and the resources to safeguard the city against flooding, they chose not to do so. The best way to begin to more completely understand why the Romans made such a decision is to consider the city's overall vulnerability to floods, an assessment that will be taken up in the conclusion.

Conclusion

The Romans' Failure to Make Rome Safe from Floods

Floods were indeed a serious problem for ancient Rome. Rome eventually grew into an enormous, architecturally complex city, but this densely populated, man-made urban landscape was situated on ground that was inherently marshy. Even worse, the city was located squarely in a flood plain and, in fact, had the misfortune to be positioned at the very point on the Tiber most prone to severe flooding. As this book has argued, these floods were far more frequent than has traditionally been assumed, with minor inundations taking place every four or five years, and catastrophic ones striking on average every 20–25 years. The latter could be of impressive magnitude, with their waters rising 15 m above the normal level of the river and inundating large regions of the city. As has been described, floods caused a wide range of both immediate and long-term destructive effects, including disruption of urban daily life, death of humans and livestock, the collapse of buildings, and increased incidence of disease. The Romans witnessed firsthand the harmful effects of floods and knew with a high degree of probability that these disasters would recur. Given all these facts, the question remains: why did they not do more to prevent these floods?

One way to begin explaining this failure is to perform an overall assessment of ancient Rome's vulnerability to floods in light of the information that has been presented in this book. Such a comprehensive evaluation reveals that the city possessed a number of unusual or even unique qualities that reduced its vulnerability to floods, rendered Rome and its inhabitants less susceptible to the damages produced by floods, and made the city atypically quick to recover from the effects of an inundation. There are at least five characteristics that helped to minimize Rome's vulnerability to floods: topography, construction methods, residential housing patterns, food storage, and water supply.

Topography. The highly varied topography of Rome intermingles within a constricted area several low-lying valleys and marshy depressions together with numerous small hills. Rome is famously the city of seven hills, and their presence would have been a major factor in reducing the fatalities that resulted from flooding. Not only do lines of hills surround the central area of the ancient city, but a number of escarpments are also scattered throughout the city's core. These would have provided convenient points of refuge to which the inhabitants of the city could have fled. Almost every point within the Aurelianic walls is less than a few hundred meters from high ground; even if someone were in the center of the Campus Martius, sanctuary on a hill was little more than a kilometer distant. Although relatively small, the hills of Rome tend to have fairly steep slopes, so that a person fleeing floodwaters could have quickly climbed to an elevation that was safe. Thus, while one was never far from the danger posed by the Tiber, one was also never far from reaching safety on a hill. The two situations that tend to result in large numbers of deaths are floodwaters that rise very rapidly, such as flash floods, and floods that strike in a flat terrain that offers nowhere to run to. The latter are common in China, where appalling death tolls are routinely caused by flooding of the Hwang He (Yellow) and Yangtze (Chang) rivers, which flow through vast, featureless plains that supply no points of refuge when the waters rise.[1] At Rome, on the other hand, the proximity of numerous hills offered ready sanctuary from floodwaters, and while the level of the Tiber can rise rapidly, such increases are measured in hours rather than minutes, allowing time for the city's inhabitants to reach high ground.[2]

Construction Methods. At first glance, it seems odd that the Romans erected the majority of their important public buildings in a flood zone. However, while some Roman construction materials, such as sun-dried brick, were highly susceptible to damage by water, major public monuments were typically built using materials and methods that rendered them invulnerable to destruction by floods. Floods usually cause serious damage to buildings either by undermining their foundations or because structural components are made out of materials that can be harmed by immersion in water. However, important buildings such as temples, basilicas, and theaters were often erected on top of massive concrete foundations many meters in depth, which defied scouring and undermining by floodwaters. In addition, by the early Empire, the buildings themselves were composed of various materials, such as kiln-dried brick, concrete, rubble, and stone, that were neither easily degraded nor destroyed by water. Often they were also heavily overengineered, with extremely thick walls well suited to withstanding the horizontal stresses that might be placed upon them by deep floodwaters. While some decorative features of these structures, such as plastered and painted walls, might have been damaged by floods, the basic structures themselves were relatively immune. Because much of their ornamentation took the form of inlaid precious stones, carved architectural elements, and stone statuary, even the decoration of these buildings was highly resistant to damage by floodwater.

The marble floors and walls of monumental Roman buildings would also have facilitated the cleaning-up and drying-out process, since mud or debris deposited by floods could have been sluiced away with clean water. Usually one of the greatest problems with postflood cleanup is that commonly used organic building materials such as wood are very hard to sanitize and readily retain flood-borne contaminants. When timbers are used to form the internal structural components of walls, they can also be extremely difficult to dry out and may suffer permanent degradation of their solidity through immersion in water. The stone, concrete, and brick that composed the walls of major public works, however, would have been much less susceptible to these threats.[3] As testimony to the construction methods used in these structures, no major public monument (other than the special case of bridges) is known to have been destroyed by a flood, although the ancient sources plainly placed a high priority on reporting damage to buildings. The popular image of ancient Rome is a city built of shining marble, and as well as enhancing its aesthetic appeal, this characteristic of the city gave very practical benefits as well.

Residential Housing Patterns. The varied topography of the city also made it possible for Rome's elites to choose whether they wanted to live on low or high ground, and they overwhelmingly elected to place their private dwellings atop hills. This ensured that the class that dominated decision making at Rome, as well as authoring nearly all of our extant primary sources, did not, as a group, suffer the destructive effects of flooding in its own homes. Certainly there were some elites who lived in low-lying areas, but there does appear to have been a very strong preference for locating *domus* on hills. During the Republic, certain hills, especially the Palatine, had well-established reputations as the favored dwelling places of Rome's powerful families. The development of the imperial palace complex atop the Palatine during the Empire ensured that the emperor's lodgings would be similarly safe from inundation. A substantial percentage of the rest of Rome's populace had to buy or rent lodgings in the remaining valleys and lowlands and thus would have suffered greatly from flooding, but on the whole these were not people who had much of a say in determining political and economic policy. Rome was a severely stratified society with a very small group of elites controlling the vast majority of wealth and power, who could—and did—overwhelmingly choose to situate their homes in places where they would not have to worry about experiencing danger or loss when the Tiber rose.

Food Storage. The manner in which the food supply mechanism of ancient Rome was organized harbored considerable potential for disaster. The huge population was dependent on hundreds of thousands of tons of imported grain that, during the brief summer sailing season, had to reach Italy, where it was stored in giant warehouses for distribution throughout the year. The whole system was precarious, with little surplus or room for error. If the stock of stored food was lost, the city faced famine. For ease of transport, most of the great *horrea* that contained the grain were situated in the flood plain close to the Tiber. Stored grain is extremely sensitive to moisture, and immersion in floodwater would not only have spoiled the grain through waterborne organic contaminants but would also have encouraged the growth of potentially fatal molds.

Given this precarious situation, every major flood should have resulted in food shortage or even famine. While there are a few clear instances of food shortage subsequent to inundations, such incidents are neither as severe nor as common as might be expected. A possible explanation can be found in the particular design of large Roman *horrea,* which resembled enclosed rectangular fortresses with high walls and often only one narrow external opening. The standard grain *horrea* design—which included a series of separate, small rooms clustered around a courtyard, unusually thick walls, ventilation windows placed high on the walls, and raised floors—might have made it possible for such buildings to protect their precious contents from minor to moderate floodwaters. The unique features of these structures have often been explained as being dictated by security concerns, but they are equally well designed to safeguard the city's vital stored grain supply from the threat of many floods.

Water Supply. Contamination of a city's water supply by floodwaters carrying sewage and corpses is usually one of the most problematic aftereffects of floods. During modern floods, the provision of clean drinking water is usually the highest priority of relief efforts but also one of the most challenging. This is due to the fact that cities typically draw their drinking water from local reservoirs, wells, or treatment facilities that, once contaminated by floodwater, are extremely difficult to clean and disinfect. Once again, the particular characteristics of ancient Rome's water supply system would have helped the city to recover from floods unusually quickly. While some water was obtained from local wells and springs, the majority of Rome's water was brought from hillside springs many kilometers distant, and thus would have been unaffected by contamination from floods. The gravity-powered supply system of aqueducts, *castella,* and pipes was a continual-flow linear network. These characteristics would have expedited its recovery from contamination, since clean water would have constantly been flowing in one direction through the system to flush out the contaminated sections. Even at the height of a flood when much of the city was underwater, residents could have readily located clean drinking water by going to the nearest distribution point that was just above the level of the floodwaters; there, they would have found a constant flow of fresh water. Thus Rome's water supply would both have continued to operate at least partially even during a flood, and would have been quick to recover after the waters subsided.

The large drains that lay under Rome's streets, which normally carried away the used water from this system, were another important component in the city's rapid recovery after an inundation. On the one hand, while these drains would have reversed during a flood, allowing the water access to low-lying parts of the city, once the waters receded, their large capacity would have helped to drain away floodwaters quickly and, just as importantly, would have prevented large stagnant pools from forming that might otherwise have persisted for weeks. In marked contrast to modern cities, the vital infrastructure of ancient Rome was both more resistant to damage from flooding and quicker to resume operation.[4]

In the introduction to this book, three goals were identified that progressively moved from determining (as much as possible) the facts about floods in ancient Rome to exploring how the Romans viewed these disasters. The first goal was simply to gather together and present what is known about ancient Roman floods from contemporary accounts. This information was then coupled with later hydrological observations of the Tiber in order to define the basic characteristics of Tiber floods: their extent, duration, seasonality, frequency, and magnitude. As a result, it has been possible to create a map of the city that estimates which regions were most prone to inundation and to describe the principal attributes of these floods. One important conclusion that has resulted from analysis of these data is that floods struck the city far more often than has previously been suggested.

Once the fundamental parameters of floods at Rome had been established, the second goal of this study was to identify and describe the full range of effects that such floods would have caused. As has been shown, floods produced serious short-term effects such as death, injuries, loss of property, and the destruction of buildings, but also an array of long-term problems, most notably weakened structures, food shortages, and disease. The third goal was to explore the way the Romans responded to these floods, including the various means they either considered or attempted to avert or lessen floods, how the threat of inundations affected the development of the urban landscape, the link between floods and religion, and, finally, the attitude of the Romans toward these floods. This investigation has inevitably led to one question: why didn't the Romans do more to prevent flooding when they had the means to do so?

An answer may begin to be found in the five characteristics of the city, listed previously, that combined to decrease the vulnerability of the city to floods, to lessen the destructive scope of inundations when they did occur, and to facilitate the city's rapid recovery from them. Individually these five factors may not seem that significant, but collectively they helped to make living with floods more acceptable. This is especially true from the perspective of Rome's elites, who were sheltered from many of the most destructive aspects of inundations. They were the ones with the power to undertake measures to prevent inundations, but they were also the group least subject to the harmful effects of flooding. There are several important additional factors that contributed to this equation. A relative lack of concern on the part of the state for the suffering of the primary victims of flooding coupled with the possibilities for urban renewal that could result from a flood's destructiveness contributed to a lack of motivation for the Romans in charge to take decisive action. Finally, uncertainty over the best method for flood prevention and religious scruples over altering the Tiber also played a role in the inability to commit to a comprehensive flood prevention scheme. In the end, the Romans' failure to make their city safer from flooding cannot be ascribed to any single cause, but rather arises from the combination of a large number of factors.

Ancient Romans learned to live with the intermittently destructive nature of their unpredictable river and to adapt to its rhythms. Rome was the largest and most complex man-made urban environment of the preindustrial age, but even in the heart of such a setting, the inhabitants could not control occasional eruptions of nature's fury into the artificial landscape of stone and brick. When these incursions happened, however, the city proved to be surprisingly resilient, and the Romans' attitude toward inundations was also marked by commendable flexibility. As the incident of the flooding of Balbus's theater that began this book illustrates, when nature intruded into the city, the Romans were prepared to adapt to the circumstances and carry on as best as possible. While it would be an overstatement to say that the great metropolis of ancient Rome lived in harmony with the Tiber, there existed at the very least an uneasy truce; unlike today, when unruly rivers are viewed solely as objects to be tamed, the Romans were willing to cede a measure of independence to Father Tiber. Despite its very real potential for destruction, the Romans maintained toward the river in their midst an attitude of acceptance of its transgressions as well as respect for its power.

Appendix I

List of Major Floods at Rome, 414 BC–AD 2000

Table A.1 includes historically attested major floods from 414 BC to AD 2000. For ancient through Renaissance floods, at least one primary source is listed. From 1702 onward, almost all the floods are known from measurements taken at Ripetta.[1] For floods that are additionally attested by one or more flood markers, this information is also noted under "Source" along with the number of markers erected commemorating that flood. When known, the height of the floodwaters is given. The accuracy of the listed flood heights increases over time, from approximations for the medieval floods, to more reliable numbers derived from flood markers or early flood measurements, to the modern, highly accurate measurements recorded at Ripetta in Rome. From 1702 onward, all the heights given are from measurements taken at Ripetta. For the period 1871–1999, all instances when the water level reached 13.00 masl at Ripetta are included even though not all of these resulted in flooding in the city due to the presence of the embankment walls.[2] From 1947 to 2000, no flood reached a height of 13 masl.[3] The modern Tiber embankment walls were constructed between approximately 1875 and 1925.

Many other authors have compiled similar lists. The most recent and complete of these appear in the appendixes of Bersani and Ben-

Appendix I

civenga (2001), the tables in Bersani and Bencivenga (2003), the article by Alessandroni and Remedia (2002), the tables in Bencivenga et al. (1995), the text of Di Martino and Belati (1980), and the tables of Frosini (1977). Not all authors are in agreement on the list of floods at Rome. I have included in my list floods that are known from a variety of different sources, including literary and epigraphic ones, but I have attempted to include only those floods for which the sources seem reasonably reliable. Nevertheless, some of the floods, particularly those before 1700, must be regarded as at least somewhat speculative.

Table A.1.
Major Floods at Rome, 414 BC to AD 2000

Date	Height (masl)	Source
414 BC		Livy 4.49.2–3
363 BC		Livy 7.3.2
241 BC		Augustine, *De Civitate Dei*, 3.18; Orosius 4.11.6
215 BC		Livy 24.9.6
203 BC		Livy 30.26.5
202 BC		Livy 30.38.10–12
193 BC		Livy 35.9.2–3
192 BC		Livy 35.21.5–6
189 BC		Livy 38.28.4
181 BC		Plutarch, *Numa* 22.4
156 BC		Iulius Obsequens 16
60 BC		Cassius Dio 37.58.3–4
54 BC		Cassius Dio 39.61.1–2; Cicero, *Ad Quintum fratrem* 3.7.1
44 BC		Horace, *Carmina* 1.2.1–20
32 BC		Cassius Dio 50.8.3
27 BC		Cassius Dio 53.20.1
23 BC		Cassius Dio 53.33.5
22 BC		Cassius Dio 54.1
13 BC		Cassius Dio 54.25.2
AD 5		Cassiodorus, *Chronicon* 604; Cassius Dio 55.22.3

(*continued*)

Table A.1. (Continued)

Date	Height (masl)	Source
12		Cassius Dio 56.27.4
15		Tacitus, *Annales* 1.76; Cassius Dio 57.14.7–8
36		Cassius Dio 58.26.5; Zonaras 11.3
69		Plutarch, *Otho* 4.5; Suetonius, *Otho* 8.3; Tacitus, *Historiae* 1.86
Reign of Nerva		Sextus Aurelius Victor, *Epitome* 13
Reign of Trajan		Pliny, *Epistulae* 8.17; Sextus Aurelius Victor, *Epitome* 13
Reign of Hadrian		SHA, *Hadrian* 21.6
147		SHA, *Antoninus Pius* 9.3; *Fasti Ostiensis*
162		SHA, *M. Aurelius* 8
217		Cassius Dio 79.25.5
253		Sextus Aurelius Victor, *De Caesaribus* 32
371		Ammianus Marcellinus 29.6.17–18
398		Claudian, *De Bello Gildonico* 41–43
411		Castiglione (1599b), Bonini (1663)
555		Castiglione (1599b), Bonini (1663)
570		Castiglione (1599b), Bonini (1663)
589		*De Gestis Langobardorum* 3.24
685		Bonini (1663)
716		*De Gestis Langobardorum* 6.36; *Liber Pontificalis*, Gregory II, 6
725		*Liber Pontificalis*, Gregory II, 1
778		Bonini (1663)

(*continued*)

Appendix I

Table A.1.   (Continued)

Date	Height (masl)	Source
791 December 20		*Liber Pontificalis,* Adrian I, 22
844 November 22		*Liber Pontificalis,* Sergius II, 22
856 January		*Liber Pontificalis,* Benedict III, 22
860 October 30		*Liber Pontificalis,* Nicholas, 15
860 December 27		*Liber Pontificalis,* Nicholas, 15
1180 January.16		
1230 February 2	>16	Marker
1277 November 6	>16	2 markers
1310 January	>15	Cod. Vat. Lat. 6880 f. 60 ss
1345 November	>15	
1376 December	17.00	
1379 November 9	17.00	Marker
1415 October 31	>15	
1422 November 30	17.32	Marker
1438 November 2	17.22	
1476 January 8	17.41	Marker
1485 November 25	>15	
1488 March 13	>15	
1495 December 5	16.88	9 markers
1514 November 13	>16	Marker
1530 October 8	18.95	9 markers
1557 September 15	18.90	3 markers
1589 November 4	>15	Marker
1589 November 10	>16	Marker
1598 December 24	19.56	19 markers
1606 January 23	18.27	Marker
1637 February 22	17.55	Marker
1647 December 7	16.41	Marker
1660 November 5	17.11	2 markers
1686 November 6	16.00	2 markers
1688	>15	Marker
1700 November	>15	2 markers
1702 December	15.41	
1742 January	15.02	
1750 December	15.58	
1783 February 17	14.49	

(continued)

Table A.1. (Continued)

Date	Height (masl)	Source
1784 December 17	14.69	
1786 January 5	14.41	
1789 November 10	14.55	
1805 February 2	16.42	5 markers
1809	15.47	
1836 February 5	14.20	
1843 February 7	15.34	
1844 February 27	>14	
1845 November 10	14.04	
1846 December 10	16.25	Marker
1851 November 10	14.04	
1855 February 17	14.79	
1855 March 28	14.90	
1858 December 3	14.07	
1863 January 20	14.92	
1870 December 29	17.22	47 markers
1871 January 25	13.40	
1871 November 10	13.41	
1872 December 13	13.04	
1873 November 1	13.98	
1875 December 5	13.96	
1878 November 16	15.35	Marker
1879 May 4	13.12	
1879 December 1	13.75	
1880 November 23	13.40	
1885 January 13	13.85	
1885 April 10	13.48	
1887 December 24	13.90	
1888 February 22	13.06	
1888 March 20	13.72	
1890 March 20	13.30	
1892 March 16	13.84	
1896 October 22	13.75	
1898 April 2	13.44	
1899 December 17	13.54	
1900 April 8	13.38	
1900 November 22	13.12	

(*continued*)

Appendix I

Table A.1. (Continued)

Date	Height (masl)	Source
1900 December 2	16.17	6 markers
1902 February 5	14.39	
1903 December 8	14.02	
1905 May 16	13.45	
1905 November 25	14.12	
1907 November 11	13.80	
1908 January 31	13.00	
1909 February 13	13.00	
1910 April 11	13.10	
1914 December 16	13.05	
1914 December 25	13.78	
1915 January 3	13.29	
1915 February 15	16.08	2 markers
1915 February 24	13.70	
1915 April 3	13.20	
1915 November 4	13.65	
1916 November 20	13.38	
1916 December 20	13.82	
1917 January 19	13.90	
1917 January 29	13.48	
1917 March 8	14.25	
1919 January 9	14.28	
1923 December 9	14.95	
1925 March 2	13.10	
1928 October 31	13.83	
1929 January 4	14.90	
1929 November 19	13.52	
1933 December 30	13.06	
1934 December 16	14.40	
1935 March 3	13.73	
1936 March 2	13.87	
1937 December 17	16.84	4 markers
1941 February 5	13.32	
1941 February 23	13.18	
1947 February 6	14.53	

Appendix II

The Modern Tiber Embankments

By the end of the 19th century, the city of Rome had suffered more than 2,500 years of flooding, and throughout this time, dozens of schemes to prevent these floods were proposed, started, attempted, discussed, and discarded before measures were at last taken to render it reasonably safe from inundation. Between 1876 and 1910, the Tiber was canalized between large vertical embankments that extended along the entire course of the Tiber within the city.[1] Since that time, the city has been free from major episodes of flooding.

A combination of several different factors was required to create the necessary impetus to finally do something about the city's vulnerability to floods. First among these was the destructive flood that struck on December 27, 1870.[2] Probably the best-documented flood in Roman history, it came at a time when Rome had not suffered a flood of such magnitude for more than 200 years. The areas affected by this flood are well known since at least 47 flood markers from the 1870 inundation were placed on buildings throughout the city. Also, this flood was intensively studied by contemporary engineers who, among other actions, in the aftermath of the flood had red lines exactly recording the high-water marks painted on buildings. The 1870 flood measured a peak of 17.22 masl at the Ripetta station hydrometer and 13.85 masl

Appendix II

at the Ripa Grande gauge. It lasted several days, covered much of the Campus Martius, severely disrupted the life of the city, and left behind a foul layer of mud and sewage.

The timing of this flood was significant because it struck only a few months after Rome had been declared the capital of the newly unified Italian state. With its new status as Roma Capitale, the city once again had an important symbolic role on the international stage. Thus it was a great embarrassment for the fledgling country when its capital city was revealed as being helpless before the destructive power of its own river. The time was also ripe for major civic projects, because there was a general perception that a great international city such as Rome aspired to be had to have monumental architecture as a visual expression of its status. The model for such a city and its architecture was Paris, with its broad boulevards, its public monuments, and its river, the Seine, constrained within uniform and visually impressive embankments.[3]

The final element lending force to the desire to prevent future floods was again a matter of image and timing—the first visit of King Vittorio Emanuele II to his new capital city. He entered the city on December 31, 1870, planning to preside over a series of ceremonies and public festivals that would officially inaugurate Rome as the capital of his empire. When he arrived, the floodwaters were still sloshing around the low-lying streets of the city, and the stinking mud and refuse that they had deposited left much of the city unfit for use. The image of a dirty, unhygienic, disaster-prone city that Rome presented to the world on this occasion was certainly not what the Italians had hoped for and was again highly embarrassing.

As a direct result of these events, an official commission was immediately created. The members were appointed in January 1871, with the charge of rendering the city of Rome safe from Tiber flooding. One of the senators of the new state, Carlo Possenti, who was also an administrator in charge of public works, was appointed president, and the commission was filled out with 10 additional members weighted heavily toward engineers. There was no shortage of possible plans for the commission to consider. Since the Renaissance, a nearly constant flow of proposals had been written advancing various schemes to prevent Tiber flooding. Between 1531 and 1845, at least

21 monographs on the subject of Tiber floods were published that advocated a range of methods for their prevention or alleviation.[4] Many of these were similar to the ideas that the ancient Romans had considered, including a resuscitation of Julius Caesar's plan to change the course of the Tiber within or around the city, and the notion of diverting some or all of the flow of the Aniene (Anio) away from the Tiber. The commission contemplated updated versions of these proposals in addition to a host of new ones, including creating overflow canals, straightening the curves of the Tiber, building a dam or a series of dams upstream from the city, diverting the Tiber's tributaries, diverting the Tiber itself, excavating a large port within the city boundaries, widening and deepening the bed of the Tiber, and constructing different types of embankments, among them versions with vertical or gradually sloping walls. All of these schemes were evaluated, debated, and discussed in a highly public manner, with factions developing that favored one or another. The popular war hero, General Garibaldi, even became involved in the process, and emerged as a vocal advocate of the proposal to divert the course of the Tiber.

Perhaps not surprisingly, in the end, the commission settled on one of the simplest and least expensive plans. Its author was Raffaele Canevari, a hydrologic engineer and, most significantly, a member of the commission itself. He proposed enclosing the Tiber within continuous embankments along the entire course of the river within the city. The walls of the embankments would be near vertical and of a uniform height of around 18 masl throughout the central part of the city. The walls would be spaced exactly 100 m apart, and anything that obstructed the free flow of water within this canal would be removed. The digging associated with the construction of the embankments would also allow Rome's ancient, outdated drain and sewer systems to be rebuilt and modernized. Finally, wide boulevards would be created running along the embankments on both sides of the river, providing needed roadways cutting through the heart of the city. The embankments would become known as the *muraglioni* and the associated boulevards as the *lungotevere*.

There were a number of significant and controversial implications to this plan. The one that raised the greatest objections was Canevari's call to remove all obstructions in the riverbed. Among the structures

Appendix II

that his proposal targeted for dismantling or removal were the grain mills lining the banks and the Ponte Rotto, the remnants of the old Roman Pons Aemilius. Tiber Island would also be radically transformed with the course of the river diverted entirely along the eastern side of the island, causing it to become in essence an extension of Trastevere. This change would also entail the pulling down of the two ancient bridges associated with the island, the Pons Cestius and the Pons Fabricius. The outcry over this destruction of the city's historical heritage was so great that the final version of the plan adopted in 1875 allowed for the island and bridges to remain in their original forms. The regularization of the width of the Tiber at a uniform 100 m meant that some portions of the riverbed were considerably widened while others were narrowed. The construction of the *lungotevere* necessitated the demolition of wide tracts of housing, especially in the Jewish Ghetto.[5]

There were a number of delays before construction work actually

Fig. A.1. Section of the Tiber in Rome before construction of the modern embankments. Ripetta is just visible in the distance before the bend. (Fototeca Unione, American Academy in Rome, 14111F)

The Modern Tiber Embankments

Fig. A.2. Stretch of the Tiber above the Ponte Garibaldi illustrating how the steep walls of the modern embankments cut off the city from access to its river. (Photo by author)

began in early 1876. The original budget for the project was 60 million lire, although it eventually cost far more than this. The work proceeded in fits and starts, with the majority of the project completed by 1890, but the final stages were not finished until 1910 (figs. A.1, A.2).

The finished *muraglioni* and *lungotevere* have incurred much criticism.[6] The steep, near-vertical walls of the embankment effectively cut off all contact between the city and its river. They even block the sight lines so that the Tiber is now invisible to the city's inhabitants unless one walks directly up to the edge of the embankment. Such a walk is made more difficult by the presence of the *lungotevere* filled with speeding vehicles, which act as a further barrier between the city and the Tiber. The old main access point to the river, the port of Ripetta, was also completely destroyed by the embankments. The riverbed within the walls has become a kind of wasteland, visually unattractive and relatively unused by the city's inhabitants. Portions of the riverbank, especially the left bank from the Cloaca Maxima to the old Em-

Appendix II

porium district, are now inhabited by homeless people and drug addicts. These problems might have been avoided or alleviated if the embankments had been constructed with gently sloping walls rather than vertical ones. This would have preserved access to the river and retained it as a focal point of the visible topography of the city. Such an arrangement was considered by the commission but was eventually rejected because of the higher cost and greater amount of space that sloping walls would have required. Currently, various proposals continue to be circulated aimed at reintegrating the city with its river, so that the story of Rome's embankments may have further chapters yet to be written.

Appendix III

A Note on Hydrological Sources

Although the primary readership of this book is most likely ancient historians, archaeologists, and classicists, due to the subject matter, it has of necessity drawn heavily from other fields and disciplines, especially hydrology, civil engineering, and geology. In the interest of accessibility, I have tried to restrain the use of technical hydrological and engineering jargon to reasonable levels, and in sections where a book on floods aimed at engineers might have relied upon mathematical formulas to portray hydrological phenomena, I have substituted more generalized verbal descriptions. For those interested in more detailed or technical information about floods, however, this appendix suggests some starting points.

An excellent up-to-date overall introduction to floods, flood processes, and responses to flood hazards is *Floods: Physical Processes and Human Impacts,* by K. Smith and Ward (1998). This book also contains an extensive and fairly current bibliography. Other particularly useful books on floods are *Inland Flood Hazards: Human, Riparian, and Aquatic Communities,* by Wohl (2000), and *Natural Disasters: Floods,* by Miller and Miller (2000). Older, more general works include *Floods,* by Hoyt and Langbein (1955), and *Floods: A Geographical Perspective,* by Ward (1978).

Appendix III

Some other works I found informative on floods and flood prevention were *Floods and Flood Management*, edited by Saul (1992); *Risk Analysis and Uncertainty in Flood Damage Reduction Studies*, published by the Committee on Risk Based Analysis for Flood Damage Reduction, National Water Science and Technology Board (2000); *Coping with Floods*, edited by Rossi et al. (1994); *Urban Flood Loss Prevention and Mitigation*, published by United Nations (1990); and *Urban Disaster Mitigation: The Role of Engineering and Technology*, edited by Cheng and Sheu (1995).

Hydrology textbooks provide an understanding of more specialized aspects of water flow. Examples include *Elements of Physical Hydrology*, by Hornberger et al. (1998); *Groundwater Science*, by Fitts (2002); *River Morphology*, by Schumm (1972); *Urban Hydrology*, by Hall (1984); and *Urban Hydrology: A Multidisciplinary Perspective*, by Lazaro (1979).

On aspects of floods and flood control engineering, there are numerous standard reference works that contain similar information, such as *Handbook of Applied Hydraulics*, by C. Davis and Sorensen (1984); *Drainage and Flood-Control Engineering*, by Pickels (1941); *Standard Handbook for Civil Engineers*, by Merritt (1968); and *Building Construction Handbook*, by Merritt (1958). The many publications of the U.S. Army Corps of Engineers on flood control engineering also offer considerable relevant data.

On the geology of the city of Rome, an older but still valuable work is *La geologia della città di Roma*, by Ventriglia (1971). An English language summary of this material is "Geology of Rome, Italy," by Thomas (1989). A recent supplement to Ventriglia that both features a number of large maps and is particularly concerned with hydrology is *La geologia di Roma: Il centro storico*, 2 vols., edited by Funiciello (1995).

On the Tiber itself and its behavior, the ultimate source of information is the archival records of the Servizio Idrografia and the Autorità di Bacino del Tevere. For interested readers, summaries of this material as well as substantial amounts of raw numerical data can most conveniently be accessed in *Il Tevere: Le inondazioni di Roma e i provvedimenti presi dal governo Italiano per evitarle*, by Frosini (1977); *Le piene del Tevere a Roma dal V secolo a.C. all'anno 2000*, by Bersani and Bencivenga (2001); "Il regime idrologico del Tevere, con particolare riguardo alle piene nella città di Roma," by Bencivenga et al. (1995); and

A Note on Hydrological Sources

La pianificazione del Bacino del Fiume Tevere 1992–2000, by Ferranti and Paolella (2001). Finally, the various issues of the journal *Tevere,* published by the Autorità di Bacino del Tevere, contain a wealth of useful information about both the historical and current Tiber, as well as its tributaries.

At the time this book went to press, several works containing significant information relevant to the topic of floods and the Tiber were forthcoming, including *Journal of Roman Archaeology* Supplementary Series no. 61, *Imaging Ancient Rome,* edited by L. Haselberger and J. Humphrey, and several articles by A. Ammerman reporting important new finds concerning the topography of Rome.

Notes

Introduction. Floods and History

1. The general literature on floods is vast, but a good compilation of bibliography can be found in Miller and Miller (2000), which is a reference work on floods containing more than 100 pages of bibliography, excerpts from relevant United States laws on flood control, and a brief but informative overview of floods in general. A recent comprehensive survey on floods that addresses some of the technical aspects of the topic but is still very accessible to a general reader and possesses an extensive bibliography is K. Smith and Ward (1998). Older, but still useful, general works on the history of floods and flood control include Hoyt and Langbein (1955) and Ward (1978). An introduction to the more technical aspects of floods is Wohl (2000a), which also contains comprehensive and further recent bibliography. Some other general textbooks on various hydrological aspects of floods include V. Baker et al. (1988); Hall (1984); Hornberger et al. (1998); Fitts (2002); Pickels (1941); and Schumm (1972). The many handbooks on hydrology and drainage systems published by the Army Corps of Engineers contain much helpful technical data. Individual historical floods are the subjects of numerous books and articles, and again the bibliographies in Miller and Miller (2000) and K. Smith and Ward (1998) are useful starting points. For bibliography specifically on the Tiber and its floods, see chapter 1, note 1.
2. Wohl (2000b), 12–13.
3. K. Smith and Ward (1998), 23–25; Wohl (2000b), 12.

Notes to Pages 2–10

4. Wohl (2000b), 13; Miller and Miller (2000), 26; NOAA (National Oceanic and Atmospheric Administration) website (www.noaa.gov/).
5. Wohl (2000c), 491. The catastrophic August 2005 flooding of New Orleans and surrounding regions as a result of Hurricane Katrina occurred when this book was already in press. Preliminary estimates of the economic losses resulting from this event are around $100 billion, and the death toll in the United States is at least 1,400. Although I was not able to directly incorporate information from Katrina into this book, the experiences and results of this disaster only underscore the continuing danger posed by floods and the timelessness of their destructive effects on cities and people.
6. K. Smith and Ward (1998), 23.
7. Miller and Miller (2000), 1.
8. Nencini (1966), 22.
9. Miller and Miller (2000), 1.
10. Hamilton and Joaquin (2000), 478.
11. J. Cornell (1976), 5.
12. The population of ancient Rome is a much debated topic, and various methods have been employed to arrive at population totals, including calculations based on square area, dwelling density, numbers of recipients of imperial benefactions, demographic analyses, actuarial statistics, and comparative data. The current consensus of opinion seems to be that the population rose rapidly during the late Republic, peaked at around or just over 1 million in the early Empire, and then began a steady decline. A good introduction to these debates can be found in Hopkins (1978), 2–3, 96–98. Other important discussions of Rome's population include Beloch (1886), 392–412; Oates (1934); Brunt (1971), 376–88; Morley (1996), 33–46; and Purcell (1999), 135–50.
13. Some Asian cities may also have attained populations comparable to that of ancient Rome. See Rozman (1973). Rome was, at any rate, certainly the largest Western city until recent times.
14. On the city of Rome and its structures generally, see, as starting points, Aldrete (2004); Coarelli (1995); Connolly and Dodge (1998); Coulston and Dodge (2000); J. Patterson (1992); and Stambaugh (1988). Essential reference works on the city and its monuments are the successive topographical dictionaries of Platner and Ashby (1929); Richardson (1992); and Steinby (1993–2000).
15. See, for example, Anderson (1997); Favro (1996); Grandazzi (1997); Hope (2000a); and Laurence (1993, 1994).

Chapter 1. Floods in Ancient Rome

1. The literature on floods at Rome has a long history and reflects the perennial threat that these events have posed to the city. The earliest wave of

scholarship on floods dates back to the 17th century, and was perhaps prompted by several destructive floods that struck the city around that time. Among these early works are G. Castiglione, *Trattato dell'inondatione del Tevere* (1599), and F. M. Bonini, *Il Tevere incatenato ovvero l'arte di frenar l'acque corrent* (1663). (See note 4 in appendix II for a complete list of 15th- to 19th-century works on floods.)

The flood of 1870 and the construction of the Tiber embankments prompted a renewed interest in the history of Tiber floods. Chief among this set of publications is the report of the commission charged with preventing future floods: C. Possenti, *Relazioni al sig. ministro dei lavori pubblici della Commissione nominata con R. Decreto 1 gennaio 1871 per studiare e proporre i mezzi di rendere le piene del tevere innocue alla città di Roma* (1871). Also belonging to this generation of studies are S. Aubert, *Roma e l'innondazione del Tevere* (1871); R. Canevari, *Studi per la sistemazione del Tevere nel tronco entro Roma* (1875); M. Carcani, *Il Tevere e le sue inondazioni dalle origini di Roma fino ai nostri giorni* (1893); E. Celani, "Alcune iscrizioni sulle inondazioni del Tevere" (1895); Strother Ancrum Smith, *The Tiber and Its Tributaries, Their Natural History and Classical Associations* (1877); and a number of works by Alessandro Betocchi, including "Del Fiume Tevere" (1879), *Dell'idrologia del Tevere* (1875), *Efemeride della straordinaria piena del Tevere 28 e 29 dicembre 1870-novembre 1871-marzo 1872* (1873), and *Statistica del fiume Tevere nel quarantennio 1 gennaio 1822–31 dicembre 1861* (1863).

The modern era of Tiber flood studies began with the publication in 1953 of Joël Le Gall's landmark study of the Tiber, *Le Tibre: Fleuve de Rome dans l'antiquité*, and in the same year, his *Recherches sur le culte du Tibre*. *Le Tibre* has probably been the single most influential and widely known work on the Tiber, and it remains relevant today. Louise Adams Holland's *Janus and the Bridge* (1961) has much to say about the early history and development of Rome and its cults in relationship to the Tiber. Useful information is contained in Cesare D'Onofrio's books, *Il Tevere: L'isola Tiberina, le inondazioni, i molini, i porti, le rive, i muraglioni, i ponti di Roma* (1980) and *Il Tevere e Roma* (1970). Pietro Frosini's *Il Tevere: Le inondazioni di Roma e i provvedimenti presi dal governo Italiano per evitarle* (1977) brings together much technical information from many years' worth of his publications on the Tiber and remains one of the most in-depth published collections of data on the hydrology of the Tiber basin. The book *Qui arrivo il Tevere* (1980) by V. Di Martino and M. Belati is a handy compilation of information about historical floods, with particularly good illustrations of the flood markers adorning many Roman buildings. A general survey of urban problems, including floods, is offered by Ramage (1983).

In the past few decades, there has been a flurry of important work on the Tiber, mostly by Italian archaeologists. Some of this material has appeared in a number of recent books of collected articles on the Tiber, including *Il delta del Tevere* (1998), ed. Carlo Bagnasco; *Il Tevere e le altre vie d'acqua del Lazio antico* (1986), ed. Stefania Quilici Gigli; and the collection of short papers, *Tevere: Un'antica via per il mediterraneo* (1986). Other relevant recent archaeological work includes the following articles: "Lungotevere Testaccio" (1985), by C. Mocchegiani Carpano and R. Meneghini; "Lungotevere Testaccio" (1985–86), by C. Mocchegiani Carpano, R. Meneghini, and M. Incitti; and "Tevere. Premesse per una archeologia fluviale" (1982), "Indagini archeologiche nel Tevere"(1981), and "Il Tevere: Archeologia e commercio"(1984a), all by C. Mocchegiani Carpano.

A brief but excellent survey of Tiber floods, including up-to-date hydrological information, is the article by M. Bencivenga, E. Di Loreto, and L. Liperi, "Il regime idrologico del Tevere, con particolare riguardo alle piene nella città di Roma" (1995). In collaboration with P. Bersani, Bencivenga followed up this article with the short monograph, *Le piene del Tevere a Roma dal V secolo a.C. all'anno 2000* (2001), and the identically titled article in the journal *Tevere,* "Le piene del Tevere a Roma dal V secolo a.C. all'anno 2000" (2003). Other recent works on Tiber floods include Maria G. Alessandroni and Gianrenzo Remedia, "The Most Severe Floods of the Tiber River in Rome" (2002); and Catherine Bustany, "Problèmes méthodologiques pour la cartographie des incendies et catastrophes naturelles dans la Rome antique" (2001), her website http://aphgcaen.free.fr/conferences/bustany.htm, and, with N. Géroudet, *Rome, maîtrise de l'espace, maîtrise du pouvoir* (2001), 33–45.

A recent lavishly illustrated book about the Tiber that features much information about floods and the city's relationship with the Tiber generally is *Il Tevere e Roma: Storia di una simbiosi,* by Maria Margarita Segarra Lagunes (2004). Other recent richly illustrated books that are aimed at a general or tourist audience but that nevertheless contain useful information, maps, illustrations, and photographs are *Il viaggio del Tevere,* by Marco Scataglini (2004); *Guida Insolita, ai misteri ai segreti, alle leggende e alle curiosità del Tevere il fiume di Roma,* by Claudio Rendina (2003); the issue of *ROMArcheologica, Il Tevere,* by C. Mocchegiani Carpano (2002); and the catalog to the exhibition, "Tibre-Seine: Deux villes deux fleuves," ed. Luisa Cardilli and Sartorio (1985). In addition, since 1996 the Autorità di Bacino del Tevere has been publishing the journal *Tevere,* which, while it focuses primarily on contemporary issues concerning the Tiber and its tributaries, also occasionally features articles on the history of the river, including floods, and in general contains much relevant hydrological information. A large volume published as a supplement to the journal and entitled *La pianificazione del Bacino del Fiume Tevere 1992–2000,* ed. Carlo Ferranti and Adriano Paolella (2001), is also of considerable technical interest.

Some ongoing projects relevant to the subject of Tiber floods include the survey work of the Tiber Valley Project (see description in H. Patterson and M. Millett, 1998), the various coring projects being conducted in many of the low-lying areas of the city of Rome by A. Ammerman and others (1990, 1996, 1998), and *Aquae Urbis Romae,* the on-line database on water-related topics at Rome organized by Katherine Wentworth Rinne (http://jefferson.village.virginia.edu/ waters/). Finally, interesting recent technical information on the Tiber and its tributaries is available on the website for the Servizio Idrografico e Mareografico Nazionale (www.dstn.it/simn/main1.html), including even some contemporary river data measured at Ripetta station in Rome (www.meteotevere.it/simn/simn/htm).

2. Ovid *Fasti* 2.381–425; Livy 1.4–7; Plut. *Rom.* 3–10; Varro *De Lingua Latina* 5.54.
3. The precise locations of the Ficus Ruminalis, the Lupercal, and the Cermalus are all somewhat problematic. For the purposes of this argument, the exact spot where the basket grounded is less important than the fact that it was clearly not on the bank of the Tiber proper but rather more inland at a site that floodwaters would have reached. On the locations of these sites, see as starting points Steinby (1993–2000) and Richardson (1992).
4. On early Rome, see as starting points C. Smith (1996); T. Cornell (1995); Pallottino (1993); Momigliano (1989); and Grandazzi (1997).
5. On foundation myths and Rome, see the works listed in the previous note, as well as Rykwert (1976); Carandini and Cappelli (2000); and Holland (1961).
6. It is interesting to note that the Tiber in flood also appears in the other great foundation myth of Rome, Virgil's *Aeneid*. In book 8, when Aeneas falls asleep on the bank of the river, Father Tiber appears to him and delivers an important prophecy. The river god identifies himself by saying, "I am the one you see touching the banks with floods" (8.62–63), and later the river god is described as soothing his swollen floodwaters (8.86–87) in order to expedite Aeneas's passage.
7. The frequency of floods is discussed in much greater detail later in chapter 2.
8. The context of accounts of floods in written sources is analyzed in more detail in chapter 6.
9. A number of modern authors have previously compiled lists of the floods in ancient Rome, and the following list is a compendium and expansion of these earlier ones. See Lugli (1953), 62–66; Le Gall (1953a), 29; Frosini (1977), 141; Di Martino and Belati (1980), 33; Gregori et al. (1988), 191–92; Bencivenga et al. (1995), 151; Bersani and Bencivenga (2001, 2003); and the list on the website dealing with natural catastro-

phes at Rome by C. Bustany (2003), http://aphgcaen .free.fr/conferences/bustany/htm. Mocchegiani Carpano (1986), 147–48, presents a table that contains several additional ancient floods, but does not offer any citations, so I have not included these in my list.

Unless otherwise indicated, translations of ancient texts are my own or adapted from standard translations (usually those found in the Loeb series of Harvard University Press).

10. For a description of this phenomenon as well as numerous historical examples, see Barber (1988), 141–44.
11. On this bridge, its architecture, and its role in Roman history, see Richardson (1992); Steinby (1993–2000); and Galliazzo (1995).
12. Le Gall (1953a), 30.
13. On the date of the flood in this poem, see Bustany (2001); Gros (1976), 18–20; Mazzarino (1966); Commager (1962); and Gallavotti (1949, cited by Gros, p. 18, n. 30).
14. For an introduction to the issues involved in dating Pliny's letters, see the comments by Syme (1958), 660–64.
15. Le Gall (1953a), 29; Frosini (1977), 141; Di Martino and Belati (1980), 33; Bencivenga et al. (1995), 151.
16. Le Gall (1953a), 29; Frosini (1977), 141; Di Martino and Belati (1980), 33; Gregori et al. (1988), 191–92; Bencivenga et al. (1995), 151; Bersani and Bencivenga (2001), 7; Bersani and Bencivenga (2003), 5.
17. These accounts are those describing the floods of 241 BC (Orosius 4.11.6; Aug. *De Civ. Dei* 3.18);193 BC (Livy 35.9.2–3); 189 BC (Livy 38.28); 54 BC (Dio 39.61.1–2); 27 BC (Dio 53.20.1); AD 15 (Tac. *Ann.* 1.76); reign of Trajan (Pliny *Epist.* 8.17); AD 371 (Am. Mar. 29.6.17–18).
18. On the extent and topography of the Campus Martius, see Coarelli (1997), especially 1–60, and Richardson (1992). The central portion of the Campus Martius was the location of the *Palus Caprae,* a swampy depression that was supposedly the site of Romulus's disappearance (Ovid *Fast.* 2.491). It was the lowest-lying section of the Campus Martius and is thought to have been approximately where the Pantheon stands today. On the Campus Martius as swampy land, see also the perceptive comments by Purcell (1996), 184–89.
19. These are the floods of 192 BC (Livy 35.21.5–6) and 193 BC (Livy 35.9.2–3).
20. These are the floods of 363 BC (Livy 7.3.2), 202 BC (Livy 30.38.10–12), and AD 12 (Dio 56.27.4).
21. On the promenade of Crassipes, see Richardson (1992), 125, entry on *Domus Daphnis.*
22. The destruction of bridges by floods is discussed in greater detail in chapter 3.
23. The citations are: 60 BC (Dio 37.58.3–4); 32 BC (Dio 50.8.3); 23 BC (Dio

53.33.5); AD 69 (Tac. *Hist.* 1.86); and AD 5 (Dio 55.22.3). The identification of the bridge damaged in this last flood as the Pons Sublicius is uncertain; see the discussion on bridges in chapter 3 for a more detailed analysis.
24. On the location of the churches and sites mentioned in these accounts, see the commentary to the translation by R. Davis (1992, 1996), and also the text and commentary by Duchesne (1981).
25. On the causes and depth of the layers of accumulated man-made debris at Rome, see Ventriglia (1971), 87–97. This volume also includes among the supplemental maps one that shows the depth of fill across the greater urban metro area of Rome.
26. On fires at Rome, see the dissertation by Rubin (2003).
27. While Monte Testaccio is the most famous such rubbish heap, there are a number of similar, if smaller, artificial mounds in the city, such as Monte Secco near the Ponte Margherita.
28. A more detailed description of ancient ground levels in areas such as the Roman Forum can be found in chapter 5, where the subject of ancient attempts to raise ground levels is discussed.
29. On this layer of fill (in particular where it is 20 m thick), see Lanciani (1897), 102.
30. On natural ground levels in the Velabrum, see Ammerman (1998). A series of cores from the Velabrum shows original ground levels of around 4–7 masl. The earliest signs of human habitation occur around the range of 6–8 masl, and the modern street levels are roughly 13–23 masl.
31. See Ammerman (1990), 637.
32. This map is derived from information in Ventriglia's (1971) map, "Carta Geologica della Città di Roma: Spessore della Coltre dei Terreni di Riporto."
33. This map was created by the author using Photoshop. It is based on information from a number of other maps and sources. The initial map was based on extrapolations from the famous map of Rome by F. Scagnetti and G. Grande, *Roma Urbs Imperatorum Aetate* (1979), the maps in U. Ventriglia, *La Geologia della Città di Roma* (1971), the photographic and topographic information in the *Atlante di Roma* produced by the Comune di Roma (1991), and the maps in D. Favro, *The Urban Image of Augustan Rome* (1996). Information on specific areas was derived from the multivolume *Lexicon Topographicum Urbis Romae,* ed. E. Steinby (1993–2000), *A New Topographical Dictionary of Ancient Rome* by L. Richardson (1992), and a large number of publications on particular sites. Subsequent to the creation of my initial map, it was rendered obsolete in 2002 by the publication of the authoritative *JRA* supplement, *Mapping Augustan Rome,* ed. L. Haselberger et al., which included topographical maps of Rome at the time of Augustus. While in most respects Haselberger's map confirmed

my own re-creation of Augustan Rome, I have now revised my map to incorporate the information from this important publication. A few instances where my map differs from Haselberger's are noted in the text. I would also like to acknowledge the collaboration of Dr. David West Reynolds of Phaeton Scientific Graphic Services in an earlier attempt to produce a topographic map of floods in ancient Rome.
34. The name of this important valley is somewhat problematic because the term Vallis Murcia seems to have been a relatively late label. In this book, it will be referred to as either the Vallis Murcia or the valley of the Circus Maximus.
35. On original ground levels, see, for example, Ammerman (1990, 1998).

Chapter 2. Characteristics of Floods

1. The discussion of general principles and terminology related to rivers and floods that follows is intended to offer a very basic introduction for readers unfamiliar with hydrology. Those already acquainted with these concepts may wish to skip this section. For the purposes of this book and to make it as accessible as possible to a nonengineer audience, I have deliberately kept the use of specialized terminology and mathematical formulas to a minimum. Readers should be aware, however, that the calculations offered here at times represent somewhat of a simplification, although slightly more refined versions would not affect any of the overall conclusions drawn from this data.

    A good general introduction to floods and associated issues is K. Smith and Ward (1998) or, on an even more basic level, Allaby (1998). Those interested in the more technical aspects of water flow can readily find this information in standard textbooks, such as Fitts (2002), on groundwater science; Wohl (2000a), on inland floods; Hornberger et al. (1998), on physical hydrology; Schumm (1972), on river morphology; and Hall (1984) and Lazaro (1979), on urban hydrology.
2. Definition taken from Ward (1978), 5.
3. See Miller and Miller (2000), 23–49, for a useful nontechnical introduction to flood types, complete with representative examples. K. Smith and Ward (1998), Ward (1978), and Hoyt and Langbein (1955) offer more detailed introductions to floods and flood types, although these are still aimed at a general readership. More in depth (as well as more technical and mathematical) discussions can be found in Fitts (2002); Wohl (2000a); Hornberger et al. (1998); and Lazaro (1979).
4. Descriptions of the hydrologic cycle can be found in any standard textbook on climate or hydrology. Lazaro (1979), 21–25, contains a nice summary of the process as it relates to floods, which I have drawn upon in the subsequent description.

the flood usually ascribed to AD 847, I have redated to 844 (*Lib. Pont.*, Serg. II, 22). For this dating, see translation and commentary by Davis (1996).

See appendix I for citations for these floods. Appendix I additionally contains a large number of post-1700 floods that reached heights between 13 masl and 15 masl. Full citations for these floods are listed very usefully and clearly by Bencivenga et al. (1995), 153–63, and in the appendixes of Bersani and Bencivenga (2001).

44. Figure 2.6 includes 82 floods. They are the same as those listed in note 43, with the addition of the flood of 1878, which reached a height of 15.35 masl. Table 2.3 only went up to 1870 because the majority of other authors writing about floods only took their data up to this point, but figure 2.6 is organized by century, and so this flood was added to the total for the 19th century.

45. See, for example, Bencivenga et al. (1995), 151–52, and Frosini (1977), 143–45, 195–98.

For another calculation of frequency over time, see the table in Alessandroni and Remedia (2002), 130. While their graph occasionally differs from mine for the reasons described in the previous note, the overall shape and pattern are very similar.

Bersani and Bencivenga (2001, 21; 2003, 8) also have a similar bar graph of floods per century. They include a larger number of floods (118), but the overall shape and distribution pattern are again very similar to mine.

46. Perhaps the best-known examples of attempts to trace changes in climate and their influence on humans are the works of H. H. Lamb (1995, 1977). The affiliated literature is large, but other useful discussions include Valensise and Colacino (1988); Colacino et al. (1988); and Wigley et al. (1981). Studies specifically examining the effects of historical climate changes on river systems or hydrology in general include Vandenberghe and Maddy (2001); Benito et al. (1998); Issar and Brown (1998); Starkel et al. (1991); and Solomon et al. (1987).

47. See, for example, Huntington (1917); Demougeot (1965); and Baynes (1943).

48. The problematic nature of relying on ancient authors to make determinations about broad climate patterns is ably pointed out by Shaw (1981).

49. For this view, see Delano Smith (1979), 278–79, and Hughes and Thirgood (1982), 202ff. Contra this interpretation, see Meiggs (1982), 376ff., and Horden and Purcell (2000), 324–41, 604–5.

50. On forests and their effects on floods, see Hewlett and Nutter (1969), chaps. 8 and 9; Susmel (1972); Leyton (1972); and Margaropoulos (1972). The discussion in Leyton of the dramatic effects that forest cover can have on the infiltration qualities of soil is particularly relevant.

51. Hewlett and Nutter (1969), 126. For another attempt to calculate how much the loss of forest cover can increase flooding, see the study of the Changbaishan region of China, where 30 years' worth of records of areas with similar rainfall but different degrees of deforestation shows that the runoff from wooded and unwooded areas is very different (Liu, 1987).
52. Leyton (1972), 332.
53. The nature of the forests near Rome and the process by which they were eventually almost all cut down are traced in detail by Meiggs (1982). See especially 218–59 and 371–403.
54. The various uses of forest products are described by Meiggs (1982). Although they perhaps present an extreme position in regards to the effects of deforestation, Hughes and Thirgood (1982) provide an excellent, concise summary of the many uses of forest products in antiquity.
55. Hughes and Thirgood (1982), 197.
56. Meiggs (1982), 373. Deforestation also seems to have been a component of Roman conquest of new regions, especially in the dense forests of northern Europe. The many scenes on Trajan's column of soldiers chopping down trees and amassing huge piles of timber provide a nice visual example of this habit.
57. Lowe et al. (1996) and Oldfield (1996), especially 349–55. Although these lakes are tangential to the Tiber basin, they are only about 25 km southeast of Rome and, due to this proximity, would have been prime areas for logging in order to supply timber to the city. Much interesting environmental data has been extracted from sedimentary studies in these lakes by the PALICLAS project (Palaeoenvironmental Analysis of Italian Crater Lake and Adriatic Sediments), whose findings are reported in a special volume of the *International Journal of Limnology* (Guilizzoni and Oldfield, 1996).
58. Although Pliny erroneously attributes this effect in part to new springs arising in areas that have been clear-cut.
59. Meiggs (1982), 379–83, collects the primary source references suggesting the at least partial recovery of Italian forests.

   While soil will quickly be lost once trees are cut down, how rapidly the land begins to generate new topsoil is dependent on how the land is used. If it is left alone, scrub vegetation will arise and start to provide roots to protect soil from erosion. Pastoralism, however, especially of goats, can be very destructive, as these animals will strip away all vegetation. On the link between goats and erosion, see Meiggs (1982), 385–86, and Hughes and Thirgood (1982), 200.

   The increase in the intensive cultivation of olive trees in the period 200 BC to 200 AD might also possibly be interpreted as evidence of soil degradation caused by the clearing of forests. Olive trees can grow on hills and in poorer and thinner soil than many other crops or trees and thus would

be suitable for cultivation on formerly forested hillsides that have lost much of their soil. On olives and their cultivation, see D. J. Mattingly (1996).
60. Population estimates of Rome are particularly contentious. The data for figure 2.7 are extrapolated from the chart in Thomas (1989), 428. Whatever the precise numbers were, all agree that the population rose quickly in the late Republic, peaking probably around 1 million for a few centuries, and then declining to well under 100,000 by circa AD 1000. Subsequently there was a gradual increase up to 1 million once again in the first half of the 20th century.
61. From 1300 to 2000, there have been 36 floods that reached estimated heights of more than 15 masl; 700 years divided by 36 yields a periodicity of 1 flood every 19.44 years. (See appendix I for list of floods.)
62. Between 250 BC and AD 250, there were 28 recorded floods; 500 years divided by 28 yields a periodicity of 1 flood every 17.85 years. (See appendix I for list of floods.)
63. Between 1700 and 2000, there were 77 recorded floods of at least 13 masl; 300 years divided by 77 yields a periodicity of 1 flood every 3.90 years. (See appendix I for list of floods.)
64. The periodicity for lesser floods was calculated by taking the total number of floods since 1700 with estimated heights of more than 13 masl (77), subtracting the number of exceptional floods with estimated heights of more than 15 masl (13), and then dividing 300 years by the remainder (64). This results in an average of 1 flood of between 13 and 15 masl every 4.69 years. (See appendix I for list of floods.)
65. This find was first published (with photo) and interpreted as a hydrometer by D. Marchetti (1892). On it, see also Le Gall (1953a), 296 and n. 2.
66. For a discussion of the depth and force of water sufficient to sweep people off their feet and to drown them, see the section on injuries and drowning in chapter 3.
67. On the problematic location of this temple, see Haselberger et al. (2002), 165, 256–57, and Richardson (1992), 244–45, 414. An inscription identifies it as being between the first and second milestones on the Via Appia (*CIL* 6.10234), and it is mentioned numerous times in connection with the road being paved as far as the temple. Livy states that the temple was somewhere beyond the Porta Capena, and Appian places the temple fully 15 stades distant from the city (Livy 7.23.3; Appian *B. Civ.* 3.41). The temple itself seems to have sat on higher ground than its surroundings, and the incline approaching it was known as the *clivus Martis* (Ovid *Fasti* 6.191–92; *CIL* 6.1270). A location near the first milestone would place it close to the later Appian Gate in the Aurelian wall, although some scholars would situate it just within this mark and others just beyond it.

A pile of marble found outside the Appian Gate may or may not be from this temple.
68. For these figures as well as a number of other high discharge rates measured between 1900 and 1991, see table 7 in Bencivenga et al. (1995), 166.
69. The reduction of the permeability of the ground caused by urban development is discussed in great detail in Montz (2000). On hydrologic effects of urban land use, see also Leopold (1971). On questions of urban flooding as it relates to city design and layout, see the informative article by Marco and Cayuela (1994).

Chapter 3. Immediate Effects of Floods

1. On the range of urban rituals staged in ancient Rome, see Aldrete (1999), especially 102–3, and n. 5 (187–88) with extensive further bibliography.
2. Old, but still illustrative, is the chapter on furniture in Mau (1899), 361–74.
3. The problem of floodwaters bearing contaminants that result in illness is dealt with in more detail in chapter 4 in the subsection on disease.
4. Marco (1994), 354–55. The damage caused to possessions is plotted as a function of depth, and typically creates an S-shaped curve. For floods of 0–0.8 m, damage is relatively mild, but it then increases very sharply, leveling off again at more than 1.0 m. Once depths reach 1.0 m, nearly everything that can be ruined usually has been, so that it does not make a great deal of difference how much higher the water reaches.

    While applying modern damage assessment data to ancient Rome is obviously speculative, it does seem to be a common phenomenon across cultures and time that people keep their most used and most valuable possessions at about waist height, where they are most easily accessible.

    For another attempt to estimate and quantify modern urban flood damages, see Appelbaum (1985).
5. K. Smith and Ward (1998), 47.
6. "Cum Tiberis abundasset et res mutas multorum in aliena aedificia detulisset, interdictum a praetore datum, ne vis fieret dominis, quo minus sua tollerent ferrent, si modo damni infecti repromitterent" (Dig. 39.2.9.1, Ulpian 53 *ad ed.*).
7. The topic of the psychological effects caused by the loss of personal property is treated in detail in chapter 4.
8. The most famous instance of boats being destroyed on the Tiber is the 200 vessels that were sunk in AD 62 at the mouth of the Tiber (Tac. *Ann.* 15.18). These seem to have been destroyed by a storm coming in from the sea rather than by a flood of the river. At the same time, another 100 watercraft were consumed in a fire at Rome. Because enough boats ap-

parently remained that the loss of 300 did not seem to result in a food shortage, this incident suggests, if nothing else, the vast numbers of watercraft plying their trade on the Tiber.
9. Alexander (1993), 524 and 545.
10. On Roman farm animals and methods of animal husbandry, see K. D. White (1970), 272–331.
11. Destruction or damage to structures is the most common feature of the flood accounts. That this was the primary focus of the ancient authors is confirmed by the study of R. F. Newbold (1982), who analyzed 94 primary source accounts of ancient disasters, including earthquakes, fires, and floods. He discovered that the most common feature of these narratives was a description of damage to buildings, found in 42% of the accounts.
12. *Aedificia* is used by Orosius (4.11.6), Livy (35.21.5–6), Tacitus (*Ann.* 1.76), and the author of the life of Marcus Aurelius (SHA *M. Aur.* 8) in describing the damage caused by the floods of 241 BC, 192 BC, AD 15, and AD 162.
13. The term *insula* itself is somewhat problematic as it can mean either an entire city block or an individual building. In addition, the much-cited figure from the fourth-century Regionary Catalog of more than 40,000 *insulae* in the city of Rome seems hard to believe unless *insulae* is loosely interpreted as referring to almost any sort of multiunit dwelling. On this issue, see Anderson (1997), 306–7, and Stambaugh (1988), 338, n. 6.
14. On this sort of social stratification, see Anderson (1997), chap. 6; Reynolds (1996); Stambaugh (1988); Hermansen (1978); and Packer (1971). On *insulae* in general, see these works, but particularly Packer (1971) and Anderson (1997).
15. On Cicero as a landlord and his attitude toward his tenants, see Frier (1978, 1980). It is estimated that Cicero and his brother alone might have been the landlords of up to 2,300 of the inhabitants of Rome (Frier, 1978, 6, n. 19).
16. See Frier (1977, 1978, 1980) on the use of managers and middlemen in running rental properties.
17. Existing Roman staircases at Pompeii and Ostia usually seem to have steps of 20–25 cm in height, with an incline of around 40 degrees (although ones as steep as 65 degrees are known). Using these typical dimensions, a 200-step climb would suggest the building had 13–16 stories, which seems difficult to believe and makes one suspect that the number of stairs is inflated due to satiric exaggeration. In satire, while numbers can be inflated, to be most effective they need to remain within the realm of possibility, and a building with even one-third this number of steps would still be an impressively tall structure. On Roman stairways, see Adam (1994), especially 200–205.

18. On these *insulae* at Rome, see Packer (1971), 75–76, with further bibliography. The upper stories of *insulae* would have been made out of the lightest materials and so would not have survived. Thus a building with five solidly made stories extant today easily could have had several more lighter-built floors in antiquity.
19. Some other evidence for the height of these structures can be inferred from mentions of items being tossed out of high windows to the detriment of pedestrians below (Juv. 3.270; *Digest* 9.3.5.1–2, 9.3.5.7), as well as the passage in Aulus Gellius (15.1.2) describing a group of friends on the Cispian Hill watching a huge *insula* "built high with many stories" being consumed by a raging conflagration.
20. It is obviously difficult to guess how many people lived in a typical room or building. Packer (1971, chap. 4) offers some estimates for buildings at both Ostia and Rome. He concludes that even in much smaller and less densely urbanized Ostia, there was a minimum of 31 structures housing at least 100 inhabitants each, and that the larger Ostian *insulae* held close to 300. Based on the descriptions of the size of some of Rome's structures, they might have housed several times this number.
21. On rents being exorbitant in ancient Rome even for mediocre lodgings, see, for example, the comments of Juvenal (3.166) and Martial (4.37). On rents and leases, see Frier (1977, 1980).
22. A good introduction to the Roman use of clay, and brick manufacture in general, is Adam (1994), 58–65. See also Vitruvius's comments on bricks and clay in book 2 of his *De Architectura*.
23. For an informative basic introduction to Roman lime used in construction and its manufacture, see Adam (1994), 65–73. Similarly, on mortar and its use, see Adam (1994), 73–81. For Roman sources on these topics, see the discussion in book 2 of Vitruvius. Cato (*De Ag.* 44) also includes a substantial account of lime production.
24. I thank Dr. David West Reynolds for making this observation. His comments were also helpful in formulating the section on Roman construction methods generally.
25. On the poor quality of the construction of many of Pompeii's walls, see Adam (1994), 73–76.
26. For an introduction to the Roman use of clay, sun-dried bricks, and wattle-and-daub construction, see Adam (1994), 58–62.
27. On Roman timber-frame construction, see Adam (1994), 122–24.
28. See Adam (1994), 122–24, with illustrations.
29. On this debate, see nearly any standard work on Roman architecture, such as Adam (1994) or Sear (1982).
30. On this view, see Boëthius (1960), 155–56, refuted by Packer (1971), 77–78.
31. A 1976 UN survey of 67 large cities found that on average 44% of the

Notes to Page 113

population of these cities were housed in shantytowns (Bairoch, 1988, 473). On shantytowns in general, for a brief summary, see Bairoch (1988), 471–74; for a more extensive analysis, see Dwyer (1975).
32. Bairoch (1988), 472–73.
33. On the formation of "Neza" and its subsequent development, see, for example, Kandell (1988), 556–59.

The various settlements in the Valley of Mexico from the ancient Aztec city of Tenochtitlan up to the current sprawling metropolis of Mexico City constitute an interesting comparative study of humans struggling to erect a densely inhabited urban setting in a flood-prone environment. For an up-to-date summary of the history of man and water in the Valley of Mexico from Tenochtitlan to today, including the great flood of 1629, see the articles in the July–August 2004 issue of the journal *Arqueología Mexicana*, which is devoted exclusively to this topic.

34. A number of recent studies that have examined the particular vulnerability of the urban poor to flooding offer interesting comparative data when one is attempting to envision similar circumstances in ancient Rome.

In 1995 Manila's squatter settlements housed an estimated 3 million inhabitants in areas that were inundated multiple times per year. Zoleta-Nantes (2000, 2003) provides an especially useful study of how floods affect the lives of the urban poor of Manila, who construct their dwellings out of "scrap and flattened metal sheets, plastic bags, cartons, and wooden boxes, old timber planks and rusty pieces of galvanized iron."

On the urban poor and flooding in Kuala Lumpur, see Chan and Parker (1996); on Calcutta, see Blaikie et al. (1994); on Delhi, see Wijkman and Timberlake (1984); on Bangladesh, see Rasid (1993), and Alexander (1993), 532–48; and on the phenomenon of the urban poor and flooding in general, see Zoleta-Nantes (2000, 2003). On the overall impact of floods on developing countries, see Alexander (1993), 523–32, and Albala-Bertrand (1993).

Other Third World cities that have been identified as harboring major shantytowns that are prone to flooding include Guayaquil, Lagos, Manila, Monrovia, Port Moresby, Recife, San Juan, Rio De Janeiro, and Port-au-Prince (Alexander, 1993, 530–31).

35. During a 2004 visit to Rome, these improvised dwellings along the Tiber seemed particularly numerous. These were especially common on the left bank in the vicinity of the Cloaca Maxima, and included not only substantial individual shacks with multiple rooms composed of fragments of lumber, sheets of metal, and cardboard, but even several small "villages" of three or four lean-tos and shelters huddled together. The indented arch in the embankment wall within which the outlet of the Cloaca Maxima lies seemed to be a particularly coveted spot due to the shelter it provides from rain, and this space housed several residents who had augmented

the overhang with sheets and boards. Other popular spots were beneath the bridges, where several additional villages of "improvised habitation" clustered.

36. On this bridge, its architecture, and its role in Roman history, see Richardson (1992); Steinby (1993–2000); Galliazzo (1995); and Holland (1961). It was built as a replacement for the original ferry across the Tiber, which had served the salt trade.

37. The citations are 60 BC (Dio 37.58.3–4); 32 BC (Dio 50.8.3); 23 BC (Dio 53.33.5); AD 69 (Tac. *Hist.* 1.86). The account of the flood of AD 5 (Dio 55.22.3) simply states that "the bridge" was destroyed, but given that the Pons Sublicius was the oldest, most famous, and most vulnerable bridge in Rome, it seems the most likely candidate.

38. On this bridge, its architecture, and its role in Roman history, see Richardson (1992); Steinby (1993–2000); and Galliazzo (1995).

39. The data cited in this paragraph are derived from the study by Abt et al. (1989). These tests took place in a laboratory flume through which water was run at varying depths and velocities. Sixty-five iterations of the experiment were run using 20 different subjects and on a variety of surfaces, including concrete, simulated turf, gravel, and steel. The subjects began each test in water of varying depth, but always with an initially slow velocity. The velocity was then gradually increased in increments of 5% until the subject lost his or her footing. The test subjects were periodically requested to attempt various types of movement in the simulated floodwater, including walking into the current, standing facing away from the current, and walking perpendicular to the current.

40. A 27-year-old female who weighed 56 kg was overthrown in water whose velocity was 1.36 m/sec and whose depth was only .52 m (Abt et al., 1989, 70).

41. Abt et al. (1989), 70.

42. Abt et al. (1989), 74.

43. Marco (1994), 355. My own experience with floodwaters, while admittedly more impressionistic than strictly scientific, also strongly suggests that the idealized environment of the laboratory renders the data derived from these trials completely inapplicable to real-life situations. In experiments traversing a stream in flood near my home, the three factors that caused the greatest difficulty were all ones not present in the laboratory experiment. These were the unevenness of the footing, the opacity of the water, and the effects of exposure to cold water. Sediment and froth on the surface rendered the water completely opaque, but by shuffling slowly along without lifting one's feet, it was possible to successfully negotiate the very uneven bed of the stream and the rocks and submerged branches within it. The moment of greatest instability occurred when I encountered a sudden pit in the streambed. The cold water also became a factor. After

about 10 minutes' immersion in the water, my legs became numb, accompanied by a perceptible decrease in muscular coordination. (Air temperature was 9.5°C.) It was relatively easy to stand in one place, more difficult to move upstream or downstream, and most difficult to move perpendicular to the direction of the current. The waters traversed ranged from a depth of 0 to .6 m, and the velocity from 0.5 m/sec near the bank to 1.3 m/sec at the deepest part of the channel.

44. Zoleta-Nantes (2000), 73–74. See also Ogden et al. (2001).
45. Dietz and Baker (1974), 307.
46. For information on the effects of hypothermia and on cold water survival, see the following websites: www.watersafety.org/hypothermia.htm; www.hypothermia-ca.com/; www.hypothermia.org/protocol.htm.
47. Di Martino and Belati (1980), 63.
48. Golaz (1993), cited in Legome et al. (1995). See also the note on this flood and the resultant injuries by Schmidt et al. (1993).
49. K. Smith and Ward (1998), 47. By comparison, the ratio of death to injury for earthquakes is estimated to be 1:3.
50. The Latin phrase is *siccandam eluviem*. It is possible that this phrase could instead be a reference to sewer cleaners, because *eluvies* can also be translated as "sewage" rather than "inundation." *Siccare*, however, is plainly "to dry up," and it makes more sense to dry up floodwaters than sewage.

Various translators of Juvenal are divided on this phrase. G. G. Ramsay's Loeb translation, for example, renders it as "draining floods," while R. Humphries opts for "cleaning out sewers," and Peter Green's Penguin edition pushes the line even further, translating it as "swamp drainage." In an article that specifically analyzes the relationship between Rome and water, Purcell (1996, 193) interprets this passage as referring to "opportunistic entrepreneurs of the corrupt city taking on the drying out of areas stricken with flood water."

51. Marco and Cayuela (1994), 712.
52. Bellotti (1998), 26. Le Gall (1953a, 22), after R. Lanciani (1897, 9), reports a figure of more than 4 million m^3 of sediment in 1871.

For a modern assessment of Tiber sedimentation and its effects on Ostia and the delta, see Bellotti (1998) and Verduchi (1998). Both of these appear in a useful collection of articles on the delta of the Tiber that addresses a number of different topics (Bagnasco, 1998).

The sedimentation load carried by the Tiber is much less than that of some rivers, such as the Yellow River in China, whose name derives from the distinctive color that its silt imparts to the waters of the river. It is estimated that the Hwang He (Yellow) River bears an annual load of 1.6 billion tons of sediment (Clark, 1982, 39).

53. Nencini (1966), 22.
54. Clark (1982), 26–28.

55. On the postflood rodent and snake menace, see standard government publications for flood cleanup workers, many of which are readily available online. For example, www.ag.ndsu.nodak.edu/flood/.
56. For example, after the Mississippi flood of 1993, there was an increase in the number of rat bites reported in Des Moines, Iowa, which had been inundated by the floodwaters (B. Baker, 1993, 26).
57. Leptospirosis is treated in more detail in chapter 4.
58. On rodents and snakes in ancient Rome, see Toynbee (1973), chaps. 17 and 21. Although these vermin are not among the most common animals depicted in ancient Roman art, a number of mosaics portray rodents scavenging for food.
59. On the disposal of corpses in Rome generally, see the articles in Hope and Marshall (2000) and Raventós and Remolà (2000). Kyle (1998) and Scobie (1986) are also relevant.
60. For an analysis of the physiological changes that a drowned body undergoes, see Barber (1988), 141–51. The buoyancy produced in corpses after death is substantial, so that even those flood victims whose bodies were weighed down or caught in subsurface debris would likely have surfaced eventually. Barber (1988, 142) recounts an example of a body that bobbed to the surface even though it was tethered to a 145-pound iron generator.
61. Barber (1988), 148.
62. On the use of the Tiber as a convenient site for the disposal of corpses and the symbolism of this, see particularly Kyle (1998), 213–41.

Chapter 4. Delayed Effects of Floods

1. This section on delayed flood damage to structures is based on precepts found in standard handbooks on civil engineering and construction materials, such as Merritt (1958, 1968).

   Particularly helpful in considering the myriad ways in which structures can be weakened and construction materials damaged is Johnson's (1965) book on the deterioration and maintenance of structures. Although his book is intended for modern engineers, its sections on the general dangers that moisture poses to materials such as timber are readily applicable to buildings in any time period.
2. In the winter, this threat may be somewhat alleviated by cold temperatures, as the fungi will normally thrive only in the temperature range of 10–38 degrees Celsius (Johnson, 1965, 242).
3. Alexander (1993), 532.
4. On famine and Rome, an excellent starting point is Garnsey (1988). In the course of a more general study of famine at Rome, he discusses most of the incidents that are listed here when floods resulted in food shortages.

5. The supply system of Rome has been much studied. For a recent overview of the system and some indications of its scale, see Aldrete and Mattingly (1999, 2000), with further bibliography. On the grain supply and its administration, see in particular Rickman (1980); Garnsey (1988); and Sirks (1991).
6. The three main wheat groups are the einkorns, the emmers, and the spelts. The einkorn group includes the original wild wheat, *triticum monococcum*. Among the emmers and the spelts, wheats are further subdivided into hulled and naked varieties. The naked wheats do not actually have exposed kernels; rather the name refers to the fact that the kernels are not tightly enclosed and are much more easily separated from the chaff. In naked wheats, the stem, or rachis, of the plant is typically strong, but in hulled wheats, it breaks before the kernels come out of the hull, again complicating the sorting procedure. Because it is easier to make bread flour from naked wheats, these eventually became more popular during the classical era. Similarly, by the high Empire, *triticum vulgare* had become favored because of its suitability for making fine flour. It is sometimes difficult to equate ancient terminology regarding grains and flours with modern classification systems. On this issue as well as all other aspects of wheats in antiquity, see Jasny (1944). Rickman provides a nice summary of the different varieties of wheat that were grown (1980, 4–7). On grain as a food in antiquity, see also the insightful article by Foxhall and Forbes (1982).

Barley was also widely cultivated in the ancient Mediterranean and in fact is a more versatile crop, because it requires less rainfall than wheat and can thrive in poorer soils. It does not seem to have been as favored a food for human consumption, although it would have been a principal crop for use as animal fodder. On barley, see Jasny (1944).
7. Aldrete and Mattingly (1999), 192–200.
8. On the organization of the transport of grain by ship, see the works listed in note 5. On maritime travel generally, see Casson (1971). On the relative efficiency of water versus land transportation, see A. Jones (1986), 841–45, and Duncan-Jones (1982), 366–69.

One of the flaws of the site of Rome was the lack of a good natural harbor at the mouth of the Tiber, and the river itself was only navigable up to Rome by smaller ships. This meant that the large grain freighters had to be unloaded at Rome's port of Ostia at the exposed mouth of the Tiber, and their cargoes transferred to lighters for the trip up the river to Rome. On the system of riverine transport between Ostia/Portus and Rome, see Casson (1965). Particularly during the Republic, many of the larger ships, including those of the Egyptian fleet, preferred to dock at the much better and safer harbor of Puteoli on the Bay of Naples, from which the grain was then transported to Rome. To correct this unsatisfactory arrangement,

Notes to Page 135

the emperor Claudius (and later Trajan) undertook gigantic public works at the mouth of the Tiber in order to build new artificial harbors that would safely accommodate the largest ships. On Rome's ports at the mouth of the Tiber, see Meiggs (1973) and Silenzi (1998).

9. On Rome's port facilities along the Tiber and the Emporium district, see Pavolini (2000); Meneghini (1985); Mocchegiani Carpano et al. (1985–86); Mocchegiani Carpano and Meneghini (1985); Mocchegiani Carpano (1984a); Rodríguez-Almeida (1984); Colini (1980); Castagnoli (1980); Lyngby et al. (1978); and Le Gall (1953a).

10. On Roman warehouses, the main standard work is Rickman (1971). Discussions of warehouses can also be found in Aldrete and Mattingly (1999, 2000); Hermansen (1982); and Meiggs (1973).

11. The Aventine area (Regio XIII), which would have included the Emporium district, is listed as having had 35 *horrea*. Only the Palatine (Regio X) has more, with 48. This surprisingly high number for the Palatine area has disturbed modern commentators to the extent that many have concluded that the figure must be a mistake. (See discussion in Rickman, 1971, 323–25.) As Reynolds (1996, 237–39) points out, however, they are not taking into account the size of each individual warehouse. Most of the *horrea* scattered around Rome were probably small storage sites, perhaps with only a couple of cubicles. As shown on the Severan Marble Plan, many of the *horrea* in the Emporium area were gigantic structures covering many thousands of square meters. Thus, comparing the numbers of warehouses in different regions is deceptive, because the actual storage capacity of even a couple of large Emporium warehouses might have been greater than that of dozens of small warehouses located somewhere else.

12. It is extremely difficult to come up with an accurate assessment of the storage capacity of the warehouses in Rome and Ostia due to the large number of unknown variables, among them the depth that grain was stored and uncertainty whether it was in sacks or loose. Also, it is impossible to know how many warehouses have simply disappeared leaving no trace, particularly those once located in Rome. Even the most rudimentary order-of-magnitude calculations, however, suggest how gigantic the necessary volume of storage space must have been.

The eleven *horrea* at Ostia described by Rickman (1971) collectively had approximately 15,000 m^2 of actual storage space on the ground floors (this figure does not include the space taken up by the internal courtyards, but only that within the small storage cubicles). Interestingly, the huge Horrea Galbana at Rome also contained roughly 15,000 m^2 of storage area within its ground floor rooms (again, not counting its three internal courtyards). If grains of wheat were piled loosely to a depth of 2 m within the Horrea Galbana, it could therefore hold approximately 22,500 metric tons of wheat. (Using the crude formula of 1 m^3 of wheat multiplied by .75 yields its weight in tons. For this formula, see G. White, 1999.) Compare this number to the 237,000 metric tons notional minimum annual amount of wheat that was consumed by Rome's citizens (Aldrete and Mattingly, 1999, 192–93). If we use these assumptions, this calculation suggests that approximately 10 *horrea*, each one the size of the Horrea Galbana, would have been required to house one year's supply of wheat.

Naturally if the wheat were stored to a greater or lesser depth, or if upper floors of the *horrea* were employed, the numbers would be quite different. In addition, wheat can contain widely varying amounts of other materials, such as chaff, that take up space. Finally, the moisture content of the wheat itself can greatly affect its volume. Nevertheless, even crude calculations such as these suggest the massive scale both of Rome's imports and of the infrastructure that developed to accommodate them.

13. Much of the specific factual material in the following discussion of moisture and mold in stored grain is derived from the large online databases of information intended for use by farmers that are maintained by the extension programs of a number of midwestern state universities, including those of Minnesota, Iowa, and Wisconsin. Some of the most useful specific web pages consulted include: http://extension.unm.edu/distribution/cropstystems/DC6959.html; www.public-health-uiowa.edu/GPCAH/FFLOOD4.htm; www.extension.umn.edu/administrative/components/wi_flood02_grainbins.html.
14. Matossian (1989), 6–7.
15. On the formation and propagation of mycotoxins in stored grains and the health problems that can result, see Trenholm et al. (1988), J. Smith and Moss (1985), Scott et al. (1985), Uraguchi and Yamazaki (1978), and the publications on mycotoxins issued by the World Health Organization (1979) and the Food and Agriculture Organization of the United Nations (1977). On mycotoxins and history, see Matossian (1989).
16. The relationship between mycotoxins and Western history has been explored in a book by Matossian (1989). She examines the ergot epidemics of the Middle Ages and later and argues that the hallucinogenic effects of ergotism could have been a factor in episodes of mass psychosis such as the witch persecutions of early modern Europe and Salem.
17. Matossian (1989), 2.
18. There is no known flood at Rome for the year AD 62 or even for several years preceding this date. It is tempting to speculate, however, that Nero's action is suggestive of an otherwise unattested flood around this date that caused the ruination of the stored food supplies.
19. On the range of disease-causing organisms that would have been found in floodwaters in ancient Rome, see the detailed description in the section of this chapter on disease.

20. The flood in this case lasted for 11 days and took place in May 1979 in Minnesota. See Meronuck (2002).
21. On insects in stored grain, see Cotton (1963), especially 84–85, on the increase in insect activity as a result of increased moisture.
22. Wilke (2002).
23. On these raised floors, see Rickman (1971), 293–97.
24. On oil and wine as foods, see Aldrete and Mattingly (1999, 2000); Amouretti (1986); Mattingly (1996); and Tchernia (1986).
25. An idea of the scale of this trade is suggested by the hill of Monte Testaccio in the Emporium district, an artificial promontory 50 m high, 180 m wide, and 250 m long, made up of millions of broken olive oil amphorae. See Rodríguez-Almeida (1984).
26. At Ostia, four structures have been excavated that contain huge *dolia*, or clay jars, partially embedded in the ground. The largest of these areas holds more than 100 such *dolia*, which have an average capacity of around 900 liters.
27. For more detailed descriptions of Roman burial practices and urban sanitation, see the collection of essays *Sordes Urbis*, ed. Raventós and Remolà (2000), as well as Aldrete (2004); J. Patterson (2000); Hope (2000b); Bodel (2000, 1999, 1994); Lindsay (2000); Allara (1995); Scobie (1986); and Toynbee (1971).
28. Bodel (2000), 129.
29. On sanitation and sewage at Rome, see in particular the classic article by Scobie (1986). Other discussions include the articles in *Sordes Urbis*, ed. Raventós and Remolà (2000), as well as J. Patterson (2000) and Bodel (2000).
30. Scobie (1986), 413.
31. The structure of the subsequent list of disease-causing organisms in sewage is derived from the list in table 1 in Berry et al. (1994), 11.

    Tartakow and Vorperian (1981) provide detailed chapters describing the characteristics of, sources of infection for, methods of prevention of and treatment of, and some historical information on each of the major waterborne diseases. On the symptoms and treatment of these diseases, see also Tierney et al. (2003) and Larson (1990).

    Another book that covers most of these diseases, but from the perspective of examining their influence upon the course of history, is Cloudsley-Thompson (1976). An interesting study of the interrelationship among disease, agriculture, animal husbandry, and history is Diamond (1997).
32. Curriero et al. (2001), 1194.
33. Curriero et al. (2001).
34. On the history of cholera, see Cloudsley-Thompson (1976), 131–36.
35. Berry et al. (1994), 10.
36. Any standard manual such as those issued by the Federal Emergency

Management Agency (FEMA) or by local public health officials for dealing with flood cleanup will detail these procedures. They are also described in Berry et al. (1994).
37. On moisture's role in preserving disease-causing organisms, see Ehlers and Steel (1943), 19.
38. On molds causing serious illness following floods in the United States, see the report in the *Journal of the American Medical Association* by Marwick (1997).
39. For a detailed overview of mosquito characteristics, habits, and diseases, see P. Mattingly (1969). On the same topics and control mechanisms as they are related to sanitation, a useful (if old) summary is provided in Ehlers and Steel (1943), chaps. 10 and 11. On mosquitoes and history, see Cloudsley-Thompson (1976).

    On malaria-carrying mosquitoes specifically, see P. Mattingly (1969); May (1961); and Delano-Smith (1979), 384–88. On malaria in the ancient world, see Sallares (2002); Brunt (1971), appendix III.18, 611–24; and Cloudsley-Thompson (1976), 85–93.
40. On malaria in the ancient world in general, and especially in Italy, see Sallares (2002); Brunt (1971), appendix III.18, 611–24; and Cloudsley-Thompson (1976), 85–93. On malaria and mortality at Rome specifically, see Scheidel (1994).
41. For examples, see the discussion in Brunt (1971), 618–19.
42. W. H. S. Jones (1907), for example, ascribes the decline of Greece to the arrival of malaria. For different degrees of more cautious perspectives, see Cloudsley-Thompson (1976), 85–93, and Brunt (1971). For primary source citations and discussion of possible famous Roman malaria victims, see Brunt (1971), 617.
43. There is probably a time-lag effect in this peak whereby the people who died in the fall were actually infected during the summer. On the seasonality of mortality and its link to disease, especially malaria, see Sallares (2002); Scheidel (1993); and Shaw (1996).
44. A number of these accounts are usefully collected in Sallares (2002), 201–34. For example, Giovanni Doni in 1667 described regions of Rome that were particularly dangerous in terms of the risk of contracting malaria. These included the Campus Martius, the region between the Aventine and the Tiber, around the Ostian gate, and the Leonine region (p. 209). In a 1881 treatise on malaria at Rome, G. Bacelli similarly identifies high risk areas including, among others, nearly all of Trastevere below the Janiculum, the region around Monte Testaccio, and the valley between the Palatine and the Caelian hills (p. 206).
45. Russac (1986). Cited in K. Smith and Ward (1998), 48–49.
46. Alexander (1993), 527.
47. Telleria (1986). Cited in K. Smith and Ward (1998), 48.

48. On the role of flies as disease vectors, see the enormous book on this subject by Greenberg (1971), as well as the accounts in Tartakow and Vorperian (1981) and Cloudsley-Thompson (1976).
49. Information about the causes, symptoms, and spread of leptospirosis is readily available in any up-to-date disease handbook. The information presented in this paragraph is drawn primarily from the 2003 edition of *CMDT* (*Current Medical Diagnosis and Treatment*), ed. Lawrence Tierney et al. The data on recent outbreaks of leptospirosis are derived from news stories, including those available in the CNN online archives, such as http://archives.cnn.com/2000/ASIANOW/southeast/ 07/27/thailand.rats.ap/, and from other contemporary sources, such as www.emedicine.com/emerg/byname/leptospirosis.htm.
50. Siddique et al. (1991), 311.
51. Siddique et al. (1991), 312.
52. Siddique et al. (1991), 313.
53. Alexander (1993), 527.
54. Sikander (1983), 102. On the vulnerability of the poor in Third World countries to health hazards during and after floods, see also Blaikie et al. (1994), especially chap. 6.
55. The most dramatic example in modern United States history occurred during the great flood of 1993, when the Des Moines, Iowa, metropolitan area lost its water supply due to flooding. This left approximately 300,000 people without water for drinking, cleaning, or waste disposal. It took a week before water supply was restored for nonconsumption purposes and a full three weeks before the tap water was judged sufficiently free of contaminants to be safe for drinking. The extraordinary efforts that had to be made to provide emergency supplies of water to the affected population are described by B. Baker (1993).
56. For these figures from Peru as well as similar ones from Ecuador, Bangladesh, and the Sudan, see the studies cited by K. Smith and Ward (1998), 47–49. One study conducted in Bolivia after flooding in 1983 found a 70% increase in cases of salmonella poisoning due to fecal contamination of the water (Alexander, 1993, 526).
57. Goubert (1986) provides a fascinating study of the growth of awareness of the link between health and clean water in the 19th century. Although focusing primarily on France, this book makes many useful comparative observations on attitudes toward sanitation and urban water supply.

One of the more alarming attitudes existing prior to the scientific realization that exposure to feces constitutes a health hazard was the perception that filth and excrement were actually beneficial to health and even therapeutic. Thus farmers placed dunghills near their dwellings, butchers reveled in the offal of the animals they slaughtered, the smell of excrement was touted as a defense against plague, and sewers were

opened up by the authorities to promote public health (Goubert, 1986, 58–59).
58. The literature on the water supply system of Rome is vast. A concise recent overview of Rome's water supply can be found in Dodge (2000), which also contains a useful bibliography of more specialized further reading. All the statistics cited in this paragraph are taken from this article. The volume of the flow of water is a particularly problematic and contentious issue, and the estimates offered by modern scholars vary widely. Dodge also supplies a balanced and brief introduction to these debates.
59. Attempts have been made by scholars to analyze the psychological stresses resulting from living in the large, crowded, disease-ridden, and disaster-prone city of ancient Rome. See, for example, the analysis of E. Ramage (1983), especially 81–84. He suggests that both poor and wealthy urban dwellers experienced constant feelings of anxiety due to their environment and that many felt "ground down" by life in the city.
60. There is a large literature on the subject of the psychological effects of disasters in general, as well as a number of specific studies attempting to measure such effects among victims of various floods. Much of this literature repeats the same general observations and conclusions, and while I have provided at least one specific citation for each of the main points discussed in this section, I could just as easily have cited a much larger number of other works supporting or illustrating the same points.

    Therefore, instead of burdening the text with a myriad of repetitious citations, I have opted to list below in one place all the relevant studies that were consulted for this section. These include: DeWolfe (2000); Penning-Rowsell and Tapsell (2002); Tapsell and Tunstall (2000); Fullerton and Ursano (1997); Tobin and Ollenburger (1996); Rossi et al. (1994); Hovanitz (1993); Bryant (1991); Drabek (1986); Luketina (1986); Raphael (1986); Laube and Murphy (1985); Powell and Penick (1983); Haas et al. (1977); and Barton (1969).
61. Bryant (1991), 262; Drabek (1986), 132–42.
62. Drabek (1986), 136–38.
63. For various examples of inflation during food crisis as well as a discussion of deliberate hoarding and speculation in the grain market, see Garnsey (1988).
64. Bryant (1991), 265.
65. Raphael (1986), 118–19.
66. Bryant (1991), 268–69.
67. Powell and Penick (1983), 272.
68. Powell and Penick (1983), 273.
69. Tapsell and Tunstall (2000), 176; Penning-Rowsell and Tapsell (2002), 381.

70. Penning-Rowsell and Tapsell (2002), 381.
71. Tobin and Ollenburger (1996), 343.
72. Hovanitz (1993).
73. While the majority of researchers, including those cited in this section, believe that floods produce considerable short- and long-term psychological problems in people who experience them, this opinion is not unanimous. Based on analysis of the 1984 floods in Southland, Australia, Luketina (1986) argues that these claims are unsubstantiated and that many of the conditions ascribed to floods are the result of other traumatic events predating the flood.
74. High estimate: Tobin and Ollenburger (1996), 340. Low estimate: Tapsell and Tunstall (2000), 184.
75. Powell and Penick (1983), 273–75.
76. Tobin and Ollenburger (1996), 354.
77. Tapsell and Tunstall (2000), 183.
78. Tapsell and Tunstall (2000), 181.
79. Bryant (1991), 264.
80. Bryant (1991), 264–65.
81. See Polybius's famous description (6.53–54) of a Roman funeral for a vivid illustration of the importance of these masks. He claims that they played a key role in inculcating virtue in young Romans.
82. Zoleta-Nantes (2000). For similar experiences in developing countries, see the citations in chapter 3, note 34.
83. Tapsell and Tunstall (2000), 181–82.
84. Bryant (1991), 264.
85. McCarroll et al. (1997); DeWolfe (2000); Raphael (1986).
86. Raphael (1986), 6–9; DeWolfe (2000), 9–12.
87. The subsequent summary of phases is a conflation of the systems described in DeWolfe (2000); Gruntfest (1994); Raphael (1986); Drabek (1986); and Barton (1969).
88. Haas et al. (1977), 2–4.
89. Haas et al. (1977), 4–23.
90. For a general survey of the duties of the various officials and organizations listed in this paragraph, see Robinson (1992), with further bibliography.
91. On fires at Rome, including disaster responses, see the dissertation by Lucas Rubin (2003). See also E. Ramage (1983). On aftereffects of fires in ancient Rome, see Newbold (1974).

Chapter 5. Methods of Flood Control

1. Today there is also considerable attention paid to nonstructural methods of flood management, such as forecasting, warning systems, prepared-

ness, disaster aid, insurance, and land use planning. For a survey of these methods, see Gruntfest (2000).
2. Watson and Biedenharn (2000), 381. For more detailed descriptions of these categories and the various flood control methods they contain, see, for example, K. Smith and Ward (1998) or Miller and Miller (2000).
3. On the seasonality of Rome's rainfall and of Tiber inundations, see chapter 1.
4. Ammerman (1998), 220–21. The Velabrum coring project is part of a broader series of ongoing investigations into the topography of archaic Rome being conducted by Albert Ammerman. This work has done much to clarify our understanding of central Rome in its early stages. See Ammerman (1990, 1996, and 1998).
5. Ammerman (1998), 219.
6. For a brief survey of information on the Cloaca Maxima, see the entries in Richardson (1992) and Steinby (1993–2000). For more detailed recent studies, see Bauer (1989) and Mocchegiani Carpano (1984b).

   The classic work on the Roman sewers is Narducci (1889). Pietro Narducci was an engineer involved in the reconstruction of the Roman sewer system that took place as part of the construction of the current Tiber embankments, and he made the first modern exploration of the ancient Roman system.

   An analysis of the sewers from a symbolic standpoint is offered by Gowers (1995). Other relevant scholarship on the Roman sewers, or on related topics, includes Reimers (1989, 1991); Scobie (1986); R. Lanciani (1890, 1897); Robinson (1992); the articles in Raventós and Remolà (2000); and Lagunes (2004), 85ff.

   A number of interesting color photographs of various interior portions of the Cloaca Maxima can be found in Pavia (2000).
7. On this drain and its associated stream, see Haselberger et al. (2002), 92; Humphrey (1986), 67; Mocchegiani Carpano (1984b); and the entries on the Circus Maximus and on the "Cloaca iuxta Circum" in Steinby (1993–2000), vol. 1.
8. See, for example, fig. 3 in Mocchegiani Carpano (1984b).
9. On this stream and its associated drain, see Coarelli (1997), 148–55; Narducci (1889), 34–39; Haselberger et al. (2002), 190; Mocchegiani Carpano (1984b); Richardson (1992), 290; and the entry for "Petronia Amnis" in Steinby (1993–2000), vol. 4.
10. See the article and accompanying map by Mocchegiani Carpano (1984b).
11. See, for example, Lanciani (1897), 30.
12. On Roman aqueducts as well as the problems in estimating flow, see chapter 4, note 58. On the continual problem posed by buildup of refuse in a sewer system, see the comparable experience of the Parisian sewers described by Reid (1991).

13. The two-directional movement that was possible through the sewers is also illustrated by anecdotes concerning fish and vermin that were able to travel from the Tiber up the sewer system into the city. Juvenal (*Sat.* 5.104–6), for example, describes a Tiber pike negotiating the Cloaca Maxima as far as the Subura district. The idea of sewers as subterranean invasion routes for vermin seems to have spawned the Roman equivalent of urban legends. Aelian (*HA* 13.6) tells of an opportunistic octopus who nightly forged its way up out of a sewer and into the house of a fish merchant in order to raid the stock of preserved fish.
14. Ammerman bases his suggestion on a reinterpretation of the stratigraphic section from Gjerstad's excavation at the "Equus Domitiani." The layers in question are strata 23–28. Gjerstad dates the first paving of the Forum to 575 BC, while Colonna argues for a much earlier date of 650 BC. For a more detailed discussion of these issues along with relevant bibliographic citations, see Ammerman (1990).
15. On the complicated history (and for extensive bibliography) of the Forum Romanum, see Coarelli (1983, 1992); Richardson (1992); and Steinby (1993–2000).
16. Even viewed from the front, where the Pantheon is apparently at ground level, this is deceptive, because buried beneath the modern street is the original building's podium and stairways leading up to the entrance.
17. On these *cippi,* the *Horologium,* and the actions by Vespasian, Domitian, and Hadrian, see Boatwright (1987); Buchner (1976, 1980); Rodríguez-Almeida (1979–80); and Romanelli (1933). All the numbers cited in this paragraph are derived from Boatwright.
18. This observation was made by Albert Ammerman in personal correspondence with the author.
19. Recent excavations that have uncovered what appear to be river embankments erected during Rome's early history considerably further inland than the current course of the Tiber suggest that these temples may have been yet even more vulnerable (Ammerman, personal correspondence). Even if only on a seasonal basis, if the Tiber once flowed many meters further toward the Palatine and Capitoline hills than at present, as these discoveries suggest, then these temples would have been precariously situated right on the bank of the river, making flood proofing more of a priority.
20. Cicero's account of the plan is actually secondhand since it was told to him by G. Capito, a houseguest at his villa in Tusculum. There is an earlier reference in his correspondence leading up to the actual description of the plan. At the beginning of July, he writes to Atticus (*Att.* 13.20) that he does not understand the current proposals for improving the city but would very much like to hear about them. In a letter (*Att.* 13.35) dating to after the scheme's description, he relates further details that he had ap-

parently heard, including the identity of the architect who will plan the work. Cicero is quite disapproving of this choice and sneers that the man has only been in Rome for two years but is already being entrusted with the enlargement of the city.
21. On this plan, see the discussions in Le Gall (1953a), 113–16; Favro (1996), 73–76; and Lagunes (2004), 117–29.

    Favro (p. 74, fig. 40) includes a map illustrating a possible route for Caesar's canal dug in front of the Vatican outcropping and rejoining the Tiber near the Porta Portuensis. She points out that such a plan would have caused considerable economic disruption due to the increases and decreases in property values that would have resulted, and that it would also have been problematic in religious terms since it would have affected a number of sacred sites. Lagunes (p. 117) offers a similar diagram. On religious questions, see Le Gall (1953a), 115.
22. Caesar's plan to divert the Tiber around the city of Rome was by no means the last time that such ideas were contemplated. The flood of 1870 prompted many suggestions for protecting the city from inundation, including a plan sponsored by Giuseppe Garibaldi in which the Tiber would have been routed east of the city in a broad loop. Other possible components of this plan included reworking the entire Tiber delta region and constructing navigable canals linking Rome and the sea. Lagunes (2004, 117–29) includes analysis and a map (p. 122) depicting schemes dating from the Renaissance and later to divert the Tiber in various ways. On Garibaldi's scheme, see also De Filippi (1994, 255–61), which includes a map showing the proposed canals and new channel route.
23. On these canals generally, and the inscriptions by which we know of them, see Meiggs (1973), 488–89, and Le Gall (1953a), 131–34.
24. The inscription reads: "Ti. Claudius Drusi f. Caesar Aug. Germanicus pontif. max. trib. potest. VI cos. design. IIII imp. XII p.p. fossis ductis a Tiberi operis portus caussa emissique in mare urbem inundationis periculo liveravit" (*CIL* 14.85).
25. Meiggs (1973), 159–60.
26. Le Gall (1953a), 133–34.
27. Meiggs's (1973, 488) preferred restored text reads "fossam fecit qua inundationes Tiberis adsidue urbem vexantes rivo perenni arcerentur." He also notes an alternate reconstruction of "fossam novam fecit" that would make it clear that this project was a different one from Claudius's canal.
28. Le Gall (1953a, 121) concludes that the effect of this diversion would have been negligible.
29. The creation of a canal system to disperse the water is Le Gall's interpretation (1953a, 121–22) of this problematic passage. He also points out that this scheme would have imperiled some excellent farmland, and for this reason alone seems ill-conceived.

30. Coccia and Mattingly (1992), 215.
31. See Le Gall (1953a, 121–23), who calculates that the Nera accounted for only 1/13th of the Tiber's output.
32. On religion and water generally, and especially on the sacred identity of the Tiber and associated numinous spots, see Le Gall (1953b) and Holland (1961).
33. For a survey of more than 20 known Roman dams built in sites ranging from Spain to the Near East, see Schnitter (1983).
34. On these dams at Subiaco, an image of one of which was apparently preserved in a Renaissance painting, see N. Smith (1970).
35. N. Smith (1970).
36. On this passage in Suetonius, and on Augustus's actions concerning the Tiber in general, see Le Gall (1953a), 117–19.
37. On some later efforts and technologies concerned with dredging the Tiber, see Lagunes (2004), 94–105.
38. The theme of the Tiber as a method of disposing of human and animal corpses is examined in detail by Kyle (1998), 213–41. See also Gowers (1995).
39. Interestingly, the mention of dredging occurs in the text of a letter from the emperor to the prefect of the grain supply, which the author of this life in the SHA is supposedly quoting verbatim (SHA *Aur.* 47).
40. On the general characteristics, as well as the advantages and disadvantages, of floodwalls, see Ward (1978), 144–49.
41. Le Gall, writing in the late 1940s and early 1950s, begins his description of ancient Rome's embankments by lamenting the sparse nature of the evidence and its incomplete publication (1953a, 194). Since then, there have been a number of important publications, mostly Italian, which have done much to clarify our knowledge about the embankments and port facilities of the city. (See the bibliography in the next note.) It is still an area, however, where significant uncertainties remain, especially in regards to the earlier forms of the ports and river embankments.
42. For a general overview of the supply system and a discussion of its scale, see Aldrete and Mattingly (1999), with further bibliography.

On the port facilities of Rome, a convenient starting point is the detailed treatment of this topic by Le Gall (1953a), 194–204. His discussion, while complete for its time, needs to be supplemented by more recent work. The 1980 volume of *MAAR* on the seaborne commerce of Rome contains two useful and well-illustrated articles by Castagnoli (1980), 35–42, on port facilities at Rome generally, and by Colini (1980), 43–53, on the port near the Forum Boarium. Other important publications on this topic include three articles with overlapping content focusing on the Roman embankments still visible along the Lungotevere Testaccio, by Meneghini (1985), Mocchegiani Carpano and Meneghini

(1985), and Mocchegiani Carpano et al. (1985–86). A good summary of the role of the Tiber as a conduit for commercial transportation, which also covers the ports at Rome, is Mocchegiani Carpano (1984a). See also Fant (2001), specifically on docks and yards at Rome related to the transportation of marble. The brief survey of port facilities that follows is derived from these works.

43. For depictions of these fragments, see Rodríguez-Almeida (1981).
44. A detailed account of the history, development, and duties of the curator of the Tiber can be found in Le Gall (1953a), 135–85. Le Gall includes a useful table of the various name changes undergone by this office (p. 148), as well as the names and careers of the known men associated with this office from AD 15 to the third century (pp. 137–45). Among these was Pliny the Younger, who served as *curator alvei Tiberis et riparum cloacarum urbis* from AD 103 to 111 (Pliny *Ep. De Caes.* 13.12; *CIL* 5.5262, 14.88). Le Gall is also particularly useful in providing references to the many inscriptions that mention the curators or their assistants.

   A briefer but more up-to-date summary of the Roman administrative offices concerned with the Tiber, sewers, and water supply is offered by Robinson (1992), 85–104. See also the comprehensive study of Sirks (1991) on the structure of the overseas transportation system serving Rome.

   The basic overview of the *curatores* that follows is derived primarily from the works listed above. For a broader temporal overview of Tiber administration from the *curatores* onward, see Lagunes (2004), chap. 5.
45. The *cippi* related to the Tiber are extensively described and analyzed by Le Gall, who has attempted to reconstruct several phases of river development and surveys on the basis of sets of *cippi* erected at the same time. The two most comprehensive of these reorderings seem to date to Augustus and Trajan. On these *cippi*, see Le Gall (1953a), 149–73.
46. On extent of jurisdiction, see Le Gall (1953a), 175–76. Le Gall points out (on p. 175) that various inscriptions from Ostia demonstrate that the jurisdiction of the curators extended to the mouth of the river (*CIL* 14.192, 254, 4704a–c, 5320, 5384).
47. On public and private boundaries, see Le Gall (1953a), 176–78, and 175–81 for a more detailed account of the various duties of the curators.
48. On the *cippi* and the shifting Tiber, see Le Gall (1953a), 149–73, and Taylor (2000), 80–83. The course of the Tiber appears to have settled into a rough approximation of its modern bed around the second century AD, and today is rigidly constrained by the 19th century embankments.
49. On the relationship between the *curator alvei Tiberis et riparum* and the boatmen guilds, see Meiggs (1973), 303–4, and Le Gall (1953a), 180–81. Le Gall believes that the curator exerted some control over the guilds, their finances, and their activities. Meiggs, however, doubts that the cu-

rators really had much supervisory control in general over these guilds and thinks that the three inscriptions in question are all specific situations where a guild wished to construct a building on the banks of the river and so had to seek the permission of the curator. On the basis of the meager evidence, either interpretation is possible.
50. On these inscriptions, see Le Gall (1953a), 179–80. One additional, very fragmentary inscription may also record a similar instance of repairs undertaken by the curator (CIL 6.31795).
51. Le Gall (1953a), 179.
52. Le Gall (1953a), 178–79.
53. On the Ostian office, see Le Gall (1953a), 182–83.
54. On the assistants to the curator and the rest of his staff generally, see Le Gall (1953a), 181–83.

Chapter 6. Roman Attitudes toward Floods

1. While figure 6.2 uses the same contour lines as the earlier map of Augustan-era Rome, many of the buildings depicted were obviously not built until later. I have not attempted to update this map to reflect the topography of any specific later date because the date selected would be arbitrary and the resulting map would contain too much guesswork to be reliable.

   Some of the obvious general changes in the topography of the city from the Augustan era to, for example, the time of Constantine would include the cutting away of the spur between the Capitoline and Quirinal to accommodate the imperial fora, a general raising of the ground level by 2–5 m in the Campus Martius (especially along its northern fringe), and a similar rise in the ground levels of other low-lying regions, including the Roman Forum, Forum Boarium, and the valley of the Circus Maximus. During a major flood, such as the 20 masl one depicted here, however, none of these alterations would meaningfully change the areas affected. A flood of such magnitude would have inundated almost exactly the same parts of the city whether it occurred at the time of Augustus or of Constantine. For the purposes of the general urban analysis in this chapter, it is only necessary to determine whether an area was ever vulnerable to flooding: in other words, does a given structure lie on ground that would have been reached by the waters of a major flood? For this limited question, this map is therefore adequate. It should be noted, however, that for lesser floods of 10–15 masl, the changes in topography over this time span would have resulted in significantly different areas being affected by inundation.
2. I would like to thank the anonymous Johns Hopkins reviewer for suggesting the analogy between bath development and aqueducts in terms of shifting population centers. The general insight that large public Roman

baths appear to have been built with consideration for floods was discovered jointly with David West Reynolds while working together on an early version of the maps depicting flooding in ancient Rome. Finally, Richard Talbert suggested to me the potential for baths to serve as refugee centers.

3. On this sort of vertical stratification as well as the complex nature of Roman neighborhoods with intermingled building types, see Anderson (1997); Stambaugh (1988); Reynolds (1996); and Packer (1971). On neighborhoods at Rome, particularly with attention to administrative and religious perspectives, see Lott (2004).

4. On the Regionary Catalogs, see Jordan (1907); Nordh (1936); Von Gerkan (1949); Hermansen (1978); and Reynolds (1996).

5. On questions of density and problems associated with the terms *insulae* and *domus* in the Regionary Catalogs, see, particularly, Hermansen (1978).

6. The information on density of *domus* and *insulae* is taken from Reynolds (1996), who has calculated the densities of various building types in all fourteen Augustan regions. Stambaugh (1988, 338, n. 7) offers a more basic calculation of ratios of *domus* and *insulae* per region.

7. To come up with these statistics, the *domus* listed in Richardson's *New Topographical Dictionary of Ancient Rome* (1992) were combined with those identified by Witherstine (1926) in her article on where Romans lived.

W. Eck (1999) earlier performed a similar analysis of where Roman senatorial *domus* were located also using a combination of literary and archaeological evidence. He, however, divided up senatorial *domus* distribution by the 14 Augustan regions. While some of the Augustan regions are roughly equivalent to hills or valleys, others contain areas of both high and low ground. It was therefore necessary to perform a separate analysis which attempted to more precisely distinguish *domus* location by elevation, as I have done here. I have not gone into a detailed source analysis since Eck already provides a very useful and complete discussion of the problems associated with using the available types of literary and archaeological evidence for *domus* location.

It should be noted that a number of the *domus* locations are speculative, often being based on where lead pipes bearing individuals' names were uncovered, and many others are the subject of sometimes heated academic debates. While further excavations or different interpretations might cause the exact numbers of houses in a given area to be increased or decreased, the overall trends are so overwhelming that such fine adjustments to the data would not affect the general conclusions.

There are an additional 15 *domus* whose existence is known, but whose locations are either completely uncertain or extremely tenuous.

These *domus* were not included in the totals. I also did not count a few dwellings of extremely early date (e.g., Romulus's or Numa's supposed houses), as well as those dated to after c. AD 450. Even if these had been included, they would have numbered no more than a half dozen.

One problem with these figures is that some of the *domus* identified as being on a certain hill might actually have been located on the slopes of that hill, perhaps even on the lower slopes, where they might have been subject to inundation by high waters. For the majority of the *domus*, it is not possible to locate their positions precisely enough to determine just where on a hill they were situated. Rome's hills tend to rise fairly steeply so that even homes on the lower slopes of the hills would have gained enough elevation to take them beyond the reach of most floods. On important residential hills such as the Palatine and Aventine, the slopes that face the Tiber both descend to the lowest elevation and rise most steeply. Few houses could have been built on these inclines. The more gradual back slopes of these hills, where it would have been more likely to find a number of homes, have elevations high enough that *domus* placed there would have been above flood level. Even if a number of these *domus* were actually situated on the sides of hills in locations where floodwaters could have reached them, rather than on the crests, the overall pattern would still hold, if perhaps not in such an extreme fashion.

It should be noted that these are absolute numbers, not density figures, which would have to be adjusted by the square areas of the respective regions. Doing so, however, would only make more extreme such contrasts as the fact that the relatively small area of the Palatine contained five times as many known *domus* as the vast expanse of the Campus Martius.

8. See Reynolds (1996), who comments on this juxtaposition (235 and fig. 4.21).
9. A useful summary of some of the many links between water, religion, and magic in the ancient world can be found in Holland (1961), 8–20. A number of the following examples are derived from there.
10. More than one third of curse tablets whose provenance is known come from wells, fountains, or baths (Bruun, 1992, 78). On water and curses in the Roman world, and on water as a malign force generally, see Bruun (1992).
11. The link between bridges and victory monuments and the interpretation of these works as a triumph over nature is explored in detail by Kleiner (1991).
12. Flood as portent: 414 BC (Livy 4.49.2–3); 363 BC (Livy 7.3.2); 202 BC (Livy 30.38.10–12); 193 BC (Livy 35.9.2–3); 192 BC (Livy 35.21.5–6); 156 BC (Iul. Obseq. 16); 60 BC (Dio 37.58.3–4); 54 BC (Dio 39.61.1–2); 54 BC (Cic. *Ad Quint. fr.* 3.7.1); 44 BC (Hor. *Carm.* 1.2.13–20); 32 BC

(Dio 50.8.3); 27 BC (Dio 53.20.1); 23 BC (Dio 53.33.5); 22 BC (Dio 54.1); AD 5 (Dio 55.22.3); AD 15 (Tac. *Ann.* 1.76); AD 15 (Dio 57.14.7–8); AD 36 (Dio 58.26.5); AD 69 (Plut. *Otho* 4.5); AD 69 (Tac. *Hist.* 1.86); Nerva (Sex. Aur. Victor *Epit.* 13); AD 147 (SHA *Ant.* 9.3); AD 217 (Dio 79.25.1–5).

See also Le Gall (1953, 62–65), who lists and comments on 14 floods as portents.

13. In a study of ancient authors' accounts of natural disasters, Newbold (1982) found that 28% of the time the disaster was interpreted as constituting a portent. The authors analyzed in this study were Thucydides, Diodorus, Livy, Tacitus, and Dio, and the disasters noted were earthquakes, fires, and floods. Newbold found a total of 94 accounts of natural disasters in these authors.

    On natural disasters in general in the ancient world and how ancient authors described them, see Newbold (1982), the essays in Olshausen and Sonnabend (1998) and Sordi (1989), and, at Rome, Bustany and Géroudet (2001), 33–46, and the website of Bustany: http://aphgcaen.free.fr/conferences/bustany.htm. On natural disasters in Italy, see Martinis (1987).

14. Floods caused by divine wrath: 363 BC (Livy 7.3.2); 60 BC (Dio 37.58.3–4); 54 BC (Dio 39.61.1–2); 54 BC (Cic. *Ad Quint. fr.* 3.7.1); 44 BC (Hor. *Carm.* 1.2.13–20); 22 BC (Dio 54.1); AD 15 (Tac. *Ann.* 1.76); AD 69 (Plut. *Otho* 4.5); AD 69 (Tac. *Hist.* 1.86).

15. Attempts to propitiate the gods: 363 BC (Livy 7.3.2); 193 BC (Livy 35.9.2–3); 192 BC (Livy 35.21.5–6); 156 BC (Iul. Obseq. 16); 54 BC (Dio 39.61.1–2); 22 BC (Dio 54.1); AD 15 (Tac. *Ann.* 1.76); AD 69 (Tac. *Hist.* 1.86).

16. Floods included among lists of other portents: 202 BC (Livy 30.38.10–12); 193 BC (Livy 35.9.2–3); 156 BC (Iul. Obseq. 16); 32 BC (Dio 50.8.3); 23 BC (Dio 53.33.5); 22 BC (Dio 54.1); AD 5 (Dio 55.22.3); AD 15 (Dio 57.14.7–8); AD 69 (Plut. *Otho* 4.5); AD 147 (SHA *Ant.* 9.3); AD 217 (Dio 79.25).

17. An example is the way in which the author of the "Life of Antoninus Pius" in the *Historia Augusta* mentions the flood of AD 147: "The following misfortunes and prodigies occurred in his reign: the famine that we have just described, the collapse of the Circus, an earthquake that destroyed towns in Rhodes and of Asia (all of which, however, the emperor restored in splendid fashion), and a fire at Rome that consumed 340 tenements and dwellings. The town of Narbonne, the city of Antioch, and the forum of Carthage also burned. Besides, the Tiber flooded its banks, a comet was seen, a two-headed child was born, and a woman gave birth to quintuplets. There was seen, moreover, in Arabia, a crested serpent larger than usual size that ate itself from the tail to the middle; and also in Arabia

there was a pestilence, while in Moesia barley sprouted from the tops of trees. And besides all this, in Arabia four lions grew tame and of their own accord yielded themselves to capture" (SHA *Ant.* 9.1–5).

18. Floods listed among other natural disasters: 203 BC (Livy 30.26.5); 202 BC (Livy 30.38.10–12); 193 BC (Livy 35.9.2–3); 192 BC (Livy 35.21.5–6); 156 BC (Iul. Obseq. 16); 60 BC (Dio 37.58.3–4); 32 BC (Dio 50.8.3); 23 BC (Dio 53.33.5); 22 BC (Dio 54.1); AD 5 (Dio 55.22.3); AD 15 (Dio 57.14.7–8); AD 36 (Dio 58.26.5); Nerva (Sex. Aur. Victor *Epit.* 13); Hadrian (SHA *Had.* 21.6); AD 147 (SHA *Ant.* 9.3); AD 217 (Dio 79.25); AD 398 (Claud. *De Bel. Gild.* 41–43).

19. Floods in Livy linked to the gods: 414 BC, 363 BC, 202 BC, 193 BC, 192 BC. Floods in Livy not linked to the gods: 215 BC, 203 BC, 189 BC. Floods in Dio linked to the gods: 60 BC, 54 BC, 32 BC, 27 BC, 23 BC, 22 BC, AD 5, AD 15, AD 36, AD 217. Floods in Dio not linked to the gods: 13 BC, AD 12.

20. The exact meaning in this context of Tiberius's "preferring secrecy on earth as in heaven" (*perinde divina humanaque obtegens*) is somewhat problematic. It is probably a reference to the recurrent motif in Tacitus of depicting Tiberius as inscrutable and secretive. It could be read, however, as indicating that Tiberius accepted a divine causation for the flood but for some reason did not wish this to be explicitly revealed.

21. Such mixed attitudes of piety and practicality are by no means exclusive to the ancient or pre-Christian world, as reflected in the popularity of the slogan "Praise the Lord and pass the ammunition." Alleged to have originally been spoken by an American army chaplain during the attack on Pearl Harbor in 1941, it has attained use beyond this specific context.

22. If 350 million HS seems excessive for a public works project, consider the 288 million HS that were expended by Domitian merely to provide gilding on the Capitol (Plut. *Public.* 15.3).

Unfortunately, ancient authors do not often provide information about the expense of construction projects at Rome. The numbers cited here are among the only ones known for major projects in or around Rome. To augment the paucity of known building costs for the city of Rome, one can look beyond the capital. For example, Duncan-Jones (1982, 157) offers a list of building expenses for structures in Italy and Africa. This study reveals that the cost of simple temples in small towns was in the range of hundreds of thousands of sesterces, and even modest baths and libraries seem to have been very expensive; for instance, Antoninus Pius's bath in Ostia cost more than 2 million HS, and Pliny donated 1 million HS toward his library in Comum.

Emperors were, and still are, often criticized for their excessive expenditure on games, yet these costs are trivial when compared with building expenses. The largest known amount spent on a single game was only

4 million HS (by Hadrian; SHA *Had.* 3). Even allowing for the fact that some of the more extravagant games probably cost more than 4 million HS, major building projects seem to have been on a totally different order of magnitude from games, and, indeed, even from the grain dole. In fact, the only expense that seems to have been on the same order of magnitude as a major building project is annual military expenditure. Even when the costs of pay for legionaries, officers, auxiliaries, praetorians, urban cohorts, retirement bounties, and the navy are included, the total still seems to be comparable with the cost of the Claudian aqueducts. K. Hopkins (1980, 124–25) offers a figure of 450 million HS for the annual military budget, and although this number is open to debate, it does suggest an order of magnitude comparable with a major public works project. While some might argue that such a comparison is deceptive because the military expense is an annual figure whereas the aqueducts took many years to complete, it should be kept in mind that the aqueducts were just one of many building projects under way at the same time, of which at least two—the Fucine Lake project and the Ostian harbor—were of similar scale.

23. The labor-intensive nature of ancient construction may also have contributed to these projects being desirable as a form of imperial benefaction. Much of the labor was unskilled and was most likely provided by free workers rather than slaves. By utilizing some of the otherwise underemployed urban plebs on such construction projects, emperors were providing an important social and economic benefaction to the inhabitants of the capital. In this context, Vespasian's rejection of a labor-saving construction device is telling. He explained to the machine's inventor that he would not adopt it because "You must let me feed the poor plebs" (Suet. *Vesp.* 18). A similar example of employment being perceived as a form of benefaction involves the 18,000 workers on the Great Temple at Jerusalem (Joseph. *Ant.* 219–23). On free labor and public works at Rome, see Brunt (1980).

24. For a more detailed comparison between ancient and modern disaster narratives, see Newbold (1982).

25. On Jewish and foreign cult centers in the Transtiberim region, see the entries for "Transtiberim" and "Synagogue" in Steinby (1993–2000) and Haselberger et al. (2002). On cults in this region, see Savage (1940). On Jews at Rome in general, see Leon (1960).

26. In many Third World countries, the urban regions closest to a river, where flooding is most severe, are clearly recognized slum zones occupied by the poorest inhabitants or by ostracized classes. On this phenomenon in a variety of Third World countries, see the works listed in notes 31, 33, and 34 of chapter 3.

27. It is important to note that, in general, ancient Rome was much less sub-

divided into clearly identifiable rich and poor neighborhoods than is common today. On the whole, there was considerable intermingling of classes, and class stratification was often more pronounced along the vertical dimension (wealthier tenants in lower-floor apartments, poorer ones on the higher levels) than the horizontal one. On this phenomenon, see Stambaugh (1988); Purcell (1994); and Reynolds (1996). Nevertheless, there do seem to have been a few exceptions to this overall trend, such as the strong upper-class dominance of residential housing on the Palatine, the disreputable and lower-class nature of the Subura, and the concentration of foreigners in the Transtiberim. On ethnicity and Roman neighborhoods, see Duff (1928) and the individual entries for various regions of the city in Steinby (1993–2000); Richardson (1992); and Haselberger et al. (2002). On neighborhood organization, with an emphasis on religion and imperial patronage, see Lott (2004).

28. There are a number of statutes from Roman towns prohibiting the demolition of existing buildings, and such laws have been inferred for Rome as well. The intent of some of these seems to have been to ensure that the land did not fall into disuse (which likely would not have been a problem in Rome). There also appear to have been problems arising from buildings being intentionally demolished in order to recover and reuse valuable components within them. Owners seem to have been allowed to tear down existing buildings in order to replace them with more valuable ones. This appears to be the case in the famous letter of Cicero (*Att.* 14.9.1) regarding some crumbling tenements he owned at Puteoli, in which he expressed the hope of evicting the current residents, rebuilding the structures in more luxurious form, and then being able to collect higher rents. Even when this was the intent, it seems that owners first had to seek permission from the appropriate official and that there was some degree of uncertainty regarding whether such a request would be granted. Therefore, builders or developers had, at the very least, to contend with a certain degree of bureaucratic interference and delay before they could demolish a structure. Thus, destruction due to flooding would have conveniently expedited the process. New land would also have opened up for development when, for example, the owner of a small shop destroyed by flooding could not afford to rebuild and so had to sell his property. On the laws regarding demolition at Rome and in other cities and the uncertainties regarding these statutes, see Garnsey (1976); Phillips (1973); and Rainer (1987). A more recent summary of the issue is included in Robinson (1992), 42–46.

Conclusion. The Romans' Failure to Make Rome Safe from Floods

1. The destructiveness of these floods is exacerbated because centuries of the building up of earthen embankments has resulted in places where the

Notes to Pages 233–241

rivers (within their artificial containments) now flow at a higher level than surrounding areas. Thus, when the embankments are overtopped, the water runs downhill into the lower-lying surrounding regions.

2. In accounts of Tiber floods after the Roman period, larger death tolls often occur during nocturnal floods. Floods whose waters began rising after nightfall could attain high enough levels during the course of the night to trap unwary people in their homes and prevent them from reaching points of safety. Even in such cases, the recorded death tolls are in the low thousands, in contrast to the tens or even hundreds of thousands who routinely drown in inundations of the great Chinese rivers. For narratives of post-Roman Tiber floods, see Di Martino and Belati (1980).

3. As discussed in chapter 6, large bath complexes, the one type of major public building that may have been highly vulnerable to flood damage due to their complex plumbing, seem, whenever possible, to have been placed on higher ground out of reach from floodwaters.

4. The comparison with modern urban infrastructure is revealing. Uniquely for a preindustrial city, ancient Rome possessed a population equivalent to that of a modern city. It also shared many of the stereotypical characteristics of large modern cities, both negative (crowding, crime, poverty, alienation) and positive (diversity, opportunity, wealth, culture). For these reasons, analyses of ancient Rome have frequently used modern cities as comparisons, but it is necessary to keep in mind some of the crucial differences as well. One of these is that while Rome might have been the size of a modern metropolis, it did not share the same delicate infrastructure with its attendant vulnerabilities to flooding. When a city today has its power grid disrupted by a flood, its social, economic, and political activities are paralyzed, and the restoration of proper functioning is a prolonged and expensive process. All the vital networks necessary to the ordinary operation of modern cities and their inhabitants that provide communication, transportation, water, waste disposal, and power are highly vulnerable to disruption by flooding. Although ancient Rome was a large, complex city, its vital infrastructure was far more robust and quick to recover, either because it simply did not possess some networks (e.g., power, communication) or because those that existed were simpler and more resilient (e.g., water supply, waste removal). On the vulnerability of large urban centers to natural disasters generally, see Albala-Bertrand (1993) and Mitchell (1999).

Appendix I. List of Major Floods at Rome, 414 BC–AD 2000

1. For a discussion of exceptions to this, see Bersani and Bencivenga (2001), 13–25.
2. For approximately the last century and a half, when the measurements taken have included not only the height that the floodwaters at Rome

reached but also their velocity, it is possible to calculate more correctly the true magnitude of floods as expressed in m³/sec.

Such an analysis has been done by Bersani and Bencivenga (2001), 35–61. They identified 55 instances between 1921 and 2000 when floods had a discharge of at least 1,400 m³/sec. The greatest recorded discharge for this period was 2730 m³/sec during the flood of December 1937, which also had the highest recorded water level of 16.84 masl. Discharge and height do not always coincide in this way, however. For example, the flood of February 17, 1976, recorded a discharge of 2050 m³/sec (the fourth largest measured between 1921 and 2000) but reached a height of only 12.72 m (the 17th highest for the same period). Thus, although this flood was a borderline "extraordinary" flood as measured by discharge, it was only in the "ordinary" range by height.

Although technically speaking, discharge is a more accurate measure of a flood's magnitude, in appendix I the decision whether to include floods has been made on the basis of height because reliable discharge data are really only available for the 19th century onward.

3. From 1947 to 2000, there were 12 floods that, although they failed to reach a height of at least 13 masl, nevertheless attained discharges of more than 1500 m³/sec and thus could have been included in the list of significant floods at Rome given in appendix I. (See note 2 above.) These were the floods of: February 27, 1951; December 23, 1960; January 6, 1961; December 30, 1964; September 3, 1965; February 17, 1969; February 17, 1976; February 18, 1979; February 27, 1984; February 2, 1986; November 22, 1991; and December 9, 1992.

For detailed information about these floods and other instances of floods with magnitudes greater than 1400 m³/sec, see Bersani and Bencivenga (2001), 42–49.

Appendix II. The Modern Tiber Embankments

1. For good overviews of the convoluted history of the Tiber embankment project, convenient modern summaries are provided by the masters thesis of Courtenay (2003) and in Frosini (1977). See also Cardilli and Sartorio (1985), 128–31. Important contemporary accounts, although lacking the benefit of historical hindsight, include the report authored by the members of the commission of 1871 (C. Possenti, 1871) and the publications of those advocating various specific plans: Tomei (1871); Rullier (1873); Baccarini (1875); Zucchelli (1879); Amadei (1875); Grimelli (1876); Filopanti (1875); and Vescovali (1880). See also the 1875 publication by Canevari himself.
2. On the flood of 1870, see the detailed accounts in Di Martino and Belati (1980) and Frosini (1977).
3. On the symbolic roles of Roma Capitale and the embankment project it-

self, see the detailed discussion in Courtenay (2003). He also examines the project in terms of modernity, national identity, and its long-term effects on the topographies (both literal and symbolic) of the city of Rome.
4. These include Gomez (1531); Modio (1556); Bacci (1558); Castiglione (1599a, 1599b); Mora (1600); Lambardi (1601); Breccioli (1607); Pinadoro (1608); Ferreri (1608); Domenichi (1609); Castelli (1642); Raggi (1662); Bonini (1663); Meyer (1685); Fontana (1694); Pascoli (1740); Chiesa and Gamberini (1746); Rasi (1827); P. Lanciani (1829); Fea (1835); and Cialdi (1845).
5. The destruction of much of the Jewish Ghetto necessitated by Canevari's plan was viewed by many at the time as an additional benefit of the project and as a desirable form of urban renewal. On this aspect of the plan, see the discussion in Courtenay (2003). On earlier issues with the river and the Jewish Ghetto, see Lagunes (2004), 229–34.
6. A nice summary and analysis of these criticisms are provided by Courtenay (2003). He also argues that some of the stereotypical criticisms leveled against Canevari's embankments are the result of a romanticized and erroneous view of the use and role of the Tiber during the centuries just prior to their construction.

Bibliography

Abt, S. R., et al. (1989). "Predicting Human Instability in Flood Flows." In *Hydraulic Engineering: Annual Proceedings of the National Conference Sponsored by the Hydraulic Division of the American Society of Civil Engineers*, 70–76. New York: American Society of Civil Engineers.

Adam, Jean-Pierre. (1994). *Roman Building: Materials and Techniques*. Trans. Anthony Mathews. Bloomington: Indiana University Press.

Albala-Bertrand, J. M. (1993). *Political Economy of Large Natural Disasters with Special Reference to Developing Countries*. New York: Oxford University Press.

Aldrete, Gregory S. (2004). *Daily Life in the Roman City: Rome, Pompeii, and Ostia*. Greenwood Daily Life through History Series. Westport, Conn.: Greenwood Press.

———. (1999). *Gestures and Acclamations in Ancient Rome*. Ancient Society and History Series. Baltimore: Johns Hopkins University Press.

Aldrete, Gregory S., and D. J. Mattingly. (2000). "The Feeding of Imperial Rome: The Mechanics of the Food Supply System." In *Ancient Rome: The Archaeology of the Eternal City*, ed. Jon Coulston and Hazel Dodge, 142–65. Oxford University School of Archaeology Monograph 54. Oxford.

———. (1999). "Feeding the City: The Organization, Operation, and Scale of the Supply System for Rome." In *Life, Death, and Entertainment in the Roman Empire*, ed. D. S. Potter and D. J. Mattingly, 171–204. Ann Arbor: University of Michigan Press.

Alessandroni, Maria G., and Gianrenzo Remedia. (2002). "The Most Severe Floods of the Tiber River in Rome." In *The Extremes of the Extremes: Extraor-*

dinary Floods, ed. Árni Snorrason, Helga Finnsdóttir, and Marshall Moss, 129–132. IAHS Publication no. 271. Wallingford, Oxfordshire: International Association of Hydrological Sciences.

Alexander, David. (1993). *Natural Disasters.* New York: Chapman and Hall.

Allaby, Michael. (1998). *Floods.* New York: Facts on File.

Allara, A. (1995). "*Corpus* et *cadaver,* la 'gestion' d'un nouveau corpus." In *La mort au quotidien dans le monde Romain,* ed. F. Hinard, 69–79. Paris: De Boccard.

Amadei, Luigi. (1875). *Memoria riassuntiva sul progetto del Tevere del generale Garibaldi.* Rome: G. B. Paravia.

Ammerman, Albert J. (1998). "Environmental Archaeology in the Velabrum, Rome: Interim Report." *Journal of Roman Archaeology* 11: 213–23.

———. (1996). "The Comitium in Rome from the Beginning." *American Journal of Archaeology* 100: 121–36.

———. (1990). "On the Origins of the Forum Romanum." *American Journal of Archaeology* 94: 627–45.

Amouretti, M.-C. (1986). *Le pain et l'huile dans la Grèce antique.* Paris: Belles Lettres.

Anderson, James C. (1997). *Roman Architecture and Society.* Baltimore: Johns Hopkins University Press.

Appelbaum, Stuart. (1985). "Determination of Urban Flood Damages." *Journal of Water Resources Planning and Management* 111, no. 3: 269–83.

Atlante di Roma: La forma del centro storico in scala 1:1000 nel fotopiano e nella carta numerica. (1991). Venice: Marsilio Editore.

Aubert, Spirito. (1871). *Roma e l'innondazione del Tevere. Considerazione dell'arch. Spirito Aubert.* Rome: Tipografia Delle Belle Arti.

Baccarini, Alfredo. (1875). *Sull'altezza di piena massima nel Tevere urbano e sui provvedimenti contro le inondazioni.* Rome.

Bacci, Andrea. (1558). *Del Tevere, della natura et bontà dell'acque et delle inondationi.* Rome.

Bagnasco, Carlo, ed. (1998). *Il delta del Tevere: Un viaggio fra passato e futuro.* Rome: Fratelli Palombi Editori.

Bairoch, Paul. (1988). *Cities and Economic Development: From the Dawn of History to the Present.* Trans. Christopher Braider. Chicago: University of Chicago Press.

Baker, Bobby. (1993). "Water, Water Everywhere . . . and Not a Drop to Drink." *Journal of Environmental Health* 56, no. 4: 25–27.

Baker, Victor. (2000). "Paleoflood Hydrology and the Estimation of Extreme Floods." In *Inland Flood Hazards: Human, Riparian, and Aquatic Communities,* ed. Ellen Wohl, 359–77. New York: Cambridge University Press.

Baker, Victor, R. Craig Kochel, and Peter Patton, eds. (1988). *Flood Geomorphology.* New York: John Wiley & Sons.

Barber, P. (1988). *Vampires, Burial and Death: Folklore and Reality.* New Haven: Yale University Press.

Barton, Allen. (1969). *Communities in Disaster: A Sociological Analysis of Collective Stress Situations.* Garden City, N.Y.: Doubleday.
Bauer, H. (1989). "Die Cloaca Maxima in Rom." *Mitteilungen des Leichtweiss-Instituts für Wasserbau der Technischen Universität Braunschweig* 103: 45–67.
Baynes, N. H. (1943). "The Decline of the Roman Empire in Western Europe. Some Modern Explanations." *Journal of Roman Studies* 33: 29–35.
Bellotti, Piero. (1998). "Il delta del Tevere: Geologia, morfologia, evoluzione." In *Il delta del Tevere: Un viaggio fra passato e futuro,* ed. Carlo Bagnasco, 19–29. Rome: Fratelli Palombi Editori.
Beloch, J. (1886). *Die Bevölkerung der griechisch-römischen Welt.* Leipzig.
Bencivenga, M., E. Di Loreto, and L. Liperi. (1995). "Il regime idrologico del Tevere, con particolare riguardo alle piene nella città di Roma." In *La geologia di Roma: Il centro storico,* 2 vols., ed. Renato Funiciello, 123–72. Memorie Descrittive della Carta Geologica d'Italia, vol. 50. Rome: Istituto Poligrafico e Zecca dello Stato.
Benito, G., V. R. Baker, and K. J. Gregory, eds. (1998). *Palaeohydrology and Environmental Change.* New York: John Wiley & Sons.
Berry, M., et al. (1994). "Suggested Guidelines for Remediation of Damage from Sewage Backflow into Buildings." *Journal of Environmental Health* 57, no. 3: 9–15.
Bersani, Pio, and Mauro Bencivenga. (2003). "Le piene del Tevere a Roma dal V secolo a.C. all'anno 2000." *Tevere,* no. 22: 4–9.
———. (2001). *Le piene del Tevere a Roma dal V secolo a.C. all'anno 2000.* Rome: Servizio Idrografico e Mareografico Nazionale.
Betocchi, Alessandro. (1879). "Del fiume Tevere." In *Monografia della Città di Roma e della Campagna Romana,* 1:197–264. Rome: Tipografia Elzeviriana.
———. (1875). *Dell'idrologia del Tevere. Osservazioni del Prof. Alessandro Betocchi.* Rome: G. B. Paravia.
———. (1873). *Efemeride della straordinaria piena del Tevere 28 e 29 dicembre 1870-novembre 1871-marzo 1872. Nota del Prof. Alessandro Betocchi.*
———. (1863). *Statistica del fiume Tevere nel quarantennio 1 gennaio 1822–31 dicembre 1861.* Rome: Tipografia delle Belle Arti.
Blaikie, P., T. Cannon, I. Davis, and B. Wisner. (1994). *At Risk: Natural Hazards, People's Vulnerability, and Disasters.* New York: Routledge.
Boatwright, Mary Taliaferro. (1987). *Hadrian and the City of Rome.* Princeton, N.J.: Princeton University Press.
Bodel, John. (2000). "Dealing with the Dead: Undertakers, Executioners and Potter's Fields in Ancient Rome." In *Death and Disease in the Ancient City,* ed. Valerie Hope and Eireann Marshall, 128–51. New York: Routledge.
———. (1999). "Death on Display: Looking at Roman Funerals." In *The Art of Ancient Spectacle,* ed. B. Bergmann and C. Kondoleon, 258–81. Studies in the History of Art 56. Washington, D.C.: National Gallery of Art.
———. (1994). "Graveyards and Groves: A Study of the *Lex Lucerina.*" *American Journal of Ancient History* 11: 1–133.

Bibliography

Boëthius, A. (1960). *The Golden House of Nero.* Ann Arbor: University of Michigan Press.

Bonini, F. M. (1663). *Il Tevere incatenato ovvero l'arte di frenar l'acque correnti.* Rome.

Breccioli, F. (1607). *Discorso sopra le cause dell'inondatione del Tevere in Roma con li rimedi per evitarla.* Urbino.

Brunt, P. A. (1980). "Free Labor and Public Works at Rome." *Journal of Roman Studies* 70: 81–100.

———. (1971). *Italian Manpower, 225 BC–AD 14.* Oxford: Oxford University Press.

Bruun, Christer. (1992). "Water as a Cruel Element in the Roman World." In *Crudelitas: The Politics of Cruelty in the Ancient and Medieval World,* ed. Toivo Viljamaa, Asko Timonen, and Chritian Krötzl, 74–80. Gesellschaft zur Erforschung der materiellen Kultur des Mittelalters. Krems. Austria.

Bryant, Edward. (1991). *Natural Hazards.* New York: Cambridge University Press.

Buchner, E. (1980). "Horologium Solarium Augusti. Bericht über die Ausgrabungen 1979/1980." *Mitteilungen des deutschen archäologischen Instituts, Römische Abteilung* 87: 355–73.

———. (1976). "Solarium Augusti und Ara Pacis." *Mitteilungen des deutschen archäologischen Instituts, Römische Abteilung* 83: 319–65.

Bustany, Catherine. (2003). http://aphgcaen.free.fr/conferences/bustany.htm.

———. (2001). "Problèmes méthodologiques pour la cartographie des incendies et catastrophes naturelles dans la Rome antique." *Cahiers de la Maison de la Recherche en Sciences Humaines de Caen,* no. 25 (Feb.): 11–44.

Bustany, Catherine, and Noëlle Géroudet. (2001). *Rome, maîtrise de l'espace, maîtrise du pouvoir de César aux Antonins.* Paris: Éditions Seli Arslan.

Canevari, Raffaele. (1875). *Studi per la sistemazione del Tevere nel tronco entro Roma.* Rome: Tip. e lit. del Giornale del Genio civile.

Carandini, A., and R. Cappelli, eds. (2000). *Roma: Romolo, Remo e la fondazione della città.* Milan: Electa.

Carcani, M. (1893). *Il Tevere e le sue inondazioni dalle origini di Roma fino ai nostri giorni.* Rome.

Cardilli, Luisa, Lucia Cavazzi, and Giussepina Sartorio, eds. (1985). *Le Tibre: Tibre-Seine, deux villes deux fleuves.* Rome: Edizioni Carte Segrete.

Casson, Lionel. (1971). *Ships and Seamanship in the Ancient World.* Princeton, N.J.: Princeton University Press.

———. (1965). "Harbour and River Boats of Ancient Rome." *Journal of Roman Studies* 55: 31–39.

Castagnoli, F. (1980). "Installazioni portuali a Roma." In *The Seaborne Commerce of Ancient Rome,* ed. J. H. D'Arms and E. C. Kopff, 35–42. Memoirs of the American Academy in Rome 36. Rome.

Castelli, B. (1642). *Della misura delle acque correnti.* Rome.

Castiglione, G. (1599a). *Tiberis inundatio anni MDIIC.* Rome: Typ. Nicolai Mutii.
———. (1599b). *Trattato dell'inondatione del Tevere.* Rome.
Celani, E. (1895). "Alcune iscrizioni sulle inondazioni del Tevere." *Bullettino della Commissione Archaeologica Comunale di Roma:* 283–300.
Chan, N. W., and D. J. Parker. (1996). "Response to Dynamic Flood Hazard Factors in Peninsular Malaysia." *Geographical Journal* 162, no. 3: 313–25.
Cheng, F. Y., and M.-S. Sheu. (1995). *Urban Disaster Mitigation: The Role of Engineering and Technology.* New York: Elsevier Science.
Chiesa, A., and B. Gamberini. (1746). *Delle cagioni e de' rimedi delle inondazioni del Tevere.* Rome.
Cialdi, Alessandro. (1845). *Delle barche a vapore e di alquante proposizioni per rendere più sicura e più agevole la navigazione del Tevere e della sua foce in Fiumicino, ragionamento.* Rome: Tipografia delle Belle Arti.
Clark, Champ. (1982). *Flood.* Alexandria, Va.: Time-Life Books.
Cloudsley-Thompson, J. L. (1976). *Insects and History.* New York: St. Martin's Press.
Coarelli, F. (1997). *Il Campo Marzio: Dalle origini alla fine della repubblica.* Rome: Edizioni Quasar.
———. (1995). *Roma.* Guide archeologiche Laterza 6. Rome: Laterza.
———. (1992). *Il Foro Romano: Periodo Repubblicano e Augusteo.* 2nd ed. Rome: Edizioni Quasar.
———. (1983). *Il Foro Romano: Periodo Arcaico.* Rome: Edizioni Quasar.
Coccia, S., and D. J. Mattingly. (1992). "Settlement History, Environment and Human Exploitation of an Intermontane Basin in the Central Apennines: The Rieti Survey 1988–1991, Part I." *Papers of the British School at Rome* 60, n.s., 47: 213–89.
Colacino, M., et al. (1988). "Climate as a Historiographical Problem." In *Past, Present and Future Trends in Geophysical Research,* ed. Wilfried Schröder, 212–49. Bremen-Roennebeck: Interdivisional Commission on History of IAGA.
Colini, A. M. (1980). "Il Porto fluviale del Foro Boario a Roma." In *The Seaborne Commerce of Ancient Rome,* ed. J. H. D'Arms and E. C. Kopff, 43–53. *Memoirs of the American Academy in Rome* 36. Rome.
Commager, Steele. (1962). *The Odes of Horace: A Critical Study.* New Haven, Conn.: Yale University Press.
Committee on Risk Based Analysis for Flood Damage Reduction, National Water Science and Technology Board. (2000). *Risk Analysis and Uncertainty in Flood Damage Reduction Studies.* Washington, D.C.: National Academy Press.
Connolly, P., and H. Dodge. (1998). *The Ancient City.* Oxford: Oxford University Press.
Corazza, A., and L. Lombardi. (1995). "Idrogeologia dell'area del centro sto-

rico di Roma." In *La geologia di Roma: Il centro storico,* 2 vols., ed. Renato Funiciello, 173–211. Memorie Descrittive della Carta Geologica d'Italia, vol. 50. Rome: Istituto Poligrafico e Zecca dello Stato.

Cornell, James. (1976). *The Great International Disaster Book.* New York: Charles Scribner's Sons.

Cornell, T. J. (1995). *The Beginnings of Rome.* New York: Routledge.

Cotton, Richard. (1963). *Pests of Stored Grain and Grain Products.* Minneapolis: Burgess Publishing.

Coulston, Jon, and Hazel Dodge, eds. (2000). *Ancient Rome: The Archaeology of the Eternal City.* Oxford University School of Archaeology Monograph 54. Oxford.

Courtenay, W. T. (2003). "Un fiume per Roma Capitale: The Socio-Political Landscape of the Tiber Embankment, 1870–1910." Master's thesis, University of Wisconsin-Madison.

Curriero, Frank, et al. (2001). "The Association between Extreme Precipitation and Water-borne Disease Outbreaks in the United States, 1948–1994." *American Journal of Public Health* 91, no. 8: 1194–99.

Davis, C. V., and K. Sorensen, eds. (1984). *Handbook of Applied Hydraulics.* 3rd ed. New York: McGraw-Hill.

Davis, Raymond, ed. (1996). *The Lives of the Ninth-Century Popes (Liber Pontificalis): The Ancient Biographies of Ten Popes from A.D. 817–891.* Liverpool: Liverpool University Press.

———, ed. (1992). *The Lives of the Eighth-Century Popes (Liber Pontificalis): The Ancient Biographies of Nine Popes from A.D. 715 to A.D. 817.* Liverpool: Liverpool University Press.

De Filippi, Rita. (1994). "Giuseppe Garibaldi e il progetto di deviazione del Tevere." In *Roma: La città dell'acqua,* 255–61. Rome: Edizioni De Luca.

Delano Smith, C. (1979). *Western Mediterranean Europe: A Historical Geography of Italy, Spain and Southern France since the Neolithic.* New York: Academic Press.

Demougeot, E. (1965). "Variations climatiques et invasions." *Revue historique* 233: 1–22.

DeWolfe, Deborah. (2000). *Training Manual for Mental Health and Human Service Workers in Major Disasters.* Rockville, Md.: U.S. Dept. of Health and Human Services.

Diamond, Jared. (1997). *Guns, Germs, and Steel: The Fates of Human Societies.* New York: W. W. Norton.

Dietz, Park, and Susan Baker. (1974). "Drowning: Epidemiology and Prevention." *American Journal of Public Health* 64, no. 4: 303–12.

Di Martino, V., and M. Belati. (1980). *Qui arrivo il Tevere: Le inondazioni del Tevere nelle testimonianze e nei ricordi storici.* Rome: Multigrafica Editrice.

Dodge, Hazel. (2000). "Greater than the Pyramids: The Water Supply of Ancient Rome." In *Ancient Rome: The Archaeology of the Eternal City,* ed. Jon

Coulston and Hazel Dodge, 166–209. Oxford University School of Archaeology Monograph 54. Oxford.
Domenichi, Cesare. (1609). *Della innondatione del Teuere et del suo rimedio.* Rome: Guglielmo Facciotto.
D'Onofrio, Cesare. (1980). *Il Tevere: L'isola Tiberina, le inondazioni, i molini, i porti, le rive, i muraglioni, i ponti di Roma.* Rome: Romana Società Editrice.
———. (1970). *Il Tevere e Roma.* Rome: Ugo Bozzi.
Drabek, T. E. (1986). *Human System Responses to Disaster: An Inventory of Sociological Findings.* New York: Springer-Verlag.
Duchesne, Louis. (1981). *Le Liber Pontificalis: Texte, introduction et commentaire.* Paris: E. de Boccard.
Duff, A. M. (1928). *Freedmen in the Early Roman Empire.* Oxford: Clarendon Press.
Duncan-Jones, R. (1982). *The Economy of the Roman Empire: Quantitative Studies.* 2nd ed. New York: Cambridge University Press.
Dwyer, D. J. (1975). *People and Housing in Third World Cities: Perspectives on the Problems of Spontaneous Settlements.* New York: Longman.
Eck, W. (1999). "*Cum dignitate otium:* Senatorial *domus* in Imperial Rome." *Scripta Classica Israelica* 16: 162–90.
Ehlers, V., and E. Steel. (1943). *Municipal and Rural Sanitation.* 3rd ed. New York: McGraw-Hill.
Fant, J. C. (2001). "Rome's Marble Yards." *Journal of Roman Archaeology* 14: 167–98.
Favro, Diane. (1996). *The Urban Image of Augustan Rome.* New York: Cambridge University Press.
Fea, Carlo. (1835). *Compendio storico delle poste specialmente romane antiche e moderne.* Rome.
Ferranti, Carlo, and Adriano Paolella, eds. (2001). *La pianificazione del Bacino del Fiume Tevere 1992–2000.* Rome: Gangemi Editore.
Ferreri, G. P. (1608). *Pianta et profili di Gio. Paolo Ferreri Architetto fatto sopra l'inondatione del Tevere in Roma.* Rome.
Filopanti, Quirico. (1875). *Sulle bonifiche romane proposte dal generale.* Rome.
Fitts, Charles. (2002). *Groundwater Science.* London: Academic Press / Elsevier Science.
Fontana, Carlo. (1694). *Discorso del Cav. Carlo Fontana . . . sopra le cause delle inondazioni del Tevere antiche e moderne a danno della città di Roma.* Rome: Stamp. della Rev. Cam. Apostolica.
Food and Agriculture Organization of the United Nations. (1977). *Perspective on Mycotoxins.* FAO Food and Nutrition Paper 13. Rome: Food and Agriculture Organization of the United Nations.
Foxhall, L., and H. A. Forbes. (1982). "Sitometreia: The Role of Grain as Staple Food in Classical Antiquity." *Chiron* 12: 41–90.
Frier, Bruce W. (1980). *Landlords and Tenants in Imperial Rome.* Princeton, N.J.: Princeton University Press.

———. (1978). "Cicero's Management of His Urban Properties." *Classical Journal* 74: 1–6.

———. (1977). "The Rental Market in Early Imperial Rome." *Journal of Roman Studies* 67: 27–37.

Frosini, Pietro. (1977). *Il Tevere: Le inondazioni di Roma e i provvedimenti presi dal governo Italiano per evitarle.* Accademia Nazionale dei Lincei Commissione di Studio delle Calamità Naturali e della Degradazione dell'Ambiente, vol. 13. Rome: Accademia Nazionale dei Lincei.

Fullerton, Carol, and Robert Ursano, eds. (1997). *Posttraumatic Stress Disorder: Acute and Long-Term Responses to Trauma and Disaster.* Washington, D.C.: American Psychiatric Association.

Funiciello, Renato, ed. (1995). *La geologia di Roma: Il centro storico.* 2 vols. Memorie Descrittive della Carta Geologica d'Italia, vol. 50. Rome: Istituto Poligrafico e Zecca dello Stato.

Galliazzo, Vittorio. (1995). *I Ponti Romani.* 2 vols. Treviso: Edizioni Canova.

Garnsey, Peter. (1988). *Famine and Food Supply in the Graeco-Roman World: Responses to Risk and Crisis.* New York: Cambridge University Press.

———. (1976). "Urban Property Investment." In *Studies in Roman Property,* ed. M. I. Finley, 123–36. New York: Cambridge University Press.

Gigli, Stefania Quilici, ed. (1986). *Il Tevere e le altre vie d'acqua del Lazio antico: Settimo incontro di studio del Comitato per l'Archeologia Laziale.* Quaderni del Centro di Studio per l'Archeologia Etrusco-Italico 12; Archeologia Laziale VII, 2. Rome: Consiglio Nazionale delle Ricerche.

Golaz, A. (1993). *Public Health Service Memorandum re: Missouri Floods, 1993.*

Gomez, L. (1531). *De prodigiosis Tiberis inundationibus ab Urbe condita ad annum 1531.* Rome.

Goubert, Jean-Pierre. (1986). *The Conquest of Water: The Advent of Health in the Industrial Age.* Trans. Andrew Wilson. Princeton, N.J.: Princeton University Press.

Gowers, Emily. (1995). "The Anatomy of Rome from Capitol to Cloaca." *Journal of Roman Studies* 85: 23–32.

Grandazzi, Alexandre. (1997). *The Foundation of Rome: Myth and History.* Trans. Jane Marie Todd. Ithaca, N.Y.: Cornell University Press.

Greenberg, Bernard. (1971). *Flies and Disease.* Vol. 1: *Ecology, Classification and Biotic Associations.* Princeton, N.J.: Princeton University Press.

Gregori, G. P., et al. (1988). "The Analysis of Point-like Historical Data Series." In *Past, Present and Future Trends in Geophysical Research,* ed. Wilfried Schröder, 146–211. Bremen-Roennebeck: Interdivisional Commission on History of IAGA.

Grimelli, Geminiano. (1876). *Sistemazione del Tevere secondo i principii e le norme di Giulio Cesare e di Giuseppe Garibaldi.* Rome: Società tipografica, antica tipografia Soliani.

Gros, Pierre. (1976). *Aurea Templa: Recherches sur l'architecture religieuse de Rome à l'époque d'Auguste.* Rome: École française de Rome.

Gruntfest, Eve. (2000). "Nonstructural Mitigation of Flood Hazards." In *Inland Flood Hazards: Human, Riparian, and Aquatic Communities,* ed. Ellen Wohl, 394–410. New York: Cambridge University Press.

———. (1994). "Flood Disaster Relief, Rehabilitation and Reconstruction." In *Coping with Floods,* ed. Giuseppe Rossi, Nilgun Harmancioglu, and Vujica Yevjevich, 723–31. Boston: Kluwer Academic Publishers.

Guilizzoni, P., and F. Oldfield, eds. (1996). *Palaeoenvironmental Analysis of Italian Crater Lake and Adriatic Sediments (PALICLAS).* Special issue of Memorie dell'Istituto Italiano di Idrobiologia, *International Journal of Limnology,* vol. 55. Verbania Pallanza: Istituto Italiano di Idrobiologia.

Haas, J. Eugene, et al. (1977). *Reconstruction Following Disaster.* Cambridge, Mass.: MIT Press.

Hall, M. J. (1984). *Urban Hydrology.* London: Elsevier Applied Science Publishers.

Hamilton, Douglas, and Alejandro Joaquin. (2000). "Urban Planning for Flood Hazards, Risk, and Vulnerability." In *Inland Flood Hazards: Human, Riparian, and Aquatic Communities,* ed. Ellen Wohl, 469–88. New York: Cambridge University Press.

Haselberger, Lothar, and John Humphrey, eds. (2006). *Imaging Ancient Rome: Documentation—Visualization—Imagination. Journal of Roman Archaeology* Supplementary Series no. 61. Portsmouth, Rhode Island.

Haselberger, Lothar, et al., eds. (2002). *Mapping Augustan Rome. Journal of Roman Archaeology* Supplementary Series no. 50. Portsmouth, Rhode Island.

Hermansen, G. (1982). *Ostia: Aspects of Roman City Life.* Edmonton: University of Alberta Press.

———. (1978). "The Population of Imperial Rome: The Regionaries." *Historia* 27, no. 1: 129–68.

Hewlett, John, and Wade Nutter. (1969). *An Outline of Forest Hydrology.* Athens: University of Georgia Press.

Hirschboeck, Katherine. (1988). "Flood Hydroclimatology." In *Flood Geomorphology,* ed. Victor Baker, R. Craig Kochel, and Peter Patton, 27–49. New York: John Wiley & Sons.

Hirschboeck, Katherine, L. L. Ely, and R. A. Maddox. (2000). "Hydroclimatology of Meteorologic Floods." In *Inland Flood Hazards: Human, Riparian, and Aquatic Communities,* ed. Ellen Wohl, 39–72. New York: Cambridge University Press.

Holland, Louise Adams. (1961). *Janus and the Bridge.* Papers and Monographs of the American Academy in Rome, vol. 21. Rome: American Academy in Rome.

Hope, Valerie. (2000a). "The City of Rome: Capital and Symbol." In *Experiencing Rome: Culture, Identity and Power in the Roman Empire,* ed. J. Huskinson, 63–93. New York: Routledge.

———. (2000b). "Contempt and Respect: The Treatment of the Corpse in Ancient Rome." In *Death and Disease in the Ancient City,* ed. Valerie Hope and Eireann Marshall, 104–27. New York: Routledge.

Hope, Valerie, and Eireann Marshall, eds. (2000). *Death and Disease in the Ancient City.* New York: Routledge.

Hopkins, Keith. (1980). "Taxes and Trade in the Roman Empire (200 B.C.–A.D. 400)." *Journal of Roman Studies* 70: 101–25.

———. (1978). *Conquerors and Slaves.* Cambridge: Cambridge University Press.

Horden, Peregrine, and Nicholas Purcell. (2000). *The Corrupting Sea: A Study of Mediterranean History.* Oxford: Blackwell Publishers.

Hornberger, George, Jeffrey Raffensperger, Patricia Wiberg, and Keith Eshleman. (1998). *Elements of Physical Hydrology.* Baltimore: Johns Hopkins University Press.

Hovanitz, Christine. (1993). "Physical Health Risks Associated with Aftermath of Disaster: Basic Paths of Influence and Their Implications for Preventative Intervention." In *Handbook of Post-Disaster Interventions,* ed. R. Allen, 213–54. A special issue of the *Journal of Social Behavior and Personality* 8, no. 5. San Raphael, Calif.

Hoyt, William, and Walter Langbein. (1955). *Floods.* Princeton, N.J.: Princeton University Press.

Hughes, J. Donald, and J. V. Thirgood. (1982). "Deforestation in Ancient Greece and Rome: A Cause of Collapse." *Ecologist* 12, no. 5: 196–208.

Humphrey, John. (1986). *Roman Circuses: Arenas for Chariot Racing.* Berkeley: University of California Press.

Huntington, E. (1917). "Climatic Changes and Agricultural Decline as Factors in the Fall of Rome." *Quarterly Journal of Economics* 31: 173–208.

Issar, Arie, and Neville Brown, eds. (1998). *Water, Environment and Society in Times of Climatic Change.* Dordrecht: Kluwer Academic Publishers.

Jasny, Naum. (1944). *The Wheats of Classical Antiquity.* Johns Hopkins University Studies in Historical and Political Science, series 62, no. 3. Baltimore: Johns Hopkins University Press.

Johnson, Sidney. (1965). *Deterioration, Maintenance, and Repair of Structures.* New York: McGraw-Hill.

Jones, A. H. M. (1986). *The Later Roman Empire, 284–602: A Social, Economic, and Administrative Survey.* 2 vols. Baltimore: Johns Hopkins University Press. Originally published by Basil Blackwell (Oxford, 1964).

Jones, W. H. S. (1907). *Malaria: A Neglected Factor in the History of Greece and Rome.* Cambridge: Cambridge University Press.

Jordan, H. (1907). *Topographie der Stadt Rom im Altertum.* Rome: L'Erma di Bretschneider. Reprint, 1970.

Kandell, Jonathan. (1988). *La Capital: The Biography of Mexico City.* New York: Henry Holt.

Kleiner, Fred. (1991). "The Trophy on the Bridge and the Roman Triumph over Nature." *L'Antiquité Classique* 60: 182–94.

Kyle, Donald G. (1998). *Spectacles of Death in Ancient Rome*. New York: Routledge.
Lagunes, Maria Margarita Segarra. (2004). *Il Tevere e Roma: Storia di una simbiosi*. Rome: Gangemi Editore.
Lamb, H. H. (1995). *Climate, History and the Modern World*. 2nd ed. New York: Routledge.
———. (1977). *Climate: Present, Past and Future*. Vol. 2: *Climatic History and the Future*. London: Methuen.
Lambardi, Carlo. (1601). *Discorso di Carlo Lambardi architetto civile, et militare, sopra la causa dell'innondatione di Roma dell'opinioni del volgo, con cinque rimedii che concorrono per assicurar Roma dall'innondationi*. Rome: Appresso Stefano Paolini.
Lanciani, Pietro. (1829). *Sulla necessità di rimuovere l'impedimento al corso del Tevere formato dallo scarico delle immondezze*. Rome: Dalla Tipografia di Crispino Puccinelli.
Lanciani, Rodolfo. (1897). *The Ruins and Excavations of Ancient Rome*. Reprint, New York: Bell Publishing Company, 1979.
———. (1890). "La Cloaca Massima." *Bullettino della Commissione Archeologica Comunale di Roma*: 95–102.
Larson, David, ed. (1990). *Mayo Clinic Family Health Book*. New York: William Morrow.
Laube, Jerri, and Shirley Murphy. (1985). *Perspectives on Disaster Recovery*. East Norwalk, Conn.: Appleton-Century-Crofts.
Laurence, Ray. (1994). *Roman Pompeii: Space and Society*. New York: Routledge.
———. (1993). "Emperors, Nature and the City: Rome's Ritual Landscape." *Accordia Research Papers* 4: 133–51.
Lazaro, Timothy. (1979). *Urban Hydrology: A Multidisciplinary Perspective*. Ann Arbor, Mich.: Ann Arbor Science Publishers.
Le Gall, Joël. (1953a). *Le Tibre: Fleuve de Rome dans l'antiquité*. Paris: Presses Universitaires de France.
———. (1953b). *Recherches sur le culte du Tibre*. Paris: Presses Universitaires de France.
Legome, Eric, Amy Robins, and Douglas Rund. (1995). "Injuries Associated with Floods: The Need for an International Reporting Scheme." *Disasters* 19, no. 1: 50–54.
Leon, Harry. (1960). *The Jews of Ancient Rome*. Philadelphia: Jewish Publication Society of America.
Leopold, Luna. (1971). "The Hydrologic Effects of Urban Land Use." In *Man's Impact on Environment*, ed. Thomas Detwyler, 205–16. New York: McGraw-Hill.
Leyton, L. (1972). "Forests, Flooding and Soil Moisture." In *Piene: Loro previsione e difesa del suolo (Rome, 23–30 Nov. 1969)*, 327–39. Accademia Nazionale dei Lincei, vol. 169. Rome.
Lindsay, Hugh. (2000). "Death-Pollution and Funerals in the City of Rome."

In *Death and Disease in the Ancient City*, ed. Valerie Hope and Eireann Marshall, 152–73. New York: Routledge.

Liu, Y. (1987). "The Influence of Variation in Forest Cover on Design Floods." In *Analysis of Extraordinary Flood Events*, ed. W. H. Kirby et al., 367–74. Special issue of *Journal of Hydrology*, vol. 96. Amsterdam: Elsevier.

Lott, J. Bert. (2004). *The Neighborhoods of Augustan Rome*. Cambridge: Cambridge University Press.

Lowe, J. J., et al. (1996). "Pollen Stratigraphy of Sediment Sequences from Lakes Albano and Nemi (near Rome) and from the Central Adriatic, Spanning the Interval from Oxygen Isotope Stage 2 to Present Day." In *Palaeoenvironmental Analysis of Italian Crater Lake and Adriatic Sediments (PALICLAS)*, ed. P. Guilizzoni and F. Oldfield, 71–98. Special issue of Memorie dell'Istituto Italiano di Idrobiologia, *International Journal of Limnology*, vol. 55. Verbania Pallanza: Istituto Italiano di Idrobiologia.

Lugli, G., ed. (1953). *Fontes ad Topographiam: Veteris Urbis Romae Pertinentes*, vol. 2, bks. 5–7. Rome: Università di Roma Istituto di Topografia Antica.

Luketina, Francis. (1986). "The Psychological Effects of Floods." *Soil and Water*, no. 1: 21–24.

Lyngby, H., M. Polia, and G. P. Sartorio. (1978). "Richerche sulla porta flumentana." *Opuscula Romana* 8: 33–52.

Marchetti, D. (1892). "Frammento di un antico pilastro per misurare le acque del Tevere." *Bullettino della Commissione Archeologica Comunale di Roma* 20: 139–49 and pl. VI.

Marco, Juan. (1994). "Flood Risk Mapping." In *Coping with Floods*, ed. Giuseppe Rossi et al., 353–73. Boston: Kluwer Academic Publishers.

Marco, Juan, and Angel Cayuela. (1994). "Urban Flooding: The Flood-Planned City Concept." In *Coping with Floods*, ed. Giuseppe Rossi et al., 705–21. Boston: Kluwer Academic Publishers.

Margaropoulos, P. (1972). "Forests, Flood-Flow and Sedimentation: Need for Reevaluation of Their Relationships." In *Piene: Loro previsione e difesa del suolo (Rome, 23–30 Nov. 1969)*, 341–63. Accademia Nazionale dei Lincei, vol. 169. Rome.

Martinis, Bruno. (1987). *Le calamità naturali in Italia: Origine, prevenzione, rimedi*. Milan: Mursia Editore.

Marwick, C. (1997). "Floods Carry Potential for Toxic Mold Disease." *Journal of the American Medical Association* 277, no. 17: 1342.

Matossian, Mary Kilbourne. (1989). *Poisons of the Past: Molds, Epidemics, and History*. New Haven: Yale University Press.

Mattingly, D. J. (1996). "First Fruit? The Olive in the Roman World." In *Human Landscapes in Classical Antiquity*, ed. G. Shipley and J. Salmon, 213–53. Leicester-Nottingham Studies in Ancient Society, vol. 6. London: Routledge.

Mattingly, P. F. (1969). *The Biology of Mosquito-Borne Disease*. London: George Allen and Unwin.

Mau, August. (1899). *Pompeii: Its Life and Art.* Trans. Francis Kelsey. New York: Macmillan.
May, J. M. (1961). "The Ecology of Malaria." In *Studies in Disease Ecology.* New York: Hafner Press.
Mazzarino, Santo. (1966). "Le alluvioni 54 a.C./23 a.C., il cognome *Augustus,* e la data di Hor. *Carm.* I.2." *Helikon* 6: 621–24.
McCarroll, James, Carol Fullerton, and Robert Ursano. (1997). "Exposure to Traumatic Death in Disaster and War." In *Posttraumatic Stress Disorder: Acute and Long-Term Responses to Trauma and Disaster,* ed. Carol Fullerton and Robert Ursano, 37–58. Washington, D.C.: American Psychiatric Association.
Meiggs, Russell. (1982). *Trees and Timber in the Ancient Mediterranean World.* New York: Oxford University Press.
———. (1973). *Roman Ostia.* 2nd ed. New York: Oxford University Press.
Meneghini, Roberto. (1985). "Attività e installazioni portuali lungo il Tevere. La riva dell'*Emporium.*" In *Misurare la Terra: Centuriazione e coloni nel mondo romano. Città, agricoltura, commercio: Materiali da Roma e dal suburbio,* ed. R. Bussi and V. Vandelli, 162–272. Modena: Edizioni Panini.
Meronuck, Richard. (2002). "A Study of Damaged Wheat and Barley in a Flooded Bin." www.extension.umn.edu/distribution/cropsystems/DC6959.html.
Merritt, Frederick, ed. (1968). *Standard Handbook for Civil Engineers.* New York: McGraw-Hill.
———, ed. (1958). *Building Construction Handbook.* New York: McGraw-Hill.
Meyer, Cornelis. (1685). *L'arte di restituire a Roma la tralasciata navigazione del suo Tevere.* Rome: Nella Stamperia del Lazzari Varese.
Miller, E. Willard, and Ruby Miller. (2000). *Natural Disasters: Floods; A Reference Handbook.* Contemporary World Issues series. Santa Barbara, Calif.: ABC-CLIO.
Mitchell, James K., ed. (1999). *Crucibles of Hazard: Mega-Cities and Disasters in Transition.* New York: United Nations University Press.
Mocchegiani Carpano, C., ed. (2002). *Il Tevere.* Tredicesimo Itinerario, ROMArcheologica Guida Alle Antichità della Città Eterna. Rome: Elio de Rosa editore.
———. (1986). "Le inondazioni del Tevere nell'antichita." In *Tevere: Un'antica via per il mediterraneo,* 147–48. Exhibition catalogue for exhibit held at S. Michele a Ripa, Rome, Apr. 21–June 29, 1986. Rome: Istituto poligrafico e zecca dello Stato.
———. (1984a). "Il Tevere: Archeologia e commercio." *Bolletino di Numismatica* 2–3: 21–81.
———. (1984b). "Le cloache dell'antica Roma." In *Roma Sotterranea,* ed. Roberto Luciani, 164–78. Rome: Fratelli Palombi Editori.
———. (1982). "Tevere. Premesse per una archeologia fluviale." *Bollettino d'Arte,* suppl. 4: 150–65.

———. (1981). "Indagini archeologiche nel Tevere." *Quaderni del Centro di Studio per l'archeologia etrusco-italica* 5: 142–55.

Mocchegiani Carpano, C., and R. Meneghini. (1985). "Lungotevere Testaccio." *Bullettino della Commissione archeologica comunale di Roma* 90: 86–95.

Mocchegiani Carpano, C., R. Meneghini, and M. Incitti. (1985–86). "Lungotevere Testaccio." *Bullettino della Commissione archeologica comunale di Roma* 91: 560–95.

Modio, G. B. (1556). *Il Teuere*. Rome: Apresso a Vincenzo Luchini.

Momigliano, A. (1989). "The Origins of Rome." In *The Cambridge Ancient History*, vol. 7, part 2: *The Rise of Rome to 220 B.C.*, ed. F. W. Walbank, A. E. Astin, M. W. Frederiksen, and R. M. Ogilvie, 52–112. Cambridge: Cambridge University Press.

Montz, B. E. (2000). "The Generation of Flood Hazards and Disasters by Urban Development of Floodplains." In *Floods*, ed. D. J. Parker, 1:116–27. New York: Routledge.

Mora, D. (1600). *Sopra la inondatione del Tevere in Roma*. Rome.

Morley, N. (1996). *Metropolis and Hinterland: The City of Rome and the Italian Economy, 200 BC–AD 200*. New York: Cambridge University Press.

Narducci, Pietro. (1889). *Sulla fognatura della città di Roma*. Rome: Forzani E. C. Tipografi del Senato.

Nencini, Franco. (1966). *Florence: The Days of the Flood*. New York: Stein and Day.

Newbold, R. F. (1982). "The Reporting of Earthquakes, Fires and Floods by Ancient Historians." *Proceedings of the African Classical Association*, no. 16: 28–36.

———. (1974). "Some Social and Economic Consequences of the A.D. 64 Fire at Rome." *Latomus* 33: 858–69.

Nordh, A. (1936). *Prolegomena till den romerska regionskatalogen*. Goteborg: Elanders boktryokeri aktiebolag.

Oates, W. J. (1934). "The Population of Rome." *Classical Philology* 29: 101–16.

Ogden, Cynthia, et al. (2001). "Emergency Health Surveillance after Severe Flooding in Louisiana, 1995." *Prehospital and Disaster Medicine* 16, no. 3: 138–44.

Oldfield, F. (1996). "The PALICLAS Project: Synthesis and Overview." In *Palaeoenvironmental Analysis of Italian Crater Lake and Adriatic Sediments (PALICLAS)*, ed. P. Guilizzoni and F. Oldfield, 329–57. Special issue of Memorie dell'Istituto Italiano di Idrobiologia, *International Journal of Limnology*, vol. 55. Verbania Pallanza: Istituto Italiano di Idrobiologia.

Olshausen, Eckart, and Holger Sonnabend, eds. (1998). *Naturkatastrophen in der Antiken Welt*. Stuttgarter Kolloquium zur Historischen Geographie des Altertums 6, 1996. Stuttgart: Franz Steiner Verlag.

Packer, James. (1971). *The Insulae of Imperial Ostia*. Memoirs of the American Academy in Rome 31. Rome: American Academy in Rome.

Pallottino, M. (1993). *Origini e storia primitiva di Roma*. Milan: Rusconi.

Pascoli, L. (1740). *Il Tevere navigato e navigabile: In cui si prova con autorità evidenti e non sospette che ne' tempi passati sin da sua scaturigine si navigava.* Rome: Antonio de' Rossi.

Patterson, H., and M. Millett. (1998). "The Tiber Valley Project." *Papers of the British School at Rome* 66: 1–20.

Patterson, John R. (2000). "On the Margins of the City of Rome." In *Death and Disease in the Ancient City,* ed. Valerie Hope and Eireann Marshall, 85–103. New York: Routledge.

———. (1992). "The City of Rome: From Republic to Empire." *Journal of Roman Studies* 82: 186–215.

Pavia, Carlo. (2000). *Guida di Roma sotteranea.* Rome: Gangemi Editore.

Pavolini, Carlo. (2000). "Il fiume e i porti." In *Roma Antica,* ed. Andrea Giardina, 163–81. Rome: Laterza.

Penning-Rowsell, Edmund, and Sue Tapsell. (2002). "Coping with Extreme Floods: Warnings, Impacts and Response." In *The Extremes of the Extremes: Extraordinary Floods,* ed. Árni Snorrason, Helga Finnsdóttir, and Marshall Moss, 379–83. IAHS Publication no. 271. Wallingford, Oxfordshire: International Association of Hydrological Sciences.

Phillips, E. J. (1973). "The Roman Law on the Demolition of Buildings." *Latomus* 32: 86–95.

Pickels, George. (1941). *Drainage and Flood-Control Engineering.* 2nd ed. New York: McGraw-Hill.

Pinadoro, T. (1608). *Designo e discorso per li rimedii dell'inondatione del Tevere et allagamenti di Roma.* Rome.

Platner, S. B., and T. Ashby. (1929). *A Topographical Dictionary of Rome.* London: Oxford University Press.

Possenti, Carlo. (1871). *Relazioni al sig. ministro dei lavori pubblici della Commissione nominata con R. Decreto 1 gennaio 1871 per studiare e proporre i mezzi di rendere le piene del tevere innocue alla città di Roma.* Rome: Tipografia Cenniniana.

Powell, Barbara, and Elizabeth Penick. (1983). "Psychological Distress Following a Natural Disaster: A One-Year Follow-Up of 98 Flood Victims." *Journal of Community Psychology* 11, no. 3: 269–76.

Purcell, Nicholas. (1999). "The Populace of Rome in Late Antiquity: Problems of Classification and Historical Description." In *The Transformations of Urbs Roma in Late Antiquity,* ed. W. V. Harris, 135–62. *Journal of Roman Archaeology* Supplementary Series no. 33. Portsmouth, Rhode Island.

———. (1996). "Rome and the Management of Water: Environment, Culture and Power." In *Human Landscapes in Classical Antiquity,* ed. G. Shipley and J. Salmon, 180–212. New York: Routledge.

———. (1994). "The City of Rome and the *Plebs Urbana* in the Late Republic." In *The Cambridge Ancient History,* vol. 9: *The Last Age of the Roman Republic,* 2nd ed., ed. J. Crook, A. Lintott, and E. Rawson, 644–88. New York: Cambridge University Press.

Raggi, F. (1662). *Il Tevere incatenato ovvero l'arte di frenare le acque correnti.* Rome.

Rainer, J. M. (1987). "Zum SC Hosidianum." *Tijdschrift voor Rechtsgeschiedenis* 55: 31–38.

Ramage, Edwin. (1983). "Urban Problems in Ancient Rome." In *Aspects of Graeco-Roman Urbanism: Essays on the Classical City,* ed. Ronald Marchese, 61–92. BAR International Series 188. Oxford.

Ramírez, Jorge A. (2000). "Prediction and Modeling of Flood Hydrology and Hydraulics." In *Inland Flood Hazards: Human, Riparian, and Aquatic Communities,* ed. Ellen Wohl, 293–333. New York: Cambridge University Press.

Raphael, Beverley. (1986). *When Disaster Strikes: How Individuals and Communities Cope with Catastrophe.* New York: Basic Books.

Rasi, G. B. (1827). *Sul Tevere e sua navigazione da Fiumicino a Roma.* Rome: Nella Tipografia Perego-Salvioni.

Rasid, H. (1993). "Preventing Flooding or Regulating Flood Levels? Case Studies on Perception of Flood Alleviation in Bangladesh." *Natural Hazards* 8, no. 1: 39–57.

Raventós, Xavier Dupré, and Josep-Anton Remolà, eds. (2000). *Sordes Urbis: La eliminación de residuos en la ciudad Romana.* Monografías de la Escuela Española de Historia y Arqueología en Romano 24. Rome: L'Erma di Bretschneider.

Reid, Donald. (1991). *Paris Sewers and Sewermen: Realities and Representations.* Cambridge, Mass.: Harvard University Press.

Reimers, Pontus. (1991). "Roman Sewers and Sewerage Networks—Neglected Areas of Study." In *Munuscula Romana: Papers Read at a Conference in Lund (Oct. 1–2, 1988) in Celebration of the Re-opening of the Swedish Institute in Rome,* ed. Anne-Marie Leander Touati, Eva Rystedt, and Örjan Wikander, 111–16. Stockholm: Swedish Institute in Rome.

———. (1989). "Opus Omnium Dictu Maximum: Literary Sources for the Knowledge of Roman City Drainage." *Opuscula Romana* 17, no. 10: 137–41.

Rendina, Claudio. (2003). *Guida Insolita ai misteri, ai segreti, alle leggende e alle curiosità del Tevere il fiume di Roma.* Rome: Newton & Compton Editori.

Reynolds, David West. (1996). "Forma Urbis Romae: The Severan Marble Plan and the Urban Form of Ancient Rome." Ph.D. diss., University of Michigan.

Richardson, L. (1992). *A New Topographical Dictionary of Ancient Rome.* Baltimore: Johns Hopkins University Press.

Rickman, Geoffrey. (1980). *The Corn Supply of Ancient Rome.* Oxford: Clarendon Press.

———. (1971). *Roman Granaries and Store Buildings.* Cambridge: Cambridge University Press.

Robinson, O. F. (1992). *Ancient Rome: City Planning and Administration.* New York: Routledge.

Rodríguez-Almeida, E. (1984). *Il Monte Testaccio: Ambiente, storia, materiali.* Rome: Edizioni Quasar.

———. (1981). *Forma Urbis Marmorea.* 2 vols. Rome: Edizioni Quasar.

———. (1979–80). "Il Campo Marzio settentrionale: *Solarium* e *Pomerium.*" *Atti della Pontificia Accademia Romana di Archeologia, Rendiconti:* 51–52.

Romanelli, P. (1933). "II.-Roma. Reg. IX—Via della Torretta.—Cippi del pomerio." *Notizie degli Scavi di Antichità:* 240–44.

Rossi, Giuseppe, Nilgun Harmancioglu, and Vujica Yevjevich, eds. (1994). *Coping with Floods.* Boston: Kluwer Academic Publishers.

Rozman, G. (1973). *Urban Networks in Chi'ing China and Tokugawa Japan.* Princeton, N.J.: Princeton University Press.

Rubin, L. (2003). "De Incendiis Urbis Romae: The Fires of Rome as an Urban Transformative Process." Ph.D. diss., SUNY-Buffalo.

Rullier, I. (1873). *La deviazione del Tevere.* Rome.

Russac, P. A. (1986). "Epidemiological Surveillance: Malaria Epidemic Following the Niño Phenomenon." *Disasters* 10: 112–17.

Rykwert, Joseph. (1976). *The Idea of a Town: The Anthropology of Urban Form in Rome, Italy and the Ancient World.* Cambridge, Mass.: MIT Press.

Sallares, Robert. (2002). *Malaria and Rome: A History of Malaria in Ancient Italy.* New York: Oxford University Press.

Saul, A. J., ed. (1992). *Floods and Flood Management.* Boston: Kluwer Academic Publishers.

Savage, S. M. (1940). "The Cults of Ancient Trastevere." *Memoirs of the American Academy in Rome* 17: 26–56 and pls. 1–4.

Scataglini, Marco. (2004). *Il viaggio del Tevere.* Rome: Edizioni Iter.

Scheidel, W. (1994). "Libitina's Bitter Gains: Seasonal Mortality and Endemic Disease in the Ancient City of Rome." *Ancient Society* 25: 151–75.

Schmidt, W., et al. (1993). "Morbidity Surveillance Following the Midwest Flood—Missouri, 1993." *Morbidity and Mortality Weekly* 42, no. 41: 797–98.

Schnitter, N. (1983). "Barrages Romains." In *Journées d'Études sur les Aqueducs Romains/Tagung über Römische Wasserversorgungsanlagen, Lyon (26–28 mai 1977),* ed. J.-P. Boucher, 333–47. Paris: Société d'Edition "Les Belles Lettres."

Schumm, Stanley, ed. (1972). *River Morphology.* Benchmark Papers in Geology Series. Stroudsburg, Pa.: Dowden, Hutchinson & Ross.

Scobie, Alex. (1986). "Slums, Sanitation, and Mortality in the Roman World." *Klio* 68: 399–433.

Scott, P. M., H. L. Trenholm, and M. D. Sutton, eds. (1985). *Mycotoxins: A Canadian Perspective.* Ottawa: National Research Council of Canada.

Sear, Frank. (1982). *Roman Architecture.* Ithaca, N.Y.: Cornell University Press.

Shaw, Brent. (1996). "Seasons of Death: Aspects of Mortality in Imperial Rome." *Journal of Roman Studies* 86: 100–138.

———. (1981). "Climate, Environment, and History: The Case of Roman North Africa." In *Climate and History: Studies in Past Climates and Their Impact on Man*, ed. T. M. L. Wigley, M. J. Ingram, and G. Farmer, 379–403. Cambridge: Cambridge University Press.

Siddique, A. K., A. H. Baqui, A. Eusof, and K. Zaman. (1991). "1988 Floods in Bangladesh: Pattern of Illness and Causes of Death." *Journal of Diarrhoeal Diseases Research* 9, no. 4: 310–14.

Sikander, A. S. (1983). "Floods and Families in Pakistan—A Survey." *Disasters* 7, no. 2: 101–6.

Silenzi, Maurizio. (1998). *Il porto di Roma: Storia e ricostruzione urbanistica del progetto architettonico, sociale e politico dell'imperatore Claudio per la realizzazione del Portus Romae*. Rome: Newton and Compton editori.

Sirks, Boudewijn. (1991). *Food for Rome: The Legal Structure of the Transportation and Processing of Supplies for the Imperial Distributions in Rome and Constantinople*. Amsterdam: J. C. Gieben.

Smith, Christopher John. (1996). *Early Rome and Latium: Economy and Society, c. 1000 to 500 BC*. Oxford: Oxford University Press.

Smith, John E., and Maurice Moss. (1985). *Mycotoxins: Formation, Analysis and Significance*. New York: John Wiley & Sons.

Smith, Keith, and Roy Ward. (1998). *Floods: Physical Processes and Human Impacts*. New York: John Wiley & Sons.

Smith, Norman. (1970). "The Roman Dams of Subiaco." *Technology and Culture* 11, no. 1: 58–68.

Smith, Strother Ancrum. (1877). *The Tiber and Its Tributaries: Their Natural History and Classical Associations*. London: Longmans, Green.

Solomon, S. I., M. Beran, and W. Hogg, eds. (1987). *The Influence of Climate Change and Climatic Variability on the Hydrologic Regime and Water Resources*. IAHS Publication no. 168. Wallingford, Oxfordshire: International Association of Hydrological Sciences.

Sordi, Marta, ed. (1989). *Fenomeni naturali e avvenimenti storici nell'antichità*. Milan: Università Cattolica del Sacro Cuore.

Stambaugh, J. E. (1988). *The Ancient Roman City*. Baltimore: Johns Hopkins University Press.

Starkel, L., K. J. Gregory, and J. B. Thornes, eds. (1991). *Temperate Palaeohydrology: Fluvial Processes in the Temperate Zone during the last 15,000 years*. New York: John Wiley & Sons.

Stedinger, Jery. (2000). "Flood Frequency Analysis and Statistical Estimation of Flood Risk." In *Inland Flood Hazards: Human, Riparian, and Aquatic Communities*, ed. Ellen Wohl, 334–58. New York: Cambridge University Press.

Steinby, E. M., ed. (1993–2000). *Lexicon Topographicum Urbis Romae*. Vols. 1–6. Rome: Edizioni Quasar.

Susmel, L. (1972). "Vegetazione forestale e caratteri idrofisici del suolo." In

Piene: Loro previsione e difesa del suolo (Rome, 23–30 Nov. 1969), 311–26. Accademia Nazionale dei Lincei, vol. 169. Rome.

Syme, Ronald. (1958). *Tacitus.* 2 vols. Oxford: Clarendon Press.

Tapsell, S. M., and S. M. Tunstall. (2000). "The Health Effects of Floods: The Easter 1998 Floods in England." In *Floods,* ed. D. J. Parker, 1:172–87. New York: Routledge.

Tartakow, I. J., and J. H. Vorperian. (1981). *Foodborne and Waterborne Diseases: Their Epidemiologic Characteristics.* Westport, Conn.: Avi Publishing Company.

Taylor, Rabun. (2000). *Public Needs and Private Pleasures: Water Distribution, the Tiber River, and the Urban Development of Ancient Rome.* Rome: L'Erma di Bretschneider.

Tchernia, A. (1986). *Le vin de l'Italie romaine.* Rome: École française de Rome.

Telleria, A. V. (1986). "Health Consequences of the Floods in Bolivia in 1982." *Disasters* 10: 88–106.

Tevere: Un'antica via per il mediterraneo. (1986). Exhibition catalogue for exhibit held at S. Michele a Ripa, Rome, Apr. 21–June 29, 1986. Rome: Istituto poligrafico e zecca dello Stato.

Thomas, Robert G. (1989). "Geology of Rome, Italy." *Bulletin of the Association of Engineering Geologists* 26, no. 4: 415–76.

Tierney, Lawrence, Stephen McPhee, and Maxine Papadakis, eds. (2003). *Current Medical Diagnosis and Treatment.* New York: Lange Medical Books–McGraw-Hill.

Tobin, Graham, and Jane Ollenburger. (1996). "Predicting Levels of Postdisaster Stress in Adults Following the 1993 Floods in the Upper Midwest." *Environment and Behavior* 28, no. 3: 340–57.

Tomei, G. B. (1871). *Piene del fiume Tevere; riposta dell'ingegnere.* Rome: Presso l'Accademia.

Toynbee, J. M. C. (1973). *Animals in Roman Life and Art.* Baltimore: Johns Hopkins University Press.

———. (1971). *Death and Burial in the Roman World.* Baltimore: Johns Hopkins University Press.

Trenholm, H. L., et al. (1988). *Reducing Mycotoxins in Animal Feeds.* Agriculture Canada Publication 1827E. Ottawa: Communications Branch, Agriculture Canada.

United Nations. (1990). *Urban Flood Loss Prevention and Mitigation.* U.N. Water Resources Series no. 68. New York: United Nations.

Uraguchi, Kenji, and Mikio Yamazaki, eds. (1978). *Toxicology, Biochemistry and Pathology of Mycotoxins.* New York: John Wiley & Sons.

Valensise, M. R., and M. Colacino. (1988). "The Impact of Climate and Environment on History: Implications, Methodologies, Sources." In *Past, Present and Future Trends in Geophysical Research,* ed. Wilfried Schröder, 126–45. Bremen-Roennebeck: Interdivisional Commission on History of IAGA.

Vandenberghe, J., and D. Maddy, eds. (2001). "The Response of River Systems to Climate Change." *Quaternary International* 79: 1–3.

Ventriglia, U. (1971). *La geologia della città di Roma*. Rome: Amministrazione Provinciale di Roma.

Verduchi, Patrizia. (1998). "L'insediamento storico Ostiense." In *Il Delta del Tevere: Un viaggio fra passato e futuro*, ed. Carlo Bagnasco, 66–78. Rome: Fratelli Palombi Editori.

Vescovali, Angelo. (1880). *Le inondazioni sotterranea di Roma e la sistemazione del Tevere*. Rome: Forzani.

Von Gerkan, A. (1949). "Grenzen und Grössen der vierzehn Regionen Roms." *Bonner Jahrbücher* 149: 5–65.

Ward, Roy. (1978). *Floods: A Geographical Perspective*. New York: John Wiley & Sons.

Watson, Chester, and David Biedenharn. (2000). "Comparison of Flood Management Strategies." In *Inland Flood Hazards: Human, Riparian, and Aquatic Communities*, ed. Ellen Wohl, 381–93. New York: Cambridge University Press.

White, Graham. (1999). "Grain Storage." Farming Systems Institute, Department of Agriculture of Western Australia, file no.: FS99302, www.agric.wa.gov.au/ento/publications/fs99302.html.

White, K. D. (1970). *Roman Farming*. Ithaca, N.Y.: Cornell University Press.

Wigley, T. M. L., M. J. Ingram, and G. Farmer, eds. (1981). *Climate and History: Studies in Past Climates and Their Impact on Man*. Cambridge: Cambridge University Press.

Wijkman, A., and L. Timberlake. (1984). *Natural Disasters: Acts of God or Acts of Man?* London: Earthscan.

Wilke, Bill. (2002). "Managing Flooded Grain Bins." University of Minnesota Extension, www.extension.umn.edu/administrative/ disasterresponse/components/wi_flood02_grainbins.html.

Witherstine, Ruth. (1926). "Where the Romans Lived in the First Century B.C." *Classical Journal* 21: 566–79.

Wohl, Ellen, ed. (2000a). *Inland Flood Hazards: Human, Riparian, and Aquatic Communities*. New York: Cambridge University Press.

———. (2000b). "Inland Flood Hazards." In *Inland Flood Hazards: Human, Riparian, and Aquatic Communities*, ed. Ellen Wohl, 3–36. New York: Cambridge University Press.

———. (2000c). "Floods in the 21st Century." In *Inland Flood Hazards: Human, Riparian, and Aquatic Communities*, ed. Ellen Wohl, 491–94. New York: Cambridge University Press.

World Health Organization. (1979). *Mycotoxins*. Environmental Health Criteria 11. Geneva: World Health Organization.

Zoleta-Nantes, Doracie B. (2003). "Differential Impacts of Flood Hazards among the Street Children, the Urban Poor, and Residents of the Wealthy

Neighborhoods in Metro Manila, Philippines." *Mitigation and Adaptation Strategies for Global Change* 7: 239–66.

———. (2000). "Flood Hazard Vulnerabilities and Coping Strategies of Residents of Urban Poor Settlements in Metro Manila, The Philippines." In *Floods,* ed. D. J. Parker, 1:69–88. New York: Routledge.

Zucchelli, Giacomo. (1879). *Relazione che accompagna il progetto di una nuova inalveazione del Tevere attraverso i prati di Castello . . . : allo scopo di preservare la città di Roma dai danni delle allagazioni di detto fiume.* Rome: Tipografia del Senato.

Index

Actium, 22
aedile, urban, 163, 198
Aemilius Lepidus, Marcus, 194
Aemilius Paullus, Lucius, 194
Aeneas, 10, 261n6
Agrippa, Marcus Vipsanius, 165, 178; and sewer renovations, 170, 172
Alba Longa, 10, 11
Amazon River, 60
Amulius (king), 10, 11
Ancus Marcius, 115
animals, 20, 30, 82, 142; carcasses of, 128, 189–90; dangerous, 127; hunts of, 25, 96; of Mars, 10–11. *See also specific animals*
Anio (Aniene) River, 29, 54, 58; dams of, 188–89; diversion of, 249
Antoninus Pius (emperor), 30
apartments/apartment buildings. *See insulae*
Apennines, 54, 153
Aqua Anio Novus, 189, 227
Aqua Claudia, 153, 227
Aqua Marcia, 227
aqueducts, 4, 81, 151–53, 172, 208; administrative oversight of, 163; cost of, 227, 296–97n22; development of over time, 210–11; resistance of to floods, 236; volume of water supplied by, 174–75. *See also individual aqueducts (under "Aqua")*
Ara Pacis, 180
Arch of Septimius Severus, 36
Arno (Arnus) River, 126, 131, 185–87
Arruntius, Lucius, 26, 185–87, 199, 224
Asinius Gallus, Gaius, 198, 224
Augustus (emperor), 25, 43, 50, 67, 148, 227; curator of Tiber appointed by, 199; dredges Tiber, 125, 189, 190, 191; famine alleviated by, 132, 162; Forum repaved by, 178; *insulae* height regulated by, 106; omens concerning, 24, 220; Rome rebuilt by, 5, 112, 180; *vigiles* organized by, 164
Aurelian (emperor), 125, 191–92
Aurelius, Marcus: aids flood victims, 132–33, 162; flood during reign of, 30
Aventine Hill: depth of fill on, 41; *domus* on, 214; and Remus, 11; storm damage on, 23

325

Index

bacteria, 3, 62, 127, 144
Balbus, Lucius Cornelius, and flood of his theater, 4, 5, 25, 37, 49, 83, 95, 104
Bangladesh, 102, 113, 150
baptism, 218
barley, 279n6, 296n17
baths, at Rome, 151, 175, 294n10; of Agrippa, 208–9; of Caracalla, 208–10; complexity of, 208; of Constantine, 209–10; of Decius, 209–10; of Diocletian, 208–10; location of and floods, 208–11; of Nero, 208–9; as refugee centers, 211; of Sura, 209–10; of Titus, 209–10; of Trajan, 209–10; water use of, 152; wood use of, 76
Bede, the Venerable, 32–33
benefactions, imperial: employment as, 297n23; to fire victims, 164–65; to flood victims, 30, 162–64; for games, 296–97n22; for public works, 296–97n22
blizzards, 3
boats/ships: damaged/destroyed by floods, 19, 100–101, 272–73n8; food brought to Rome by, 134, 135, 136, 182, 279–80n8; possession of in law, 100; as transportation during floods, 5, 24, 25, 26, 31, 32, 63, 82, 93–95, 133; unloading facilities for, 194–96, 279–80n8; variety of at Rome and Ostia, 100. *See also* ferries/ferrymen
Bolivia, 149, 284n56
Bosphorus, 218
Brazil, 150
bricks: problems with manufacture of, 108–10, 111; process of making, 108; transition from sun-dried to fired, 110, 112, 234; vulnerability of to floods, 117
bridges: destroyed/damaged by floods, 18, 19, 23, 24, 27, 38, 103, 115–16; hydrometers on, 81–82; structure of, 115–16; as symbolic conquest of water, 218. *See also* individual bridges (under "Pons")
brothels, 230
buildings: collapse of, 40, 102–18, 121, 131; damaged by floods, 129–31; demolition of, 298n28; monumental public, 104. *See also* construction techniques; *and specific construction materials and structures*
burial clubs, 142

Caelian Hill: as alternate site for Equirria, 38, 79, 96; *domus* on, 214
Caesar, Gaius Julius: and bridge over Rhine, 218; death of, 22, 67; and malaria, 148; Roman projects of, 181–82, 198; and siege of Massilia, 137; and Tiber diversion scheme, 182–84, 249, 289nn21–22
Calcutta, 113
calendar, Roman, 69, 95
Caligula (emperor), 164, 218
Campus Martius, 4, 165; as built up region, 89; as *domus* site, 214–15; drainage of, 173; embankments along, 195–96; fill (artificial) in, 41, 178, 180, 292n1; as floodplain, 33–35, 41, 45, 46, 47, 48, 49, 176, 178–80, 206, 208; floods of, 18, 27, 33–35, 37, 38, 39, 79, 83, 96, 248; ground levels of, 41, 178, 180, 292n1; lacking in high ground, 122, 233; as malarial region, 283n44; as marginalized area, 113; as market site, 205; original marshy nature of, 54, 168, 262n18; and Tiber diversion scheme, 182–83; Tiber shifts and, 200; transformed by Augustus, 5
canals: to bypass Rome, 182–84, 289nn21–22; across Corinthian isthmus, 181; as flood control, 181; at mouth of Tiber, 182, 184, 185, 289n22
Canevari, Raffaele, 249
Cannae, Battle of, 223
Capito, Ateius, 26, 185–87, 199, 224
Capitoline Hill, 12, 18, 39; cut away for construction, 292n1; depth of fill on, 41; *domus* on, 214; during floods, 49; as residential site, 167
Carinae Hill, 214
castella, 151, 152, 236

Index

cattle: corpses of as hazard, 128; drowned in floods, 17, 18, 29, 82, 100, 101, 102; markets for, 205
censors, 198
ceremonies. *See* rituals/ceremonies
Cermalus, 12
chamber pots, 142
channel course, alteration of, 167, 181
channel improvement, 166–67, 181, 189
charcoal, 76
Charon, 218
Chiani (Clanis) River, 185, 187
children, 120, 151
China, floods in, 3, 122, 233, 298–99n1; and deforestation, 270n51; and disinhumation of corpses, 18
cholera, 145
Christianity, 218
Cicero, Marcus Tullius, 187; as landlord, 106, 273n15, 288–89n20, 298n28
cippi, 180, 198–200
Circus Maximus: drainage of, 171–72; floods of, 16, 17, 25, 35, 36, 63, 67, 83, 84, 95, 96, 220; ground level change in, 292n1; low-lying nature of, 44, 46, 49; original swampy nature of, 54, 206; sturdy construction of, 104
Cispian Hill, 214
cities, 2, 3; as intensifying flood effects, 85–89; vulnerable infrastructure of, 299n4; and zoning, 211–12
Ciudad Nezahualcoyotl, 113
Claudius (emperor): Aqua Anio Novus built by, 189, 227; flood control efforts of, 184, 185; Fucine Lake drained by, 227, 228; new harbor at Ostia created by, 184, 228, 279–80n8
clay: in bricks, 108, 110; vulnerability of to water, 111, 117; in wattle-and-daub construction, 110
cleanup, after flood, 123–28, 129, 234
climate, change in over time, 73–74
Cloaca Maxima, 8, 170–71, 177, 205, 251, 275n35, 287n6; convoluted course of, 219; development of, 170–71; and floodwaters, 47, 175; and vermin, 288n13

clothing, 119; contaminated by floodwater, 98, 146; and hypothermia, 121; owned by typical Roman, 97
cold temperature of water, as hazard during floods, 120, 121, 157, 276–77n43. *See also* hypothermia
cold weather/temperatures, 278n2; and mold growth, 136
Colline Gate, 95
Colosseum. *See* Flavian Amphitheater
comitium, 205
concrete: as construction material, 108, 109, 171, 234; increasing runoff, 87, 124; and moisture, 130
construction projects: expense of, 296n22; labor for, 297n23
construction techniques, 104–18, 233–34. *See also specific construction materials*
corpses: buoyancy of, 128, 278n60; disinhumed by floods, 18; as health hazard after floods, 3, 122, 123, 128, 236; in streets of Rome, 142, 143; thrown in Tiber, 128, 189–91; unrecovered, after floods, 160. *See also* sanitation
Crassipes, Promenade of, 37
criminals, thrown in Tiber, 190
crops, 101–2. *See also* food
curatores aquarum, 163, 202
curators of the Tiber and its banks: assistants of, 201; and boundary demarcation, 199, 200; and building/maintenance of port facilities, 200, 201, 292n50; censors as, 198; and disaster relief, 163; and dredging, 125–26, 192, 201; and guilds, 200, 291–92n49; maintaining navigability of Tiber, 198, 201; Ostian offices of, 201
curia, 132, 205
curse tablets, 218, 294n10

dams: broken, 51, 118; as flood control, 166, 167; to prevent Tiber floods, 187, 249; Roman, 188–89
Danube River, 218
Darius, 218

Index

death, 159; by disease, 143–45; by drowning, 151; by earthquakes, 277n49; by ergot, 137; by flood, 2, 3, 20, 121, 122, 299n2; from injuries, 122–23; by leptospirosis, 150; by malaria, 148; by meningitis, 144; by mold, 136, 137; by parasites, 145; seasonality of at Rome, 148; by starvation, 132

debris: blocking river channels, 166, 167; dangers posed by in floodwaters, 115, 119, 120, 123; fires result in, 40; in floodwaters, 3, 29, 98–99, 100, 126; raises ground level, 40, 177. *See also* fill

decontamination, 146, 162–63

deforestation: in China, 270n51; and Roman conquest, 270n56; of Tiber drainage basin, 74, 75–77, 266n22, 270–71n59; and Tiber floods, 70, 74–77

Delhi, 113

diarrhea, 144, 145, 150, 151

disasters, natural: ancient, 30, 132; attitudes toward, 229; death as a result of, 2, 3; exploited for gain, 155–56, 285n63; psychological trauma and, 154–60; recovery/reconstruction after, 160–65; reporting of, 222, 229–30, 295n13. *See also* earthquakes; fires; floods; Tiber floods

discharge, of rivers, 52–53, 81, 85, 167. *See also* floods

discharge, of Tiber, 59, 60, 61, 85, 265–66n16, 266nn20–21, 299–300n2. *See also* Tiber floods; Tiber River

disease, 3; and floods, 98, 118, 127–28, 141–54; from mold, 136–38

divers, 201

dogs, 142

dolia, 141, 282n26

Domitian (emperor), 180, 296n22

domus (houses): design of, 124–25; destroyed by floods, 103; distribution of, 213–16, 293–94n7; and elites, 235; lack of latrines in, 142; number of, 212

drainage basin, Tiber, 54, 56–58, 61, 265n11; anthropogenic changes to, 74; deforestation of, 70, 74, 75–77; divisions of, 56; erosion in, 77; pluviometric regime of, 58; rainfall in, 58, 59, 265n15. *See also* Tiber River

drainage basins, 53, 54

drains, ancient Roman, 173–77, 237, 249. *See also* sewers of Rome

dredging: of rivers, 166, 189; of the Tiber, 125, 189, 191–92, 201

drowning, 118–22, 151; alcohol and, 120; and cold, 120–21

drying out, 147, 234, 277n50

dysentery, 145, 147

earthquakes, 3, 222, 273n11, 295n17

Egypt, 1, 221

embankments, 192; ancient Roman, 193, 194, 195, 196, 200, 202, 225; in China, 298–99n1; disadvantages of, 166; failure to build in antiquity, 225–31; modern Roman (*muraglione*), 80, 113, 197, 225, 226, 241, 247–52; Tiber, 113, 287n6

emotions, 154–60

emperors, 4, 235; dwellings of, 217. *See also individual emperors*

employment: as imperial benefaction, 297n23; loss of due to floods, 27, 92–93, 132; on public works, 225–26, 227, 297n23

Emporium district, 251–52; as commercial district, 134, 135, 205, 230, 280n11; flood-prone nature of, 38, 44–45, 46, 49; and food supply of Rome, 134, 135, 205, 280n11; port facilities in, 194, 195, 225

entertainment centers, Roman, 206–7

Equirria, 38, 67, 79, 96

ergot (St. Anthony's Fire), 136–37, 281n16

erosion, 131, 266n22, 270n59

Esquiline Hill, 41, 214, 216

Euphrates River, 1

evaporation, 51, 52, 62, 75, 124

excrement, 113; attitudes toward, 284–85n57; contaminating floodwater, 143, 145, 146, 175, 236, 248,

328

284n56; contaminating urban water systems, 151–54, 236–37; flies and, 149; harmful organisms in, 143–45, 146–47; and Roman sewers, 173–75; in streets of Rome, 142, 143, 248. *See also* sanitation; urine

famine, due to floods, 27, 31, 38, 131–41, 155–56, 235, 236. *See also* food; supply system of Rome

farms, 1, 228, 284n57; destroyed by floods, 16, 17, 18, 29, 101, 102, 103; modern, 281n13

Father Tiber (god). *See* Tiber, Father

Faustulus, 11

Federal Emergency Management Agency (FEMA), 282–83n36

ferries/ferrymen, 168–69, 200, 218

fill, 40–42, 177–81

fires: aid to victims of, 164–65; in ancient Rome, 17, 23, 106, 112, 132, 164, 272n8, 273n11; efforts to combat, 163; Great (of AD 64), 40, 106, 112, 155, 165; as omen, 222, 295n17; rubble from raises ground level, 40

fish, in sewers, 288n13

Flavian Amphitheater (Colosseum), 44, 49, 176, 206, 228

flies, 149

flood control (general), 2; by channel modification, 181, 189; by drainage, 170; by embankments and levees, 192–93; methods of, 166–67, 286–87n1

flood control of Tiber in ancient Rome: attitude toward, 202–3, 222–25; benefits of, 228–31; by canalization, 184–85; by construction of dams, 188–89; cost of, 225–28; by diverting river, 182–84; by diverting tributaries, 185–87; by drainage, 167–77; by dredging, 189–92; by embankments, 193–98; problems with, 187–88, 202–3; by raising ground level, 177–81; religious issues and, 187, 188, 225; Roman administration and, 198–202. *See also* Tiber floods

flood of 1870, 247–48; construction of embankments prompted by, 248–49; hydrograph analysis of, 64–65; and Tiber flooding, 259n1, 289n22. *See also* Tiber floods

floodplains, 3, 85, 87; benefits of living in, 1; in China, 3, 122; in Egypt, 1; in Mesopotamia, 1; poor live in, 113; Rome in, 4, 12

floods (in general), 51; in Bangladesh, 102, 113, 150; in Bolivia, 284n56; in Brazil, 150; catastrophic, 53; in China, 3, 18, 122, 270n51, 277n52; cities intensifying effects of, 85–89; and civilization, 1; and crops, 1; and dam failure, 51, 118; deaths and, 2, 3, 118–21, 123; and disease, 143–46; duration of, 61–63; economic cost of, 2, 3, 63, 258n5; in Egypt, 1; flash, 51, 118, 233; in Florence, 3, 126, 131; frequency analysis of, 71–72; and Gilgamesh, 10; health hazards and, 3, 98; hundred-year, 71–72; hydrograph depiction of, 52–53; hydrologic cycle and, 51–52; in India, 102, 113, 127; and injuries, 118, 120, 122–23, 150; magnitude of, 71–72, 81; in Malaysia, 113; media coverage of, 156, 229; in Mexico, 275n33; of Noah, 10; in Philippines, 113, 120, 150, 159, 275n34; and property destruction, 98; psychological effects of, 154–65; recovery and reconstruction after, 160–65; reporting of, 229–30, 273n11; in Thailand, 150; types of, 51; in U.S., 1, 2, 18, 121, 123, 144, 145, 147, 156, 258n5, 278n56, 283n38, 284n55; warning of, 162. *See also* flood control (general); floodplains; floodwaters; Tiber floods

flood walls, 166, 192–93

floodwaters: contaminated, 143; drowning in, 118–23; force of, 2, 82, 88, 99, 113–15, 126, 139, 140; and sediment, 126; walking in, difficulty of, 276n39, 276–77n40

Florence, 54, 187; flooded in 1966, 3, 126, 131

Index

food: contaminated/destroyed by floods, 62, 98, 101–2, 131–41, 146; distributed to flood victims, 162, 165; shortage of, 27, 38, 101, 155–56. *See also* famine; supply system of Rome
fora, imperial, 49, 205, 212
foreigners, 229, 230, 298n27. *See also* marginalized groups
Forma Urbis. *See* Marble Plan, Severan
Forum, Roman: changes in ground level of, 41, 177–78, 205, 292n1; dogs drag corpse through, 142; *domus* near, 214, 215; drainage of, 170, 176; flood-prone nature of, 44, 46, 47–48, 49, 205; floods of, 22, 31, 35, 39, 83, 96, 121, 179; as important cross-roads, 169; malarial nature of, 148; as marketplace, 205; marshy nature of, 170, 176, 205; springs in, 55
Forum Boarium: embankments along, 194, 195; flood-prone nature of, 35, 43, 46, 49, 169, 206; ground level raised in, 292n1; original swampy nature of, 54; as site of commerce, 169, 205
Forum of Augustus, 205; elevation of, 84; Ludi Martiales held in, 25, 36, 83, 84, 96
Forum of Trajan, 112, 216, 228
fountains: contaminated by floods, 151; curse tablets found in, 294n10; as part of water supply system, 151–52; washing streets, 143, 152, 175
freedmen, 201
Frontinus, 81, 189
Fucine Lake, 181, 227–28, 297n22
Fulvius Flaccus, Quintus, 194
Fulvius Nobilior, Marcus, 194
funerals, 95, 158, 286n81
fungi, 130, 147, 278n2
furniture: damaged/destroyed by floods, 98, 99, 146; owned by Romans, 97

Gabinius, Aulus, 221
Garamantes, 5
garbage: housing built from, 112, 275n34; mounds of, 263n27; raises ground level, 40; thrown into streets, 142, 143; thrown into Tiber, 189–91
Garibaldi, Giuseppe, 249, 289n22
goats, and erosion, 270n59
gods. *See* religion
Golden House of Nero, 165, 228
government, Roman, response to disasters, 162–65
Gracchus, Gaius, 190
grain: destroyed by floods, 27, 38, 101, 132; distributions of, 132, 165, 280–81n1; dumped in Tiber, 138, 190–91; price controls on, 155, 165; selling of, 155–56; storage of, 136–40, 236; types of, 133–34, 279n6; vulnerability of to moisture, 136–40, 235. *See also* food; supply system of Rome
grain dole, 133, 297n22. *See also* supply system of Rome
grief, 158, 159
ground levels of Rome, 40–50, 79–80, 205, 225; in Campus Martius, 178, 180; changes in, 40, 292n1; raised to control floods, 177–80, 202; in Roman Forum, 177–78

Hadrian (emperor), 178, 180
Hadrian's Wall, 228
Haiti, 149
Hellespont, 218
Hepatitis A, 144
Herculaneum, 97, 111
hills of Rome, 4; benefits of living on, 215–16; changes in levels of, 41; elite preference for living on, 113, 214–17, 235, 293–94n7; as refuge during floods, 122, 233. *See also individual hills*
holidays, 95
homeless, the: forced into low-lying regions, 113; and improvised shelter, 112–13, 275n34, 275–76n35; living along Tiber, 251–52, 275n35; as result of floods, 2; unburied, in ancient Rome, 142. *See also* marginalized groups
Homer, 221
Horologium, 180

330

horrea (Roman warehouses): capacity of, 280–81n12; design of, 135, 137, 236; in flood-prone region, 38, 46, 49, 136, 139, 194, 195, 205; flood-resistant design of, 139–41, 235–36; and floods, 138–39; location of, 134–36; number of, 280n11; size of, 135. *See also* supply system of Rome
Horrea Galbana, 134, 135, 140, 280–81n12
Horrea Lolliana, 195
horse races, 25, 38, 67, 79, 84, 96
housing, 4, 112, 113, 297–98n27; location of and floods, 211–17. See also *domus*; *insulae*; shantytowns
hurricanes, 3, 53, 258n5
Hwang He (Yellow) River, 3, 122, 233, 277n52
hydrographs, 52–53
hydrologic cycle, 51–52
hydrometers, 72, 85; ancient Roman, 81–82; Egyptian, 81. *See also* Ripetta
hydrostatic pressure, 114
hypothermia, 120–21, 276–77n43
hysteria, 155

Ice Age, Little, 74
imagines, 158, 286n81
India, 102, 127, 145
infiltration, by water, 124, 266n22, 269n50
infrastructure, 4, 227, 237, 299n4
insects, 138, 147–48. *See also* flies; mosquitoes
insulae (Roman apartment buildings): collapse in floods, 27, 103, 231; design of, 124–25; destroyed in fire, 295n17; distribution of, 213, 216; garbage and excrement thrown from, 142, 274n19; height of, 4, 106–7, 273n17, 274nn18–19; location of, 213, 216; mold, mildew, and fungi in, 147; number of, 212–13; number of inhabitants in, 274n20; as problematic term, 273n13; as refuge during floods, 31, 133; regulations concerning height of, 106–7; as residences for the poor, 4, 97, 105; shoddy construction of, 105–6, 107–8, 109, 110, 112; stratification of classes within, 212, 297–98n27; trapping floodwaters, 125; vermin in, 127–28. *See also* housing
Interamnate (Terni), 186
interflow, 52

Janiculum Hill, 41, 47
Jews/Jewish Quarter of Rome, 113, 230, 250, 301n5. *See also* marginalized groups
Julius Ferox, Tiberius, 200
Jupiter (god), 21–22

Katrina, Hurricane, 258n5
Kuala Lumpur, 113

labor, on construction projects, 297n23. *See also* employment
Lacus Curtius, 168
lares, 158
Largo Argentina, 5, 178
latrines, 142. *See also* excrement; urine
law, Roman: and building height restrictions, 106–7; and building wall width restrictions, 108; and demolition of buildings, 231, 298n28; and objects thrown from windows, 142, 274n19; and possessions lost in floods, 99–100; and price limits on food, 155, 165; and river banks, 191
leptospirosis, 127, 149–50
levees, 166, 192
London, size of, 4
looting, 156
Ludi Apollinares, 17, 63, 67, 95, 97
Ludi Martiales, 25, 67, 83, 96
lungotevere, 194, 249, 250, 251
Lupercal, 12

malaria: after floods, 118, 149; influencing history, 148; link with mosquitoes, 147, 148; at Rome, 148, 149, 283n44
Manila: experiences of flood victims in, 120, 159; floods in, 113, 275n34

Index

Marble Plan, Severan, 135, 195, 216, 280n11
Marcius Censorinus, Gaius, 198
Marcus Aurelius (emperor), 30, 132, 162
marginalized groups, 250; forced to settle in floodplains, 113, 230–31, 297n26. *See also* foreigners; Jews/Jewish Quarter of Rome; poor, the
markers, Roman flood, 55, 56, 64; for Flood of 1870, 247; illustrations of, 56, 259n1; number of per flood listed, 244–46; record flood depths, 72, 85, 241. *See also* Tiber floods
markets, 38, 205
Marmore Falls, 186–87
Mars (god), 10, 11
marshes. *See* swamps/marshes
Massilia, 137
Mausoleum of Augustus, 178, 180
meningitis, 144
Mesopotamia, 1
Mexico City, 112, 113; floods of, 275n33
Mississippi River, 1
mold, 62, 235; as cause of illness after floods, 136–39, 147, 283n38; in grain, 136–39
monsoons, 53
Monte Fumaiolo, 54
Monte Testaccio, 40, 134, 263n27, 282n25
mortar, Roman, problems with mixing, 108, 109, 110, 117, 130
mosquitoes, 147–49
mud: contaminated by floodwater, 127, 143; left by Flood of 1870, 248; left by floods, 98, 99, 123, 125, 126, 234; left by Florence flood, 3, 126. *See also* sediment
Mulvian Bridge, 182–83
mycotoxins, 136–37; and history, 281n16

natural disasters. *See* disasters, natural
Nera (Nar) River: Roman plan to divert from Tiber, 185–87; as tributary of Tiber, 54, 57, 58, 290n31
Nero (emperor): building height restrictions imposed by, 106; dams built on Anio by, 188–89; Golden House built by, 165; grain dumped in Tiber by, 138, 190, 281n18; grain prices regulated by, 155; rebuilding Rome after Great Fire, 112, 165
New Orleans, 18, 258n5
nighttime, floods during, 156–57, 299n2
Nile River, 1
Nilometers, 81
Numitor, 10

octopi, in sewers, 288n13
olive oil, 141
olive trees, 270–71n59
omens, divine: birds as, 11; of Caesar's death, 22; context of reports of, 221–24, 229, 295n13, 295–96n17; floods as, 16, 24, 26, 27, 79, 97, 219–24, 229, 295n13, 295–96n17; natural disasters as, 295n13, 295–96n17; of Octavian's rise, 24, 220; of Tiberius's death, 219; types of, 221–22, 295–96n17
Ostia, 40, 54, 199, 273n17; administrators at, 201; and canals, 182; cost of, 297n22; as flood-prone, 140, 141; as harbor of Rome, 100, 125, 134, 135, 136, 141, 165, 181, 182, 279–80n8, 297n22; and population density, 274n20; volume of warehouses of, 280–81n12, 282n26. *See also* port facilities at Rome; Portus; supply system of Rome
Otho (emperor), 27, 38, 67
oxen, 102

Palatine Hill: defensible nature of, 167, 215; depth of fill on, 41; as desirable address, 216, 235; *domus* on, 214; emperor's palace on, 216, 235; during floods, 49; and foundation myth of Rome, 11, 12; as residential site, 167, 216
Palus Caprae, 46, 168, 262n18
panic, 155
Pantheon: in flood-prone location, 37,

332

94, 262n18; ground levels rise around, 178, 288n16
parasites, internal, 127, 144–45, 150
Parthia, 30
penates, 158
Peru, 149
Petronia Amnis, 173
Philippines, 150
Piazza di Spagna, 41
Piazza Pilota, 41
Piazza Venezia, 41
Pincian Hill, 214
Piscina Publica, 37, 49, 84
plebs, urban, 297n23
pluviometers, 58
podia of temples, 180–81
pomerium, 34, 46, 180
Pompeii, 97; poor construction of buildings at, 109, 111; staircases known from, 273n17
Pompey (Gnaeus Pompeius Magnus), 132, 162
Pomptine Marshes, 181–82
Pons Aemilius: damaged by floods, 19, 38, 115–16; proposal to dismantle ruins of, 250
Pons Cestius, 250
Pons Fabricius, 24, 87, 88, 250
Pons Sublicius, 115; destroyed by floods, 19, 20, 23, 24, 27, 38, 115; as earliest bridge, 115, 116; embankments near, 194
Ponte Flaminio, 42
Ponte Rotto. *See* Pons Aemilius
Ponte Sisto, 82
poor, the: and districts of Rome, 212, 230, 297–98n27; as flood victims, 229, 230, 231, 275n34; housing of, 112, 113, 212; and labor, 297n23; and slum districts, 297n26. *See also* marginalized groups
Porta Appia, 84
Porta Flumentana, 17, 18, 35, 49, 115
portents. *See* omens, divine
port facilities at Rome, 193, 194, 196, 290–91n42; administrators of, 198. *See also* Ostia; Portus

Portus, 125, 135, 182, 279–80n8
Possenti, Carlo, 248
Postumius Albinus, Aulus, 194
poverty. *See* wealth and poverty contrasted
power grid, electric, 123, 154, 299n4
Praetorian Guard, 163
prefect of the grain supply (*Prefectus Annonae*), 163, 201
pressure: exerted by dry grain, 139; exerted by floodwater, 139; exerted by wet grain, 139
property, personal: destroyed/damaged by floods, 97, 98, 100, 158, 272n4; difficulty of salvaging after floods, 98, 99, 100, 118, 123; emotional attachment to, 158, 159; of poor and wealthy Romans, 97
prostitution, 230
psychological effects of disasters, 154–60
Ptolemy (king), 221
public works, 234; costs of, 225–27; in provinces, 228; as source of prestige, 227
pumps, 124, 154
Puteoli, 182, 279n8, 298n28

quays, at Rome, 193–96, 198, 200–201, 205. *See also* Ostia; port facilities at Rome; Portus; supply system of Rome
Quirinal Hill, 41, 214

rain/rainfall, 2, 266n22; and disease, 145; heavy, 18, 51–53, 58, 113, 265n15. *See also under* drainage basin, Tiber
rats/ratbites, 127, 128, 149, 278n56, 278n58
Reate (Rieti), 186
recovery/reconstruction after disasters, 160–65
Regia, 22, 23, 35, 49, 179
Regionary Catalogs, 135, 212, 213, 273n13
regions of Rome, 14; Augustan, 213, 280n11, 293n7

333

religion, 190, 208; and floods, 95–97, 187–88, 219–25; and water, 217–19. *See also* omens, divine
Remus, 10–13, 35, 70
rescue of flood victims, 156, 161–65
rescue workers, 150, 155, 160, 161–65
reservoirs, 51, 151, 153, 166, 167, 188, 236
revetments, 167
Rhea Silvia, 10
Rhine River, 218
riots, 132
Ripetta: port of, 250, 251; Tiber measurements recorded at, 55, 56, 59, 60, 85, 241, 247, 261n1
rituals/ceremonies, 5; disrupted by floods at Rome, 5, 19, 25, 35, 95–97; familial, 158; range of at Rome, 95. *See also* Equirria; funerals; Ludi Apollinares; Ludi Martiales
rivers: altering course of as religious offense, 218–19, 225; as boundaries, 218; bridging of as symbolic, 218. *See also individual rivers*
Roma Capitale, 248
Rome, 6, 248; Augustan regions of, 213; buildings of, 4; as capital, 228; changes in topography of, 292n1; commercial centers of, 169, 204, 205, 207, 213, 216; disruption of daily life of, 92–97; earliest settlement at, 13; entertainment centers of, 204, 206–7, 213, 216; flood effects intensified in, 89; in floodplain, 12; foundation of, 10–13; geology of, 55; ground levels of, 40–50, 79–80, 177–81; hills of, 4, 41, 44, 122; lack of zoning in, 212; location of, 55; markets of, 205; marshy site of, 54–55, 167–69; neighborhoods of, 212, 213; patterns of building locations in, 204–17; political centers of, 204–5, 207, 213, 216; population of, 3, 4, 78–79, 133, 210–11, 258n5, 271n60; ports and docks of, 46, 94, 193–96, 198, 200–201, 290n42; quick recovery from floods of, 234–38; religious structures of, 4, 204, 207–8, 213, 216; resistance to floods of, 233–38; topography of, 39–43, 122, 167, 204, 233, 235; vulnerability to floods of, 232–37; water supply system of, 151–54. *See also* port facilities at Rome; sewers of Rome; supply system of Rome; water supply system of Rome
Romulus (king), 35, 70; and foundation of Rome, 10–13; house of, 294n7; site of disappearance of, 262n18
runoff, 52, 54, 70, 87, 266n22

sailing season in Mediterranean, 134, 191, 235
salmonellosis, 144, 284n56
Salto (Himella) River, 186
sanitation: in ancient Rome, 142, 143, 145, 146, 150, 151, 152, 169, 170, 173, 174, 175, 189, 190; and disease, 144–54, 284–85n57. *See also* corpses; excrement; garbage; sewers (general); sewers of Rome; urine
satire, 273n17
saturation point, 52, 54
sediment: enriches soil, 1, 102; in floodwater, 98, 125; ground levels raised by, 40, 55; in Hwang He River, 277n52; opacity of floodwater caused by, 120; and reservoirs, 167; in Tiber, 126, 277n52
Seine River, 248
senate/senators, 26, 132, 205
Servilius Vatia Isauricus, Publius, 198
Servizio Idrografico, 56, 254, 265n11
sewage. *See* excrement; urine
sewers (general): backing up during floods, 3; as combined drainage and sewage systems, 170; in France, 284n57; and illness after floods, 151; leptospirosis common to workers in, 149–50
sewers of Rome, 208, 277n50; admiration for, 173; carcasses thrown in, 128; contaminating floodwaters, 143, 150; development of, 170–73; as drains, 142, 169–77, 205; limitations of, 173–74; as pathways for floods, 175, 184; rebuilt in 19th century, 249,

Index

287n6; and vermin, 288n13. *See also* Cloaca Maxima; sanitation

shantytowns: in ancient Rome, 112, 113; in flood-prone areas, 113; materials used to construct, 112, 275n34; modern, 112, 113, 159, 274–75n31, 275n33, 275n34, 275–76n35. *See also* housing; marginalized groups; poor, the

ships. *See* boats/ships

shops: destroyed by floods, 21, 103; in *insulae*, 105, 216

slaves, 163, 229, 297n23

snakes, bites of, 123, 127

snowmelt and Tiber levels, 59, 71, 75

soil: absorption of water by, 52, 59, 75, 87; dryness of in summer, 60, 70; Mediterranean, 52; porosity of, 52, 62; renewal of by floods, 1

soldiers: and deforestation, 270n56; and disaster relief, 163; pay for, 297n22

speakers' platforms, 205

spillways, 166

springs: at Rome, 54, 55, 152, 167, 173, 236; as sacred 218, 236

squatter settlements. *See* shantytowns

stairs, 106–7, 143, 273n17

St. Peter's Basilica, 39

streets of Rome: broadened after Great Fire, 165; cleaning of, 175; corpses in, 142; during floods, 89, 93, 143; garbage and excrement in, 142–43, 149; narrowness of, 89. *See also* individual streets (under "Via")

stress, 156, 157, 160, 285n59

Styx, River, 218

Subiaco (Sublaquem), 188–89

Subura district, 143, 216, 288n13; as densely inhabited, 49, 212; *domus* in, 215; as lower-class, 212, 230, 298n26

summer, 131, 267n36; anomalous Roman floods during, 69–71, 77; dry season during, 58, 169; lack of floods during, 66; low water level during, 26, 61, 191; and putrefaction, 128; as sailing season, 134, 191, 235

supply system of Rome, 133–35; administrators involved with, 200–201; geographic locations involved in, 205–6; port facilities for, 193, 194, 195; resistance of to floods, 235–36. *See also* famine; food; grain; grain dole; Ostia; port facilities at Rome; Portus

swamps/marshes: and foundation story of Rome, 11–12; and malaria, 148, 283n44; in Rome, 8, 11–12, 54–55, 148–49, 167–69, 204, 205, 206, 262n18, 277n50. *See also* Palus Caprae; Pomptine Marshes

Sybilline Books, 26, 221, 224

symbolic perspectives, 6

symbols/symbolism: photographs as, 158; Roman religious, 158; Rome as national, 248, 300–301n3; topography and, 6; water and, 218

tabernae. *See* shops

tanneries, 230

Tarquinius Priscus (king), 170

Tarquinius Superbus (king), 170

Tarracina, 182

Temple of Deified Caesar, 179

Temple of Janus, 180–81

Temple of Juno, 180–81

Temple of Jupiter Optimus Maximus, 50, 207

Temple of Mars on Via Appia, 37, 49, 84–85, 271n67

Temple of Portunus, 180–81

Temple of Spes, 180–81

Temple of Vesta, 22, 23, 35, 49, 180–81

temples, 35; location of, 208; podia of and floods, 180–81. *See also* individual *temples*

Tenochtitlan, 275n33

Thailand, 150

theaters: destroyed by floods, 19, 103, 114; floods of, 4, 5, 83, 95, 238; location of, 206–7; sturdy construction of, 104

Theodosius I (emperor), 32–33

Theodosius III (emperor), 32–33

Tiber, Father (god), 217; delivers prophecy, 261n6; representation of, 13; reverence for, 187, 219, 239

335

Index

Tiber Commission, 19th century, 248–51, 259n1
Tiber commissions, ancient, 26, 70, 185, 186, 187–88, 199, 224
Tiber floods, 5, 6; aid to victims of, 30; attitudes of Romans toward, 5, 6, 9, 202–3, 217–31, 238–39; backflowing through sewers, 175; classification of, 266n20; cleaning up after, 123–28; and collapse of buildings, 102–18; damaging buildings, 129–31; death by, 20, 118–23; deforestation and, 70, 74–77; destroying personal property, 97–100; difficulty dating, 69; and disease, 141–54; disrupting daily life by, 92–97; and distribution of public buildings in Rome, 205–17; and distribution of residential buildings in Rome, 204, 211–17; as divine punishment, 220–23; duration of, 61–66; economic effects of, 92–93, 100; elites' safety from, 235, 238; and famine, 131–41; and food spoilage, 131–41; foundation of Rome and, 10–12; frequency of, 14, 71–81, 232, 269n45; history of scholarship of, 258–61n1; injuries from, 118–23; lack of concern for victims of, 238; magnitude of, 71–73, 77, 81–89, 232, 242–46; map depicting 10 masl, 45; map depicting 15 masl, 47; map depicting 20 masl, 48; and marginalized groups, 230–31; medieval, 38–39, 55, 63–64, 78, 83, 241, 243–244; misdated, 32–33; as omens, 219–25, 229; postclassical schemes to prevent, 248–49; primary source accounts of, 13–33, 78, 229–30; primary victims of, 230–31; problems with reconstructing effects of, 91–92; psychological effects of, 154–65; public monuments' invulnerability to, 234–35; rainfall and, 53–54; recovery and reconstruction after, 162–65; and religion, 187–88, 217, 219–25; reporting of, 72–81, 221–25, 229–31; Roman beliefs about cause of, 184, 188, 296n20; Romans' failure to prevent, 225–31, 232, 237–38, 239; Rome's quick recovery from, 234–38; Rome's resistance to, 233–38; Rome's vulnerability to, 232–33; seasonality of, 66–71, 168, 267n31, 267n33; in summer, 69–70; twentieth-century, 64, 65, 80; typical cause of, 54; and urban renewal, 230–31. *See also* discharge, of Tiber; drainage basin, Tiber; flood control of Tiber; markers, Roman flood; Tiber River
Tiber Island, 24, 46, 115, 116; legendary formation of, 190–91; plan to join to Trastevere, 250; river crossing below, 54
Tiberius (emperor), 25; death of foretold by flood, 219; flood victims aided by, 164; grain prices limited by, 155; rational response of to floods, 224, 296n20; Tiber commission appointed by, 26, 70, 185, 199, 224
Tiber River: administrative oversight of, ancient, 198–202; average levels of, 266n21; corpses and garbage thrown into, 142, 189–91; course of, 54, 291n48; criminals thrown in, 190; cut off from city by embankments, 251; delta of, 126, 277n52, 289n22; discharge of (average), 59, 61, 266n20, 299–300n2, 300n3; diverting course of, 182–84, 289nn21–22; dredging of, 189, 191–92, 201; early course of, 288n19; grain dumped in, 190–91; length of, 54; level of bed of, 41; low water level of during summer, 26, 61, 191; measurement of water levels along, 56; natural shifting of course of, 200; origins of, 54; pollution of, 174; rainfall and, 58–60; religion and, 187–88, 217–25; snowmelt and, 59, 71, 75; statistics of, 54, 60; transportation and, 76; width regularization of, 250. *See also* discharge, of Tiber; drainage basin, Tiber; flood control of Tiber; Tiber floods
tidal waves, 51
Tigris River, 1
toads, 137

tornadoes, 3
Trajan (emperor): bridges Danube, 218; building heights restricted by, 107; canals built by, 184, 185; and curators of the Tiber, 199; harbors built by, 279–80n8
Trajan's Column, 270n56
transportation. *See* Ostia; port facilities at Rome; Portus; supply system of Rome
Transtiberim (Trastevere), 41, 183, 250; docks along, 195; *domus* in, 215; flood-prone nature of, 38, 45, 46, 47, 48; *horrea* in, 135–36; Jews in, 230; as marginalized area, 113, 230, 298n27; swamps in, 54
Trasimeno (Trasumennus), Lake, 186
Trastevere. *See* Transtiberim
trauma, psychological. *See* psychological effects of disasters
travel, interruption of, 63
tsunamis, 51
Turano (Tolenus) River, 186
typhoid fever, 144, 147, 149

United States, floods in, 1, 145, 258n5, 283n38, 284n55
urban renewal, floods and, 298n28, 301n5
urine: human, 143, 144; rat, 127, 149–50

Valerius Messalla Niger, Marcus, 198
Vallis Murcia (Valley of the Circus Maximus), 36; depth of fill in, 41; drainage problems in, 176; flood-prone nature of, 44, 47, 177; floods of, 84; problematic name of, 264n34; streams in, 167–68
Vatican hills, 182–83
Velabrum: flood-prone nature of, 35, 43, 44, 46, 49; inhabitants of, 230; original ground level of, 41, 263n30; original swampy nature of, 168–69; raised ground levels in, 46, 47, 263n30
Veline Lakes, 186–87
Velino (Avens) River, 186
vermin, 175
Verus (emperor), 30, 132, 162

Vespasian (emperor): and employment of plebs, 297n23; meal of interrupted by scavengers, 142; *pomerium* changed by, 180; single Tiber curator appointed by, 199
Vestal Virgins, 10, 23
Via Appia, 21, 36–37, 44, 227
Via Flaminia, 27, 38, 49
Via Labicana, 41
Via Lata, 39, 83
Via Tritone, 41
Victory monuments, 23, 218
vigiles, 163, 164
Viminal Hill, 214
viruses, 127, 144
Vitellius (emperor), 67
Vitruvius, 107
Vittorio Emanuele II (king), 248
Volga River, 60
Vulcanalia, 67
vultures: as omen, 11; as scavengers, 142

warehouses. *See horrea*
warm weather/temperatures, 138, 139, 149; and mold growth, 136, 138
water: flowing vs. still, 217; Holy, 218; and hydrologic cycle, 51–54; hydrostatic pressure of, 114; and magic, 218; pressure of moving, 114; Roman reverence for, 9, 217–19
water, standing or stagnant: drainage of at Rome, 124, 176, 237; after floods at Rome, 11, 27, 124, 148, 149, 176, 237; and mosquitoes, 147, 148, 149; as problem after floods, 62, 124, 149. *See also* swamps/marshes
water filtration plants, 153, 154, 236
water supply (of cities), 151–52; contaminated by floods, 151, 154, 163, 236, 284n55, 284–85n57
water supply system of Rome, 151–52, 236–37; administration of, 163; drawbacks of, 175; resistant to contamination, 152–54
water table, 167
wealth and poverty contrasted, 97, 105, 106, 111, 113, 212, 235, 297–98n27
wells, 153, 236

337

Index

wheat, 133, 280–81n12; types of, 279n6. *See also* food; grain; supply system of Rome
winter, 128, 131, 278n2; avoidance of sailing during, 134; floods during, 11, 26, 61, 66–71, 120–21; and putrefaction, 128; rainy season during, 58, 168–69, 178
wolf, Capitoline, 10–11, 13
wood, 234, 270n56; as construction material, 75, 99, 111, 130; rot in, 130; uses of by Romans, 75–76
woodpecker, 10

Xerxes, 218

Yangtze River, 233
Yellow River. *See* Hwang He River

zoning, urban, 211–12

ABOUT THE AUTHOR

Gregory S. Aldrete is Professor of History and Humanistic Studies at the University of Wisconsin–Green Bay. He is the author of five books, including *Gestures and Acclamations in Ancient Rome* and *Daily Life in the Roman City: Rome, Pompeii, and Ostia*.

ANCIENT SOCIETY AND HISTORY

The series Ancient Society and History offers books, relatively brief in compass, on selected topics in the history of ancient Greece and Rome, broadly conceived, with a special emphasis on comparative and other nontraditional approaches and methods. The series, which includes both works of synthesis and works of original scholarship, is aimed at the widest possible range of specialist and nonspecialist readers.

Published in the Series:
Eva Cantarella, *Pandora's Daughters: The Role and Status of Women in Greek and Roman Antiquity*
John E. Stambaugh, *The Ancient Roman City*
Giovanni Comotti, *Music in Greek and Roman Culture*
Géza Alföldy, *The Social History of Rome*
Mark Golden, *Children and Childhood in Classical Athens*
Thomas Cole, *The Origins of Rhetoric in Ancient Greece*
Stephen L. Dyson, *Community and Society in Roman Italy*
Suzanne Dixon, *The Roman Family*
Alison Burford, *Land and Labor in the Greek World*
Steven H. Lonsdale, *Dance and Ritual Play in Greek Religion*
J. Donald Hughes, *Pan's Travail: Environmental Problems of the Ancient Greeks and Romans*
C. R. Whittaker, *Frontiers of the Roman Empire: A Social and Economic Study*
Nancy Demand, *Birth, Death, and Motherhood in Classical Greece*
Elaine Fantham, *Roman Literary Culture: From Cicero to Apuleius*
Kenneth W. Harl, *Coinage in the Roman Economy, 300 B.C. to A.D. 700*
Christopher Haas, *Alexandria in Late Antiquity: Topography and Social Conflict*
James C. Anderson, jr., *Roman Architecture and Society*
Matthew R. Christ, *The Litigious Athenian*
Gregory S. Aldrete, *Gestures and Acclamations in Ancient Rome*
H. A. Drake, *Constantine and the Bishops: The Politics of Intolerance*
Tim G. Parkin, *Old Age in the Roman World: A Cultural and Social History*
Thomas S. Burns, *Rome and the Barbarians, 100 B.C.–A.D. 400*
Michael Kulikowski, *Late Roman Spain and Its Cities*
Gregory S. Aldrete, *Floods of the Tiber in Ancient Rome*